# *Building Strategies for College Reading*

## *A Text with Thematic Reader*

Jane L. McGrath

*Paradise Valley Community College*
*A Maricopa Community College*

Prentice Hall, Englewood Cliffs, New Jersey 07632

*Library of Congress Cataloging-in-Publication Data*

McGrath, Jane L.
    Building strategies for college reading : a text with thematic
reader / Jane L. McGrath.
        p.   cm.
    Includes index.
    ISBN 0-13-043894-4
    1. College readers.   2. Reading (Higher education)   I. Title.
PE1122.M268   1995
808'.0427—dc20                                          94-32425
                                                             CIP

Editorial/production supervision
    and interior design: Patricia V. Amoroso
Acquisitions editor: Maggie Barbieri
Editor-in-chief: D. Anthony English
Manufacturing buyer: Robert Anderson
Cover design: Deluca Design

 © 1995 by Prentice-Hall, Inc.
A Simon & Schuster Company
Englewood Cliffs, NJ 07632

*Credits and copyright acknowlegments appear on pages 425-428,
which constitute an extension of the copyright page.*

Printed in the United States of America

10   9   8   7   6   5   4   3   2   1

ISBN 0-13-043894-4

PrenticeHall International (UK) Limited, *London*
Prentice-Hall of Australia Pty. Limited, *Sydney*
Prentice-Hall Canada Inc., *Toronto*
Prentice-Hall Hispanoamericana, S.A., *Mexico*
Prentice-Hall of India Private Limited, *New Delhi*
Prentice-Hall of Japan, Inc., *Tokyo*
Simon & Schuster Asia Pte. Ltd., *Singapore*
Editora Prentice-Hall do Brasil, Ltda., *Rio de Janeiro*

# Contents

## 9   DECIDE WHAT TO DO WITH THE AUTHOR'S INFORMATION   *186*

## THEME 1:   STAYING HEALTHY IN AMERICA   *202*

## THEME 2:   LIVING IN A THROWAWAY SOCIETY   *259*

## THEME 3: "DOING PHILOSOPHY" IN EVERYDAY LIFE  *302*

## THEME 4: WORKING IN A GLOBAL ECONOMY  *342*

# *Preface to the Instructor*

Over the last century, at least 600 texts and workbooks have been published and used in college reading programs. So why another text? I've written this text for two reasons. The first reason is to move forward with the paradigm shift taking place in reading instruction.

Since the work of Skinner and others in the 1950s, the teaching of reading has conformed to the paradigm of behaviorism with a deficit model of instruction. First, we administered a standardized exam to diagnose what skill a student lacked, e.g., finding the main idea. Then we tried to remediate that skill. Now, however, research indicates that teaching discrete reading skills does not necessarily transfer to or improve a student's ability to master real assignments in other college courses. Thus, as reading educators, we're moving away from this fragmented, component skills approach to a more holistic approach in which we perceive reading as an interactive, dynamic, cognitive process.

In this new paradigm, we view students as energetic participants in the reading process. We encourage them to approach reading as an interactive process in which success depends on the match between the writer's skill and knowledge and the reader's skill and knowledge. We ask students to see the reading process as dynamic—variable, depending on the task.

Our intent is to have students become independent learners able to accomplish the tasks they encounter in college. We know that the organization and orientation of college texts and reference materials are significantly different from those of the commonly read narrative. We also know that students transfer new strategies more naturally to their own work when they practice on tasks they perceive to be real. Therefore, the second reason for this text is to provide authentic reading tasks for students.

To meet these goals, this text approaches reading as a holistic, complex process, not as a series of discrete, simplistic skills. And, because strategic reading is essential for successful readers, this text encourages students to select and practice reading and study strategies using typical college prose.

Although there is still much discussion about the differences between a skill and a strategy, I consider a skill to be an accomplished technique whereas a strategy is an action a reader consciously selects to achieve a particular goal. Strategies are means to an end.

## THE ORGANIZATION OF THIS TEXT

The text's overall design is to encourage students to: (1) develop a plan—clarify their purpose, activate their own knowledge, and set goals; (2) actively implement their plan, drawing from a repertoire of learning and reading strategies; (3) review what they've gathered—consolidate, integrate, and review information, and decide what else they need to know; and (4) develop a new plan and continue the cycle. It asks students to view reading and learning as an ongoing process rather than as a one-shot activity.

**Chapters.**   The nine chapters investigate the skills of successful comprehension. I encourage students to adapt and use a variety of strategies to help them fulfill their purpose. Each chapter contains instruction, examples, and at least four practice readings with authentic tasks.

**Themes.**   The four thematic units, both in content and tasks, contain typical college expository prose. Each thematic unit contains a full textbook chapter along with six to eight pieces centered on a unifying topic. Each piece relates to the text chapter and builds on previous readings to expand understanding of the theme and students' relationship to it.

Questions in the thematic units are consistent with the paradigm shift. While some questions require the recall of specific information, others are more process-oriented—helping to dispel the black-and-white concept of the nature of comprehension. Use of this combination of product- and process-oriented assessments encourages students to analyze their own strengths and needs in concert with the instructor.

Throughout the text, emphasis is given to identifying the author's purpose, understanding vocabulary in context, differentiating among different levels of information, and making valid inferences. Varied writing assignments provide another forum for students to interact with the concepts they are learning.

**Instructor's Manual.**   An Instructor's Manual is available. It includes

- course syllabus recommendations
- presentation ideas
- information about reading selections
- suggested answers for exercises
- additional reading selections to use as quizzes for each of the nine chapters
- transparency masters

In addition, a brief synopsis of Project Read Aloud—the award-winning community service project for developmental reading students—and a complete *Project Read Aloud Student Handbook* is included.

## Acknowledgments

Although my name appears as the author of *Building Strategies for College Reading,* countless women and men have contributed to its creation and publication.

I am exceedingly grateful to my students of the last twenty-five years who have taught me volumes about the process of reading. They have, directly and indirectly, shown me how critical it is to work on authentic tasks.

Numerous colleagues across the Maricopa Colleges deserve credit and thanks. Over the years their knowledge, philosophies of teaching and learning, and experiences have provided meaningful insight into the realities of successful college reading. Special recognition must be given to Sally Rings, who generously provided time, energy, and support for this project.

I also want to thank the reviewers of this edition for their willingness to share their wisdom to make this a more useful tool for students:

| | |
|---|---|
| Margaret Bagwell | St Louis Community College at Florisannt Valley |
| Sharon Gavin | Salem Community College |
| Bertilda Garnica Henderson | Broward Community College |
| Clare Hite | University of South Florida |
| Anita Podrid | Queens College |
| Mari Valentenyi | John Tyler Community College |

The cadre of dedicated professionals at Prentice Hall is wonderful. Thanks to Kim Byrne and Carol Wada (the original acquisitions editor) for believing in a new paradigm and in my ability to deliver a relevant product, and to Phil Miller, Patricia Amoroso, and Maggie Barbieri for seeing the project through to completion. I'm indebted to Joan Polk in college editorial for acting as my anchor and for her sensible and efficient assistance throughout the writing and production process.

And, finally, my profound gratitude goes to Larry McGrath, my husband and partner in all of life's adventures. Without his continuing encouragement and assistance, this book would not exist.

# *Preface to the Student*

Reading is the process of making meaning out of the 26 squiggles we call the alphabet. It is more than just knowing how to say words. [Reading is the active thinking process of understanding an author's ideas, connecting those ideas to what you already know, and organizing all the ideas so you can remember and use them.]

And, as you know, the demands of reading academic material are enormous—from studying a text assignment to prepare for class, to reading a magazine article for a discussion group, to reviewing for an exam. In fact, research by Anderson and Armbruster (1984)* shows that a single text page can have as many as 50 separate but connected ideas. As a result, you are faced with sorting and understanding hundreds of ideas every time you sit down to study. But don't be discouraged. It is not an impossible task.

[ You can build a repertoire, or inventory, of reading and study strategies that help you identify, understand, organize, and remember the information you need. Strategies are tools or techniques you consciously select to complete tasks accurately and efficiently. ]

Just learning about the strategies won't be enough, however. As an analogy, consider Jake. For the last month, Jake has been trying to shed a few pounds of extra weight and get in shape. He's learned that some strategies for reaching his goals include eating a low-fat diet and exercising regularly. He thinks about the strategies often and enjoys talking to his friends about his new fitness plan. He has just finished reading a book about planning healthy meals and he's made some sacrifices in his budget so he can buy a top-of-the-line exer-

*"Studying," by T. H. Anderson and B. B. Armbruster, in P. D. Pearson (ed), *Handbook of Reading Research* (pp. 657–679), New York: Longman.

cise bike. Unfortunately, Jake hasn't lost any flab. Why? Because even though he's learned several strategies, he still spends his evenings eating chocolate cupcakes in front of the television. Until Jake starts actually using the strategies—eating right and riding the bike—he won't make much progress toward his goals.

Don't be like Jake. As you discover new reading and study strategies, apply them. Try them out in your classes and at work. Adapt them to fit your needs. Add them to your repertoire of strategies and use them *consistently*.

# About the Author

Jane L. McGrath currently teaches reading, English, and computer applications courses at Paradise Valley Community College in Arizona. She has taught in the Maricopa Community Colleges for 25 years. She earned her undergraduate degrees in education and mass communications and her Ed.D. in reading education from Arizona State University. In 1991, McGrath was named *Innovator of the Year* by the Maricopa Colleges and the League for Innovation in Community Colleges for Project Read-Aloud, a college-community service program. She has also received *Outstanding Citizen* awards from the cities of Phoenix and Tempe for her community service work. In addition to teaching, McGrath is a freelance writer. She and her husband, Larry, a professional photographer, combine talents on a wide range of projects from travel articles, to cookbooks, to technical pieces for the high-performance automotive industry. She is a member of the National Association of Developmental Educators and the College Reading and Learning Association.

## About You

I hope you will help me improve future editions of this book by taking a few minutes to answer these questions. Please send your comments to me at College Reading Development Group, Prentice Hall, 113 Sylvan Avenue, Englewood Cliffs, NJ 07632.

If this is not your first college course, what other courses have you taken?

What courses are you taking along with this reading course?

List two strategies or chapters that have proven useful.

List two strategies or chapters that haven't worked for you.

Which chapters did you cover in class?

Which Themes did you cover in class?

List two articles that you enjoyed.

List one article that was difficult to read.

List one article that you thought was boring.

If I were to develop a new Thematic Unit, what should it be about?

What courses do you plan to register for next term?

I'd appreciate any comments or suggestions you have about the text.

# 1

## *Adopt a Plan»Do»Review»Cycle for Academic Reading*

Everyone looks for ways to be more successful. American executives strive to compete with aggressive foreign competitors, teachers seek ways to enrich student learning, and students like you search for ways to improve academic performance.

So, how can you, like a company president or a college professor, improve your chances for success? First, realize that whether your goal is to improve performance on a widget production line or a sociology final exam, the basic blueprint can be the same: You plan what you need to do; you implement your plan; and you review how well you did. Then, since goals such as zero defects or, in your case, understanding more of what you read, can't always be met the first time you complete your plan, you view reading as a cycle instead of a one-shot activity.

To use this cycle to become more successful at reading for learning means that each time you have an assignment, you will *plan* before you begin, you will *do* your reading actively, you will *review* what you have read, and you will continue to *plan, do,* and *review* until your comprehension goals are met. This chapter introduces you to a variety of reading and study strategies that you can draw from to build your personal repertoire of strategies. Remember, a strategy is an action that you consciously select to achieve a particular goal. Strategies are means to an end.

---

### Chapter 1 Content Objectives

- determine why you should develop a plan before beginning to read
- identify the purpose of pre-reading strategies
- identify ways to monitor comprehension
- list and explain fix-up strategies
- explain why review is necessary and identify review strategies
- explain how successful readers use a plan»do»review cycle

---

### Plan»Do»Review»Cycle

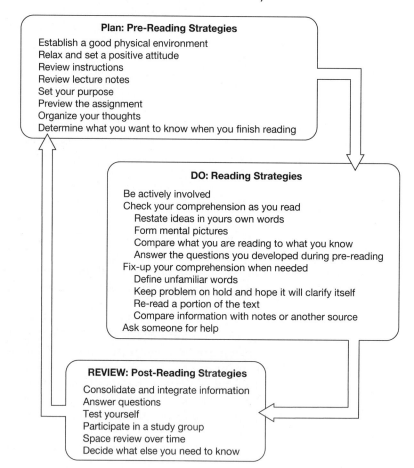

**Plan: Pre-Reading Strategies**

Establish a good physical environment
Relax and set a positive attitude
Review instructions
Review lecture notes
Set your purpose
Preview the assignment
Organize your thoughts
Determine what you want to know when you finish reading

**DO: Reading Strategies**

Be actively involved
Check your comprehension as you read
    Restate ideas in yours own words
    Form mental pictures
    Compare what you are reading to what you know
    Answer the questions you developed during pre-reading
Fix-up your comprehension when needed
    Define unfamiliar words
    Keep problem on hold and hope it will clarify itself
    Re-read a portion of the text
    Compare information with notes or another source
Ask someone for help

**REVIEW: Post-Reading Strategies**

Consolidate and integrate information
Answer questions
Test yourself
Participate in a study group
Space review over time
Decide what else you need to know

## Why Do I Need to Develop a Plan for Every Assignment?

*Task 1:* Read this paragraph from a stockbroker's newsletter.

Writing or selling Options against stock you already own is a strategy that is conservative and usually works well in a trading market. An Option is either a call (a right to buy 100 shares of stock at a specified price in the future) or a put (a right to sell 100 shares of stock at a specified price in the future). Thus an Option buyer or seller who owns no stock (called uncovered or naked) is a speculator who is looking at making large percentage returns on a small amount of invested capital in a short time. This individual would be paying the Option premium to us, the covered writer.

How successfully did you complete Task 1? How do you know if you were successful?

You may not have been very confident of your success. Unless you have a working knowledge of the stock market, the content of the paragraph as a whole is hard to understand. In addition, since you didn't have a specific purpose for reading, it was probably difficult to know if you understood what was expected.

*Task 2:* Read this same paragraph from a stockbroker's newsletter to find out whether writing Options against your own stock is considered a risky or a conservative strategy.

Writing or selling Options against stock you already own is a strategy that is conservative and usually works well in a trading market. An Option is either a call (a right to buy 100 shares of stock at a specified price in the future) or a put (a right to sell 100 shares of stock at a specified price in the future). Thus an Option buyer or seller who owns no stock (called uncovered or naked) is a speculator who is looking at making large percentage returns on a small amount of invested capital in a short time. This individual would be paying the Option premium to us, the covered writer.

How successfully did you complete Task 2? How do you know if you were successful?

I suspect you evaluated yourself "very successful" on Task 2. You found the information you were looking for—that writing Options against your own stock is a conservative strategy—in the first sentence. You clearly knew you had achieved your goal, and you stopped reading.

As you can see, even given the same paragraph, the reading requirements can be very different. So you begin every reading assignment by developing a plan.

Base your plan on the reading assignment's two critical factors: (1) your specific purpose for reading the assignment, such as answering questions, preparing for lecture, or reviewing for an exam; and (2) how difficult the material is for you, considering elements such as the vocabulary and your knowledge about the topic. You have a better chance of success when you plan.

## WHAT PLANNING OR PRE-READING STRATEGIES CAN I USE?

Pre-reading strategies are tactics to give you a head start on good comprehension. They prime your brain. Pre-reading strategies include:

***Establishing a good physical environment.*** Place yourself in surroundings that help your ability to concentrate on reading. Make certain that you have good lighting. Use a comfortable chair that encourages good posture and a ready-to-work attitude, and that allows you to hold or rest the book easily.

***Relaxing and setting a positive mental attitude.*** Set yourself up to be successful. Arrange your schedule to do your study-reading when you are at your best mentally. Have confidence in yourself; know that you can read successfully and accomplish the goals that you set.

***Reviewing instructions.*** Check any comprehension guidelines you have been given such as "Read this in preparation for tomorrow's lecture," or "Read to see how this author differs from what I've said today," or "Review all of the material we covered in preparation for the exam."

***Reviewing any lecture notes.*** Reread any notes you have taken on this topic, looking for topics or ideas you need to clarify, words you need to define, or names and dates you need to fill in. Once you have completed your reading, you will need to combine the information in your notes with the information from your reading.

***Setting your purpose.*** There are different purposes for reading, and to be successful you must match the way you read with your purpose. For instance, reading for enjoyment does not require the full understanding that reading in preparation for a psychology lecture requires, which, in turn, is different from reading for a chemistry exam. When you take time to clarify your purpose before you begin to read, you are more likely to read and understand successfully, and less likely to waste time.

***Previewing the assignment.*** Looking over the material before you begin to read is like looking at a completed jigsaw puzzle before you start trying to put individual pieces together. When you preview an assignment, you

- read the chapter objectives
- read headings and subheadings
- read introductory and concluding paragraphs
- read boldface and italic words and phrases
- highlight and clarify unfamiliar vocabulary
- examine graphics
- review end-of-chapter summaries and questions.

In short, you take advantage of anything that will help to give you a general understanding of the organization and core ideas.

***Organizing your thoughts.*** First, based on the chapter objectives and headings/subheadings, jot down the major topics. Then, write a few words about what you know on each of the topics.

***Clarifying what you want to know when you finish reading.*** If you don't read to find out something specific, you probably won't find out anything specific. One way to read for something specific is to phrase the chapter's objectives or headings/subheadings as questions and then read to answer those questions.

For example, if you were assigned the following selection, "Caring About Kids: When Parents Divorce," you could use some of the planning strategies this way.

*Plan*

1. Find an environment that allows for maximum concentration.
2. Allot time to complete the assignment; then relax and adopt a positive attitude.
3. Review the professor's instructions (such as "Read this to prepare for tomorrow's lecture on Divorce in the United States").
4. Set your purpose: Read to identify the main concepts and to understand the vocabulary.
5. Preview the assignment:

# *Caring About Kids: When Parents Divorce*

### THE DIVISION OF SCIENTIFIC AND PUBLIC INFORMATION, NATIONAL INSTITUTE OF MENTAL HEALTH

## INTRODUCTION

[1]Divorce: the breakup of a family. More than one-third—actually 40 percent—of all marriages in the United States now end in divorce. Although legally a separation of two people, divorce is, in reality, a family affair because more than half of all divorces involve children. Divorce ends the role of spouse; it doesn't end that of parent.

## WORKING OUT ISSUES

[2]Couples seeking a divorce will not always find it easy to reach agreement on issues that affect their children, but they should attempt to do so before telling their children about the impending separation. Children, even very young children, need to be prepared for the divorce. They need information about where they will live, who will take care of them, where they will go to school, and whatever other issues are of major concern to them.

## CUSTODY ISSUES

[3]When parents struggle over custody or are inconsistent in the arrangements agreed upon, problems are increased. When a child becomes the prize in a parental tug of war, the results can be emotionally damaging, causing the child to feel more insecure, angry, and guilty. The sooner parents face up to and work out custody details, the better the chances are that a child's anxiety about the divorce and his own future will begin to fade.

[4]Parents should carefully balance their own needs with those of the children. For example, the decision to keep the family home for

the children's sake may cause a financial hardship. Or, if the family can't afford to buy a second car, it may be necessary for one parent to move closer to public transportation.

[5]Once the primary plans are made, many other issues need to be settled. How can the responsibility of child care and living expenses be fairly divided? Who will care for the children? Where? How? If both parents share expenses, how and when? Who will pay for medical care, insurance, transportation, food, and clothing? How will college costs be shared? Where will children spend holidays and vacations? And finally, will the visitations and responsibilities change as the children get older?

## TYPES OF CUSTODY

[6]Custody is a responsibility as well as a right. It becomes obvious, when trying to consider the best interests of everyone involved, that there are no perfect answers. Custody does not have to be an all-or-nothing decision, however. There are a number of options available for sharing responsibility.

[7]***Single Parent Custody.*** Neither parent relinquishes parenthood, but it is decided that one parent should be physically in charge.

[8]***Joint Custody.*** Parents legally share responsibility for the children. The details of shared responsibility can be worked out in various ways.

[9]***Split Custody.*** When there is more than one child in the family, children may be divided between parents. For example, the older children may live with the father and the younger with the mother, or the boys with the father and the girls with the mother.

[10]***Other Arrangements.*** Single parents sometimes share responsibilities of parenting with other adults or grandparents so that a supervising adult is present at all times.

6. Organize thoughts (use headings/subheadings to help organize the author's ideas and what you already know):

   **INTRODUCTION:**

   - number of divorces—I'm not surprised by the number of divorces quoted; at least $\frac{1}{3}$ of my friends' parents and my parents' friends are divorced.
   - divorced people are still parents—I've seen movies where people who are getting divorced try to reassure the kids that the divorce won't affect them.

   **WORKING OUT ISSUES**

   - parents need to "get their act together" before involving children.

### CUSTODY ISSUES

- parents can make things worse for children—read to see how to avoid problems!

### TYPES OF CUSTODY

- several custody options—The only type of custody I know about is where the mother has custody of the children. I wonder what other types are allowed?

7. Determine what you want to know when you finish reading:

    a. What is the current divorce rate in the U.S.?

    b. How/when should couples work out custody issues?

    c. What are some major custody issues?

    d. What are the four types of custody?

Once you have developed your plan, you are ready to begin reading.

## What Do I Do Once I Start to Read?

Did you ever fall asleep while playing tennis or while you were watching your favorite television show? Probably not. How about while you were reading? Probably. What makes the difference? Your active involvement.

Active physical and mental involvement keeps you interested and committed. When you become passive, you rapidly lose interest and drift away. So, to read successfully you must be an active, thinking participant in the process.

### HOW CAN I CHECK MY COMPREHENSION AS I READ?

As an active reader, you use comprehension monitoring, or checking, strategies to make certain that your understanding is satisfactory for your purpose. Comprehension monitoring strategies include:

***Restating ideas in your own words.*** At the end of a sentence or paragraph, rephrase the idea in your own words.

***Forming mental pictures.*** Build a mental picture of what the author is describing.

***Comparing what you are reading to what you know.*** Ask yourself how this new information fits with what you know. Does it reinforce your previous knowledge? Does it contradict what you previously thought? Does it add new information?

***Answering questions.*** Connect what you are reading to the questions you need to answer.

## IF I DON'T UNDERSTAND WHAT I'M READING, WHAT CAN I DO?

If you discover that you do not understand what you are reading, use one of these fix-up strategies to get yourself back on track. Fix-up strategies include:

*Defining unfamiliar words.* Make certain that you understand the words the author uses. If an unfamiliar word isn't defined in the context or the text's glossary, check your lecture notes or, a dictionary, or even ask someone.

*Using chapter objectives and headings/subheadings.* Reread the objectives and headings/subheadings to see if there are ideas or concepts that can help you to understand.

*Reviewing related graphics.* Review all associated graphics and their explanations to see if they clarify the text information.

*Rereading a portion.* Try reading the sentence or paragraph a second time with the specific goal of clarifying your question.

*Keeping the problem on hold and hoping that it will clarify itself.* If the problem lies in only one sentence or paragraph, you may decide to mark it and continue reading. It is possible that the next sentence or paragraph will help your understanding.

*Comparing information with notes or another source.* Read about the topic or idea in your notes or in another book to see if a different approach helps your understanding.

*Asking someone.* After you have clarified the vocabulary, reread the objectives, headings/subheading, graphics, and unclear passages; review the other information you have on the topic or idea; if you still don't understand what you need to, ask someone for help. Potential resources may include your professor, a teaching assistant, a tutor, or a classmate.

For example, having developed a plan for the sample selection above, you could use some of the comprehension monitoring and fix-up strategies this way.

*Do*

8. Begin reading.
9. Monitor comprehension by answering the four questions in your plan:

    a. What is the current divorce rate in the U. S.? (40%)

    b. How/when should couples work out custody issues? (Couples should agree on issues that affect their children before telling them about the separation/divorce.)

    c. What are major custody issues? (Major custody issues include: where the child will live, responsibility of child care, living expenses, extra expenses, college costs, holidays and vacations, and changes as children get older.)

    d. What are the four types of custody? (1. single parent [problem: don't understand "neither parent relinquishes"])

10. Fix-Up strategy: define relinquishes—gives up. Although neither parent gives up custody, one parent takes charge. Now, understandable.
11. Continue reading for other types of custody arrangements (2. Joint custody, 3. Split custody, and 4. Other arrangements.)
12. Finished reading.

Even though you have finished reading (meaning you have understood what you set out to understand) your cycle is not complete. To successfully read for learning, you must review what you have read.

## If I Understand What I've Read, Why Do I Have to Review?

Think about when you first learned to do something like drive a car, type, or play the guitar. If you practiced daily, you found yourself doing a little better each day. If, however, you didn't practice for two or three weeks, you had probably forgotten so much that you needed to start with some of the basics again.

It doesn't matter how old we are; without review, we forget information very quickly. In fact, without good review at regular intervals, you will probably forget as much as 80 percent of what you have read.

### HOW CAN I REVIEW EFFECTIVELY?

Review strategies help you put information into perspective and help you to remember it. To be most effective, your review sessions should be spaced out over time. Arrange your first review session within 24 hours of reading and continue to review the information on a regular schedule. Reviewing periodically helps you commit information to your long-term memory.

Some review strategies include:

*Rereading thoughts you've organized and questions you've answered during reading.* Make use of the work you did during your planning and reading.

*Answering questions.* Write out or talk through the answers to the questions that you set out in your plan.

*Consolidating and integrating information.* Combine your knowledge with what you've gained from reading and your lecture notes to form one coherent picture.

*Participating in a study group.* Join a group of classmates to talk about what you have read. Try reviewing concepts, sharing notes, and taking practice tests with one another.

*Testing yourself.* Make up a test on the material or have a classmate make one up and test yourself. Make a set of Question-and-Answer flash cards for a convenient carry-along review tool by writing the question on one side of a 3″ × 5″ card and the answer on the reverse side.

For example, using the sample, "Caring About Kids," and having developed a plan and read the selection to achieve your plan, you could use these review strategies.

*Review*

13. Make up and take a test covering the necessary information.
14. Correct the test.
15. Review the information at least once before the next lecture.

## Why Should I Do Anything Else?

Occasionally, on small assignments or familiar material, you will achieve your reading comprehension goals at the end of one plan»do»review cycle. On the other hand, when you're reviewing, don't be surprised to discover gaps in your knowledge. When you do, just develop a new plan that will help you fill in the gaps. Reread the portion of the assignment you need to get the information and then review, making sure to integrate the new information with what you already have.

As mentioned in the Preface, reading is thinking. Successful reading for learning requires that you understand what an author says, and that doesn't happen without continuing effort.

---

### REVIEW QUESTIONS

*Review Questions*

1. Explain why you should develop a plan before you begin reading.
2. Identify the purpose of pre-reading activities and list three pre-reading activities.
3. What are two ways to monitor your comprehension?
4. What are two fix-up strategies for improving poor comprehension, and when should you use them?
5. Explain why review is necessary, and list two review strategies.
6. Explain how you can use a plan»do»review»cycle to be more successful.

*Think and Connect Questions*

7. Re-read the *Preface to the Student*. List two topics that were covered in both the *Preface* and this chapter. Why do you think these topics are in both places?
8. Where do you normally do your reading/studying? Do you think that environment helps or hurts your comprehension? How could you improve your environment?

*Application Exercises*

9. Using one text section from one of your other textbooks, implement the plan»do»review»cycle: develop a plan for reading, read, review, and continue the cycle until you have met your goal.

10. When you are having difficulty comprehending what you are reading, one of the fix-up strategies you can use is to ask someone for help. For each of your classes, identify at least two resources you can call on. After you have checked with your sources, list when and where they are available, and how to contact them.

---

### USE YOUR STRATEGIES: EXERCISE 1

---

# *Nutrition for the '90s*

### AMY KEATING, M.S., R.D.

*For this exercise, assume your instructor has asked you to read this selection as part of your preparation for tomorrow's introductory lecture on good nutrition. (1) Prepare a plan that includes what you will read during preview, how you will organize your thoughts, and four questions you will answer. (2) Tell how you will read to complete your plan (be sure to include answers to your planning questions). (3) Describe the review strategies you will use to prepare for the lecture.*

[1]You may know the merits of healthy eating. But often wanting to eat right and actually doing so are two separate things. For many, understanding how to eat right is the real challenge because the recommendations for good nutrition appear more complex than they actually are. Although several health organizations issue a variety of dietary recommendations, the basic message regarding diet and health are the same: Consume a diet low in fat, cholesterol and sodium and high in complex carbohydrates and dietary fiber to reduce the risk of chronic disease.

[2]To put these strategies into practice the focus should be on the big picture—the total diet over time. Here is a brief overview of major dietary concerns.

### A WORD ON VARIETY

[3]Variety is not only the spice of life, it is also the secret to making sure you get the more than 40 nutrients you need each day. No one food supplies all the essential nutrients. That is why it is important to eat several types of food each day to get all the nutrients you need for good health. Choosing from the five food groups every day—Fruits, Vegetables, Grains, Meat and Dairy Products, with an assortment of foods within these groups, can help you get the variety you need.

### CUT BACK ON FAT
### AND CHOLESTEROL

[4]Health authorities recommend that Americans reduce total dietary fat intake to no more than 30% of total daily calories. This guideline should apply to your total diet over time, not individual

|  | MEN | WOMEN | DIETERS |
|---|---|---|---|
| Calories/Day | 2400 | 1800 | 1400 |
| Drop last digit | 240 | 180 | 140 |
| Divide by 3 = | | | |
| FAT Grams/Day | 80 | 60 | 47 |

foods. One way to monitor your fat intake is to determine your DAILY FAT TARGET. This is based on your calorie need which is influenced by your sex, age, weight and activity level. The following chart provides typical examples of how to calculate the daily fat gram target for men, women and dieters. Keep in mind that fat-containing foods can be balanced with lower fat foods over the course of the day.

[5]It is also recommended that we keep cholesterol intake below 300 mg per day. Remember that cholesterol is found only in foods of animal origin—meat, poultry, fish, eggs, milk and milk products.

## GO LOW ON SODIUM

[6]We get sodium from many sources, but mostly in the form of salt added to foods in processing, cooking and at the table. While we all need some sodium daily (about 500 mg) most Americans consume more than the 2400 mg per day recommended by the National Academy of Sciences. To put these numbers in perspective, just one teaspoon of salt contains about 2000 mg of sodium. Though it has not been proven that eating large amounts of sodium causes high blood pressure, many health professionals believe that reducing sodium intake is a good idea for everyone.

## EAT FIBER-RICH FOODS

[7]Nutrition authorities recommend 20–30 grams of fiber per day, but many Americans consume much less. This is because we do not eat enough vegetables, fruits and grains in our current diets. Populations like ours with diets low in these types of foods and with higher than recommended amounts of fat tend to have a high incidence of heart disease, obesity and some types of cancers.

**One Possible Plan»Do»Review Approach
for "Nutrition in the '90s"**

*Plan*

1.  Find an environment for maximum concentration.
2.  Allot time to complete the assignment, relax, and adopt a positive attitude.

3. Review the professor's instructions: "Read this for tomorrow's lecture."

4. Set your purpose: Read to identify main concepts and understand vocabulary.

5. Preview the assignment:

   - read (1) title and author, (2) two introductory paragraphs, (3) bold-faced headings, (4) table

6. Organize your thoughts (use headings/subheadings to organize):

   Introductory paragraphs:

   - basic message: Eat a diet low in fat, cholesterol, sodium and high in complex carbohydrates and dietary fiber to reduce risk of chronic disease
   - focus on "big picture"—total diet over time

   Major diet concerns:

   - variety
   - cut back on fat and cholesterol
   - go low on sodium
   - eat fiber-rich foods

7. Determine specific reading outcomes: To prepare for lecture I will read to find out:

   a. How do you get good variety in your diet?

   b. How can you cut back on fat and cholesterol?

   c. Why should you cut back on sodium?

   d. What are fiber-rich foods?

*Do*

8. Begin reading.

9. Monitor comprehension by answering the four questions in the plan:

   a. How do you get good variety in your diet? Eat from the five food groups every day.

   b. How can you cut back on fat and cholesterol? Doesn't say how to cut back; advises that fat should be no more than 30 percent of total calories, how to calculate you own daily fat target, and to keep cholesterol below 300 mg per day.

   c. Why should you cut back on sodium? Too much sodium may cause high blood pressure; reducing sodium seems to just be a good idea.

   d. What are fiber-rich foods? Fiber-rich foods include vegetables, fruits, and grains.

10. Fix-up strategy: define "high incidence of heart disease," paragraph 7: high occurrence of—more people have heart disease.

11. Finished reading.

*Review*

12. Two to four hours before lecture, reread thoughts jotted down during planning (#6) and answers to four questions (#9).

USE YOUR STRATEGIES: EXERCISE 2

# *Fractions*

ALLEN R. ANGEL

*Allen Angel teaches at Monroe Community College. This selection is from his book* Elementary Algebra for College Students, *3rd ed.*

*For this exercise, assume your instructor has asked you to read this portion of the section on "Fractions" to prepare for a quiz on basic algebraic terms. (1) Prepare a plan that includes what you will read during preview, how you will organize your thoughts, and four terms you will identify. (2) Tell how you will read to complete your plan (be sure to include answers to your planning questions). (3) Describe the review strategies you will use to prepare for your quiz.*

## FRACTIONS

»1. Learn multiplication symbols.
»2. Recognize factors.
»3. Reduce fractions to lowest terms.
»4. Multiply fractions.
»5. Divide fractions.
»6. Add and subtract fractions.
»7. Convert mixed numbers to fractions.

Students taking algebra for the first time often ask, "What is the difference between arithmetic and algebra?" When doing arithmetic, all of the quantities used in the calculations are known. In algebra, however, one or more of the quantities are often unknown and must be found.

### Example 1

A recipe calls for 3 cups of flour. Mrs. Clark has 2 cups of flour. How many additional cups does she need?

*Solution:* The answer is 1 cup.

Although very elementary, this is an example of an algebraic problem. The unknown quantity is the number of additional cups of flour needed.

An understanding of decimal numbers and fractions is essential to success in algebra. The procedures to add, subtract, multiply, and divide numbers containing decimal points are reviewed in Appendix A. Percents are also reviewed in Appendix A. You may wish to review this material now.

You will need to know how to reduce a fraction to its lowest terms and how to add, subtract, multiply, and divide fractions. We will review these topics in this section. We will also explain the meaning of factors.

»**1** In algebra we often use letters called **variables** to represent numbers. A letter commonly used for a variable is the letter $x$. So that we do not confuse the variable $x$ with the times sign, we use different notation to indicate multiplication.

---

### Multiplication Symbols

If $a$ and $b$ stand for (or represent) any two mathematical quantities, then each of the following may be used to indicate the product of $a$ and $b$ ("$a$ times $b$").

$$ab \qquad a \cdot b \qquad a(b) \qquad (a)b \qquad (a)(b)$$

---

### EXAMPLES

| *3 times 4 may be written* | *3 times x may be written* | *x times y may be written* |
|---|---|---|
| | $3x$ | $xy$ |
| 3(4) | 3($x$) | $x$($y$) |
| (3)4 | (3)$x$ | ($x$)$y$ |
| (3)(4) | (3)($x$) | ($x$)($y$) |
| 3 • 4 | 3 • $x$ | $x$ • $y$ |

»**2** The numbers or variables multiplied in a multiplication problem are called **factors.**

---

If $a \cdot b = c$, then $a$ and $b$ are **factors** of $c$.

---

For example, in $3 \cdot 5 = 15$, the numbers 3 and 5 are factors of the product 15. As a second example, consider $2 \cdot 15 = 30$. The numbers 2 and 15 are factors of the product 30. Note that 30 has many other factors. Since $5 \cdot 6 = 30$, the numbers 5 and 6 are also factors of 30. Since $3x$ means 3 times $x$, both the 3 and the $x$ are factors of $3x$.

»**3** Now we have the necessary information to discuss fractions. The top number of a fraction is called the **numerator,** and the bottom number is called the **denominator.** In the fraction $\frac{3}{5}$ the 3 is the numerator and the 5 is the denominator.

A fraction is **reduced to its lowest terms** when the numerator and denominator have no common factors other than 1. To reduce a fraction to its lowest terms, follow these steps.

> **To Reduce a Fraction to Its Lowest Terms**
> 1. Find the largest number that will divide (without remainder) both the numerator and the denominator. This number is called the **greatest common factor.**
> 2. Then divide both the numerator and the denominator by the greatest common factor.

If you do not remember how to find the greatest common factor (GCF) of two or more numbers, read Appendix B.

### Example 2

Reduce $\frac{10}{25}$ to its lowest terms.

Solution:  The largest number that divides both 10 and 25 is 5. therefore, 5 is the greatest common factor. Divide both the numerator and the denominator by 5 to reduce the fraction to its lowest terms.

$$\frac{10}{25} = \frac{10 \div 5}{25 \div 5} = \frac{2}{5}$$

---

**USE YOUR STRATEGIES: EXERCISE 3**

# *Sources of Groundwater Pollution*

### BERNARD J. NEBEL

*Dr. Nebel is a biology professor at Catonsville Community College in Maryland, where he has taught environmental science for 21 years. He is a member of several professional associations and actively supports a number of environmental organizations. This selection comes from his book* Environmental Science, *3rd ed.*

*For this exercise, assume that you have had one introductory lecture on sources of pollution and that your instructor has asked you to read this assignment before the next class. (1) Prepare a plan that includes what you will read during preview, how you will organize your thoughts, and four questions you will answer. (2) Tell how you will read to complete your plan (be sure to include answers to your planning questions). (3) Describe the review strategies you will use to prepare for the lecture and a possible quiz.*

[1]As water infiltrates and percolates through the soil, it will tend to dissolve and carry any soluble chemicals into the groundwater. The soil will not filter out chemicals that are in solution. It is the old problem of *leaching* described in earlier chapters. Consequently, the general principle is: *Any chemical used on, disposed of, spilled, or leaked onto or into the ground can contaminate groundwater* (Figure 11–2).

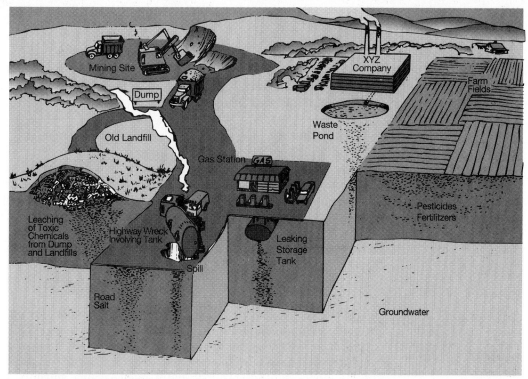

**Figure 11–2** Any chemical used, stored, spilled, or disposed of on or near the surface may leach into the groundwater. This illustration depicts some of the most significant sources of groundwater contamination.

[2]Major sources of groundwater pollution are currently recognized as the following:

[3]• Inadequate landfills and other facilities where toxic chemicals have been dumped and from which they may leach into groundwater.

[4]• Leaking underground storage tanks or pipelines. The leakage of gasoline from service station storage tanks is a particular problem.

[5]• Pesticides and fertilizers used on croplands, lawns, and gardens.

[6]• Deicing salt used on roads.

[7]• Waste oils used on dirt roads to keep dust down.

[8]• Overapplication of sewage sludges or wastewater.

[9]• Transportation spills.

[10]Of all these, inadequate disposal and use of pesticides are considered to be the most widespread threat to groundwater.

### TOXIC CHEMICALS: THEIR THREAT

[11]The most insidious of all groundwater pollution problems involves certain toxic chemicals that may go undetected because of being at very low concentrations, but which may gradually accumu-

late in the body to cause many adverse health effects including cancer.

### What Are the Toxic Chemicals?

[12]Most toxic chemicals belong to one of two classes: heavy metals or synthetic organic chemicals.

***Heavy Metals.*** [13]*Heavy metals* are metallic elements that in pure form are heavy. Lead, mercury, arsenic, cadmium, tin, chromium, zinc, and copper are examples. They are widely used throughout industry. Heavy metals are extremely toxic because, as ions or in certain compounds, they are soluble in water and may be ingested and absorbed into the body where they tend to combine with and inhibit the functioning of particular enzymes. Thus, very small amounts can have severe physiological or neurological consequences. The mental retardation caused by lead poisoning and the insanity and crippling birth defects caused by mercury are particularly well known.

***Synthetic Organics.*** [14]Recall that all the complex molecules that make up plants and animals are natural organic chemicals. In contrast, chemists have learned to make hundreds of thousands of organic (carbon-based) compounds that are the basis for all plastics, synthetic fibers, synthetic rubber, paint-like coatings, solvents, pesticides, wood preservatives, and innumerable other chemicals. Such human-made organic compounds are referred to as synthetic organic chemicals.

[15]Many synthetic organic compounds are similar enough to natural organic compounds that they may be absorbed into the body and interact with particular enzymes or other systems, but here they cause problems. The body may not be able to break them down or metabolize them in any way; they are *nonbiodegradable.* The result is that they upset the system. With sufficient doses the effect may be acute poisoning and death. However, with low doses over extended periods, the effects are even more insidious, including **mutagenic** (mutation-causing), **carcinogenic** (cancer-causing), and **tetratogenic** (birth-defect-causing) effects. In addition, they may cause serious liver and kidney dysfunction, sterility, and numerous other physiological and neurological problems.

[16]A class of synthetic organics that is particularly troublesome is the **halogenated hydrocarbons,** organic compounds in which one or more of the hydrogen atoms have been replaced by an atom of chlorine, bromine, fluorine, or iodine. These four elements are classified as *halogens;* hence the name halogenated hydrocarbons.

[17]Among all the halogenated hydrocarbons, those containing chlorine and referred to as **chlorinated hydrocarbons** are by far the most common. Such compounds are widely used in plastics (e.g., polyvinyl chloride), pesticides (e.g., DDT, kepone, and mirex), solvents (e.g., carbon tetrachlophenol), electrical insulation (e.g., PCBs or polychlorinated biphjenyls), flame retardants (e.g., TRIS), and many other products. *PCBs* and *dioxin* are examples of chlorinated hydrocarbons that are notorious for their pollution hazard. . . .

# *Rhythm*

## DANIEL T. POLITOSKE

*Daniel Politoske teaches at the University of Kansas. "Rhythm" comes from the 5th edition of his book* Music.

*For this exercise, assume your instructor has asked you to read this assignment before the next class. Your instructor often gives a quiz on terminology at the beginning of class. (1) Prepare a plan that includes what you will read during preview, how you will organize your thoughts, and four questions you will answer. (2) Tell how you will read to complete your plan (be sure to include answers to your planning questions). (3) Describe the review strategies you will use to prepare for the lecture and a possible quiz.*

[1]***Listening Preview.*** Rhythm and melody are fundamental to most music of all countries and periods. Sometimes one or the other seems to be dominant, but both often work together to create a particular musical effect. Listen to a performance of a Gregorian chant, such as the Introit of the Requiem Mass, and notice the prominence of the single melody with very free rhythm sung by a choir. Contrast that use of melody with the melody heard at the beginning of Bach's Fugue in G Minor, in which the melody is also very prominent and distinctive, but whose rhythm is heard in more regular patterns. As the opening melody and rhythm are repeated in the piece, notice how quickly they become easy to recognize because of certain recurring patterns.

## THE BASIC MATERIALS OF MUSIC

[2]An outpouring of thoughts or emotions is not in itself artistic. It must be made accessible to another person before a work of art is created. This requires organizing, disciplining, and refining the basic material.

### Sound and Time

[3]A musical work is essentially a disciplined and refined organization of sounds. The sounds that are produced unfold in time from one moment to the next. Thus, music itself may be defined very simply as *sound* organized within *time*. Indeed, the twentieth-century composer Igor Stravinsky (1882–1971) once defined music as "a speculation in terms of sound and time."

## RHYTHM

[4]When we listen for structure in music, recognizing rhythmic patterns makes the music easier to understand.

## Beats and Rhythmic Patterns

[5]*Rhythm* is music's organizing principle, and *beats* are the regular divisions of time which define rhythm. In its widest sense, rhythm is the organizing principle of the natural world and our lives also: musical rhythms were probably originally modeled after such natural phenomena as regularly recurring heartbeats, breathing, and the cycle of days and nights.

[6]One structural factor that is immediately evident to the ear is the repetition of certain rhythmic patterns. A basic rhythmic pattern of Twin-kle, twin-kle, lit-tle star is used from the beginning of the song – – – – – — The pattern is presented six times without change. You will hear this repeated rhythmic pattern even more clearly if you clap the rhythm of the song.

[7]Historians have speculated that music originated in the beating of rhythms that were used to accompany ritual. In some traditional music of African peoples, music still focuses predominantly on rhythms, often very complicated ones. In the music of many cultures, rhythmic patterns are occasionally alone, with no accompanying melody. Military drum rolls are a familiar example. The rhythmic patterns of "Twinkle, Twinkle, Little Star" can be clapped without singing the melodic patterns. In most music, however, rhythmic patters are wedded so closely to melody as to be nearly inseparable.

[8]Think of the words and rhythms of "America." For the moment, don't think of the melody:

|  |  |  | | |  |  |  | |
|------|------|-----|---|-------|------|-------|---|
| ____ | ____ | ___ | | | _____ | ____ | _____ | |
| My | coun - try | 'tis | | of | | thee, | |

| ____ | ____ | ___ | | | _____ | ____ | _____ | |
| Sweet | land | of | | li - | | ber - ty, | |

| ____ | ____ | ___ | | | _____ | | | |
| Of | thee | I | | sing. | | | |

| ____ | ____ | ___ | | | _____ | ____ | _____ | |
| Land | where | my | | fa - | | thers died, | |

| ____ | ____ | ___ | | | _____ | ____ | _____ | |
| Land | of | the | | pil - | | grim's pride, | |

| ____ | __ __ __ __ | | | _____ | ____ | _____ | |
| From | Ev - ry - | | moun - | tain | side | |

| __ __ ___ ____ | | | _____ | | | |
| Let - | free - dom | | ring! | | | |

Certain patterns of long and short tones are immediately perceived by the ear. For example, the pattern _ _ _ ____ _ ___ is heard several times. In all, this rhythm occurs four times in the song, creating a distinctive, repeated rhythmic pattern. Listen to the "Elements of Music" tape, No. 1, to hear examples of rhythm, beat, and rhythmic patterns.

## METER

### Accent

[9]A regularly recurring pulse or beat underlies most rhythmic patterns. In "Twinkle, Twinkle, Little Star" the beat is quite clear from the beginning. Also very clear is a recurring stress—or accent—on the first of every two beats. If the symbol / is used to indicate accented beats and the symbol ∪ to show weaker beats, the pattern looks like this:

| / | ∪ | / | ∪ | / | ∪ | / | ∪ |
|---|---|---|---|---|---|---|---|
| Twin - | kle, | twin - | kle, | lit - | tle | star | —; |

| / | ∪ | / | ∪ | / | ∪ | / | ∪ |
|---|---|---|---|---|---|---|---|
| How | I | won - | der | what | you | are | —. |

A second example shows recurring accents on the first of every three beats of "America":

| / | ∪ | ∪ | / | ∪ | ∪ |
|---|---|---|---|---|---|
| My | coun - | try, | 'tis | of | thee, |

| / | ∪ | ∪ | / | ∪ | ∪ |
|---|---|---|---|---|---|
| Sweet | land | of | li - | ber - | ty, |

| / | ∪ | ∪ | / | ∪ | ∪ |
|---|---|---|---|---|---|
| Of | thee | I | sing | _____ | |

### Triple and Duple Meters

[10]The pattern of accented and unaccented beats or pulses in music is called *meter*. "America" is said to be "in three," or in *triple meter,* because each accented beat marks off a set of three equal beats. "Twinkle, Twinkle, Little Star" is in "two" or *duple meter,* because each accented beat marks off a set of two equal beats. Notice that the musical accents often, but not always, coincide with the accents of the words as they would be spoken.

### Measures

[11]The ear perceives the beats in these songs in groups of three or two—that is, in *measures*. Having observed the formation of one measure, we expect similar measures will follow, all in the same metrical pattern.

[12]Most people are acquainted with the metrical patterns used in certain kinds of music. A person can easily fall into step to the meter of a march—ONE-two, ONE-two. Dances are also characterized by their meters—the waltz by its sweeping ONE-two-three and the polka by its vigorous ONE-two.

[13]In much music, beats are subdivided normally into either two or three units. A meter whose beats are subdivided into two is known as *simple.* "Ba Ba Black Sheep" is in simple duple meter, and "The First Nowell" is in simple triple meter. If the beat has three subdivisions, the meter is *compound:* "Row, Row, Row Your Boat" has a compound duple meter, as its "Merrily, merrily" section illustrates. Other meters are formed from combinations of the basic duple or triple patterns. Especially within the last century, musicians have made unusual deviations from the traditional meters. Tchaikovsky, in the second movement of Symphony No. 6 (the "Pathétique"), used a meter of ONE-two-THREE-four-five, while Béla Bartók, a Hungarian composer, sometimes used measures of seven beats. "Everything's All Right" from the musical *Jesus Christ Superstar* uses a five-beat meter, with the same ONE-two-THREE-four-five stress pattern employed by the Tchaikovsky movement.

### Syncopation

[14]One of the most delightfully surprising effects in music occurs when the meter of a work is upset—that is, when an accent is placed on a normally weak beat of half of a beat. *Syncopation,* as this is called, can be obvious, as in Gershwin's "I've Got Rhythm," or it can be very subtle, as in some folksongs, e.g., "Joe Hill." In dance music, syncopation creates a strong and distinctive rhythmic pattern. It is an essential aspect of most jazz.

[15]Meter organizes a composition into identical groups of strong and weak beats. Syncopation simply changes the placement of the strong accent to an unexpected beat. Listen to the "Elements of Music" tape, No. 2, to hear examples of duple meter, triple meter, and syncopation.

---

### CONNECTIONS

A. Think about an area of your life in which you have been wanting to improve your performance, i.e., play better tennis, stick to a monthly budget, increase your productivity at work. What have you tried recently to help you improve? Do you think the plan»do»review cycle could improve your chances for success? Why or why not? How would you start your plan to improve?

B. Using a plan»do»review»cycle to be a more successful reader asks you to approach reading differently than you have in the past. Which part(s) make the most sense to you? Why? Which part(s) are unclear or seem as if they will be the hardest to use? Do you think you will try using this approach? Why or why not?

# 2

# *Determine Who the Author Is and Why the Author Is Writing*

As suggested in Chapter 1, before you start to read an assignment you should develop a plan of action. You know that your general goal for reading this chapter is to find, practice, and master strategies that you can use to become more successful in reading for learning. But to get the most from this chapter you have to be more specific about your purpose and reading objectives.

Begin to develop your plan for this chapter by reviewing your instructor's directions and clarifying what you need to accomplish. For example, are you reading this chapter to prepare for listening to a lecture on the topic, as a follow-up to a class discussion, for information to use in completing the exercises, or a for a combination of reasons?

When you have decided why you are reading, and you are physically and mentally ready to work, you can activate additional pre-reading strategies. For example, your next step might be to read the content objectives, headings, sub-headings, and chapter-ending questions to get your thoughts focused on the content.

Highlight the definitions for this chapter's key vocabulary:

- prose
- infer and inference
- purpose
- exposition and expository
- narration and narrative
- description and descriptive
- persuasion and persuasive

Now, think about and organize the information you've gathered. One way you could do this is to write down the chapter's major topics, a few words about what you already know on each of the topics, and what you need to find out as you are reading.

Now, do the reading of this chapter.

---

**Chapter 2 Content Objectives**

- determine why it's important to know the author
- identify and define four primary reasons authors have for writing
- identify strategies for inferring author's purpose
- understand why knowing the author's purpose helps comprehension

---

## What Is My Basic Strategy for Determining Who and Why?

**As You Plan:**

1. Make certain you are ready to work.
2. Read about the author and the author's knowledge on this subject.
3. Determine the sources of the author's information.

**As You Read:**

4. Watch for references to information sources.
5. Follow the author's thoughts and clues.
6. Consider all the information.
7. Connect the author's information with your knowledge.
8. Infer the author's purpose.

**As You Review:**

9. Check validity of inferences with the information given.
10. Clarify the author's purpose.

## Why Does It Matter Who the Author Is?

Think about the last time you had to talk with someone you didn't know. Remember how difficult that first conversation was? But do you also recall how, as you learned about his or her background, job, hobbies, friends, and language, talking and understanding became easier?

This also holds true for the silent conversation that takes place between you and the author during reading. Reading without knowing the writer, like talking with someone you don't know, makes communication difficult. Find out as much as you can about who the author is, his or her knowledge of the subject, and the source of the information.

There are several ways you can get to know an author and his or her qualifications for writing. In books, look on the title page for basic data such as where the author teaches or what he or she does. Information about an author's background and professional activities is often included in the preface or in a special "About the Author" section. Journals and magazines usually run a byline and short biography. Professors and librarians can also provide background data on authors. The more comprehensive picture of the author you construct, the more insight you will have for understanding what he or she is saying.

# Why Do Writers Write?

Once you know who is writing, read to find out why he or she is writing. Because an author doesn't often directly state his or her reason for writing, you must consider the information from all the sentences and infer, or put together, the reason for writing.

Inferring a writer's purpose is not just your opinion or a wild guess. An inference is your best reasoned conclusion based on the information you are given. Valid inferences follow logically from the information the author provides. As semanticist S. I. Hayakawa says in *Language in Thought and Action,* an inference is "a statement about the unknown made on the basis of the known."

Knowing an author's reason for writing will help you understand what the author writes. Four primary purposes for writing prose (writing other than poetry) are:

»*Exposition:* the author wants to explain, set forth or make clear facts, events, and ideas

»*Description:* the author wants to paint a picture in words

»*Narration:* the author wants to tell a story

»*Persuasion/Argumentation:* the author wants to influence you—by engaging your emotions or by presenting logical arguments—to believe or feel a certain way or to take a particular action

But, just as in your own writing, authors often combine two or more purposes to clearly communicate their message. For example, an author may need to tell a story's sequence of events with vivid descriptions (but the primary purpose is still to tell you the story) or perhaps persuade you to take some action by giving you facts about the consequences of inaction (but the primary purpose is still to persuade you to act).

## WHAT IS THE PURPOSE OF EXPOSITORY WRITING?

In your textbooks, you will most often find that an author's reason for writing is exposition—to give you information about ideas, events, people, or experiences without taking sides. Examples of exposition in textbooks include: physics—how gravity works, and art humanities—listing the major paintings by Rembrandt.

To establish writing as expository, look for definitions, facts, and explanations that can be verified, rather than personal opinions. When reading exposition, have a clear purpose and concentrate on identifying main ideas first and then selecting the details that meet your purpose.

***Expository paragraph.*** John Macionis is a professor of sociology and author of numerous textbooks in the field. This excerpt comes from his text *Sociology*. The circled phrases highlight how he defines his topic and gives examples of its use. Added together, you can infer that his purpose is to give information about survey research.

## *Survey Research*

A survey is a research method in which subjects respond to a series of items or questions in a questionnaire or an interview. Perhaps the most widely used of all research methods, surveys are particularly suited to studying what cannot be observed directly, such as political attitudes, religious beliefs, or the private lives of couples. Like experiments, surveys can be used to investigate the relationship among variables. They are also useful for descriptive research, in which subject responses help a sociologist to describe a social setting, such as an urban neighborhood or gambling casino.

## WHAT IS THE PURPOSE OF DESCRIPTIVE WRITING?

When authors want you to visualize an object or a setting, they use sight, hearing, smell, taste, and touch words to create a picture that you can see in your mind. In your reading, description is often combined with exposition. Examples of description in textbooks include: political science—the detailed recounting of the sights and sounds of the exuberant celebration when the Berlin Wall came down, and American literature—Steinbeck allowing us to taste and feel the red dirt of the Oklahoma dust bowl in *Grapes of Wrath*.

To identify descriptive writing, look for details about the characteristics of people, places, and things that engage your senses. When reading description, use the author's words to build pictures in your mind.

***Descriptive paragraph.*** From the title and the words that writer-naturalist Joseph Wood Krutch uses in *Desert Year*, we learn more than just that the desert is dry. Notice how, with phrases like those circled, Krutch paints us a picture of the flower, sand, bird, and lizard. We can infer that his purpose is to sketch a picture of his beloved New Mexico desert.

## *What It Looks Like*

What one finds, after one has come to take for granted the grand general simplicity, will be what one takes the trouble to look for— the brilliant little flower springing improbably out of the bare, packed sand, the lizard scuttling with incredible speed from cactus clump to spiny bush, the sudden flash of a bright-colored bird. This dry world, all of which seems so strange to you, is normal to them.

## WHAT IS THE PURPOSE OF NARRATIVE WRITING?

In the narrative, the author tells a story. In academic reading, you will most likely read narration used with exposition; the author tells the story for a purpose or to make a point. Good expository narratives use many specific details. Examples of narration in textbooks include: American government—excerpts from a John Kennedy biography, and chemistry—what happens during combustion.

To identify narrative writing, watch for a retelling of events, situations, and experiences told in the order in which they happen. When reading narration, determine if the author is telling the story just to entertain or if he or she is making a point, explaining a process, developing an idea, or providing information.

***Narrative paragraph.*** Professor, scholar, and Pulitzer-Prize-winning author N. Scott Momaday tells of his life and the traditions of his Native American ancestors in his autobiography, *The Names.* The circled phrases point out how he uses the sequence of events to guide us along. We can infer his purpose is to tell a story.

## *The End Of My Childhood*

The day before I was to leave I went walking across the river to the red mesa, where many times before I had gone to be alone with my thoughts. And I had climbed several times to the top of the mesa and looked among the old ruins there for pottery. This time I chose to climb the north end, perhaps because I had not gone that way before and wanted to see what it was. It was a difficult climb, and when I got to the top I was spent. I lingered among the ruins for more than an hour, I judge, waiting for my strength to return. From there I could see the whole valley below the fields, the river, and the village. It was all very beautiful, and the sight of it filled me with longing.

## WHAT IS THE PURPOSE OF PERSUASIVE WRITING?

In persuasive writing, authors present information, ideas, and opinions that they hope will influence you to adopt a particular point of view, spend your money in a specific way, believe a certain concept, or do something. Authors can try to influence you by engaging your emotions or by presenting logical arguments to support their belief. For our purpose, whether an author wants to convince you through an appeal to emotions or an appeal to reason, we'll call their purpose persuasion. (As you continue with more advanced work, you will differentiate between an appeal to emotions—persuasion—and an appeal to reason—argumentation.) Examples of persuasion in textbooks include: computer programming—details on disk failure rates that make you want to keep backup disks, and health—data from the American Cancer Society on cure rates and research costs that make you want to donate money.

To identify persuasive writing, look for information and opinions that support only one side of an issue or idea. Although skilled persuasive authors indicate that they understand the other side of the issue by saying something about it, they spend their time discrediting ideas that go against their own. When reading persuasion, keep track of information without taking sides. All persuasive material is not bad and should not be discredited; you just need to recognize the author's attempt to influence you so that you can decide whether to accept the information, reject the information, or find more information on the subject before you make up your mind.

***Persuasive paragraph.*** In this preface to his book, *Quality in America: How to Implement a Competitive Quality Program,* President of Technology Research Corporation V. Daniel Hunt discusses the importance of producing quality goods. Notice, in the circled phrases, the words Hunt uses to appeal to patriotism and the desire for security to encourage readers to implement the Quality First™ program. We can infer that his purpose is to persuade the reader to take action.

# *Preface*

Producing quality goods and services is crucial not only to the continued economic growth of the United States, but also to our national security and the well-being and standard of living of each American family. America has been recognized for its leadership in producing quality products. However, in recent years, the position of America as quality leader has been challenged by foreign competition in domestic and overseas markets. Reasserting our leadership position will require a firm commitment to quality and the Quality First™ principle of continuous quality improvement. America can, and must excel in this area, setting new standards for world-class quality and competing vigorously in international markets. (™ held by Technology Research Corporation)

## CAN AN AUTHOR HAVE MULTIPLE REASONS FOR WRITING?

As mentioned earlier, an author often combines two or more purposes to communicate a message more clearly.

Harvard historian and Kennedy advisor Arthur M. Schlesinger, Jr., uses a combination of narration and exposition—using story form to tell what happened—in this excerpt from his book about Kennedy, *A Thousand Days.* What clues does Schlesinger give you?

# A Thousand Days

When they arrived at Love Field, Congressman Henry Gonzalez said jokingly, "Well, I'm taking my risks. I haven't got my steel vest yet." The President, disembarking, walked immediately across the sunlit field to the crowd and shook hands. Then they entered the cars to drive from the airport to the center of the city. The people in the outskirts, Kenneth O'Donnell later said, were "not unfriendly nor terribly enthusiastic. They waved. But they were reserved, I thought." The crowds increased as they entered the city—"still very orderly, but cheerful." In downtown Dallas enthusiasm grew. Soon even O'Donnell was satisfied. The car turned off Main Street, the President was happy and waving, Jacqueline erect and proud by his side, and Mrs. Connally saying, "You certainly can't say that the people of Dallas haven't given you a nice welcome," and the automobile turning on to Elm Street and down the slope past the Texas School Book Depository, and the shots, faint and frightening, suddenly distinct over the roar of the motorcade, and the quizzical look on the President's face before he pitched over, and Jacqueline crying, "Oh, no, no . . . Oh, my God, they have shot my husband," and the horror, the vacancy.

The first narrative clues include *When they arrived,* and *The President, disembarking, walked immediately across the sunlit field to the crowd and shook hands.* What other narrative clues do you find?

Malcolm Rohrbough, a history professor and historian of the American West, tells the story of *Aspen: The History of a Silver Mining Town* using description and exposition—word pictures and facts. What descriptive clues does Rohrbough use?

# A Thrifty Mining Camp

The mining camp of Aspen lay at the end of a horseshoe, with the open end facing west down the valley of the Roaring Fork. Contact with the world of capital, supplies, technology, and people (in the form of immigrants) lay toward the east, however, across the axis of the horseshoe, by way of mountain ranges more than fourteen thousand feet high. The camp could be approached from only two directions: west from Leadville by way of Independence Pass; north from Buena Vista via the Taylor or Cottonwood Pass.

Rather than just tell where Aspen was located on a map, Rohrbough begins drawing a word picture of the location of Aspen in the first sentence: *Aspen lay at the end of a horseshoe, with the open end facing west down the valley of the Roaring Fork.*

---

### PRACTICE: IDENTIFYING THE AUTHOR'S PURPOSE

Identify the author's purpose for writing in each paragraph.

1. Like traditional library research, there are a number of things you should do before you go on-line to do research in an electronic database. First, decide exactly what you want to know. Next, determine which database you will be using and how that database operates. Finally, write out your search strategy so that once you are on-line you can proceed through your search efficiently. (McGrath, *Magazine Article Writing Basics*)

2. Across the Great Plains, they erupt from the earth, tall and spindly with great round heads that spin and shine like galvanized bugs, twisting and clanking and spitting water. (Carrier, "Windmill Creaks Echo in West's History," *The Denver Post*)

3. . . . One of the strongest barriers to good thinking, then, is fear. Fear may show itself as anger, envy, selfishness, or hatred, but these are just expressions of our fear. And don't underrate the power of such emotions. History has shown what devastation fear and hatred among nations can wreak. Our personal fears can be just as damaging to our inner world, blinding our critical faculties with their dark energies. When we argue, then, we must be aware of what we feel as well as what we think. A good critical thinker may have to scrutinize not only the intellectual character of an argument, but its emotional temperature as well. (White, *Discovering Philosophy*)

4. The primary distinction between a bill, note and bond is the length of time, or term, the security will be outstanding from the date of issue. Treasury bills are short-term obligations issued for one year or less. Treasury notes are medium-term obligations issued with a term of at least one year, but not more than ten years. Treasury bonds are long-term obligations issued with a term greater than ten years. (Department of the Treasury)

5. By the early 1600s several religious minorities had abandoned hope of change in England and had begun to consider emigration. The first to depart was a small body of radical Puritan Separatists, the Pilgrims. In 1608 this group moved to Leiden in the Netherlands, then a refuge for religious minorities from all over Europe. For a while they prospered, but as time passed the little congregation began to fear for its survival and its orthodoxy in the face of the easygoing religious ways of the Dutch. In 1617 the Pilgrim leaders decided to move the congregation to "Virginia," where they could maintain their preferred mode of life and form of worship without distraction. (Unger, *These United States*)

---

### REVIEW QUESTIONS

*Review Questions*

1. Why is it important to know who the author is? Do you think this information is more critical for some types of material than others? Why?

2. What are some strategies for identifying an author's expertise?

3. What is an inference?

4. List and define four primary purposes for writing.

5. List at least one strategy to use for identifying each of the purposes for writing.

6. Why is understanding who the author is and what the author's purpose is for writing helpful for accurate comprehension?

*Think and Connect Questions*

7. Re-read the selections at the end of Chapter 1. Notice who the author is and determine the primary purpose for writing. Does knowing the author's background and purpose influence your willingness to accept the information? Why/why not?

8. Using one text section from one of your other textbooks and two magazine articles, identify the author and the primary purpose for writing.

*Application Exercises*

9. Using the topic "cheating on a college exam," write an expository paragraph, a persuasive paragraph, and a descriptive narrative paragraph.

10. From recent newspapers and magazines, identify articles that represent each of the primary purposes for writing, and an article in which the author has multiple purposes for writing. Try to establish who the author is.

**Note:** If you have problems with any of the exercises, use one of the fix-up strategies described in Chapter 1, such as re-reading, to get the information you need to be successful.

---

### USE YOUR STRATEGIES: EXERCISE 1

1. What can you infer best-selling author James Michener's purpose was in introducing readers of *Tales of the South Pacific* to character Luther Billis this way?

# A Boar's Tooth

The fat SeaBee was energetic and imaginative. He looked like something out of Treasure Island. He had a sagging belly that ran over his belt by three flabby inches. He rarely wore a shirt and was tanned a dark brown. His hair was long, and in his left ear he wore a thin golden ring. The custom was prevalent in the South Pacific and was a throwback to pirate days.

He was liberally tattooed. On each breast was a fine dove, flying toward his heart. His left arm contained a python curled around his muscles and biting savagely at his thumb. His right arm had two designs: Death Rather Than Dishonor and Thinking of Home and Mother. Like the natives, Luther wore a sprig of frangipani in his hair.

. . . On his left arm Billis wore an aluminum watch band, a heavy silver slave bracelet with his name engraved, and a superb wire circlet made of woven airplane wire welded and hammered flat. On his right wrist he had a shining copper bracelet on which his social security and service numbers were engraved. And he wore a fine boar's tusk.

2. What can you infer the American Dental Association's purpose is in this excerpt from their booklet "Keeping Your Dental Health: An Adult Thing to Do"?

# Periodontal Disease

What Is It? There are actually several types of periodontal disease. All are started by a bacterial infection that destroys the gums, bone and ligaments supporting the teeth. Periodontal disease progresses silently, often without pain or overt symptoms that would alert you to its presence. It may develop slowly or progress quite rapidly.

Despite unparalleled advances in dentistry and breakthroughs in research, periodontal disease remains a serious dental health problem. Nine out of ten people are afflicted by it in the course of their lives. Responsible for considerable tooth loss in adults, periodontal disease currently affects more than half of the population over age 18. After age 35, about three out of four adults develop some form of gum disease.

3. What can you infer college professors Presley, Freitas, and Jones' purpose is in this excerpt from their textbook, *An Introduction to Business Using Works?*

# Banks

By the strictest definition, the word "bank" refers to commercial banks; however, in a broader application of the term, "bank" also includes other types of financial institutions, such as savings and loan associations and credit unions. Commercial banks are banking corporations which accept demand deposits and make loans to businesses. Savings and loan associations are financial corporations set up to sell shares to individuals, the proceeds of which are mostly invested in home mortgages. The investors are paid in the form of dividends rather than interest. Credit unions are cooperative financial societies organized by a group of people to accept deposits and make loans to its members.

4. What can you infer freelance writer Alexandra Greeley's purpose is in this article written for the *FDA Consumer?*

# *Getting the Lead Out . . . of Just About Everything*

A Puerto Rican family moved here from the Caribbean with high hopes for a better life. They set up housekeeping in low-income housing in eastern Massachusetts, and four of the six children developed lead poisoning, shattering family dreams.

When questioned, the 10-year-old son answers that he lives in the state of Boston and that George Washington is president of the United States. He cannot count to 30. His younger brother with severe lead poisoning is chronically restless. He is unable to sit still, and the doctor describes him as roaming around the doctor's office like a "caged animal."

In another case, the ninth of 10 children of a well-to-do Boston family had seizures and was in a coma as a child as a result of lead poisoning. She ultimately recovered and went to school and then to college. But her history shows she had tremendous emotional difficulties throughout her life and has managed to cope only because her family had the financial resources to help.

Not fictious children, they represent but a few of the cases that John Graef, M.D., associate clinical professor at Harvard Medical School and chief of the lead and toxicology program at Children's Hospital in Boston, has encountered in his career. "I think we all get numbed by the numbers," he says. "These are real people. Statistics do not tell the whole story. . . . One of the things that worries us is that no matter where we look, there are ways for lead to enter our bodies."

Despite successful cleanup efforts—such as the reduction in the numbers of lead-soldered food cans, which the FDA has urged, and the removal of lead from gasoline—health problems caused by repeated exposure to lead continue to endanger Americans.

5. What can you infer automotive writers Jane and Larry McGrath's purpose is in this *Performance Racing Industry* magazine article excerpt?

# *Trends 2000: Positioning for Profit*

The future is bright for grassroots racing across the country—from Friday night drags and autocross to NHRA and NASCAR division racing. And all those racers are high-energy ingenious folks. They refuse to be satisfied with today's performance; they boldly search and research for the best of tomorrow.

That translates into a decade of unlimited business opportunities for high performance automotive retailers. With a proactive vitality, successful retailers are positioning themselves to increase profits well into the 21st century. "By the year 2000 we're going to look different and market our products differently," predicts Mike Oldham, Automotive Engineering, Clearwater, Florida. "We'll get rid of our old '60s look' and become more interesting and energetic," he said.

For many, however, building a long-range plan to achieve and profit from that competitive 'new look' is a mystery. To help unlock that mystery, here are the seven tactics that industry leaders forecast will propel retailers successfully into the future.

6. What can you infer the author's purpose is in this excerpt from an article on Bolivian silver mines in *Newsweek*'s Columbus issue?

# *Potosí: A Mountain That Eats Men*

They say that Huayna Cápaj, king of the Incas, discovered the silver of Potosí, the Bolivian mines that lined the pockets of Spain and the rest of Europe for two centuries. . . . The Spanish arrived "from afar" in 1545 and by the turn of the century had extracted silver equal to three times the wealth in all of Europe's reserves. In 1592, the year of peak production, the mines yielded 220 tons of precious metal. Potosí itself became the jewel of the empire, a European-style metropolis with 36 gambling houses, ballrooms and theaters. When 16th-century Spaniards referred to something invaluable, they called it "worth a Potosí."

7. What can you infer the Alaskan Tourist Board's purpose is in this paragraph excerpted from their booklet for potential tourists?

# *Alaska*

This is a land of secrets, of ancient rainforests, of timeless rituals, with creatures of the land, the air, and the sea all taking part. When nature sings her ancient songs, birds wing their way north, and majestic whales begin their annual odyssey which may encompass thousands of miles. We, too, heed inner voices and turn north when the spirit calls. This is a land of mountain spires, of mighty rivers, and of whispering breezes. Some say if you listen carefully, you'll hear it calling your name.

8. What can you infer Janson and Janson's purpose is in this excerpt from the introduction to their text *A Basic History of Art?*

# Form

Every two-dimensional shape that we find in art is the counterpart to a three-dimensional form. There is nevertheless a vast difference between drawing or painting forms and sculpting them. The one transcribes, the other brings them to life, as it were. They require fundamentally different talents and attitudes toward material as well as subject matter. Although numerous artists have been competent in both painting and sculpture, only a handful have managed to bridge the gap between them with complete success.

Sculpture is categorized according to whether it is carved or modeled and whether it is relief or free-standing. Relief remains tied to the background, from which it only partially emerges, in contrast to free-standing sculpture, which is fully liberated from it. A further distinction is made between low (bas) relief and high (alto) relief, depending on how much the carving projects. However, since scale as well as depth must be taken into account, there is no single guideline, so that a third category, middle (mezzo) relief, is sometimes cited.

9. What can you infer professors McGrath and Rings' purpose is in this course syllabus statement?

# Success

Rarely can you get something for nothing. However, according to study skills expert David Ellis, students can get nothing for something—it happens when the only thing they invest in a course is their money.

We have no magic formulas, no new discoveries, no quick-fixes. The reading and study strategies we will present have been around, in one form or another, for a long time. Some of the strategies will work for you and some will not but there is no way for you to know until you use them.

We can merely set the stage; you create learning through your own energy and action.

10. What can you infer professor Macionis's purpose is in this portion of a "Sociology of Everyday Life" segment in his *Sociology* text?

# What's in a Name? Social Forces and Personal Choice

On July 4, 1918, twins were born to Abe and Becky Friedman in Sioux City, Iowa. The first to be born was named Esther Pauline Friedman; her sister was named Pauline Esther Friedman. Today, these women are known to almost every American, but by new names adopted later: Ann Landers and Abigail ("Dear Abby") Van Buren.

These two women are not the only Americans to have changed their names to further their careers—it is a practice especially common among celebrities. At first glance, this may seem to be simply a matter of particular preference. However, examining the list below from a sociological perspective uncovers a general pattern. Historically, women and men of various national backgrounds have tended to adopt not just any name, but *English-sounding* names. Why? Because American society has long accorded high social prestige to those of Anglo-Saxon background.

---

**USE YOUR STRATEGIES: EXERCISE 2**

---

# Can Interpersonal Skills Be Taught?

## STEPHEN P. ROBBINS

*Stephen Robbins teaches organizational behavior at San Diego State University and Southern Illinois University at Edwardsville. He is also the author of the best-selling* Organizational Behavior, 4th ed. *This selection is from* Training in Interpersonal Skills.

[1]Business and public-sector organizations spend tens of millions—maybe hundreds of millions—of dollars each year on development programs to improve their managers' interpersonal skills. You'd think, therefore, that there would be little debate over whether such skills can be effectively taught. But there are diverse opinions on this question.

[2]On one side are those who view interpersonal skills as essentially personality traits that are deeply entrenched and not amenable to change (Fiedler, 1965). Just as some people are naturally quiet, while others are outgoing, the antitraining side argues that some people can work well with others while many cannot. That is, it's a talent you either have or you don't. Their case is intuitively

appealing when they single out individuals with highly abrasive interpersonal styles and propose that no amount of training is likely to convert them into "people-oriented" types. Most of their evidence, however, tends to be of this anecdotal variety.

[3]The skills advocates have an increasing body of empirical research to support their case. For instance, there is evidence that training programs focusing on the human relations problems of leadership, supervision, attitudes toward employees, communication, and self-awareness produce some improvement in managerial performance (Burke and Day, 1986).

[4]Nothing in the research suggests that skills training can magically transform the interpersonally incompetent into highly effective leaders. But that should not be the test of whether interpersonal skills can be taught. The evidence strongly demonstrates that these skills can be learned. Although people differ in their baseline abilities, the research shows that training can result in improved skills for most people.

1. Who is the author?
2. Do you think that the author is knowledgeable about the subject? Why or why not?
3. What can you infer the author's purpose for writing is?
4. What does the author want to convince you of?

---

**USE YOUR STRATEGIES: EXERCISE 3**

# *Advice to Beginning Writers*

### ROBERT L. MCGRATH

*Robert McGrath is a free-lance writer/photographer living in Irvine, California. His work appears in numerous national publications. This selection is from* Byline.

[1]Countless successful writers—and some not so accomplished—have tried to unlock the secret of their triumphs to share it with others. Obviously, there is no patented method to achieve success. What works for one person may be a washout for others. But here's a method that works for me, and perhaps it will be helpful to you. I call it SWAP—a four-part approach to achievement in your writing efforts.

[2]**S**—Studying. Writing requires a lifetime of study. Your study may be concentrated at local colleges which offer writing courses at various levels, along with occasional seminars and local writers' groups. Or it may involve reading all the books about creative writ-

ing you can find. Constant review of magazines such as *Byline, Writer's Digest, The Writer,* and others will contribute immeasurably to your study program. Read the type of material you aspire to write. Saturate yourself with it. Have at hand several basic tools: A good dictionary, a thesaurus, a market list, books on technique covering the categories you hope to sell. Use them!

[3]**W**—Writing. This, of course, is the only way to succeed. A writer must write; otherwise, he is not a writer, and cannot lay claim to the appellation. Study courses, either in classroom situations or by correspondence, can be helpful, combining study with actual writing by requiring a certain amount of discipline—otherwise often elusive. I like an additional formula: SOP-2-SOC—seat of pants to seat of chair. So Hemingway stood at the mantel to write . . . do it your way, but do it. Pen, pencil, typewriter, word processor—they're all good tools. Use them! Form the habit of writing, every day if possible. Time or place do not matter. Just do it!

[4]**A**—Ambition. Set realistic goals for yourself. Be practical. Your first effort probably won't be The Great American Novel. But an expressive poem just might find print in an obscure journal and set you on your way. Or you might be a winner in one or more of the many *Byline* contests. You'll need a certain amount of self-confidence, for without it, you'll never reach those goals. Know that you have the native ability to put words on paper—words that will be worthwhile not only to you, but to others as well. Another formula comes to mind: SYI—scratch your itch. You have that urge to write. So write . . . write . . . write.

[5]**P**—Perseverance. Never give up on something you believe in. You can succeed, but only if you refuse to toss in the towel. My files contain irrefutable proof of the value of hanging in there. My short short story, "Payment Received," won tenth place in the 1955 *Writer's Digest* contest. I figured it had to be a worthy piece. But on thirty-nine trips to various editors, it failed to make the grade. The fortieth submission was to a magazine that previously had rejected it. I goofed; otherwise, I probably wouldn't have resubmitted it to Alfred *Hitchcock's Mystery Magazine.* It was later published in a hardcover collection of Hitchcock yarns, and reprinted in two separate paperback editions of the same anthology. It was read over a South African radio station (for which I was paid). It was the subject of a *Writer's Digest* experience report. Perseverance caused its sale. Other stories have parallel records. One sold to prestigious *Stories* magazine on its fifty-fifth trip out. The record for me is a sale on the eightieth trip to an editor's desk. Believe in yourself—persevere!

[6]Try the **SWAP** plan. Results aren't guaranteed, but it's worth a try.

1. Who is the author?

2. Do you think the author is knowledgeable about the subject? Why or why not?

3. What can you infer the author's purpose for writing is?

# An American Elite:
# Thoughts on the Ladies
# and Gentlemen of West Point

## JAN MORRIS

*Jan Morris is the author of more than 20 travel books. Her most recent is* Sydney, *which was published last year. This selection is from* Travel Holiday.

¹After dark one evening I went down alone to the Plain, the great parade ground of the United States Military Academy, at West Point, New York. A moon was rising, the Hudson lay dark and velvety below, and across the grass a solitary skunk came snuffling through the dusk. Now and then aircraft winked their way overhead. A train wailed somewhere. A tug and its barges labored upstream toward Albany. A curious military-police car coasted by. There was not another soul about, down there above the river, but in the great, monastic buildings of the academy, dimly crowned by the Cadet Chapel tower, myriad lights steadily and silently burned.

²Four thousand three hundred young American men and women, I knew, were hard at work in there, steadfast before computer screens, deep into laws of ballistics, theories of economics, translations from the Russian, differential equations, historical relevancies. These men and women were to be an elite, an officer corps to lead the armies of the Republic into a world subject more than ever to American power and decision—the world of the Pax Americana. My few minutes alone there seemed to me an almost transcendental time, one of those moments of travel when history, place, and circumstance seem in collusion to proclaim some truth—if we can only discover what it is.

³The military police returned. "You okay, ma'am?" Sure, I said, quite okay, just watching the skunk.

⁴It was true that I had never seen a skunk in nature before, but actually I was contemplating the moment. I cannot deny that as a visitor from Britain I was greatly depressed just then by the condition of the United States, which seemed more than usually sunk in crime, corruption, and hypocrisy, bewildered by racism, and enervated by crackpot introspections. West Point was a world of its own, a place where the old American values counted still, where honor and duty were watch-words and to tell a lie was to betray one's heritage; a place too, so it appeared that evening, where purpose was so exactly matched by experience that the scene became an allegory.

⁵Next day I went back in daylight and saw the future elite for myself—classes of '92 to '95. Every football Saturday the entire Corps of Cadets parades in their gray uniforms between the statues of Eisenhower and MacArthur, with George Washington on his high

plinth in the middle. Some of the West Point mystique, gathering since the academy's foundation, in 1802, is then on display for any passerby to see. Ensigns flutter. A 100-piece band plays. Swords flash. Tradition's Long Gray Line is regimentally massed. And one of the place's better-known peculiarities is publicly demonstrated.

[6]The quizzing of the plebes, or freshmen (freshpersons, as the world outside West Point might call them), is a demanding ritual. There in the open air, on the parade ground, freshmen cadets are examined by upperclassmen in anything from the dates of presidents to the contents of that morning's *New York Times*. I watched it all through my binoculars. Alarming indeed were the attitudes of the examiners, as severe military snap questions were put and answers offered. Sometimes lists of names seemed to be demanded. Sometimes the freshmen seemed to be reciting poems or perhaps military regulations. Sometimes songs were ordered.

1. Who is the author?
2. Do you think the author is knowledgeable about the subject? Why or why not?
3. What can you infer the author's purpose for writing is?

---

**USE YOUR STRATEGIES: EXERCISE 5**

# *The First Americans*

## IRWIN UNGER

*Pulitzer-Prize-winning historian Irwin Unger has been teaching American history for over 25 years on both coasts. He currently teaches at New York University, where he has been since 1966. This selection is from* These United States, *5th ed.*

[1]The first Americans were migrants from eastern Siberia on the Asian mainland. Physically, they belonged to the same human stock as the modern Chinese, Japanese, and Koreans—a relationship suggested by the straight black hair, broad face, and high cheekbones of most modern American Indians. The migrants were a hunting, fishing, and gathering people who depended on roots, berries, fish, and game for food. As decreasing rainfall reduced these resources in Siberia, scholars conjecture, the native peoples gradually moved eastward seeking sustenance. Today they would be stopped by the Bering Sea, but in that distant era we know that a land bridge joined Alaska in North America to Siberia. On the eastern side of this bridge the migrants probably found more abundant food supplies and a climate milder than in their homeland. Gradually they moved southward along various routes, and by the time Europeans arrived many thousands of years later, they had spread from just below the

Arctic Ocean to Tierra del Fuego at the southern tip of South America and from the Atlantic to the Pacific. They had also grown enormously in numbers. From perhaps a few hundred or a few thousand migrants, by 1942 the Indian population of the Americas had swelled to 75 million, a figure equal to that of contemporary Europe.

[2]As their numbers grew over the centuries, the descendants of these Asian people diversified into many groups with distinct languages, cultures, and political and economic systems. By about 3000 B.C. some had begun to practice agriculture, with "maize" (corn), first developed from a grasslike native American plant, as their chief crop and the staple of their diet. They also grew tomatoes, squash, various kinds of beans, and, in South America, potatoes. Surpluses from agriculture transformed Indian life. Abundant food led to larger populations and also to more diverse societies. Not everyone was needed to produce food to sustain life, so classes of priests, warriors, artisans, and chiefs appeared. In the most fertile agricultural regions great civilizations arose with a command of technology, artistic sophistication, and political complexity comparable to the civilizations of Asia and Europe.

1. Who is the author?
2. Do you think the author is knowledgeable about the subject? Why or why not?
3. What can you infer the author's purpose for writing is?

## CONNECTIONS

A. In what classes do you think you will have to do mostly expository reading? In what classes will you probably have a mixture of types of readings? Why the differences? What impact might these differences have on the way you study for particular classes?

B. Look again at the sample readings and exercises in this chapter. Who are your two favorite authors? Why are they your favorites? Do you tend to prefer a certain type of writer (for example, writers who use description more than straight exposition)? Do your preferences seem to affect your comprehension? If so, what strategies could you use to overcome potential problems?

# 3

## *Understand the Vocabulary the Author Uses*

English is the richest language with the largest vocabulary on Earth—over 1,000,000 words. Yet the average adult has a vocabulary of only 40,000 to 50,000 words. So it's not surprising that in every reading assignment you encounter unfamiliar and confusing words.

As you develop your plan for reading this chapter, think about what you do when you run into a word you don't know. Perhaps you stop and look it up in the dictionary or find someone you can ask. What else have you tried? What do you do when the definition you found in the dictionary doesn't make sense in the context of the sentence or paragraph you're reading?

When you preview this chapter, jot down your own answer to each of the boldfaced questions. Then, as you read and gain new information, revise your answer.

Also, highlight the definitions for this chapter's key vocabulary:

- context
- context clues
- prefix
- root
- suffix
- word analysis
- literal meaning
- denotation
- connotation
- figurative language
- simile
- metaphor

---

**Chapter 3 Content Objectives**

- formulate an overall strategy for defining unfamiliar words
- understand how to use context to help define a word
- understand how to use the parts of the word to help define it
- identify other resources for defining unfamiliar words
- recognize the difference between the denotation and the connotation of a word
- recognize when words are chosen by the author for a special purpose
- recognize and understand figurative language

---

## What Is My Basic Strategy for Understanding the Author's Vocabulary?

**As You Plan:**

1. Review words that are highlighted, i.e., words in **bold face** or *italic* and words that are defined in footnotes or marginal notes.

**As You Read:**

2. Identify unfamiliar words.
3. Use context clues:

   - Look at the surrounding words: do they offer any clues?
   - Look at the rest of the sentences or paragraphs: do they offer any clues?
   - Look for other clues, such as punctuation, the author's purpose, or setting.

4. Analyze word parts:

   - Look at the word: Is it related to a known word?

5. Use your own experience.
6. Predict the possible meaning.
7. Try out the meaning in the sentence and see if it makes sense.
8. Decide if the definition makes sense, if you should try again, or if you should consult a dictionary or an expert.
9. Check for meanings beyond the literal definition.

**As You Review:**

10. Clarify any remaining definitions.
11. If it is important to your purpose, determine a way to review and remember the new words.

# How Can I Use the Context to Help Define a Word?

Most of these words are familiar: *option, trading, call, put, uncovered, naked,* and *covered.* Yet in this paragraph from the stockbroker's newsletter you read in Chapter 1, your definitions for the words probably didn't help you understand the paragraph.

Writing or selling *Options* against stock you already own is a strategy that is conservative and usually works well in a *trading* market. An Option is either a *call* (a right to buy 100 shares of stock at a specified price in the future) or a *put* (a right to sell 100 shares of stock at a specified price in the future). Thus an Option buyer or seller who owns no stock (called *uncovered* or *naked*) is a speculator who is looking at making large percentage returns on a small amount of invested capital in a short time. This individual would be paying the Option premium to us, the *covered* writer.

This is because words do not have just one, isolated meaning. Words take on meaning from their context—how they are used in conjunction with other words.

When you read this, you could either skip over the words you didn't know or try to figure out their meanings. Fortunately, active readers—readers thinking about and looking for related information—can often use clues the author provides to help them understand unfamiliar words. In fact, I just used a context clue: I defined what I meant by "active reader" and set it off with a dash (—) as your clue.

As another example, look for context clues in the stockbroker's paragraph. Considering the first two words—*Options* and *trading*—are there any words or information in the paragraph that help? Not really, so if you don't recognize them from your own experience, come back to them later. The next four of the words—*call, put, uncovered, naked*—are defined for you (parentheses are your clue). To define the final word—*covered*—the author gives the definition for its opposite—*uncovered*—as your clue.

## USING CONTEXT CLUES

Assume you are reading your astronomy text and come to the unfamiliar words *perihelion* and *aphelion.* To comprehend the passage, you must understand the words. See how you can use the context clues the author provides.

*Perihelion* is the point in the earth's orbit where the distance between the earth and the sun is at its minimum, as opposed to *aphelion.*

Here, the author defined *perihelion* directly (the point in the earth's orbit where the distance between the earth and the sun is at its minimum) and has clued you to the definition of *aphelion* by stating it is the opposite (therefore, *aphelion* must be the point in the earth's orbit where the distance between the earth and the sun is at its maximum).

In addition to using punctuation, stating a definition or an opposite, an author can provide other clues, such as giving an example or explanation, or restating the thought in more simple terms.

Making use of context clues to help define unfamiliar words is much like the work you did in Chapter 2 to infer the author's purpose. You combine all the information an author provides to determine the meaning the word has in this context. The meanings you construct through context clues are not reckless guesses; they are thoughtful suppositions supported by the author's information.

Unless the passage is extremely difficult and has too many unfamiliar words, using context clues can save you time and assure that you have the best definition for the context.

See how author John Macionis uses a variety of context clues in these passages from his text *Sociology.* As you read, look for words, phrases, and punctuation that relate to or seem to point to the unknown word.

### Gives a Specific Definition of an Important Word (*sociology*):

A distinctive perspective is central to the discipline of *sociology,* which is defined as the scientific study of human social activity. As an academic discipline, sociology is continually learning more about how human beings as social creatures think and act.

### Provides an Explanation of a New Word (*replication*):

One way to limit distortion caused by personal values is through the *replication* of research. When the same results are obtained by subsequent studies there is increased confidence that the original research was conducted objectively.

### Uses Punctuation As a Clue to Meaning of Words (*experiment, hypothesis*):

The logic of science is clearly expressed in the *experiment*—a research method that investigates cause-and-effect relationships under high controlled conditions. Experimental research tends to be explanatory, meaning that it is concerned not with just what happens but with why. Experiments are typically devised to test a specific *hypothesis*—an unverified statement of a relationship between any facts or variables. In everyday language, a hypothesis is simply a hunch or educated guess about what the research will show.

### Gives Clue to Unknown Term (*ethnography*) by Comparison to Known Term (*case study*):

Cultural anthropologists describe an unfamiliar culture in an *ethnography;* a sociologist may study a particular category of people or a particular setting as a *case study.*

### Gives Clue to New Word (*secondary analysis*) by Stating Its Opposite:

Each of the methods of conducting sociological investigation described so far involves researchers personally collecting their own data. Doing so is not always possible, however, and it is often not necessary. In many cases, sociologists engage in *secondary analysis.*

**Gives Clue to New Word** *(subculture)* **with Examples:**

When describing cultural diversity, sociologists often use the term *subculture*. Teenagers, Polish-Americans, homeless people, and "southerners" are all examples of subcultures within American societies. Occupations also foster subculture differences, including specialized ways of speaking, as anyone who has ever spent time with race-car drivers, jazz musicians, or even sociologists can attest.

---

### PRACTICE: DEFINING WORDS USING CONTEXT CLUES

Use the author's context clues to unlock the meaning of the italicized terms in these passages. Describe the context clues you used.

1. A magazine is custom-designed for its special audience. For example, *Redbook* and *Cosmopolitan* are both primarily women's magazines and may have articles on similar topics but their *slant*—their approach to the topic—is very different. Each must answer the questions and provide the information their readers expect. (McGrath, *Magazine Article Writing Basics Handbook*)

2. *Like terms* are terms that have the same variables with the same exponents. (Angel, *Elementary Algebra for College Students,* 3rd ed.)

3. Typically, work outcomes are measured in *physical units* (i.e., quantity of production, number of errors), *time* (i.e., meeting deadlines, coming to work each day), or *money* (i.e., profits, sales costs). (Robbins, *Training in InterPersonal Skills*)

4. A composer often provides a marking for *tempo,* or overall speed, to help convey the character of a composition. (Politoske, *Music*)

5. Computerphobia, the fear of computers, is apparently affecting more and more people as microcomputers continue to be plugged into more and more homes, schools, and offices throughout the land. This relatively recent phenomenon, also known as *cyberphobia,* occurs in a large proportion of students and professionals. (Fuori and Gioia, *Computers and Information Processing*)

6. One problem in treating alcoholism is that it is hard to recognize. Although a person who is *chronically* drunk, as opposed to the occasional drinker, is more suspect. (*University of California at Berkeley Wellness Newsletter,* February 1993)

## How Can I Use the Word Itself as a Clue to Its Meaning?

You can't always rely on context clues; there may not be any or they may be confusing. Another strategy you can use to define an unfamiliar word is to analyze the parts of the word—its root and any prefixes and/or suffixes—as clues to the meaning of the entire word.

The root is the basic part of a word. Additional words are sometimes made by adding a prefix at the beginning of a root word and/or a suffix at the end of a root word. Prefixes and suffixes change the meaning of the root word. A suffix can also change the way a word can be used in a sentence. Combining the meanings of the word parts helps you to understand the whole word.

When you learn the meaning of a few common word parts, you have a head start on defining other words that contain those parts. In fact, researchers estimate that for every word part you know, you have the key to unlock the meaning of about seven more words.

## USING WORD PARTS

Let's assume you are reading a different astronomy text, this one with no context clues, and you come to the unfamiliar words *perihelion* and *aphelion*. If you know, or can look up the meanings of the basic word parts, you can define the words as easily as with context clues:

*perihelion: peri* from the Greek, meaning *near* + *helios* from the Greek, meaning *the sun* = near the sun

*aphelion: apo* from the Greek, meaning *away from* + *helios* from the Greek, meaning *the sun* = away from the sun

We arrive at a similar meaning for *perihelion* and *aphelion* as when there were context clues to help. We just used a different strategy.

If you know that *apolune* means the point in the path of a body orbiting the moon that is farthest from the center of the moon, what does *perilune* mean? By combining what you already knew about *peri* (near) with the new information (*lune* means moon), you know that *perilune* means the point in the path of a body orbiting the moon that is nearest the center of the moon.

Use word parts to help define each of these words.

| | |
|---|---|
| un = not | able = capable of |
| retro = backward | spec = see |
| trans = across | anti = against |

a.  un•read•able (not capable of being read)
b.  retro•spec•tive (looking backward)
c.  trans•atlantic (across the Atlantic ocean)
d.  anti•inflammatory (against, or counteracting inflammation)

---

### PRACTICE: DEFINING WORDS USING WORD PARTS

---

The following table lists some common word parts. Use them to help you define the italicized words in these passages.

1.  It is the loss of this *biodiversity* and the loss of *unreplaceable* ancient forests that most concern environmentalists about the issue of logging in national forests. (Scott, "Hoots to Blame?")

### Roots

| | | | |
|---|---|---|---|
| aud, audit | hear | demos | people |
| graphy | writing, record | mit, miss | send |
| pathy | feeling | port | carry |
| divers | different | phob | fear |
| scribe, script | write | spec | see |
| literate, literatus | able to read and write | geront, gerento | old age |
| annus (ennal) | year | mille | 1,000 |

### Prefixes

| | | | |
|---|---|---|---|
| ec-, eco- | habitat | chiz- or schizo- | split |
| phren, phreno- | mind | il-, im-, ir- | in or into/or not |
| tele- | over a distance | mega-, meg- | large |
| trans- | across | retro- | backward |
| anti, contra, ob- | against | quadri-, quadr- | four |
| un- | not or opposite | bi-, bio- | living organisms |
| intra- | within, inside | inter- | among, between |
| semi- | half | ultra- | super, excessive |
| micro- | small | em-, en- | within |

### Suffixes

| | | | |
|---|---|---|---|
| -er, -or, -ist | one who | -ly | like |
| -ance, -ancy, -ency | act or fact of doing | -able | capable of |
| -ese | native to; originating in | -ulent | abounding in |
| -ine | having the nature of | -al | characterized by |
| -ment | action | -less | without |
| -logy | oral/written expression | -ism | manner of action |
| -ity | condition, state | -fy | make, form into |

2. In the industrialized countries, 3.3 percent of the adult population is *illiterate.* For the developing countries as a whole the figure is 35 percent, and rises as high as 60 percent in the 47 least developed countries. (Bequette, *UNESCO Courier,* January 1993)

3. In *telecommunications* we are moving to a single worldwide information network, just as economically we are becoming one global marketplace. (Naisbitt and Aburdene, *Megatrends 2000*)

4. Baca recalls her role in the beginning of the Chicano Mural Movement when she was searching for a way to express her own experience as a Hispanic American artist. Greatly influenced by the Mexican muralists, Baca discovered a means of community *empowerment.* (Estrada, "Judy Baca's Art for Peace")

5. Moving from our analysis of the term communication, we now examine the process of communication. We begin by studying a communication model and the three types of communication important to our study in this text: *intrapersonal, interpersonal,* and mass communication. (Bittner, *Each Other*)

6. The compost pile is really a teeming *microbial* farm. (Office of Environmental Affairs, *Backyard Composting*)

# If I Still Can't Figure Out the Meaning, What Other Resources Can I Use?

There will be times when you can't piece together any helpful information from the context or the structure of the word. When this happens, take the time to look the word up in the book's glossary or a dictionary, or ask one of your resource people (someone you identified in Chapter 1 as being a resource.)

A glossary is a quick, easy-to-use resource because it lists only the specific meaning of the word as it's used in the book. Not all books provide a glossary (and even those that do sometimes won't provide enough information—such as how to pronounce the word), so sometimes you will need to consult a dictionary.

A dictionary is a reliable source of all the definitions for a word, plus the correct spelling variations, pronunciations, parts of speech, and derivations. Since you will often find several definitions for a word, you must always fit the meaning you select back into the original context to be certain it makes sense.

## USING A DICTIONARY

Assume that this time you come across *perihelion* and *aphelion* in your text and you don't have any context clues and you don't know the meaning of the word parts. Looking up the words in a dictionary gives you literal meanings similar to when you used context clues or word parts.

> **a|phe|li·on** (ə fē′lē ən, -fēl′yən) *n., pl.* -**li·ons** or -**li|a** (-ə) ⟦ModL, altered (as if Gr) by Johannes KEPLER < earlier *aphelium* < Gr *apo-*, from + *hēlios,* SUN¹; modeled on L *apogaeum,* APOGEE⟧ the point farthest from the sun in the orbit of a planet or comet, or of a man-made satellite in orbit around the sun: opposed to PERIHELION

In this passage from the editors of *Syllabus,* you may have conflicting ideas about the meaning of rudimentary—does it mean low or high?

> The increasing power of the personal computer is making it possible to develop applications that are smarter and more responsive to the user. . . . Anyone who has used a spelling or grammar checker has experienced this type of application at a very *rudimentary* level. ("Advanced Technologies Lead the Way to the Future of Educational Computing," *Syllabus*)

If rudimentary is an unfamiliar word, your best resource is the dictionary.

> **ru·di·men·ta|ry** (rōō'də men'tər ē, -men'trē) **adj.** of, or having the nature of, a rudiment or rudiments; specif., *a)* elementary  *b)* incompletely or imperfectly developed  *c)* vestigial

Unfortunately, finding the correct meaning of a word in the dictionary is not always this clear-cut. Many words have more than one meaning and can be used as more than one part of speech. Each time you look up a word in the dictionary, your job is to sort through the definitions and select the one definition that best fits the context.

For example, if you look up the word *base* in a dictionary, you will find a variety of definitions.

> **base¹** (bās) **n.,** *pl.* **bas'|es** (-iz) ⟦ME < OFr *bas* < L *basis,* BASIS⟧ **1** the thing or part on which something rests; lowest part or bottom; foundation **2** the fundamental or main part, as of a plan, organization, system, theory, etc. **3** the principal or essential ingredient, or the one serving as a vehicle *[paint with an oil base]* **4** anything from which a start is made; basis **5** *Baseball* any of the three sand-filled bags *(first base, second base,* or *third base)* that must be reached safely one after the other to score a run **6** the point of attachment of a part of the body *[the base of the thumb]* **7** a center of operations or source of supply; headquarters, as of a military operation or exploring expedition **8** *a)* the bottommost layer or coat, as of paint *b)* a makeup cream to give a desired color to the skin, esp. in the theater **9** *Archit.* the lower part, as of a column, pier, or wall, regarded as a separate unit **10** *Chem.* any compound that can react with an acid to form a salt, the hydroxyl of the base being replaced by a negative ion: in modern theory, any substance that produces a negative ion and donates electrons to an acid to form covalent bonds: in water solution a base tastes bitter, turns red litmus paper blue, and, in dissociation theory, produces free hydroxyl ions: see pH **11** *Dyeing* a substance used for fixing colors **12** *Geom.* the line or plane upon which a figure is thought of as resting *[the base of a triangle]* **13** *Heraldry* the lower portion of a shield **14** *Linguis.* any morpheme to which prefixes, suffixes, etc. are or can be added; stem or root **15** *Math. a)* a whole number, esp. 10 or 2, made the fundamental number, and raised to various powers to produce the major counting units, of a number system; radix *b)* any number raised to a power by an exponent (see LOGARITHM) *c)* in business, etc., a starting or reference figure or sum upon which certain calculations are made

Select the best definition of base for each of the following sentences.

1. In the expression $4^2$, the 4 is called the *base,* and the $^2$ is called the exponent.

2. The Ionic order's most striking feature is the column, which rests on an ornately profiled *base* of its own.

3. The closing of the military *base* in the region prompted a quick economic decline.

4. Today's experiment will show whether the compound is *base* or acid.

5. Both investigation teams were working from the same *base* information.

---

**PRACTICE: SELECTING THE BEST DICTIONARY DEFINITION**

---

Each of the italicized words or phrases has multiple meanings listed in the dictionary. Select the definition that best fits the context.

1. Your career depends not only on your efforts, but also on the efforts of many other people. You cannot be successful by yourself. You can only be successful as part of a joint effort by many different people, by acting in *harmony* with other people. All through your career, you will find yourself interdependent with other people. (Johnson, *Human Relations and Your Career*)

> **har·mo|ny** (här′mə nē) ***n.***, *pl.* **-nies** ⟦ME *armony* < OFr *harmonie* < L *harmonia* < Gr < *harmos*, a fitting < IE base \**ar-* > ART, ARM¹ ⟧ **1** a combination of parts into a pleasing or orderly whole; congruity **2** agreement in feeling, action, ideas, interests, etc.; peaceable or friendly relations **3** a state of agreement or orderly arrangement according to color, size, shape, etc. **4** an arrangement of parallel passages of different authors, esp. of the Scriptures, so as to bring out corresponding ideas, qualities, etc. **5** agreeable sounds; music **6** *Music a)* the simultaneous sounding of two or more tones, esp. when satisfying to the ear *b)* structure in terms of the arrangement, modulation, etc. of chords (distinguished from MELODY, RHYTHM) *c)* the study of this structure

2. Population increases, urban growth, and devastating poverty are three of the most *acute* problems facing the world in the 21st century.

> **a|cute** (ə kyo̅o̅t′) ***adj.*** ⟦L *acutus*, pp. of *acuere*, sharpen: see ACUMEN⟧ **1** having a sharp point **2** keen or quick of mind; shrewd **3** sensitive to impressions *[acute* hearing*]* **4** severe and sharp, as pain, jealousy, etc. **5** severe but of short duration; not chronic: said of some diseases **6** very serious; critical; crucial *[an acute* shortage of workers*]* **7** shrill; high in pitch **8** of less than 90 degrees *[an acute* angle*]*: see ANGLE¹, illus. **9** INTENSIVE (sense 3)

3. Science is an important foundation of all sociological research and, more broadly, helps us to *critically* evaluate information we encounter every day. (Macionis, *Sociology,* 3rd ed.)

> **crit|i·cal** (krit′i kəl) ***adj.*** **1** tending to find fault; censorious **2** characterized by careful analysis and judgment *[a* sound *critical* estimate of the problem*]* **3** of critics or criticism **4** of or forming a crisis or turning point; decisive **5** dangerous or risky; causing anxiety *[a critical* situation in international relations*]* **6** of the crisis of a disease **7** designating or of important products or raw materials subject to increased production and restricted distribution under strict control, as in wartime **8** *a)* designating or of a point at which a change in character, property, or condition is effected *b)* designating or of the point at which a nuclear chain reaction becomes self-sustaining —**crit′i·cal|ly** *adv.* —**crit′i·cal′i|ty** (-kal′ə tē) or **crit′|i·cal·ness** *n.*

4. A *front* usually is in constant motion, shifting the position of the boundary between the air masses but maintaining its function as a barrier between them. Usually one air mass is actively displacing the other; thus the *front* advances in the direction dictated by the movement of the more active air mass. (Bergman and McKnight, *Introduction to Geography*)

**front** (frunt) *n.* ⟦ME < OFr < L *frons* (gen. *frontis*), forehead, front < IE *bhren-*, to project > OE *brant*, steep, high⟧ **1** *a*) the forehead *b*) the face; countenance **2** *a*) attitude or appearance, as of the face, indicating state of mind; external behavior when facing a problem, etc. *[*to put on a bold *front] b*) [Colloq.] an appearance, usually pretended or assumed, of social standing, wealth, etc. **3** [Rare] impudence; effrontery **4** the part of something that faces forward or is regarded as facing forward; most important side; forepart **5** the first part; beginning *[*toward the *front* of the book] **6** the place or position directly before a person or thing **7** a forward or leading position or situation ☆**8** the first available bellhop or page, as in a hotel: generally used as a call **9** the land bordering a lake, ocean, street, etc. **10** [Brit.] a promenade along a body of water **11** the advanced line, or the whole area, of contact between opposing sides in warfare; combat zone **12** a specified area of activity *[*the home *front,* the political *front]* **13** a broad movement in which different groups are united for the achievement of certain common political or social aims ☆**14** a person who serves as a public representative of a business, group, etc., usually because of his or her prestige ☆**15** a person or group used to cover or obscure the activity or objectives of another, controlling person or group **16** a stiff bosom, worn with formal clothes **17** *Archit.* a face of a building; esp., the face with the principal entrance **18** *Meteorol.* the boundary between two air masses of different density and temperature —*adj.* **1** at, to, in, on, or of the front **2** *Phonet.* articulated with the tongue toward the front of the mouth, as (i) in *bid* —*vt.* **1** to face; be opposite to **2** to be before in place **3** to meet; confront **4** to defy; oppose **5** to supply or serve as a front, or facing, of —*vi.* **1** to face in a certain direction *[*a castle *fronting* on the sea] ☆**2** to act as a FRONT (senses 14 & 15): with *for*

5. The effects created by different intensities of sound, or dynamics, are basic to all musical expression. In traditional music, we often first become aware of the impact of dynamic effects upon hearing very sudden changes from soft to loud, or vice versa. For some of us, the first awareness of musical dynamics is very obvious, as in the so-called "Surprise" Symphony of Franz Joseph Haydn (1732–1809). Here, the surprise is a *radical* change in volume, a very loud chord coming on the heels of a gentle melody. (Politoske, *Music*)

**rad|i·cal** (rad′i kəl) *adj.* ⟦ME < LL *radicalis* < L *radix* (gen. ROOT[1]⟧ **1** *a*) of or from the root or roots; going to the foun( source of something; fundamental; basic *[*a *radical* prin( extreme; thorough *[*a *radical* change in one's life] **2** *a*) fundamental or extreme change; specif., favoring basic chan social or economic structure *b*) [**R-**] designating or of any o: modern political parties, esp. in Europe, ranging from mo( conservative in program **3** *Bot.* of or coming from the root having to do with the root or roots of a number or quantity —( basic or root part of something *b*) a fundamental **2** *a*) ε holding radical views, esp. one favoring fundamental socia nomic change *b*) [**R-**] a member or adherent of a Radical *Chem.* a group of two or more atoms that acts as a single a goes through a reaction unchanged, or is replaced by a single is normally incapable of separate existence **4** *Math. a*) the i root of a quantity or quantities, shown by an expression under the radical sign *b*) RADICAL SIGN

## PRACTICE: DEFINING WORDS USING OUTSIDE RESOURCES

Define each of the italicized words or phrases and tell what resource you used to find your definition.

1. America's love affair with the automobile was never any secret in Los Angeles. Built around the car, the Californian *megalopolis* is the biggest gas guzzler in the world. Its 13 million residents drive 9 million cars over 386 million kilometers (nearly 24 million miles) a day, using up 68 million liters (nearly 18 million gallons) of gasoline and

diesel fuel, and producing 60 percent of the city's *notorious* smog. (*UNESCO Courier,* November 1992)

2. Since before the first *Gutenberg revolution,* paper has served as an indispensable all-purpose catalyst for much of one abstraction of what universities are all about: the creation, preservation, dissemination, and interpretation of data, information, and knowledge. (Lynn, "Publish Electronically or Perish," *Higher Education Product Companion*)

3. Few people could imagine that in a decade or so television would become a *preemptory force* in American culture, defining the news, reshaping politics, reorienting family life, and remaking the cultural expectations of several generations of Americans. (Gilder, *Life After Television*)

4. The automobile, one of the most *pervasive* symbols of modern culture, serves as an *apt metaphor* for the ways in which humans change the global environment. (Silver, *One Earth, One Future*)

5. Our institutions of family, religion, education, business, labor, and community are attempting to keep afloat while wrestling with both internal and external combatants. Each group's *raison d'être* is challenged constantly while it seeks acceptable canons in which to function in modern society. (Rauch, "A Quality Life Should Be Full of Values" *USA Today*)

## How Can I Use the Strategies Together While I'm Reading?

Real reading tasks don't have the obvious look of these isolated samples. To read successfully (remember that reading and understanding are synonymous terms), the variety of material required in an academic setting requires that you use strategies flexibly.

When you encounter a word that hinders your understanding, you may first check to see if there are any context clues you can use. On the other hand, if you recognize the parts of the word, perhaps that is all the clue you need. You work smarter, not harder. But you also realize that if context clues, word analysis, and your experience don't yield a probable meaning for the word, you must take time to consult an outside resource, like the dictionary.

For example, read this sentence from *Megatrends 2000,* by John Naisbitt and Patricia Aburdene. "Conceived under the influence of the next millennium, these new megatrends are the gateways to the 21st century."

You probably read the passage by combining several strategies:

• noting the context relationships between millennium and 21st century and between megatrends and gateways

• using knowledge of word parts—mille = 1,000 and mega = big

• remembering some prior knowledge—perhaps you've heard of megatrends.

Even if you used a slightly different set of strategies, when you fit the meanings together you understood that Naisbitt and Aburdene were saying "after thinking about the next thousand years—the 21st century—these are the big trends or ideas that will get us there successfully."

---

**PRACTICE: DEFINING WORDS USING CONTEXT CLUES,**
**WORD PARTS, AND OTHER RESOURCES**

---

Use your word sleuthing strategies to define the italicized words.

# *Endangered Species: Endangered Means There's Still Time*

### U.S. DEPARTMENT OF THE INTERIOR, U. S. FISH AND WILDLIFE SERVICE

[1]Since life began on this planet, countless creatures have come and gone—*rendered extinct* by naturally changing *ecological* conditions, and more recently by humans and their activities.

[2]If *extinction* is part of the natural order, and if so many species still remain, some people ask, "Why save *endangered species*? What makes a relatively few animals and plants so special that effort and money should be spent to preserve them?"

## WHY SAVE ENDANGERED SPECIES?

[3]Saving species is important to many people for a variety of reasons. People care about saving species for their beauty and the thrill of seeing them, for scientific and educational purposes, and for their ecological, historic, and cultural values.

[4]A *compelling reason* to preserve species is that each one plays an important role in an *ecosystem*—an intricate network of plant and animal communities and the associated environment. When a species becomes endangered, it indicates that something is wrong with the ecosystems we all depend on. Like the canaries used in coal mines whose deaths warned miners of bad air, the increasing numbers of endangered species warn us that the health of our environment has declined. The measures we take to save endangered species will help *ensure* that the planet we leave for our children is as healthy as the planet our parents left for us.

[5]Some species provide more immediate value to humans. For example, cancer-fighting drugs have been *derived* from the bark of a *yew* that is native to the Pacific Northwest. Chemicals used to treat diseases of nerve tissue were found in an endangered plant in Hawaii. Valuable resources such as these could be lost forever if species go extinct.

## CAUSES OF DECLINE

[6]We can no longer attribute the *accelerating loss* of our wild animals and plants to "natural" processes. *Habitat destruction* is the single most serious worldwide threat to wildlife and plants, followed

by *exploitation* for commercial or other purposes. Disease, *predation,* inadequate conservation laws, pollution, and introduction of non-native species, or a combination of these can contribute to a species' decline.

## THE LISTING PROCESS

[7]The U.S. Fish and Wildlife Service maintains the List of Endangered and Threatened Wildlife and Plants, which identifies species protected under the Endangered Species Act. The Act defines an "endangered" species as one that is in danger of extinction throughout all or a significant portion of its range. A "threatened" species is one likely to become endangered within the foreseeable future.

To understand the meaning of this passage you had to use several strategies together. For example,

*rendered extinct* (¶1): Check surrounding words for clues. Prior phrase "have come and gone" clue to general meaning. I already know extinct means gone. Predict possible meaning: "made to disappear." Fit meaning into sentence. It makes sense.

*ecological* (¶1): Check surrounding words; no strong clues. Read ahead; no specific clues. Consider topic, and that *eco* means habitat. Predict possible meaning "environmental." Fit meaning into sentence. It makes sense, but since this appears to be an important word, I should also check for a dictionary definition.

*extinction* (¶2): Check surrounding words for clues. Following phrase "and if so many species still remain" seems to be opposite to meaning of extinction. Consider it has the same root as *extinct.* Predict possible meaning: "disappearing." Fit meaning into sentence. It makes sense.

*endangered species* (¶2): Check surrounding words; no strong clues. Read ahead; locate specific definition in last paragraph. Fit meaning into sentence. It makes sense.

*compelling reason* (¶4): Check surrounding words for clues. No direct restatement but phrase "each one plays an important role" makes me think it means "good reason." Fit meaning into sentence. It makes sense.

*ecosystem* (¶4): Check surrounding clues; punctuation indicates that definition follows.

*ensure* (¶4): Check surrounding words for clues. No direct word clues but the sentence, taken as a whole, seems to suggest it's positive action. Consider the root *sure.* Predict possible meaning: "make sure." Fit meaning into sentence. It makes sense.

*derived* (¶5): Check surrounding words for clues. No direct clues but phrase "from the bark" makes me think it means "taken from or made out of." Fit meaning into sentence. It makes sense.

*yew* (¶5): Check surrounding words for clues. Prior phrase "from the bark of a" suggests it's a tree. Fit meaning into sentence. It makes sense.

List the strategies you use to define these words from paragraph 6 and your definitions.

1. accelerating loss
2. habitat destruction
3. exploitation
4. predation

## How Can a Word Mean More than Its Definition?

In this chapter we've concentrated on finding an exact literal, or denotative meaning of a word. But words often mean more than their explicit meaning or just what it says in the dictionary. Words can also suggest a variety of meanings that trigger an assortment of feelings and emotions. These associated meanings are called connotations—what the word implies to the reader. Because of these meanings beyond the literal, authors can subtly influence readers with the words they select. You should be especially wary of connotations when the author's primary purpose is to persuade.

For example, which of these descriptions do you think I prefer?

- Dr. McGrath is petite, has reddish-brown hair, and a good sense of humor.
- Dr. McGrath is a runt, has reddish-brown hair, and a good sense of humor.

Yes, even though I have a good sense of humor, I do prefer being called petite. Why? Because even though both petite and runt mean "short" in the dictionary, they make me feel differently because of their connotations. For me, the connotation of petite is positive: small and delicate. The connotation of runt, is negative: unnaturally short.

For example, consider the similarities and differences between the denotative and connotative meanings of the italicized words in each pair of passages.

Jeff was very *confident* he would get the job because he scored well on the written exam.

Jeff was very *cocky* he would get the job because he scored well on the written exam.

Because they felt so strongly about the issue, Karen and Bill took part in a *rally* at the capital.

Because they felt so strongly about the issue, Karen and Bill took part in a *demonstration* at the capital.

In everyday reading, however, you don't have two versions of the same passage to compare. Therefore, once you have determined the literal meaning, ask yourself if the word or phrase makes you feel or react—positively or negatively—beyond its meaning. Determine whether the word seems to soften the impact of the message (anti-personnel weapon instead of bomb) or intensify your reaction to the message (guerrilla fighters instead of freedom fighters). Authors choose words for their maximum impact—including their connotative meaning. You must understand both the denotative and connotative meaning of the words to fully understand the author's message. We'll take another look at how authors influence us by their choice of words in Chapter 8.

---

### PRACTICE: CONSIDERING BOTH THE CONNOTATIVE AND DENOTATIVE MEANINGS

---

Read each pair of words. List their literal definitions and then describe their connotations.

1. a. jock              b. athlete
2. a. reserved          b. inhibited
3. a. collect           b. hoard
4. a. impertinent       b. bold

Read each passage with special attention to the italicized phrases. Why do you think the author selected those words? What message does the author want you to understand? What other words or phrases could be used that would give different connotations?

1. After *unsuccessfully peddling his idea to every monarch of Western Europe,* Columbus finally interested the rulers of Spain. (Unger, *These United States,* 5th ed.)

2. By *crushing black leaders,* while *inflating the images of Uncle Toms* and celebrities from the world of sport and play, the mass media were *able to channel and control the aspirations and goals of the black masses.* (Cleaver, *Soul on Ice*)

3. To many minds, Hillary Clinton is the *quintessential yuppie mother* of the 1990s, juggling career and family with remarkable skill. (editorial, *The Arizona Republic*)

4. Exemptions from ESA (the Endangered Species Act) can be granted by the *so-called God Squad,* which is convened at the request of the U.S. Secretary of the Interior. (Berke, "The Audubon View," *Audubon*)

## What Is Figurative Language?

*From my drifting hot air balloon, the Hawaiian Islands looked like small bread crumbs floating in a full bowl of soup.*

*Enthusiasm bubbled out of petite 22-year-old Chrissy Oliver with the effervescence of a just-opened split of champagne.*

*Homelessness is a rusty blade cutting through the soul of humanity.*

Each of these statements is an example of figurative language: using words in an imaginative way to help you comprehend the message more clearly. Certainly, I could have written the statements literally: "The Hawaiian Islands look small," "Chrissy Oliver was happy to win the race," or "Homelessness causes untold problems," but I would have taken more of a chance that you would picture exactly what I wanted you to understand.

Although figurative language does not make sense literally, it does help you form a mental image, or picture, of what an author is writing about. Figurative expressions often compare something the author thinks you already know about to what he or she wants you to understand. The most basic of these comparisons are called similes (direct comparisons using the words "like" or "as") and metaphors (implied comparisons).

When a passage doesn't make sense to you at the literal level, check to see if the author is using figurative language. If so, use the author's words to draw a mental picture definition and fit that back into the context.

In this paragraph, to what does noted historian John Lukacs compare the problems of this country? What does he want you to picture and understand from the figurative expressions in this passage?

> As the great French thinker Georges Beranos once wrote: "The worst, the most corrupting lies are problems wrongly stated." To put this in biological terms: without an honest diagnosis there can be no therapy, only further decay and perhaps even death. So I must sum up seven deadly sins of misdiagnosis: seven deadly problems that now face this country because of their intellectual misstatements. (Lukacs, *Our Seven Deadly Sins of Misdiagnosis*)

Lukacs wants you to picture the nation as a sick person to whom the doctor has given the wrong diagnosis. Before the person (the nation) can be cured, the illness (the problem) has to be correctly identified.

In this paragraph, training and development specialist Ron Zemke employs two comparisons. What does he want you to picture and understand from the figurative expressions?

> The auditorium lights grow dim. A diffusion of sunrise hues washes languidly across a sweep of rear-projection screens. From beneath stage level, rising in single file like a septet of hunter's moons, come the seven letters of the sacred rite: Q-U-A-L-I-T-Y. (Zemke, "Faith, Hope and TQM," *Training,* January 1992)

In the second sentence Zemke compares the slides coming on the screen to a slow, colorful sunrise. Then, he compares the appearance of the seven (septet) letters of the word QUALITY to the wondrous appearance of large and bright (hunter's) moons. (Note: When you have difficulty understanding a part of the figurative comparison, like "hunter's moons," check with one of your resources to get the literal meaning of the expression. You must understand the literal before the figurative will make sense.)

---

### PRACTICE: UNDERSTANDING FIGURATIVE LANGUAGE

Describe what the author is comparing, and what you should picture and understand from the figurative language in each of these passages.

1. This is our hope. This is the faith that I go back to the South with. With this faith we will be able to *hew out of the mountain of despair a stone of hope.* With this faith we will be able to *transform the jangling discords of our nation into a beautiful symphony of brotherhood.* (King, Jr., "I Have A Dream," speech delivered in Washington, D.C., August 28, 1963)

2. The *performance improvement efforts* of many companies *have as much impact on operational and financial results as a ceremonial rain dance has on the weather.* (Schaffer and Thompson, "Successful Change Begins With Program Results," *Harvard Business Review,* January–February 1992)

3. *The year 2000 is operating like a powerful magnet on humanity,* reaching down into the 1990's and intensifying the decade. It is amplifying emotions, accelerating change, heightening awareness and compelling us to reexamine ourselves, our values, and our institutions. (Naisbitt and Aburdene, *Megatrends 2000*)

4. It wasn't long ago that school newspapers and campus newsletters were being churned out using slow processes that have now all but become extinct. . . . The print-oriented *classrooms of the '90s are now more or less jam-packed with computer terminals,* a *spaghetti feast of electronic wiring,* and students leaning toward computer terminals. (Morse, "Campus Publishing," *Higher Education Product Companion*)

5. *The flowering of Etruscan civilization* coincides with the Archaic age in Greece. During this period, especially near the end of the sixth and early in the fifth century B.C., Etruscan art showed its greatest vigor. (Janson and Janson, *A Basic History of Art*)

6. But time has proven that R.E. *"Ted" Turner*—Captain Outrageous to the press—is *crazy like a fox.* (Griffin and Ebert, *Business,* 2nd ed.)

---

## REVIEW QUESTIONS

*Review Questions*

1. Discuss your overall strategy for defining unfamiliar words.

2. Explain how to use context clues to help define a word and list two types of clues that authors use.

3. Explain what it means to use the parts of the word to help define it. Give one example.

4. List two other resources for defining unfamiliar words, and when you might use them.

5. State the difference between the denotation and connotation of a word. Give an example of how a word can have a connotative meaning beyond its dictionary meaning.

6. Explain why it's important to understand both the denotative and connotative meanings of words and phrases.

7. Explain the purpose of figurative language and give an example.

*Think and Connect Questions*

8. Re-read *Advice To Beginning Writers,* by Robert McGrath, Chapter 2, Exercise 3. Identify four of the unfamiliar words you came across when you first read it, and describe the strategies you used to figure them out. Now that you have some additional strategies, would you go about defining them any differently now? Why or why not?

9. Re-read *An American Elite: Thoughts on the Ladies and Gentleman of West Point,* by Jan Morris, Chapter 2, Exercise 4. Identify two figurative expressions and explain what the author wanted you to picture.

*Application Exercises*

10. From recent newspapers or magazines, select an article you think uses a word or phrase for its connotative meaning. Tell why you think the author used the language. Rewrite the word or phrase, keeping the literal meaning but changing the connotation.

---

**USE YOUR STRATEGIES: EXERCISE 1**

---

# Obsessive-Compulsive Disorder

## MARY LYNN HENDRIX

*Mary Lynn Hendrix is a science writer in the Office of Scientific Information, National Institute of Mental Health (NIMH). Scientific review was provided by NIMH staff members Thomas R. Insel, M.D.; Dennis L. Murphy, M.D.; Teresa A. Pigott, M.D.; Judith L. Rapoport, M.D.; Barry Wolfe, Ph.D.; and Joseph Zohar, M.D.*

### WHAT IS OCD?

[1]In the mental illness called *OCD* (obsessive-compulsive disorder), a person becomes trapped in a pattern of *repetitive* thoughts and behaviors that are senseless and distressing but extremely difficult to overcome. The following are typical examples of OCD:

[2]Troubled by repeated thoughts that she may have *contaminated* herself by touching doorknobs and other "dirty" objects, a teenage girl spends hours every day washing her hands. Her hands are red and raw, and she has little time for social activities.

[3]A middle-aged man is *tormented* by the notion that he may injure others through carelessness. He has difficulty leaving his home because he must first go through a lengthy *ritual* of checking and rechecking the gas jets and water faucets to make certain that they are turned off.

[4]If OCD becomes severe enough, it can destroy a person's *capacity to function* in the home, at work, or at school. That is why it is important to learn about the disorder and the treatments that are now available.

### HOW COMMON IS OCD?

[5]For many years, mental health professionals thought of OCD as a very rare disease because only a small minority of their patients had the condition. But it is believed that many of those *afflicted* with OCD, in efforts to keep their repetitive thoughts and behaviors

secret, fail to seek treatment. This has led to *underestimates* of the number of people with the illness. However, a recent survey by the National Institute of Mental Health (NIMH)—the Federal agency that supports research nationwide on the brain, mental illness, and mental health—has provided new understanding about the *prevalence* of OCD. The NIMH survey shows that this disorder may *affect* as much as 2 percent of the population, meaning that OCD is more common than *schizophrenia* and other severe mental illnesses.

1. What is Hendrix's purpose?
2. Do you think Hendrix is knowledgeable on this topic? Why or why not? What impact does the scientific review panel have on your view?
3. Write the meanings of these words and phrases and what strategies you used to get them.

a. OCD (¶1)

b. repetitive (¶1)

c. contaminated (¶2)

d. tormented (¶3)

e. ritual (¶3)

f. capacity to function (¶4)

g. afflicted (¶5)

h. underestimates (¶5)

i. prevalence (¶5)

j. affect (¶5)

k. schizophrenia (¶5)

---

**USE YOUR STRATEGIES: EXERCISE 2**

# *Hummingbirds: Jewels on Wings*

## ROBERT MCGRATH

*Robert McGrath is a freelance writer. His work appears in numerous national publications. This selection is from* FEDCO Reporter.

[1]You've probably enjoyed watching those tiny rainbow-pinioned helicopters *hover* at the feeder in your backyard—or perhaps at your neighbor's. But how much do you really know about these jewels on wings?

[2]Hummingbirds come in a variety of colors, though mostly in the same *diminutive size* that makes them stand out as among nature's most remarkable creatures.

[3]There are more than 300 kinds, but amazingly, only the ruby-throated hummingbird is found east of the Mississippi River. Western states are home to as many as 18 different types, with the bulk of the others in the family inhabiting Central and South America. None are found outside the Western Hemisphere.

[4]Their kaleidoscopic plumage has no solid color. Instead, there are tiny barbs on each feather, placed so they break and refract light, just as a mirror or a diamond will do. While the male hummingbird is more colorful than his mate, underparts of both male and female are usually gray or a variety of other shades, while head and back are often a glowing green.

[5]The birds sport so many patches of different tints, they're often named after precious jewels—ruby, topaz, emerald, amethyst-throated.

[6]Those whirring wing-beats are made possible by special hinges within their bone-structure that permit helicopter-like rapid vibrating and feathering. Suspended or backward flight requires about 54 wing-beats per second, while normal dodging, darting flight reaching 50 miles per hour takes up to 75 beats of its narrow wings.

[7]Because it uses so much energy in flight, a hummingbird goes into a *state resembling hibernation* at night when it rests from a constant labor of gathering food. When awake, its normal temperature is over 100 degrees; it falls to as low as 64 degrees when it's asleep. The hummingbird's heartbeat, however, is super fast. While human beings average 72 beats a minute, the hummer's regular rate is 615 beats a minute when in flight.

[8]The *territorial-minded* male hummingbird vigorously defends his space against other birds, cats, or even snakes. Yet, once he has selected his mate and courtship is complete, the male leaves everything else to his partner. She alone builds the solid little nest—so small a quarter placed on top of it would stick out over the edges—using plant fibers, lichens, and bark, then cementing this miniature cup with saliva glue and spider webs.

[9]It takes 21 days for the female to hatch her two pea-sized pearly eggs. She then begins the endless duty of feeding the helpless, ever-hungry chicks by herself, a task lasting three weeks, when the *fledglings* are ready to fly.

[10]Anyone with a hummingbird feeder can enjoy a thrill a minute watching these winged wonders display their *aerial antics*—the most exciting in the world of birds.

1. What is McGrath's purpose?

2. Do you think McGrath is knowledgeable to write on this topic? Why or why not?

3. Write the meanings of these words and phrases:

   a. hover (¶1)

   b. diminutive size (¶2)

   c. state resembling hibernation (¶7)

   d. territorial-minded (¶8)

   e. fledglings (¶9)

   f. aerial antics (¶10)

4. Identify and explain:

   a. 2 figurative phrases in paragraph 1

   b. 2 figurative phrases in paragraph 4

   c. 1 figurative phrase in paragraph 9

---

**USE YOUR STRATEGIES: EXERCISE 3**

# *Food Irradiation: A Scary Word*

### DALE BLUMENTHAL

*Dale Blumenthal is a staff writer for* FDA Consumer, *the magazine of the U.S. Food and Drug Administration.*

[1]*Irradiating* food to prevent illness from food-borne bacteria is not a new concept. Research on the technology began in earnest shortly after World War II, when the U.S. Army began a series of experiments irradiating fresh foods for troops in the field. Since 1963, FDA has passed rules permitting irradiation to *curb* insects in foods and microorganisms in spices, control *parasite contamination* of pork, and *retard spoilage* in fruits and vegetables.

[2]But to many people, the word irradiation means danger. It is associated with atomic bomb explosions and *nuclear reactor accidents* such as those at Chernobyl and Three Mile Island. The idea of irradiating food signals a kind of *"gamma alarm"* according to one British broadcaster. (Gamma rays are forms of energy emitted from some radioactive materials.)

[3]But when it comes to food irradiation, the only danger is to the bacteria that contaminate the food. The process damages their *genetic material,* so the organisms can no longer survive or multiply.

[4]Irradiation does not make food *radioactive* and, therefore, does not increase human exposure to radiation. The specified exposure times and energy levels of radiation sources approved for foods are *inadequate to induce radioactivity* in the products, according to FDA's Laura Tarantino, Ph.D., an expert on food irradiation. The process involves exposing food to a source of radiation, such as to the gamma rays from radioactive cobalt or *cesium* or to x-rays. However, no radioactive material is ever added to the product. Manufacturers use the same technique to sterilize many disposable medical devices.

[5]Tarantino notes that in testing the safety of the process, scientists used much higher levels of radiation than those approved for use in poultry. *But even at these elevated levels,* researchers found no toxic or cancer-causing effects in animals *consuming* irradiated poultry.

1. What is Blumenthal's purpose?

2. Do you think Blumenthal is knowledgeable on this topic? Why or why not?

3. Write the meanings of these words and phrases:

    a. irradiating (¶1)

    b. curb (¶1)

    c. parasite contamination (¶1)

    d. retard spoilage (¶1)

    e. nuclear reactor accidents (¶2)

    f. gamma alarm (¶2)

    g. genetic material (¶3)

    h. radioactive (¶4)

    i. inadequate to induce radioactivity (¶4)

    j. cesium (¶4)

    k. but even at these elevated levels (¶5)

    l. consuming (¶5)

---

### Use Your Strategies: Exercise 4

---

# What Ecosystems Are and How They Work

### Bernard J. Nebel

*Dr. Nebel is a biology professor at Catonsville Community College in Maryland where he has taught environmental science for 21 years. He is a member of several professional associations and actively supports a number of environmental organizations. This selection is from* Environmental Science, *3rd ed.*

¹In 1968 astronauts returned with photographs of the earth taken from the moon. These photographs made it clear as never before that the earth is just a sphere suspended in the void of space. It is like a self-contained spaceship on an everlasting journey. There is no home base to which to return for repairs, more provisions, or disposal of wastes; there is just the *continuous radiation* from the sun. Indeed, the term "Spaceship Earth" was *coined* by futurist Buckminster Fuller as a result of this new perspective on our planet.

²Who is at the controls of Spaceship Earth? Unfortunately, no one! But Spaceship Earth is *equipped with an amazing array of self-providing mechanisms. Enormously diverse* plant and animal species *interact* in ways such that each obtains its needs from and provides for the support of others. Air and water are constantly *repurified and recycled.* Then there are self-regulating mechanisms as well, which tend to keep all the systems in balance with each other.

³But now problems are arising. In particular, the *human species is multiplying out of all proportion to others.* This is placing greater and greater demands on all systems and, at the same time, it is undercutting their productivity through pollution and over exploitation. The *natural regulatory mechanisms* are being upset. It is clear that such behavior aboard Spaceship Earth *cannot be sustained without catastrophic consequences.* Nor can we afford the happy-go-lucky luxury of trial-and-error learning when the fate of the whole world is at stake. We must gain an understanding of how Spaceship Earth works and then we must learn to conduct our activities within this context.

⁴Here in Part I our objective is to provide a general framework of understanding concerning the way our spaceship works. This understanding is gained through a study of natural ecosystems: what they are, how they function, how they are regulated, and how they develop and change. In keeping with the scientific method, we shall approach each area by describing the basic observations that have been made and showing how these observations have led to the formation of operating theories and principles. Finally, the understanding of these theories and principles will enable us to see more clearly where current trends are headed and *how certain human activities must be modified if modern society is to be sustained.*

1. What is Nebel's purpose for this section?
2. What does he compare the earth to, and why?
3. Write the meaning of these words and phrases.

    a. continuous radiation (¶1)
    b. coined (¶1)
    c. equipped with an amazing array of self-providing mechanisms (¶2)
    d. enormously diverse (¶2)
    e. interact (¶2)
    f. repurified and recycled (¶2)
    g. human species is multiplying out of all proportion to others (¶3)
    h. natural regulatory mechanisms (¶3)
    i. cannot be sustained without catastrophic consequences (¶3)
    j. how certain human activities must be modified if modern society is to be sustained (¶4)

# Drop the Ball on Sports Metaphors in Political Coverage

### ELLEN GOODMAN

*Ellen Goodman is a syndicated columnist with the* Boston Globe. *Her articles appear in newspapers around the world. This selection appeared in the* Boston Globe.

¹The crocuses are a-blooming, the Ides of March and the Ides of Super Tuesday are here. So, by all these *portents,* it must be time for my *quadrennial plea against the use of sports metaphors in writing, speaking and thinking about politics.*

²This has been a long, personal and so far entirely *futile* attempt on my part to have an impact on the *rhetoric of democracy.* By my calculations, politics has been described as the great American sport ever since the first election was called a race and the candidate became a winner.

## PLAY-BY-PLAY ANALYSIS

³But sports reached a saturation point in the '80s when politicians began to sound like the Wide World of Sports, and the media turned from analysis to play-by-play. One favorite *mixed sports metaphor* came in 1984 from Lawton Chiles, now the governor of Florida, who described the "game plan" for the presidential debates this way: "It's like a football game. . . . Mondale can't get the ball back with one big play. But the American people love a horse race. I would advise him not to knock Reagan out."

⁴Well, as expected, the 1992 campaign began with the usual assortment of slam-dunks, knockout punches, end runs and hard balls. But something happened after the campaign left New Hampshire and *relative civility.* While I was trying to get out of the locker room, we ended up in the trenches.

⁵The metaphors switched from sports to war. The *political coverage reads less like Sports Illustrated than Soldier of Fortune.*

⁶We have campaign "assaults" and "attacks." The Super Tuesday states are "battlegrounds." The candidates "snipe" and "take aim" at each other. Jerry Brown is accused of using "slash-and-burn" tactics. Paul Tsongas is "under fire." And Pat Buchanan is a man who will "take no prisoners."

## PLAYING FIELD TO KILLING FIELD

[7]How did this primary get off the playing field and onto the killing field? Kathleen Jamieson, political wordsmith and dean of the University of Pennsylvania's Annenberg School of Communication, says that war images creep in as a campaign gets, well, hostile.

[8]"When you are playing fairly within the rules of the game, the sports metaphors fit. The war metaphor is much more negative. It doesn't assume fair play or a referee."

[9]If words are the way we frame our ideas, *the war metaphor is more than rhetoric*. It forces us to talk and think about elections as if they were *lethally combative events* in which the object was to kill the enemy and declare victory. In the end, the war metaphor produces a victor or a commander-in-chief. But not necessarily a governor, or a leader, or a problem-solver.

[10]War talk doesn't allow the candidates to describe or stand on common ground. "It doesn't assume the goodwill and integrity of the other side," says Ms. Jamieson. "It doesn't talk about common good and collective ends. It assumes one person is right and the other's wrong."

## SEARCH-AND-DESTROY MISSION

[11]As for the media and the metaphor, fighting words frame the campaign as a search-and-destroy mission. It is not a coincidence that attack ads make the headlines. Nor is it a coincidence, says Ms. Jamieson, that men are much more likely to talk like warriors and write like war correspondents.

[12]Ms. Jamieson herself has been trying to elaborate a different political campaign language. She first played with a *courtship metaphor* since the candidates do woo the electorate and pledge forms of fidelity. That was, to put it mildly, fraught with sexual undertones.

[13]In New Hampshire, a focus group came up with the *metaphor of an orchestra*. The government is, after all, a collective entity that needs a leader to keep things in harmony. This had a nice ring, but it didn't hit all the right notes.

[14]Now Ms. Jamieson is toying with a metaphor that would picture the campaign as a quest. In the *vernacular* of the "quest" metaphor, the candidates would overcome "tests" that reveal their "character."

[15]The campaign would become a "search" for answers, not for the *soft underbelly of an opponent*.

[16]The point is to shift the verbal focus from strategy—"Is he doing what's necessary to win?"—to problems—"Does he understand them, can he solve them?" Her own quest for this "quest" metaphor has just begun. Any ideas are welcome in our metaphor mailbag.

[17]In the meantime, in the spirit of candidates and those who

cover them, *block that war metaphor.* Tackle it if you must. There are already enough bodies on the combat field, careers blown to smithereens and land mines planted for the fall election. All we have learned so far this election year is that politics is hell.

1. What is Goodman's purpose?

2. Write the meanings of these words and phrases:

   a. portents (¶1)

   b. quadrennial plea against the use of sports metaphors (¶1)

   c. futile (¶2)

   d. rhetoric of democracy (¶2)

   e. mixed sports metaphor (¶3)

   f. relative civility (¶4)

   g. political coverage reads less like *Sports Illustrated* than *Soldier of Fortune.* (¶5)

   h. the war metaphor is more than rhetoric (¶9)

   i. lethally combative events (¶9)

   j. courtship metaphor (¶12)

   k. metaphor of an orchestra (¶13)

   l. vernacular (¶14)

   m. soft underbelly of an opponent (¶15)

   n. block that war metaphor (¶17)

### CONNECTIONS

A. Think about the reading demands you have this semester. Discuss how important you think your ability to understand the authors' language is to successful comprehension. How important do you think understanding vocabulary is when you are listening to a lecture?

B. Describe a time when you used a particular word, in writing or speaking, because of its connotation. What was your purpose? Were you successful? Has anyone successfully convinced you to do or not do something by their choice of words?

# 4

# *Identify What the Author Is Writing About*

A significant reason for developing a plan before you begin to read academic material is to make certain you set specific purposes for reading—to decide what you want to find out as you read. When you read for learning, your purpose will usually include finding the author's main ideas. This is because a main idea is the framework that holds all the information together.

During your preview of this chapter, think back to a recent reading assignment where your purpose was to determine the main idea of the chapter. How did you begin your search? What did you look for? How did you know when you had found a main idea? When you found what you thought was a main idea, did you stop reading?

Highlight definitions for this chapter's key vocabulary:

- paragraph
- topic
- controlling thought
- main idea
- thesis
- directly stated main idea
- implied main idea
- multi-paragraph selection

---

**Chapter 4 Content Objectives**

- identify the main idea of a paragraph, whether it is directly stated or implied
- rephrase an author's main idea into a complete sentence using your own words
- identify the thesis of a multi-paragraph selection
- rephrase an author's thesis into a complete sentence using your own words

---

## What Is My Basic Strategy for Identifying What the Author Is Writing About?

**As You Plan:**

1. Understand the vocabulary.
2. Identify the topic—ask who or what it is about.
3. Identify the controlling thought—ask what the author wants you to know about the topic.
4. Consider what you know about the topic and the controlling thought, being careful not to allow your prior knowledge to distort what you read.
5. Combine the topic and controlling thought and predict the main idea.

**As You Read:**

6. Actively search for information that helps to clarify and refine your prediction about the main idea.

**As You Review:**

7. Revise and restate the main idea.

## How Can I Identify the Main Idea of a Paragraph?

Assume that 30 students in your English class are asked to write a paragraph on college grading systems. Would all 30 paragraphs tell your professor the same thing? Probably not. Although you would all write on the same topic, you would each focus on a specific thought. One of you might focus on the differences between high school and college grading systems, another on how college grading systems have changed over the years, another on the unfairness or worthwhileness of grades, while someone else might focus on the differences among college grading systems. The specific thought you selected—your controlling idea—is what makes your paragraph unique.

A paragraph is a group of related sentences that support and explain one main idea. Readers often mistake the topic—the who or what—for the main idea. But the topic is only a part of the author's idea. The main idea of a paragraph is the combination of the topic and the controlling thought—what the author wants you to know or understand about the topic.

To identify the main idea of a paragraph, find the topic by answering the question "Who or what is the author writing about?" and then clarify the controlling thought by answering "What does the author want me to know or understand about the topic?"

As stated earlier, the main idea is the frame that holds a paragraph together. Without understanding the main idea, you only have bits and pieces of details. It's very difficult to understand the relationships among the information without the main idea.

## DIRECTLY STATED MAIN IDEAS

Often, in expository and persuasive material, an author states his or her main idea in a sentence in the paragraph. This main idea sentence, or topic sentence, states the topic and controlling thought and clearly focuses the reader's attention on the author's message.

A topic sentence is often the first sentence in a paragraph, helping to prepare the reader for the rest of the paragraph. However, it can appear anywhere in a paragraph. It can be in the middle of the paragraph, tying the beginning and ending together; at the end of the paragraph, as a summary; or even split between two sentences in the paragraph.

No matter where the topic sentence is located, your strategy for finding and understanding the main idea is the same:

- identify the topic—ask who or what it is about
- identify the controlling thought—ask what the author wants you to know about the topic
- consider what you know about the topic and controlling idea, being careful not to allow your prior knowledge distort what you read
- combine the topic and controlling thought and identify the topic sentence
- rephrase the sentence in your own words

For example, identify the topic, the controlling thought, and then the main idea in this excerpt from Barker and Barker's *Communication* text.

> In a class where a professor used the sound "uh" some 20 times during the first five minutes of class, students could hardly help keeping count. The problem was that the professor didn't test the class on his "uhs," and many students didn't pass the test on the lecture. Of course it's easy to blame speakers for their sins. As effective listeners, however, we can't afford to let such mannerisms keep us from getting important points from the message. Focusing on the important elements in the communication setting rather than on the speaker's mannerisms is a much more profitable expenditure of listening energy. (Barker and Barker, *Communication*)

Who or what are Barker and Barker writing about? *listening*

What do they want you to understand about listening? *that you should pay attention to what someone says, not how they say it*

In this paragraph, the main idea is directly stated in the last sentence. However, to make sure you understand the author's main idea, you should rephrase the topic sentence in your own words. For example, "To be an effective listener, you should pay attention to what a speaker says and not how he or she says it."

Read this paragraph to determine Grassian's main idea.

> Aristotle's sexist view is still shared by many people. For example, it is not uncommon to hear people say, "No woman should ever be President of the United States; women are too emotional for such responsibilities." Such a claim reflects the still common belief that the sex of an individual is highly correlated with psychological characteristics and, as such, may be used as an indicator of an individual's capacity to perform certain tasks. As a result of this belief, women are often treated unequally in our society. (Grassian, *Moral Reasoning*)

Who or what is Grassian writing about? *many people still share Aristotle's sexist views*

What does he want you to understand about the fact that many people still share Aristotle's sexist views? *that it results in women often being treated unequally*

In this paragraph, the main idea is split between the first and last sentence of this paragraph. Write one sentence that expresses the main idea.

The following is the opening paragraph from the "Weather and Climate" section in *Introduction to Geography* by Bergman and McKnight. Like many opening paragraphs, this one contains both the thesis for the entire section and a main idea for this paragraph. To find the main idea of this paragraph, identify the topic (who or what most of the paragraph is about), the controlling thought, and then the main idea.

> The Earth is different from other known planets in a variety of ways. One of the most notable differences is the presence around our planet of a substantial atmosphere with components and characteristics that are distinctive from those of other planetary atmospheres. Our atmosphere makes life possible on this planet. It supplies most of the oxygen that animals must have to survive, as well as the carbon dioxide needed by plants. It helps maintain a water supply, which is essential to all living things. It serves as an insulating blanket to ameliorate temperature extremes and thus provide a livable environment over most of the Earth. It also shields the Earth from much of the sun's ultraviolet radiation, which otherwise would be fatal to most life forms. (Bergman and McKnight, *Introduction to Geography*)

Although the first sentence sounds like a possible main idea statement, it does not contain the answer to our two questions.

Who or what are Bergman and McKnight writing about? *the atmosphere*

What do Bergman and McKnight want you to understand about the atmosphere? *that its presence (the atmosphere's) is one of the Earth's most notable differences among known planets*

Thus, the first sentence, which is the most general, is actually the thesis for the entire section. (The remaining paragraphs in the text section cover other ways that the Earth is different from other planets.)

The second sentence, which answers our two questions, contains the main idea.

---

### PRACTICE: IDENTIFYING DIRECTLY STATED MAIN IDEAS

Identify the main idea in each paragraph.

1. To be successful in school, students must be able to understand and remember information presented in classroom lectures. This is not an easy task. In order to learn from a lecture, students need to engage in a number of different cognitive tasks. They must focus their attention on the lecture while it is being delivered, understand the ideas presented, organize the content in some manner, accurately store the new material in their memory, and be able to recall it at a later time, such as on an exam. (King, "Reciprocal Peer-Questioning" *The Clearinghouse*)

2. We created our twenty-four-hour society, in part, as a way to cut costs, a way to squeeze more output from our scarce resources. Even the most rudimentary cost-benefit analysis shows that it is far cheaper to build one facility or one assembly line and operate it twenty-four hours a day, seven days a week, than to build four facilities or assembly lines and operate them only forty hours a week. More product can be manufactured in that single continuous operation, because daily start-ups and shutdowns are eliminated, and the savings on the capital costs of the equipment are enormous, particularly if by turning your facility or assembly line into a continuous facility you increase the opportunity for automation and thus reduce the need for personnel. (Moore-Ede, *The Twenty-Four-Hour Society*)

3. The economic status of the aged has been a topic of great interest to researchers and policymakers for many years. The conventional wisdom formerly was that the economic status of the aged was low. In recent years that view has been replaced by the conventional wisdom that the aged are well off. The former view led to sentiment for increases in government assistance, while the latter view has led to cutbacks. Both views, however, are too simplistic. The assessment of the economic status of the aged is far more complex than most popular articles and analyses suggest. (Radner, "The Economic Status of the Aged," *Social Security Bulletin,* Fall 1992)

4. In spite of the good intentions of many writers, fictional characters are predominantly white and do not accurately portray reality. The population of the United States consists of about 12 percent blacks, 8.2 percent Hispanics, 2.1 percent Asians, and 2 percent Native Americans, and 20 percent of all people have a disabling condition—but most fiction portrays quite a different reality. (Seger, *Creating Unforgettable Characters*)

5. Hormonal changes in adolescents increase the size of skin oil glands and change the amounts of oil produced. In many teenagers, pores become blocked, causing some form of acne or skin blemishes on the face, back and chest. Some form of acne occurs in 80 to 90 percent of all teenagers. Inadequate washing, eating certain foods, and the use of

moisturizers have little to do with causing acne, although certain foods may aggravate the condition. Acne is caused by skin oils, not dirt or moisturizers. (Greenberg and Dintiman, *Exploring Health*)

# What Can I Do If the Main Idea Isn't Directly Stated?

Sometimes, especially in descriptive and narrative pieces, an author doesn't directly state the main idea. The author leaves it up to the reader to piece together the information from all the sentences and infer, or put together, the main idea. The author implies; you infer.

Like determining the author's purpose or defining a word through context, to infer an unstated main idea, you combine what the author says directly, the author's clues, and your own knowledge. Inferring a main idea requires your best reasoned conclusion based on the information you are given.

## IMPLIED MAIN IDEAS

Even when there isn't a topic sentence, your basic strategy for finding the main idea is the same: You identify the topic and controlling thought. Then, however, instead of locating a topic sentence, you combine the topic and controlling thought into your own main idea statement.

For example, in this paragraph from *Who Are the Investment Swindlers?* by the National Futures Association (NFA), there isn't one sentence that directly states the main idea. But when you add together the title and what is directly stated, you can infer the main idea.

> They are a faceless voice on the telephone. Or a friend of a friend. They may perform surgery on their victims' savings from a dingy back office or boiler-room or from an opulent suite in the new bank building. They may wear three-piece suits or they may wear hard hats. They may have no apparent connection to the investment business or they may have an alphabet-soup of impressive letters following their names. They may be glib and fast-talking or so seemingly shy and soft-spoken that you feel almost compelled to force your money on them. (National Futures Association, *Who Are the Investment Swindlers?*)

Who or what is the NFA writing about? *who are investment swindlers*

What do they want you to understand about investment swindlers? *that there is no single description of them; they can be anybody*

Thus we can infer that the main idea is: *There is no single description for investment swindlers; anybody could be one.*

Identify the topic of this paragraph by The President's Committee on Employment of the Handicapped. Again, there isn't one sentence that directly states the main idea, but when you add together what is directly stated, you can infer the main idea.

In 1943 Public Law 16 significantly advanced vocational rehabilitation services for veterans. A year later, the G.I. Bill of Rights provided veterans with allowances for educational training, loans for the purchase and construction of homes, farms, and business property, and compensation for periods of unemployment. Benefits were continued and enlarged in subsequent years in response to the Korean and Vietnam wars. (The President's Committee on Employment of the Handicapped, *Performance*)

Who or what is the Committee writing about? *government services for veterans*

What do they want you to understand about government services for veterans? *an increasing array of benefits have been offered since 1943*

Thus we can infer that the main idea is: *Since 1943 the government has provided an increasing array of benefits for veterans.*

---

### PRACTICE: IDENTIFYING IMPLIED MAIN IDEAS

Write the main idea of each paragraph.

1. In the Dick and Jane readers some of us remember from our childhoods, a family consisted of a married couple, two or three well-behaved children, and a dog and a cat. Father wore suits and went out to work; mother wore aprons and baked cupcakes. Little girls sat demurely watching little boys climb trees. Home meant a single-family house in a middle-class suburban neighborhood. Color the lawn green. Color the people white. Family life in the textbook world was idyllic; parents did not quarrel, children did not disobey, and babies did not throw up on the dog. (Delfattore, *What Johnny Shouldn't Read—Textbook Censorship in America*)

2. On the job you will periodically face challenges not directly related to the work you do. Prejudice and discrimination based on factors such as age, sex, race, ethnicity, and disability are common problems. Sexual harassment—any uninvited verbal or physical behavior related to sexuality—is of concern in today's work environment. Knowing what to do if you are confronted and then making wise choices can lessen the trauma. Being sensitive to others in the work environment so that you don't unwittingly create problems is most advisable. Refraining from sexist or racist comments and language may require effort, but it is the fair and decent way to behave. Challenging your own stereotypes and eliminating personal prejudice will make this easier. Acceptance and equal treatment of others are keystones of positive human relations. (Hanna, *Person to Person: Positive Relationships Don't Just Happen*)

3. A famous figure in sixteenth-century English history, Thomas More lived from 1478 to 1535. He was the son of judge John More and was an unusually talented individual. Legend has it that More was marked for greatness even as a youth. Educated at Oxford University and London's Lincoln Inn, More began his career as a lawyer after giving up the idea of being a monk. More developed an active law practice, he was visible in London politics, and he established a reputation as a Renais-

sance humanist through his writings in literature, history, and philosophy. He is best known to most people, however, for being a member of the court of King Henry VII. More held a series of posts and ultimately rose to the important position of Lord Chancellor. (White, *Discovering Philosophy*)

4. The day before I was to leave I went walking across the river to the red mesa, where many times before I had gone to be alone with my thoughts. And I had climbed several times to the top of the mesa and looked among the old ruins there for pottery. This time I chose to climb the north end, perhaps because I had not gone that way before and wanted to see what it was. It was a difficult climb, and when I got to the top I was spent. I lingered among the ruins for more than an hour, I judge, waiting for my strength to return. From there I could see the whole valley below, the fields, the river, and the village. It was all very beautiful, and the sight of it filled me with longing. (Momaday, *The Names*)

5. The Federal Clean Air Act mandates that employers with more than 100 employees who are located in selected metropolitan areas reduce car commuting by 25 percent by 1996. Consequently, many U.S. corporations, nonprofit organizations and government agencies are taking a new look at the option of telecommuting—having some of their employees regularly work from home a few days a week, connected to the office via computer and modem. (Conroy, "Away from Their Desks," *Compuserve Magazine*)

## How Can I Be Sure I Have Identified the Main Idea of a Paragraph?

If you aren't certain you have selected the main idea of the paragraph, try this strategy: after each sentence of the paragraph, read your main idea sentence. If you have identified the main idea, your sentence will unify all of the other sentences of the paragraph into a coherent unit. Your sentence will be more general than all the other sentences. It will sum up the other sentences.

---

### PRACTICE: IDENTIFYING MAIN IDEAS IN PARAGRAPHS

Use your strategy for finding the main idea:

- Do I understand the vocabulary the author is using?
- Who or what is this paragraph about?
- What does the author want me to know about this topic?
- What do I know about this topic and controlling thought?
- When I combine the topic and controlling thought, what do I think the main idea is?
- What information can I find that helps me clarify and refine my prediction about the main idea?
- Can I state the main idea in my own words?

1. Business education has undergone more change in the last ten years than it has in the last century. The education reform movement, recent technological innovations, increasing cultural diversity in the workforce, and the emergence of the global marketplace have all had a dramatic impact on the office support curriculum. Businesspersons and educators alike are trying to cope with what Tom Peters calls "a world turned upside down." What was appropriate just a few years ago must be continually evaluated and updated to keep pace with the rapidly changing workplace. (Jaderstrom, White, and Ellison, "The Changing Office Support Curriculum: Preparing Students for the Future," *The Balance Sheet*)

2. Since all of my recommendations call upon you to prepare for speaking by writing out, in some form, what you wish to say, it is, first of all, of great importance to recognize that what is written to be read has a radically different character from what is written to be heard. The remarkable difference between listening and reading—the one requiring you to keep moving forward irreversibly with the flow of speech, the other allowing you to proceed at your own pace and to go forward or backward at will by simply turning the pages—demands that you accommodate what you write for listening, as contrasted with what you must do for readers. (Adler "Preparing and Delivering a Speech," *How to Speak, How to Listen*)

3. "Manners makyth man," wrote the poet William of Wykeham. Ah—but what makyth the manners? We might, perhaps, venture "Mother makyth manners"—along, of course, with a dash of early experience and more than a little spicing of genetic inheritance. The relative roles of "nature" versus "nurture" caused much bitter argument in scientific circles in recent years. But the flames of the controversy have now died down, and it is generally accepted that, even in the lower animals, adult behavior is acquired through a mix of genetic make-up and experience gained as the individual goes through life. The more complex an animal's brain the greater the role that learning is likely to play in shaping its behaviour, and the more variation we shall find between one individual and another. Information acquired and lessons learned during infancy and childhood, when behaviour is at its most flexible, are likely to have particular significance. (Goodall, "Mothers and Daughters," *Through a Window*)

4. Ozone-destroying chemicals are extremely stable, so they last in the atmosphere for many decades. That means even if production of all chlorofluorocarbons (CFSs) and halons stopped today, the chemicals already in the atmosphere would go on destroying ozone well into the 21st century. And because large quantities of these chemicals are contained in existing air conditioners and refrigerators, from which they continue to escape through malfunction or intentional venting, it may be a century before the ozone layer has built itself back up. (Cooper "Ozone Depletion," *CQ Researcher*)

5. Of all the traditional presentation media, 35mm slides promise to make the best impression on an audience. There is something attention-grabbing and impressive about seeing well-executed color slides on a big screen. At the same time, slides are the greatest challenge to produce from the desktop (computer). Creating 35mm slides is not a solo activity like running the company newsletter off a laser printer.

Making slides requires either additional hardware in the form of a slide recorder, and maybe even another computer. (Thompson, "Sliding Home," *PC Publishing & Presentations*)

## How Can I Identify the Thesis of a Multi-Paragraph Selection?

A multi-paragraph selection, like an essay or text chapter, is a group of related paragraphs—each with a main idea—that support and explain one thesis, or overall main idea. The thesis of a multi-paragraph selection is the umbrella idea that unifies the main ideas of all the paragraphs.

Just as the main idea is the frame that holds the sentences of a paragraph together, the thesis is the frame that holds the many paragraphs of the essay or chapter together. If you don't identify the thesis, you have a series of ideas with nothing to connect them.

The thesis sentence is often stated in the first paragraph to prepare the reader for the rest of the chapter. However it can appear anywhere in the chapter or, like the main idea of a paragraph, it may not be directly stated at all. It may be up to you to put all of the author's ideas together and infer the thesis.

No matter where the thesis is located, your strategy for finding it is the same:

- identify the topic—ask who or what the entire selection is about
- identify the controlling thought—ask what the author wants you to know about the topic
- consider what you know about the topic and controlling idea
- combine the topic and controlling thought and identify the thesis

### PRACTICE: IDENTIFYING THE THESIS OF A MULTI-PARAGRAPH SELECTION

# *Special Nutritional Needs of Athletes and Active Individuals*

## JERROLD S. GREENBERG AND GEORGE B. DINTIMAN

*Jerrold Greenberg teaches at the University of Maryland. George Dintiman teaches at Virginia Commonwealth University. This selection is from* Exploring Health: Expanding the Boundaries of Wellness.

[1]Athletes and active individuals have a few special nutritional needs to meet the demands of *vigorous* activity, to prevent heat exhaustion and heat stroke and to maximize and store energy from food.

## MORE CALORIES

[2]If you are neither losing nor gaining weight and have sufficient energy, you are probably taking in the correct number of calories daily. Weigh yourself at the same time and under the same conditions daily, preferably upon rising. If no weight gain or loss is occurring, there is no need to keep complicated records in *caloric intake and expenditure.* In general, very active male college-age athletes need approximately 25 to 27 calories per pound compared to 20 to 21 per pound for female athletes. Moderately active individuals need approximately 20 to 23 (males) and 16 to 18 (females) calories per pound. *Sedentary* individuals, on the other hand, need approximately 15 to 18 (males) and 11 to 12 (females) calories per pound.

## MORE WATER

[3]To avoid dehydration, electrolyte imbalance, and heat-related disorders, as well as early fatigue, it is necessary to *hydrate* approximately fifteen minutes before exercising by drinking 12–48 ounces of cold water (one to four glasses), then drinking water freely during and after exercise. Since thirst will underestimate your needs, you must form the habit of drinking *when no thirst sensations exist.*

## PROPER NUTRITION

[4]*Electrolytes*—water, sodium, potassium, and chloride—lost through sweat and water vapor from the lungs should be replaced as rapidly as possible. It is the proper balance of each electrolyte that prevents dehydration, cramping, heat exhaustion, and heat stroke. Too much salt without adequate water, for example, actually draws fluid from the cells, *precipitates nausea,* and increases potassium loss. Although water alone will not restore electrolyte balance, it is the single most important element in preventing heat-related disorders. Eating extra portions of potassium-rich foods several days before a contest and using extra table salt is all most individuals need. If commercial electrolyte drinks are used, they should be diluted with twice the normal amount of water to reduce the sugar content. Lower sugar content will speed absorption time and prevent the body's release of insulin and possible reduction of quick energy.

## IRON SUPPLEMENTS

[5]Iron deficiency can lead to a loss of strength and endurance, early fatigue during exercise, loss of visual perception, and impaired learning. Needs vary according to age, activity level, and sex. Iron is the only nutrient that adolescent female and male athletes need in greater quantity.

1. What is Greenberg and Dintiman's purpose?
2. Define these words or phrases:

   a. vigorous (¶1)

   b. caloric intake and expenditure (¶2)

   c. sedentary (¶2)

   d. hydrate (¶3)

   e. when no thirst sensations exist (¶3)

   f. electrolytes (¶4)

   g. precipitates nausea (¶4)

3. What is the thesis of the selection?
4. What is the main idea of each paragraph?

## REVIEW QUESTIONS

*Review Questions*

1. What is your strategy for identifying the main idea of a paragraph?
2. Why is it important to restate the main idea in your own words?
3. What is your strategy for identifying the thesis of a multi-paragraph selection?

*Think and Connect Questions*

4. Re-read "Sources Of Groundwater Pollution," Chapter 1, Exercise 3. What is the author's purpose? State the thesis in your own words.
5. Re-read "Endangered Species," in Chapter 3. What is the author's purpose? State the thesis in your own words. Write the main ideas of paragraphs 3–5.

*Application Exercises*

6. Select three paragraphs in a current reading assignment from another class. Identify the main idea of each paragraph.
7. You have been told to write a paragraph on the topic of health care costs. Decide what your controlling thought will be and write a topic sentence (main idea) for your paragraph.

## USE YOUR STRATEGIES: EXERCISE 1

Define the italicized words. Write the main idea of each paragraph in your own words.

1. The causes of asthma are surprisingly *elusive*. It is known, Kaliner says, that about half of asthma cases in adults and some 90 percent in children appear to involve allergies. For these victims, avoiding offending substances such as sulfite preservative, animal hair and shellfish can help prevent attacks. In others, cold air, cigarette smoke, stress, menstruation, even perfume, can trigger an episode. The afflic-

tion runs in families, and recent work shows that heredity plays an important though unspecified role. Nearly half of all children with asthma are less troubled by it as years go by. *(Newsweek)*

2. At times we half-heartedly make efforts to remember facts that stand out, and completely miss the speaker's main points. This habit has also been referred to as "majoring in minors." Unless we listen with an intent to understand the *essence* of the message, we may fall into the habit of picking and choosing only selected tidbits to process and remember. When we put these bits together at the end of the presentation or conversation, we may find that we have a totally incorrect perception of what the speaker was trying to get across. (Barker and Barker, *Communication*)

3. Couples seeking a divorce will not always find it easy to reach agreement on issues that affect their children, but they should attempt to do so before telling their children about the *impending* separation. Children, even very young children, need to be prepared for the divorce. They need information about where they will live, who will take care of them, where they will go to school, and whatever other issues are of major concern to them. (NIMH, *Caring About Kids: When Parents Divorce*)

4. A *compelling* reason to preserve species is that each one plays an important role in an ecosystem—an intricate network of plant and animal communities and the associated environment. When a species becomes endangered, it indicates that something is wrong with the ecosystems we all depend on. Like the canaries used in coal mines whose deaths warned miners of bad air, the increasing numbers of endangered species warn us that the health of our environment has declined. The measures we take to save endangered species will help ensure that the planet we leave for our children is as healthy as the planet our parents left for us. (U.S. Department of the Interior, U.S. Fish and Wildlife Service, *Endangered Species*)

5. Overweight is a hefty problem in the United States. It's estimated that 24 percent of men and 27 percent of women in this country—about 34 million Americans—are obese. And sometimes it seems that there are 34 million different diets or diet products promoted to combat the problem. The latest to win the nation's *fervent* attention is a revival of a sort—a return to very low calorie diets, generally 400 to 800 calories per day. *(FDA Consumer)*

6. In countries where two or more languages *coexist*, confusion often arises. In Belgium, many towns have two quite separate names, one recognized by French speakers, one by Dutch speakers, so that the French Tournai is the Dutch Doornik, while the Dutch Luik is the French Liège. The French Mons is the Dutch Bergen, the Dutch Kortrijk is the French Courtrai, and the city that to all French-speaking people (and indeed most English-speaking people) is known as Bruges (and pronounced "broozsh") is to the locals called Brugge and pronounced "broo-guh." Although Brussels is officially bilingual, it is in fact a French-speaking island in a Flemish lake. (Bryson, *Mother Tongue*)

7. You may know the merits of healthy eating. But often wanting to eat right and actually doing so are two separate things. For many, understanding how to eat right is the real challenge because the recom-

mendations for good nutrition appear more *complex* than they actually are. Although several health organizations issue a variety of dietary recommendations, the basic message regarding diet and health are the same: Consume a diet low in fat, cholesterol and sodium and high in complex carbohydrates and dietary fiber to reduce the risk of chronic disease. (Keating, "Nutrition for the '90s")

8. Despite the rich variety of *indigenous* local cultures around the globe, the world is increasingly coming to look like one place. In consumer goods, architecture, industrial technology, education, and housing, the European model is pervasive. (Bergman and McKnight, *Introduction to Geography*)

9. Breathing. It may be something you never think about or it may be your major focus when you're meditating, swimming laps, *trekking* at high altitudes, or having an asthma attack. In any case, it is a remarkable physical process that provides our bodies with the oxygen we need for metabolism and eliminates metabolism's waste product, carbon dioxide. (Vernick, "Every Breath You Take," *Good Housekeeping*)

10. As water infiltrates and percolates through the soil, it will tend to dissolve and carry any soluble chemicals that are in solution. It is the old problem of leaching described in earlier chapters. Consequently, the general principle is: Any chemical used on, disposed of, spilled, or leaked onto or into the ground can *contaminate* groundwater. (Nebel, *Environmental Science*)

---

### USE YOUR STRATEGIES: EXERCISE 2

---

# *Who Am I?*

### DAVID W. JOHNSON

*David Johnson teaches at the University of Minnesota. This selection is from* Human Relations and Your Career, *3rd ed.*

[1]How you describe yourself as a person is your identity. Your identity is a consistent set of attitudes that defines who you are. These attitudes contain both a view of how you are similar to other people and a view of how you are *unique* as a person. The world can change. Other people can change. Your career can change, but there is something about yourself that stays the same. And that something is your identity.

[2]There are three ways you build your identity. The first is by comparing yourself with other people. The second is by trying to be like people you admire. And the third is by taking on social roles.

[3]Being part of a cooperative effort allows you to compare yourself with others. It is within cooperative relationships that you increase your self-awareness (by finding out how other people see you). Through cooperating with people, you become aware of how you are similar to and different from others. The better you know other

people, the clearer you will be about your identity. The more feedback you receive from other people, the better you will know yourself as a person. It is from your cooperative relationships that you find out whether you are an emotional or unemotional person, whether you are *diplomatic* or blunt, or whether you are sensitive or nonsensitive as a person. From hearing about other people's attitudes, you become more aware of your own attitudes. By sharing experiences and feelings, you become more self-aware. Cooperation promotes the type of relationships in which you can get to know other people and yourself.

4A second way you build your identity is by deciding who you want to be like. Everyone has people they like, admire, and see as unusually competent or powerful. You will want to be like such people. So you will adopt their attitudes and actions. One of the interesting things about wanting to be like other people whom you admire is that the people do not have to be real. They can be *fictional* or fantasy persons! You may decide that you want to be like a character in a movie. You may decide that you want to be like a person in a book. Most of the people you will want to be like, however, will be people you cooperate with. Your parents, older brothers and sisters, older friends, and even teachers are all people you may wish to be like in certain ways. You can strengthen your identity by choosing people with positive qualities and trying to develop the same qualities in yourself.

5A third way you build your identity is by taking on a *stable set* of social roles. A social role is a set of actions that other people expect of you. Examples of social roles are the roles of student, friend, spouse, sibling, child, parent, and citizen. Every social role has a set of expected actions. The social roles you take on help tell you who you are as a person. The more stable your social roles, the more stable your identity will be.

1. What is Johnson's purpose?
2. Define these words or phrases:

   a. unique (¶1)

   b. diplomatic (¶3)

   c. fictional (¶4)

   d. stable set (¶5)

3. Write the thesis of the selection.
4. Write the main ideas of paragraphs 3, 4, and 5.

# *Computers of the '90s: A Brave New World*

## NEWSWEEK STAFF

[1]"There is zero doubt," says Nick Donofrio, vice president for development of IBM's entry-systems division, "that the computers of the future will be more *user friendly*." In fact, as much as 50 percent of the added power of tomorrow's computers will go to make the machines easier to use. The *"graphical interface"* popularized by the Apple Macintosh (in which symbols such as a trash can replace commands such as "delete") will become a standard feature; chances are good that the once controversial "mouse" will also become the universal tool for *navigating* across the computer screen. Computer makers will vie to make their machines visually pleasing and fun to use, but that's just the start. Along with visual cues, computers almost certainly will develop their own voices.

[2]Chatty computers have been possible for years, but the technology has been expensive, the applications limited. Early on, marketers realized that an office filled with computers jabbering away in mechanical tones would be a tough sell. But with their new power, computers can now produce very pleasing human voices, complete with Texas drawl or sultry *intonations*. And sometimes talk is useful. Future computer programs will probably coach novice users by talking them through complicated procedures: "To erase that word, hit the backspace key. No. Not that one, the one next to it." And travelers may be able to dial their computers from the road and hear the day's *electronic mail* read aloud.

[3]Computers will begin to understand speech as well, although that's proven far tougher than mimicking regional accent. One of the best speech recognition systems thus far, developed at Carnegie Mellon, can understand about 1,000 words of English spoken by anyone. Computers that have been "trained" to understand only one voice can manage a much wider vocabulary—although most experts agree that the dictation-taking computer is still a decade away. Jobs—whose NeXT computer will someday offer *voice-recognition software*—suggests that to ensure security and privacy, future computers may turn on only when they hear the sound of their boss's voice.

[4]Talking computers may find their warmest welcome in university language labs. Computers are already important tutors: "My prediction," says Frank Ryan, director of Brown University's language lab, "is that in no more than two years, all the grammar taught in our French classes will be taught by computer." But that's just a start. Brown, Dartmouth, MIT and Stanford are all exploring even more ambitious ways to put computers to work in language instruction. One current program shows computer-controlled film clips of French or Russian speakers shopping or going apartment hunting; the on-screen speakers regularly pause to ask questions. The student responds by typing an answer that the computer either accepts

or corrects. Once computers can speak *fluently,* however, the computer itself—rather than taped humans—will *interact* with the student. Language teachers expect to have computers that will read, with correct pronunciation, each sentence a student types even using Chinese or Russian characters.

[5]Friendlier computers will transform grade schools as well. A recent Office of Technology Assessment study concluded that modern classrooms are far less computerized than offices or factories. Part of the reason is limited funding, but overburdened teachers also resist the added hassle of bulky and inconvenient hardware. Simpler computers will mean that both teachers and kids can begin to use them as daily tools rather than special-purpose drill-and-practice machines. At The Open School in Los Angeles, an Apple-financed research project called Vivarium aims to make computers as natural a part of the curriculum as pencil and paper. Computers are recessed under the desks but are visible through transparent desktops—out of the way, yet always accessible. Last year, says Apple research fellow Alan Kay, 300 kids, some as young as five, learned a program called Hypercard. Kids use it to do their homework, take class notes, make drawings, even create data bases, on easy-to-use software. "Children are very good at computers," he says, "and computers make the kids look and feel smarter."

[6]The physical shape of computers will become friendlier as well. They'll almost certainly shrink; already, you can buy a laptop computer as powerful as an IBM desktop machine that will fit in a 9-by-12 manila envelope. New flat-screen displays from Japan are so sharp and crisp they appear almost like a sheet of paper; within a few years such screens will be the equal of bulky cathode-ray tubes in both color and clarity. Apple's Kay says the portable computer will be so compact and convenient that owners will even make their grocery lists on it and then carry the machine along to the store. Mitch Kapor, founder of Lotus Development Corp., believes some computers will lack keyboards altogether; owners will hand write their thoughts on a small tablet. Further out, says Andrew Lippman of MIT's Media Lab, computers may even be sewn into clothing. "Maybe we'll have *computational jackets,*" he says. "They'll whisper in your ear." Regardless of form, says Apple VP of advanced technology Lawrence Tesler, one thing is clear: "Sooner or later, more people will carry their computers around than keep them fixed to a desk."

1. What is the author's purpose?
2. Define these words/phrases:

   a. user friendly (¶1)   f. voice-recognition software (¶3)

   b. graphical interface (¶1)   g. fluently (¶4)

   c. navigating (¶1)   h. interact (¶4)

   d. intonations (¶2)   i. computational jackets (¶6)

   e. electronic mail (¶2)

3. Write the thesis of the selection.
4. Write the main ideas of paragraphs 2, 3, 4, and 5.

# Theories of Human Behavior

## JERROLD S. GREENBERG AND GEORGE B. DINTIMAN

*Jerrold Greenberg teaches at the University of Maryland. George Dintiman teaches at Virginia Commonwealth University. This selection is from* Exploring Health.

[1]Why do people adopt certain health-related behaviors and not others? Although many *theories* have been proposed to explain why people behave as they do, no one knows for sure. The theories described below, however, are often cited as the most adequate explanations of why some people smoke cigarettes and others do not, and generally why some people behave in a healthy way and others do not. This is no magic list, though. Your instructor or other sources can provide you with additional theories of human behavior.

## HIERARCHY OF NEEDS

[2]Abraham Maslow proposed that human beings behave in ways that are designed to satisfy certain needs. Further, there exist levels of needs, and the high-level needs do not *emerge* until the low-level needs are satisfied.

[3]Until hunger and thirst (physiological needs) are satisfied, you will not be concerned with safety. In fact, if you need food badly, you might even chase a lion away from a *felled prey*. Until you feel safe and secure (safety needs), you will not be concerned with others loving you. Until you are loved (love needs), you will not be concerned about whether others respect you (esteem needs). And until you are respected by others, you will not care whether you can achieve your potential (self-actualization needs).

[4]In our society, most of these needs are met to some degree. However, the degree to which they are met varies and consequently our behavior varies. Some of us might display sexual behavior that is *contrary to our nature* because of our need for love. Others might conform to friends' drug behavior because of the need for esteem.

## FORCE FIELD THEORY

[5]According to Kurt Lewin, human behavior is characterized by a *constant tension* between *driving and restraining forces*. When one set of forces becomes stronger than another, you behave one way. When the other set of forces becomes stronger, you behave another way.

[6]For example, you might want to lose weight but you live with someone who eats high-calorie foods. If the attraction of these foods is stronger than your desire to lose weight, your diet goes down the drain.

## ADJUSTMENT THEORY

[7]Others believe that human beings are constantly striving to adjust to their environments. The adjustment is needed to maintain an *equilibrium* necessary for a healthy existence. When the environment places us in *disequilibrium* we behave in ways designed to right ourselves. Thus, when a student enters college and leaves home for the first time, he or she seeks to replace the family with close friends. To acquire these friends might mean joining college organizations, taking drugs, or acquiring other behaviors designed to restore equilibrium.

1. What is Greenberg and Dintiman's purpose?
2. Define these words or phrases:

    a. theories (¶1)

    b. emerge (¶2)

    c. felled prey (¶3)

    d. contrary to our nature (¶4)

    e. constant tension (¶5)

    f. driving and restraining forces (¶5)

    g. equilibrium (¶7)

    h. disequilibrium (¶7)

3. Write the thesis of the selection.
4. Write the main ideas of paragraphs 2, 5, and 7.

---

### CONNECTIONS

A. In the first four chapters of this text you have read paragraphs and multi-paragraph selections about many subjects, e.g., ecology, nutrition, sociology, and business. In your other classes, at work, and at home, you read about many other subjects. In which subjects is the reading easiest for you? In which subjects is it most difficult? By that I mean, when is it easiest or hardest for you to identify the main idea? Why do you think that is true? What do you think you can do to make the hardest reading easier?

B. Based on the reading assignments you have done for your classes during the last few weeks, how important is it for you to understand the vocabulary the author uses? What do you do when you encounter an unfamiliar word? Is what you do different in any way than what you did six months ago? Why or why not?

# 5

## *Establish How the Author Develops the Ideas*

Indisputably, understanding main ideas is crucial to comprehension. For some purposes, such as preparing to listen to a lecture, knowing the main ideas may be all you need to be successful. But many times, just understanding the main ideas will not provide enough information to meet your purpose. When your purpose for reading requires a more detailed understanding, such as answering questions, writing a paper, or learning the steps in a procedure, you must go beyond the thesis and main ideas and be able to identify the details you need.

As you plan for this chapter, think about how you decide what is important to remember. Do you try to remember everything you read? Do you try to remember more details in some subjects than in others? Do you vary the amount of detail you try to remember depending on what you are going to do with the information?

Highlight definitions for this chapter's key vocabulary:

- major supporting detail
- minor supporting detail
- signal words
- methods of development

> **Chapter 5 Content Objectives**
>
> - identify and understand different kinds of details
> - determine the relationships among details and/or sentences
> - identify and understand the use of signal words
> - understand how the way an author develops and supports the thesis and/or main idea can help comprehension
> - use signal words, punctuation, and the methods authors use to develop and support thesis and/or main ideas as clues to understanding

## What Is My Basic Strategy for Establishing How the Author Develops Ideas?

**As You Plan:**

1. Understand the vocabulary.
2. Predict the thesis and/or main idea.
3. Determine how much detail you need to know.

**As You Read:**

4. Actively search for information that helps to clarify and refine your prediction about the thesis and/or main idea.
5. Highlight useful signal words.
6. Determine the relationships among details and/or sentences.
7. Determine if the way the author develops the thesis and/or main idea helps you to understand the details.
8. Use the author's signal words, punctuation, and development as clues to help you identify information and ideas you need.

**As You Review:**

9. Revise and restate the thesis and/or main idea.
10. Restate the supporting details you need to fulfill your purpose.

## How Can I Identify and Understand Different Kinds of Details?

Remember what Veit, Gould, and Clifford said about writing in one of the practice paragraphs in Chapter 4:

> If stating an idea were enough, there would be no books or essays. Each piece of writing would consist of only a topic sentence. Of course more is needed. Writers must explain, expand and support their ideas. Sometimes facts or logic are called for, sometimes the

narration of events, and sometimes examples, illustrations, and reasons. A mathematics textbook calls for clear, step-by-step reasoning, with many examples and exercises to reinforce each lesson. New interpretations of historical events call for background information, direct evidence, and support from authoritative sources. The way that an author chooses to develop a main idea depends on the work's purpose and its intended audience.

The work you did in Chapter 4 reinforced the concepts that: (1) a multi-paragraph selection has only one thesis, (2) there may be any number of paragraphs in the selection but each paragraph has only one main idea, (3) a paragraph my contain any number of sentences and thus any number of major and minor details.

A major supporting detail is a specific piece of information that directly supports and explains a main idea. A minor supporting detail is a very specific piece of information that supports and explains a major detail.

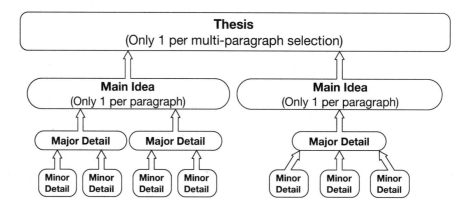

Being able to distinguish among the thesis, main idea, major supporting detail(s), and minor supporting detail(s) and determine how they relate to one another, is critical for the reader who is reading to fulfill a specific purpose and to be able to remember what he or she has read. Identifying the relationships among the ideas and/or sentences helps you make connections among ideas and improve comprehension.

For example, take another look at the opening paragraph from Bergman and McKnight's "Weather and Climate" chapter. We established in Chapter 4 that sentence one is the thesis for the entire section and sentence two is the main idea for this paragraph. Now, read to see what additional information the authors provide.

[1]The Earth is different from other known planets in a variety of ways. [2]One of the most notable differences is the presence around our planet of a substantial atmosphere with components and characteristics that are distinctive from those of other planetary atmospheres. [3]Our atmosphere makes life possible on this planet. [4]It supplies most of the oxygen that animals must have to survive, as well as the carbon dioxide needed by plants. [5]It helps maintain a water supply, which is essential to all living things. [6]It serves as an insulating blanket to ameliorate temperature extremes and thus provide a livable environment over most of the Earth. [7]It also shields the Earth

from much of the sun's ultraviolet radiation, which otherwise would be fatal to most life forms.

How do the details they provide support and explain the main idea?

Sentence 3 directly supports the main idea, therefore it is a major detail. Sentences 4–7 give examples of the major detail, therefore they are minor details.

  Sentence 4—supplies oxygen and carbon dioxide
  Sentence 5—helps maintain water supply
  Sentence 6—insulation from temperature extremes
  Sentence 7—shield from ultraviolet radiation

Now that you have identified several different levels of information, how much of it should you remember? Just the thesis? The thesis and main idea? The thesis, main idea, and the major detail? The thesis, main idea, major detail, and the four examples?

How much you need to remember about what you read depends on your purpose for reading. If this had been an actual geography assignment, you would have decided as part of your plan specifically what you needed to find out as you read. For example, if you were reading this chapter as preparation for a lecture, you might have decided to concentrate only on the thesis and main idea. On the other hand, if you were preparing for an extensive exam on the chapter, you might have decided you needed to memorize several levels of detail, including the examples.

Reread this paragraph from Macionis's *Sociology.* Like many authors, Macionis often combines major and minor details in one sentence. Identify his main idea and distinguish between major and minor supporting details.

[1]A survey is a research method in which subjects respond to a series of items or questions in a questionnaire or an interview. [2]Perhaps the most widely used of all research methods, surveys are particularly suited to studying what cannot be observed directly, such as political attitudes, religious beliefs, or the private lives of couples. [3]Like experiments, surveys can be used to investigate the relationship among variables. [4]They are also useful for descriptive research, in which subject responses help a sociologist to describe a social setting, such as an urban neighborhood or gambling casino.

Main idea: A survey is a research method in which subjects respond to a series of items or questions in a questionnaire or an interview.

### Sentence 2:

*Major*—widely used, suited to studying what can't be observed
  *Minor*—such as political attitudes, religious beliefs, private lives

### Sentence 3:

*Major*—like experiments, used to investigate relationships among variables

*Sentence 4:*

*Major*—useful for descriptive research where subject helps describe social setting

> *Minor*—such as urban neighborhood or gambling casino

To help you understand the relationships among the details and/or sentences, an author uses a variety of clues including signal words, punctuation, and paragraph structure.

## What Are Signal Words and Phrases?

Signal words are words or phrases an author uses to point you in a specific direction of thought or to alert you to particular types of information. These words can be clues for identifying different kinds of details.

In the Macionis paragraph above, you used several signal words and phrases to point you to different types of information.

> *is a*—to alert you to a definition
>
> *are particularly suited to*—to point out a use of surveys
>
> *such as*—to alert you to examples
>
> *Like*—to point out a similarity
>
> *also*—to point out an additional use of surveys
>
> *such as*—to alert you to examples

Signal words that can point to major details include words such as: central, principal, chief, major, main, key, primary, and significant.

Signal words that suggest a continuation of the same type of thought include: and, too, in addition, moreover, or, also, furthermore, as well as, besides, in other words, and another.

Words that signal a recap of the author's ideas include phrases like: in summary, in conclusion, and to sum up.

Other signal words and phrases are used to guide you through a paragraph or multi-paragraph selection. These additional signal words are listed later in this chapter with each of the methods of development.

---

### PRACTICE: DETERMINING THE RELATIONSHIPS AMONG DETAILS AND/OR SENTENCES

---

1. [1]The origin of the term "Baroque" is uncertain. [2]Possibly it derives from the Portuguese word *barroco,* an irregularly shaped pearl. [3]Or it may have come from the Italian word *baroco,* a far-fetched syllogistic argument. [4]Or perhaps it came from the name of a sixteenth-century Italian painter, Frederigo Barocci. (Politoske, *Music*)

   a. What is the main idea?

   b. What is the relationship of sentences 2–4 to sentence 1? Do they summarize, introduce a contrast, or provide an illustration or example? Explain.

c. What is the relationship of sentence 4 to sentences 2 and 3? Does it define, summarize, introduce a contrast, or continue the thought? Explain.

2. [1]Couples seeking a divorce will not always find it easy to reach agreement on issues that affect their children, but they should attempt to do so before telling their children about the impending separation. [2]Children, even very young children, need to be prepared for the divorce. [3]They need information about where they will live, who will take care of them, where they will go to school, and whatever other issues are of major concern to them. (NIMH, *Caring About Kids: When Parents Divorce*)

   a. What is the main idea?

   b. What is the relationship of sentence 3 to sentences 1 and 2? Does it define a term, introduce a contrast, or provide an illustration or example? Explain.

   c. Does sentence 3 contain major or minor details? Explain.

3. [1]Various behavioral theories have been studied as they relate to health. [2]Ideas and concepts such as self-efficacy, locus of control, and health locus of control are becoming more widely understood. [3]Self-efficacy refers to a person's appraisal of his or her own ability to change or to accomplish a particular task or behavior. [4]Locus of control refers to a person's perceptions of forces or factors that control his or her destiny. [5]Health locus of control focuses specifically on those factors that influence health. [6]These constructs influence how we view ourselves and also how we behave or seek to change behaviors. (Donatelle and Davis, *Access to Health*)

   a. What is the main idea?

   b. What is the relationship of sentence 2 to sentence 1? Does it define, summarize, introduce a contrast, or provide an illustration or example? Explain.

   c. What is the relationship of sentences 3–5 to sentence 2? Do they define, continue the same thought, or provide an illustration or example? Explain.

4. [1]Many (of the North American Indian) tribes were skilled in handicrafts, making beautiful pottery, light and swift birchbark canoes, and implements of copper. [2]Some wove a kind of cloth from the inner bark of trees. [3]Others, however, lived very simply, with few artifacts. [4]The numerous peoples of California, for example, blessed with a mild climate and abundant food, made do with simple clothing and crude houses. [5]Only their beautiful basketwork revealed their skills with materials. (Unger, *These United States*)

   a. What is the main idea?

   b. What is the relationship of sentence 3 to sentences 1 and 2? Does it define, summarize, introduce a contrast, or continue the same thought? Explain.

   c. What word does Unger use in sentence 3 to signal its purpose?

5. [1]It is estimated that advertisers in the United States now spend more than $57 billion each year, compared with $1.69 billion spent in 1935,

according to census reports. [2]As the nation's gross national product (GNP) has risen beyond $2.6 trillion, advertising expenditures have kept pace, ranging close to 2 percent of the GNP each year. [3]Advertising, with its marketing aids of sales promotions, product design, point-of-purchase displays, product publicity, and public relations, thus plays an obvious role in the growth of the nation's economy. (Agee, Ault, and Emery, *Introduction to Mass Communications*)

a. What is the main idea?

b. What is the relationship of sentence 3 to sentences 1 and 2? Does it define, summarize, introduce a contrast, or provide an illustration or example? Explain.

6. [1]Mechanical industries that processed tobacco, grain, soap, and canned foodstuffs dramatically increased their output through the use of continuous-process machinery. [2]A cigarette-making machine developed in 1881 was so productive that just fifteen of them satisfied America's entire annual demand for cigarettes. [3]Procter & Gamble developed a new machine for mass-producing Ivory soap. [4]Diamond Match began using a machine that produced and boxed matches by the billions. [5]Industries that distilled and refined petroleum, sugar, animal or vegetable fats, alcohol, and chemicals reaped enormous savings from new heat and chemical technologies, giant furnaces, whirling centrifuges, converters, and rolling and finishing equipment. [6]Standard Oil, American Sugar Refining, and Carnegie Steel, among others, gained unprecedented efficiencies. [7]Metalworking industries benefited from larger and more efficient machine tools and a wider variety of semifinished materials. [8]International Harvester and Singer Sewing Machine expanded their production far beyond the imaginings of past generations. (Reich, *The Work of Nations*)

a. What is the main idea?

b. What is the relationship of sentences 2–4 to sentence 1? Do they provide a contrast, or an illustration or example? Explain.

c. What is the relationship of sentence 6 to sentence 5? Does it provide a contrast, or an illustration or example? Explain.

d. What is the relationship of sentence 8 to sentence 7? Does it provide a contrast, or an illustration or example? Explain.

## How Does the Author Develop the Main Idea?

How the author develops and supports the thesis or main ideas refers to the structure he or she gives the information. Six common ways authors develop and support main ideas are example, comparison and/or contrast, division and classification, cause and effect, process, and definition.

It is useful to determine the structure, or method of development because it provides a clue to locating and sorting out the relationships among details you need. By that I mean that when you spot one of the common methods of development such as comparison/contrast, you think and read actively because you know to look for the similarities and differences the author is providing to support and explain the main idea.

Please remember, however, that discovering the author's method of development is not your reason for reading; you are just using what you can discover about the development as a clue to understanding the ideas and details you need.

## HOW DOES THE AUTHOR USE EXAMPLE?

One of the most common and easily recognized methods of development in academic material is the use of examples to support and develop the thesis or main idea.

Using this method of development, authors support and develop their general statement—the thesis or main idea—with specific, relevant examples, instances, or illustrations.

Topic sentences such as these often lead to the use of examples.

> The best strategy for staying warm is to rely on an old mountaineering technique known as layering, a method that helps the body maintain a comfortable balance between heat generated and heat lost. For example, the first layer . . . *(the reader should watch for details that give examples of layering)*

> A magazine is custom-designed for its special audience. For example, *Redbook* and *Cosmopolitan* . . . *(the reader should watch for details that give examples of magazines that are custom-designed for an audience)*

Words that signal examples or illustrations include: for example, to illustrate, for instance, such as, specifically, namely, and the abbreviations, i.e., and e.g.

Determine the main idea of this paragraph on cardiovascular diseases. What kind of details do Donatelle and Davis use to develop and support their main idea?

> We can prevent or reduce the risks for cardiovascular diseases by taking steps to change certain behaviors. For example, controlling high blood pressure and reducing our intake of saturated fats and cholesterol are two things we can do to reduce the risk for heart attacks. By maintaining our weight, lowering our intake of sodium, and changing our lifestyles to reduce stress, we can lower blood pressure. We can also monitor the levels of fat and cholesterol in our blood and adjust our diets to prevent clogging of arteries. (Donatelle and Davis, *Access to Health*)

In this paragraph, Donatelle and Davis support their main idea (we can prevent or reduce the risk of heart diseases by changing some of our behaviors) through a series of specific examples (control high blood pressure and reduce intake of saturated fats and cholesterol to reduce risk of heart attacks; maintain weight, lower intake of sodium and reduce stress to lower blood pressure; monitor fat, cholesterol and adjust diet).

## HOW DOES THE AUTHOR USE COMPARE AND/OR CONTRAST?

Compare means to tell how two things or ideas or people are alike. Contrast means to tell how two things or ideas or people are different.

Authors can choose to develop and support their main idea by giving the likenesses, the differences, or both the likenesses and differences between or among things or ideas or people.

Topic sentences such as these alert you to watch for likenesses and/or differences:

> Running for the local school board is similar to running for a major political office in many ways, but there are also important differences. *(the reader should watch for details that tell how running for school board and major office are alike and how they are different)*

> Despite the diversity of ecosystems, they are alike in some ways. *(the reader should watch for details that tell how various ecosystems are alike)*

> Although there may be some similarities between the lighting techniques of studio and outdoor photographers, their differences are critical. *(the reader should watch for details that tell how the lighting techniques are different)*

Signal words to watch for that may indicate comparison include: similarly, like, the same as, compared to, in the same way, likewise, parallels, resembles, equally, and just as.

Signal words that may indicate contrast include: but, yet, on the other hand, however, instead, nevertheless, on the contrary, unlike, in contrast to, whereas, in spite of, although, conversely, different from, rather than, and just the opposite.

Read this paragraph to determine Long's main idea. How does he develop the details he uses to support that idea?

> A computer system can also be likened to the biological system of the human body. Your brain is the processing component. Your eyes and ears are input components that send signals to the brain. If you see someone approaching, your brain matches the visual image of this person with others in your memory (storage component). If the visual image matches that of a friend, your brain sends signals to your vocal cords and right arm (output components) to greet your friend with a hello and a handshake. Computer system components interact in a similar way. (Long, *Introduction to Computers and Information Processing*)

In this paragraph, Long supports his main idea (a computer system is like a human biological system) by describing how the two systems are alike (brain is like processing component; eyes and ears are like input components; memory is like storage component; vocal cords and arm are like output components).

Read this paragraph to determine the author's main idea about Canyonlands National Park and the Grand Canyon. How are the details developed?

> For diversity, Canyonlands National Park gives even the Grand Canyon a run for its money. Its 337,570 acres range in elevation from 3,700 feet at the head of Lake Powell to more than 7,000 feet at the highest point on the south boundary above Salt Creek. Like the Grand Canyon, Canyonlands protects a great inner gorge carved by the Colorado River, with a rim high above that offers awesome views. But here, too, are flats studded with slickrock needles

and spires, an intricate system of side canyons decorated with massive stone arches, and rich archeological resources famous for fine rock art. *(The Sierra Club Guides to the National Parks)*

The authors of this paragraph develop their main idea (Canyonlands National Park is at least as diverse as the Grand Canyon) by giving information on how they are alike (they both have an inner gorge carved by the Colorado River and a high rim with an awesome view) and how they are different (Canyonlands has flats studded with slickrock needles and spires, an intricate system of side canyons decorated with massive stone arches, and rich archeological resources famous for fine rock art).

## HOW DOES THE AUTHOR USE DIVISION AND CLASSIFICATION?

Division or classification is commonly used when the author wants to break a larger subject into parts to examine how each part contributes to the whole. Additionally, when an author needs to bring order to a group of ideas, activities, or things, he or she will often divide or classify them according to their characteristics. In classification, an author uses categories or groups, not individual items.

The main idea usually identifies what will be divided or classified and often tells how many divisions will be considered. Topic sentences such as these point to division or classification of information:

We can divide the color input/output process into five areas: planning, scanning, color correction, proofing, and printing. *(the author is breaking a large topic—color input/output process—into parts; the reader should watch for details that examine each part)*

There are four basic ways to accomplish the purchase of mutual fund shares at that day's net asset value. These ways are to transfer from a money fund, with a wire transfer from your bank, through a telephone purchase, or by opening a new account by wire. *(the author is dividing ways to buy mutual funds at a specific value; the reader should watch for details that tell how each way works)*

Signal words you should watch for include: categories, classifications, groups, classes, ways, elements, features, methods, kinds, types, parts, factors, issues, reasons, and sorts.

Read this paragraph to determine Bittner's main idea. How does it appear he will develop the details of Eric Berne's approach to understanding human interaction?

The psychiatrist and proponent of transactional analysis, Eric Berne, developed an interesting approach to understanding human interaction. At the core of his approach is what he called the ego state. In the simplest terms, there are three types of ego states which are, according to Berne, present in every individual (adult state, parent state, child state). To better understand these three types in relation to what we have already been discussing about self-concept, think of them as different self-concepts which we possess and relate to at any given time. (Bittner, *Understanding Self-Concept*)

Bittner develops his main idea (the concept of the ego state is at the center of Berne's theory of human interaction) by dividing it into three types (adult state, parent state, child state). He follows this paragraph with an in-depth look at each of the three states.

## HOW DOES THE AUTHOR USE CAUSE AND EFFECT?

An author uses cause and effect—reasons and results—to tell why or how something happened and the result of the action. By using a cause-and-effect pattern of development, an author can examine the reasons for events or situations and their consequences, look at the known benefits or outcomes of a set of conditions, or predict the possible consequences of a given situation.

An author can begin with the cause(s) and give the result(s), or can begin with the result(s) and give the cause(s). There can be a single cause with multiple effects, multiple causes and a single effect, or a causal chain—where, like falling dominoes, an action results in an effect, which causes something else, which causes something else, and so on.

Topic sentences such as these alert you to look for a cause-and-effect relationship:

> Many factors contributed to the increase in college enrollments in the 1980s. *(the author gives the effect—increased college enrollment; the reader should watch for details that give the causes)*

> Although it is difficult to predict all of the long-term effects of air pollution, a few are already known. *(The author gives the cause—air pollution; the reader should watch for details that give the effects)*

Words that signal cause include: because; for this reason; due to; cause; on account of; and the phrase, if this, then this.

Words that signal a result include: as a result, since, consequently, therefore, thus, in effect, resulting, and the outcome is.

Read this paragraph to determine Strongman's main idea. How does he develop the main idea?

> Within psychology, there has been a long-standing link between personality and abnormal behavior, an understanding of the former often being regarded as important to the study of the latter. Perhaps one reason for this is the impact of the early psychoanalysts on both fields. A very brief comment therefore might be useful on some of the links between emotion and personality. (Strongman, *The Psychology of Emotion*)

Strongman develops his main idea—the effect (that there has been a long-standing link between personality and abnormal behavior) by looking at one cause (the impact of the early psychoanalysts on both fields).

## HOW DOES THE AUTHOR USE PROCESS?

When an author wants you to understand how to do something yourself or how something is or was done, he or she must give or describe the sequence of steps or behaviors needed to complete the process.

Topic sentences such as these alert you to look for a sequence of activities:

The interview, like any research, is a time-consuming process that involves a number of steps. *(the reader should watch for details that give the steps)*

The imaging technique known as ISI (Idealized Self-Image), developed by Dr. Dorothy Susskind, asks the subject to perform the following behaviors. *(the reader should watch for details that give the behaviors)*

Signal words that may indicate process include: first, second, third, . . . ; next; then; finally; eventually; following this; steps; at the start; to begin; initially; during the next minute, hour, day, year; and specific times or dates.

Read this paragraph to determine Tocquet's main idea. How does he develop and support his main idea?

For the extraction of a square root, the mental calculation broadly follows the normal method: first, you divide the number into groups of two figures, you look for the largest square contained in the first group, you carry the root as the first result and subtract this square from the first group. Next, you mentally add on to the remainder the first figure of the second group and divide the number thus obtained by twice the first figure carried; you retain this quotient as the second figure of the root required. As can be seen, the process is rather complicated and lengthy. (Tocquet, *The Magic of Numbers*)

Tocquet's supports his main idea (to mentally calculate a square root you use about the same procedure as when you calculate with pencil and paper) by giving the sequence of steps needed to complete the process. He uses two signal words—first and next—and a series of punctuation marks to help you follow the process.

## HOW DOES THE AUTHOR USE DEFINITION?

In academic material, authors often need to restrict and clarify a definition or explain their personal interpretation of the meaning of a term or concept.

This is done in a variety of ways. Common methods of providing definitions include: giving one or more dictionary definitions or one or more connotative meanings, tracing the etymology, comparing and/or contrasting the word with other terms, providing examples, and using negation—telling what it doesn't mean.

Topic sentences such as these alert you to watch for definitions:

The word "politician" has many meanings. *(the reader should watch for details that give various meanings)*

Psychologists are wary when asked to write about aggression; it is a definitional minefield. *(the reader should watch for details that give various definitions)*

Words that signal definition include: defined as, is, known, the term means, is stated as, and is used to mean.

Read this paragraph by Grassian to determine the main idea. How does he develop the details to support his idea?

The concept of euthanasia is used today with varying meanings. In its original Greek meaning, "euthanasia" meant no more than an easy and painless death (*eu* = well; *thanatos* = death) and was later extended to refer to the work of a physician in alleviating as far as possible the suffering of dying. Today, however, "euthanasia" is often used synonymously with that of "mercy killing" and as such entails the bringing about of death. *The American Heritage Dictionary* (1975) defines "euthanasia" as "the action of inducing the painless death of a person for reasons assumed to be merciful." As this definition demonstrates, central to our current concept of euthanasia is the idea that such an action be motivated by a desire to be merciful to or to do good to the recipient. As such, when most people are asked to think of a case of euthanasia they imagine a person who is dying of a painful terminal illness, such as cancer, and is given some lethal drug or injection that is meant to "put him out of his misery." (Grassian, *Moral Reasoning*)

Grassian develops and supports his main idea ("euthanasia" has different meanings) by giving five definitions of the word. He begins with the original meaning from Greek and traces the meaning through to today's usage.

## HOW DOES AN AUTHOR USE A COMBINATION OF METHODS?

Up to this point, you have been working with sample paragraphs that I have selected because they showed one method of development. But don't be misled. Much of the material you read is not this clear-cut; it does not adhere to only one method of development. Most authors use a combination of methods to develop their paragraphs, chapters, and articles.

For example, what do Donatelle and Davis want you to understand about manic depressives? What details do they provide to help you understand their idea? How do they develop the details?

Endogenous and exogenous depression are sometimes called unipolar depression because their victims suffer depression only. Conversely, victims of manic-depressive mood disorder suffer from violent mood swings. Manic depressives may be energetic, creative, vivacious, and "happy" for a time and then become severely depressed. Thus the characteristic mania of happiness followed by the melancholy of depression classifies the disorder as a bipolar affliction. Between 10 and 15 percent of the total American population is afflicted with manic-depressive mood disorders. (Donatelle and Davis, *Access to Health*)

Donatelle and Davis mainly want you to understand that manic depression is a bipolar affliction because it causes significant highs and lows. They first contrast victims of manic depression with victims of endogenous and exogenous depression (termed unipolar depression) by telling how their moods are different from each other—unipolar depressives suffer only depression; manic depressives suffer violent mood swings. Then they give an effect of this mood swing—it's classified as bipolar.

## PRACTICE: DETERMINING THE MAIN IDEA, SIGNIFICANT DETAILS, AND METHOD OF DEVELOPMENT

1. The age of the average worker has gradually increased over the past few decades. . . . This trend has affected businesses in two ways. First, older workers tend to put greater demand on a company's health insurance, life insurance, and retirement benefit programs. And second, younger workers taking the places of retirees tend to want different things from employers—things like more opportunities for self-expression or more leisure time. (Griffin and Ebert, *Business*)

    a. What is the main idea?

    b. How do Griffin and Ebert develop and support the main idea?

    c. What signal words were helpful?

    d. In what two ways has the aging of the work force affected businesses?

2. The most serious disciplinary problems facing managers undoubtedly involve attendance. For instance, in a study of two hundred organizations, 60 percent of which employed over one thousand workers, absenteeism, tardiness, abuse of sick leave, and other aspects of attendance were rated as the foremost problems by 79 percent of the respondents (Bureau of National Affairs, 1973). Importantly, attendance problems appear to be even more widespread than those related to productivity—such as carelessness in doing work, neglect of duty, and not following established procedures. (Robbins, *Training in Interpersonal Skills*)

    a. What is the main idea?

    b. What kind of details does Robbins use to support the main idea?

    c. If you were reading this paragraph to prepare for listening to a lecture, what would you concentrate on remembering?

    d. If you were reading this paragraph to prepare for taking a test, would you concentrate the same, more, or less?

3. [1]Being shy can cause many problems for adults. [2]They are often hesitant to seek out others and are excluded from social relationships. [3]Shy or withdrawn individuals are less likely to be promoted at work. [4]In addition, adults who are hesitant to talk with others are often taken advantage of by aggressive salespeople. (McGrath, *Self-defeating Behaviors*)

    a. What is the main idea?

    b. What kind of details does McGrath use to develop the main idea?

    c. What is the cause? What are the results?

    d. What is the relationship of sentence 4 to sentences 2 and 3? Does it define, summarize, introduce a contrast, continue the same thought, or provide an illustration or example?

4. To be convincing, presentation graphics must be fitted to the message and to the audience. . . . Begin with a plan. The most important part of your presentation preparation is deciding on just one primary idea with which to leave your audience. State it in a dozen words or less. Next, develop a complete outline of what you want to say.

When you've clearly identified your theme, the time, and the relative emphasis of each portion of your presentation, you can begin to create individual elements. Decide on the best way to illustrate your message for this audience. Then, draw small sketches of each overhead, slide, or handout you want to use. (adapted from Hengesbaugh, *Typography for Desktop Publishers*)

a. What is the main idea?

b. List the steps in the process described by Hengesbaugh.

5. Perhaps these (communication) difficulties arise because public speaking differs from other forms of communication in two ways. First, a public speaking situation includes two distinct and separate roles: speaker and audience. Second, in this speaker-audience relationship, the speaker carries more responsibility than does the audience. In other communication situations, speakers and listeners exchange roles and share this responsibility. (Barker and Barker, *Communication*)

a. What is the main idea?

b. How does public speaking differ from other forms of communication?

c. What often happens because of these differences?

6. We all want to have positive influence with certain people in our personal and professional lives. But how do we do it? How do we powerfully and ethically influence the lives of other people? There are three basic categories of influence: 1) model by example (others see); 2) build caring relationships (others feel); 3) mentor by instruction (others hear). (Covey, *7 Habits of Highly Effective People*)

a. What is the main idea?

b. How does Covey develop his main idea?

c. What do you predict the paragraphs that follow this one contain?

---

### REVIEW QUESTIONS

*Review Questions*

1. What is the difference between a thesis, a main idea, a major detail, and a minor detail? Why do you need to know the difference?

2. What is the purpose of signal words? Give two examples of signal words and explain how you would use them.

3. List and explain six methods authors use to develop and support their main ideas.

4. Explain how you can use author clues such as signal words, punctuation, and methods of development to help your comprehension.

*Think and Connect Questions*

5. Re-read "Endangered Species," in Chapter 3. In paragraphs 3–5, look beyond the main ideas you identified for the details that the authors provide to support them. For each of the three paragraphs, list the major supporting details and the development clues you used, such as signal words or method of development.

6. Re-read "Theories of Human Behavior" Chapter 4, Exercise 4. Identify the major details Greenberg and Dintiman used to develop and support the main ideas of paragraphs 2/3/4, and 5/6.

*Application Exercises*

7. Review the topic sentence about "health care costs" you wrote for Application Exercise 9, Chapter 4. Using the method of paragraph development that you think will best support and explain your main idea, write one paragraph. Your paragraph should include at least two major supporting details and one minor supporting detail.

8. Using your texts or other expository material, identify one paragraph in which the author develops the main idea using example, one in which the author uses comparison/contrast, one in which the author uses process, and one in which the author uses either division/classification or cause/effect.

---

**USE YOUR STRATEGIES: EXERCISE 1**

---

1. [1]Exercise has several beneficial effects. [2]It burns calories, enhances weight loss, and increases the likelihood that weight loss will be maintained. [3]It also increases metabolism, which counteracts the opposing effects of dieting, suppresses appetite, and minimizes the loss of lean tissue. [4]Aerobic exercise in particular strengthens the heart; enhances general muscle tone, strength, and elasticity; and has a positive effect on serum lipids, coronary efficiency, and blood pressure (Brownell, 1980). [5]At the same time, aerobic exercise decreases the risk of coronary artery disease, diabetes, and high blood pressure. [6]It is also associated with decreased anxiety and depression and an enhanced sense of well-being. [7]However, exercise also carries some risks. [8]If initiated by someone who is unfit or if carried to extremes, it may result in orthopedic discomfort and injury and, more rarely, may precipitate a heart attack (Haskell, 1984). (Snyder, *Health Psychology & Behavioral Medicine*)

   a. What is the main idea?

   b. How does Snyder develop and support the main idea?

   c. If you needed to remember several details in order to write your own in-class paragraph on this idea, which details would you remember? Why?

   d. What is the relationship of sentence 7 to sentence 1? Does it define, restate, introduce a contrast, continue the same thought, or provide an illustration or example?

2. [1]Computers are designed to be either special-purpose or general-purpose computing devices. [2]Special-purpose computers, also known as dedicated computers, are designed around a specific application or type of application. . . . [3]For example, the Lunar Excursion Module (LEM), which landed the first man on the moon, had a special-purpose computer on board intended to do only one thing: control the altitude or relative position of the vehicle during descent and ascent to and from the moon. . . . [4]General-purpose computers are designed to handle a variety of tasks. . . . [5]Thus the same combination of hardware

can be used to execute many different programs. [6]General purpose computers have the advantage of versatility over special-purpose computers but typically are less efficient and slower than special-purpose computers when applied to the same task. (Fuori and Gioia, *Computers and Information Processing*)

a. What is the main idea?

b. How do Fuori and Gioia develop and support their main idea?

c. What is the purpose of sentence 3?

3. Animals, known technically as fauna, occur in much greater variety than do plants. As objects of geographical study, however, they are less important than plants, for at least two reasons. First, animals are much less prominent in the landscape. Apart from extremely localized situations, animals tend to be secretive and inconspicuous, whereas the vegetation is not only fixed in position, it also serves as a relatively complete ground cover wherever it has not been removed by human interference. In addition, animals do not provide the clear evidence of environmental interrelationships that plants do. (Bergman and McKnight, *Introduction to Geography*)

a. What is the main idea?

b. How do Bergman and McKnight develop and support their main idea?

c. List the two reasons animals are less important than plants to geographical study.

4. A clause is a group of words containing both a subject and a predicate. A clause functions as an element of a compound or a complex sentence. There are two general types of clauses: the main or independent clause and the subordinate or dependent clause. The main clause (such as "it is hot") is an independent grammatical unit and can stand alone. The subordinate clause (such as "because it is hot") cannot stand alone. A subordinate clause is either preceded or followed by a main clause. *(Webster's Guide to Business Correspondence)*

a. What is the main idea?

b. How does the author develop and support the main idea?

c. If you were preparing to take a test in which you had to explain clauses and give examples, which details would you remember? Which ones would you ignore? Why?

5. The sociological perspective was sparked by three basic and interrelated changes. First, rapid technological innovation in eighteenth-century Europe soon led to the spread of factories and an industrial economy. Second, these factories drew millions of people from the countryside, causing an explosive growth of cities. Third, people in these expanding industrial cities soon began to entertain new ideas about the world, leading to important political developments. (Macionis, *Sociology*)

a. What is the main idea?

b. What development clues does Macionis use?

c. If you needed to remember the major details for a quiz, which details would you remember?

6. [1]About 300 million years ago the conditions for the subsequent formation of petroleum (mineral oil) were established in shallow coastal waters by the teeming tiny creatures and plants that lived and died in vast numbers. [2]The ooze formed on the bottom by the remains of these organisms was unable to decompose because of a lack of oxygen. [3]As a result of climatic changes, these coastal areas became buried under layers of earth, and the organic remains were subjected to high pressures and temperatures over periods of millions of years. [4]The fats, carbohydrates and proteins were thereby subjected to conditions in which they were decomposed and underwent extensive chemical changes. [5]As a result of these changes, a large number of compounds were formed which all enter into the composition of petroleum. *(The Way Things Work)*

   a. What is the main idea?

   b. How does the author develop and support the main idea?

7. A number of factors contribute to overweight and obesity in the United States population. Inactivity and overeating, in that order, are the two leading causes among both children and adults. Early eating patterns, the number of fat cells acquired early in life, metabolism, age, and environmental and genetic factors also play a significant role. (Greenberg and Dintiman, *Exploring Health*)

   a. What is the main idea?

   b. How do Greenberg and Dintiman develop and support their main idea?

8. [1]Studying philosophy helps you to develop insight into some of life's great puzzles and to fashion your own vision of what life is all about. [2]As you go through life, you will be challenged all along the way to make decisions about who you are and what's important to you. [3]What will you do with your life? [4]What career will you pursue? [5]Will you marry? [6]And if so, what kind of person? [7]Will you have children? [8]How will you rear them? [9]What will you tell them is important? [10]What are you willing to do for money and success? [11]How will you cope with the crises you will encounter in your own life or in the lives of those you love—illnesses, accidents, problems on the job or at home, death? [12]Philosophy helps you develop a sense of what life is all about and where you're going. (White, *Discovering Philosophy*)

   a. What is the main idea?

   b. How does White develop and support the main idea?

   c. What is the relationship of sentence 12 to sentence 1? Does it define, restate, introduce a contrast, continue the same thought, or provide an illustration or example?

9. The Colorado Avalanche Information Center (CAIC) in Denver advises skiers to stay alert for avalanche conditions. The threat of avalanches is greatest in the late winter because of higher snow accumulations, warmer temperatures that make snow wet and heavy, and the presence of more unstable snow layers. Avalanche conditions are more likely to occur in terrain sloping 30° or more, and during and immediately after bad weather involving snow and high winds.

   If it is not possible to stay out of such conditions, the CAIC advises skiers to stay near the end or flanks of narrow valleys and away from the middle or lower reaches, cliffs, tree stands, and gullies, where there is limited room to maneuver in an emergency. (adapted from information from the Colorado Avalanche Information Center)

a.  What is the main idea of paragraph one?

    What is the main idea of paragraph two?

b.  How does the author develop and support the main ideas?

c.  What are three conditions that increase the threat of avalanches? Why is the threat greater in the late winter? Why should skiers try to stay near the end of a narrow valley?

10.  In the early years of the new nation, two types of newspapers were developing. One was the mercantile paper, published in the seaboard towns primarily for the trading and shipping classes interested in commercial and political news. Its well-filled advertising columns reflected the essentially business interest of its limited clientele of subscribers—2000 was a good number. The other type was the political paper, partisan in its appeal and relying for reader support on acceptance of its views, rather than upon the quality and completeness of its news. Most editors of the period put views first and news second; the political paper deliberately shaped the news to fit its views. (Agee, Ault, and Emery, *Introduction to Mass Communications*)

a.  What is the main idea?

b.  How do Agee, Ault, and Emery develop and support their main idea?

c.  List the major differences between the two types of newspapers.

---

### USE YOUR STRATEGIES: EXERCISE 2

# *When X-Cold Strikes*

## ROBERT L. MCGRATH

*Robert McGrath is a freelance writer. His work appears in numerous national publications. This selection is from* Young American.

[1]X-cold is hypothermia—body temperature lowered too rapidly by chilling from wet, wind and cold. It brings quick collapse of mental and physical functions, affecting anyone, young or old.

[2]It's exception-cold, extensive-cold. X-cold happens when unexpected winter wind, rain or snow arrives. Your clothes get wet and lose up to 90 percent of their insulating value. Water is held against your body with a chilling effect, even though outside temperatures can be as high as 50 degrees Fahrenheit.

[3]Your body temperature, normally 98.6°F, drops to 94°F or below. If it cools further, it's a danger point—X-cold—because cooling to 80°F can produce death.

⁴If you know how to prevent it, X-cold won't spoil your outdoor fun. Watch for these signals:

- Chattering teeth and shivering.
- Slow, hard-to-understand speech.
- Forgetfulness, confusion.
- Fumbling hands.
- Stumbling, difficulty in walking.
- Sleepiness—The person going to sleep may never wake up.
- Exhaustion—If the person can't get up after a brief rest, X-cold has taken over.

⁵X-cold reduces reasoning power and judgment because of lack of oxygen to the brain. The affected person usually denies that anything is wrong.

⁶What can you do? Find shelter. Build a fire. Get the victim out of wind, rain, snow. Strip off wet clothing and put on dry clothes or wrap up in a sleeping bag. Give warm drinks. Avoid medicines—they may slow down body processes even more.

⁷Body heat trapped by insulating clothing is the best protection against cold. Wear loose-fitting, lightweight clothing in several layers. Put on a knit cap—more than half the body's heat can be lost through the head. That extra warmth will send added blood to your feet, making them feel more comfortable.

⁸Remember, weather may pull surprises. Unexpected changes can bring sharp wind, driving rain, snow—conditions producing X-cold.

⁹Use your head. Wear seasonal clothing. Don't let X-cold—hypothermia—keep you from enjoying our great outdoors the year around.

**Questions**

1. What is McGrath's purpose?
2. Write a sentence that expresses McGrath's thesis.
3. What is X-cold?
4. What is hypothermia?
5. In paragraph 1, what is the relationship between sentence 2 and sentence 1?
6. What is the main idea of paragraph 7?
7. What are four warning signs of hypothermia?
8. Why does hypothermia reduce a person's reasoning power?
9. What are four positive actions you can take to counteract hypothermia?
10. What is the primary action McGrath urges you to take to avoid hypothermia?

---

USE YOUR STRATEGIES: EXERCISE 3

---

# *Running the Small Business: Reasons for Successes and Failures*

## RICKY W. GRIFFIN AND RONALD J. EBERT

*Ricky Griffin teaches business at Texas A&M University. Ronald J. Ebert teaches business at the University of Missouri–Columbia. This selection is from* Business, 2nd ed.

[1a]Why do many small businesses succeed and others fail? [b]While there is no set pattern, there are some common causes of both success and failure.

[2]***Reasons for Failure.*** [a]Four common factors contribute to small business failure. [b]One major problem is managerial incompetence or inexperience. [c]If managers do not know how to make basic decisions, they are unlikely to make them effectively. [d]A second contributor to failure is neglect. [e]That is, after the glamour and excitement of the big grand opening, some *entrepreneurs* get discouraged and don't concentrate as much on their business as they should. . . . [f]Third, weak control systems can also be a cause of failure. [g]If control systems fail to alert managers to *impending problems,* they are likely to be caught unprepared to deal with them. [h]Finally, many small businesses fail because the owner does not have enough capital to keep it going. [i]New business owners are almost certain to fail if they expect to pay the second month's rent from the first month's profits.

[3]***Reasons for Success.*** [a]Likewise, four basic factors contribute to small business success. [b]One factor is hard work, drive, and dedication. [c]Owners must be committed to succeeding and willing to put in the time and effort necessary to make it happen. [d]Another factor is *market demand* for the products or services being provided. [e]If a large college town has only a single pizza parlor, a new one is more likely to succeed than if there are already thirty in operation. [f]Managerial competence is also important. [g]Successful small businesspeople have at least a *modicum of ability and understanding* of what they should do. [h]And finally, luck is often a key variable in determining whether the business succeeds or fails. [i]For example, when Debbi Fields first opened Mrs. Fields' Cookies, she literally had to give cookies away in order to tempt people to buy them. [j]Had she not found eager customers that first day she might well have given up and quit.

**Questions**

1. What is Griffin and Ebert's purpose?
2. Define each of these words or phrases from the selection.

   a. entrepreneurs (¶2)

   b. impending problems (¶2)

   c. market demand (¶3)

   d. modicum of ability and understanding (¶3)

3. What type of context clue do Griffin and Ebert use to help define market demand?
4. Write a sentence that expresses Griffin and Ebert's thesis.
5. In each sentence in paragraphs 2 and 3, identify whether the sentence is the main idea, a major detail, or a minor detail.
6. In paragraph 2, what is the relationship of sentence b to sentence a?
7. In paragraph 2, what is the relationship of sentence c to sentence b?
8. What are four common causes of failure for small businesses?
9. What are four common causes of success for small businesses?
10. What four words do Griffin and Ebert use in paragraph 2 to signal the four causes?

---

**USE YOUR STRATEGIES: EXERCISE 4**

---

# *The Benefits of the Sociological Perspective*

### JOHN J. MACIONIS

*Dr. Macionis is an associate professor of sociology at Kenyon College in Gambier, Ohio. He teaches a wide range of upper-level courses, but his favorite course is Introduction to Sociology. His doctorate is in sociology and he is the author of several articles and papers on topics such as community life in the United States, interpersonal relationships in families, effective teaching, and humor. This selection is from* Sociology, *3rd ed.*

[1]The knowledge that has been amassed within sociology is immense and can be readily applied to our lives in countless ways. There are, however, four general ways in which the sociological perspective can enrich our lives.

[2a]The first benefit of using the sociological perspective is learning that our world contains a remarkable variety of human social patterns. [b]North Americans represent only about 5 percent of the world's population, and, as the remaining chapters of this book explain, the rest of humanity lives in ways that often differ dramatically from our own. [c]As members of any society, people define their

ways of life as proper and often "natural." [d]But looking over the course of human history, and examining the world today, we find countless competing versions of correct behavior. [e]*The sociological perspective helps us to recognize human diversity and to begin to understand the challenges of living within a diverse world.*

[3]The second benefit comes from realizing that, within particular societies, people come to accept as "true" certain ideas that may or may not be factual. *The sociological perspective challenges our familiar understandings of ourselves and of others, so that we can critically reconsider what has been assumed to be "true."*

[4]As we have already seen, a good example of a widespread but misleading "truth" is that Americans are "autonomous individuals," independent of others and personally responsible for their lives. By thinking this way, we are sometimes too quick to praise particularly successful people as being personally superior to those who have not fared as well. On the other side of the coin, people who do not measure up may be unfairly condemned as personally deficient. A sociological approach encourages us to ask whether these beliefs are actually true and, to the extent that they are not, why they are so widely held.

[5]As we consider American society in global context, we might also wonder if the American conception of "success," with its emphasis on materialism rather than, for instance, spiritual well-being, is the best way by which to judge others, as well as to evaluate our own lives.

[6]The third benefit provided by the sociological perspective involves understanding that, for better or worse, American society operates in a particular and deliberate way. No one is able to live with complete disregard for society's "rules of the game." In the game of life, we may decide how to play our cards, but it is society that deals us the hand. The more effective player is generally one who better understands how the game works. Here again, sociology is valuable. *The sociological perspective allows us to recognize both the opportunities and the constraints that affect our lives.* Knowledge of this kind is power. Through it, we come to understand what we are likely and unlikely to accomplish for ourselves, and we are able to see how the goals we adopt can be realized more effectively.

[7a]Of course, the more we understand about the operation of society, the more we can take an active part in shaping social life. [b]On the other hand, with little awareness of how society operates, we are likely passively to accept the status quo. *The sociological perspective, therefore, empowers us as active members of our world.* For some, this may mean embracing society as it is; others, however, may attempt nothing less than trying to change the entire world in some way. The discipline of sociology advocates no one particular political orientation. Indeed, sociologists are widely spread across the political spectrum. But evaluating any aspect of social life—whatever one's eventual goal—depends on the ability to identify social forces and to assess their consequences. . . .

**Questions**

1. What is Macionis's purpose?

2. Write a sentence that expresses Macionis's thesis.

3. How does Macionis develop and support his thesis?

4. In paragraph 2, what is the relationship of sentence e to sentence a?

5. How do paragraphs 4 and 5 relate to paragraph 3?

6. What words does Macionis use in paragraphs 2, 3, and 6 to signal the key points?

7. What other clues—in addition to, or in place of signal words—does he use to signal key points?

8. In paragraph 7, what is the relationship of sentence b to sentence a?

9. List the benefits of the sociological perspective.

10. What percentage of the world's population do North Americans represent? Are you surprised by this percentage? Did you think it would be higher or lower? Why?

11. What does Macionis think is "a widespread but misleading 'truth' about Americans"?

12. How does Macionis think we judge success in America? Does he think it is the best criteria? Do you?

13. What political viewpoint do most sociologists hold?

14. What is necessary, according to Macionis, for us to become active members of society?

15. Assume you are going to have a short quiz tomorrow on the benefits of the sociological perspective. What details would you remember?

---

### CONNECTIONS

A. When you are reading an assignment, how do you decide what to remember? Do you vary the amount of detail you try to remember depending on what you are going to do with the information? Do some of your classes require you to remember more details than others? If so, why?

B. Are you pleased with the results of your reading and study strategies this semester? If you are pleased, what attitudes do you have and what things are you doing that help you the most? If you are not pleased with your success, what are two changes you could make this week that might help? Have you been using any of the Plan»Do»Review» Cycle? How successful is it for you?

# 6

# *Integrate Words and Graphic Information*

Because of computer technology, expository authors are using an increasing number of graphics, such as graphs, tables, charts, diagrams, and photographs, to complement and supplement their words. Rarely in academic reading do graphics stand alone. Authors use graphics to condense, clarify, illustrate, highlight, or add details that aren't covered in the text. You must be skillful in understanding the information provided by the graphic, and in integrating that information with the words.

As you preview this chapter, recall the types of graphics you have seen recently in your text assignments, in newspapers and magazines, and on television. Did you read the graphic? If so, did you understand the main idea? If you read the graphic, did you skip over the words? Did you read both the words and the graphic? Did you compare the information between the words and the graphic?

Highlight definitions for this chapter's key vocabulary:

- graphic
- graph
- table
- pie chart
- diagram
- flow chart
- caption

- row
- column
- map
- legend
- key
- scale

---

**Chapter 6 Content Objectives**

- recognize that graphics contain valuable information
- understand how to read different types of graphics
- identify and consider the source of the information used in graphics
- integrate words and graphics

---

# What Is My Basic Strategy for Integrating Words and Graphics?

**As You Plan:**

1. Read the graphic's title and subtitles.
2. Read the graphic's labels, captions, legend, key and/or scale.
3. Determine how the information is organized.
4. Answer the question, who or what is this graphic about?
5. Identify the relationships, changes, or trends represented.
6. Answer the question, what does the author want me to understand about this subject?
7. Consider the quality of the information.
8. Predict the relationship of the information in the graphic to the written information.

**As You Read:**

9. Integrate the information in the graphic with the written information.

**As You Review:**

10. Revise and restate the thesis and/or main idea.
11. Restate the supporting details that you need to fulfill your purpose.

# How Can I Understand Graphic Information?

For our purpose, a graphic is any visual representation that authors use to highlight, clarify, illustrate, summarize, or complement their text.

When you read a graphic, you must first understand the graphic's information. Just as you do with written material, consider the source or quality of the graphic's data. Information about who collected and prepared the data should be included in the graphic's caption or footnote.

Then, like reading a paragraph, identify the author's main idea and the relationships among the details.

Next, compare the information from the graphic with what is presented in the text—is it the same or are there some differences? Does the graphic highlight a portion of what is written, give an example of a concept or idea, summarize the written material, or add details not covered in the text? Finally, based on your overall purpose for reading, decide how much of the graphic's information you need to know.

# How Do I Read a Graph?

A graph uses bars or lines to show the relationships between or among quantities. Graphs can be used in almost every subject. For example, a graph can be used in a mass communications text to show the change in the number of newspapers published in the United States over the last 50 years, in a psychology text to show the divorce rates by sex and age, or in your reading class to show the distribution of grades on the last exam.

When reading a graph, you are concerned with at least two variables—one indicated, or labeled, on the vertical axis (up and down the side), and the other labeled on the horizontal axis (across the bottom). The main idea of the graph will often be summarized in its title or by the text's discussion of the graph. Captions or footnotes under the graph often give the source of the information. A key, or reference center, defines any other codes used. Two common types of graphs are bar graphs and line graphs.

## BAR GRAPH

An author can use a simple bar graph to show the comparison of quantities within a category. See how the bar graph in Example 1.1 uses data from the U.S. Census Bureau (caption), to show the number of gallons (vertical axis) of three kinds of milk (key) consumed in the United States during four different years (horizontal axis).

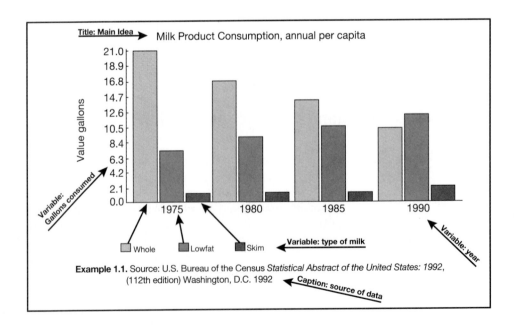

**Example 1.1.** Source: U.S. Bureau of the Census *Statistical Abstract of the United States: 1992,* (112th edition) Washington, D.C. 1992

***Stacked bar graph.*** A stacked bar graph is effective when an author wants you to concentrate on component parts of a total. See how Example 1.2 uses the same U.S. Census data and variables as Example 1.1, but focuses your attention on the changes in the proportion of each kind of milk consumed to the total consumption.

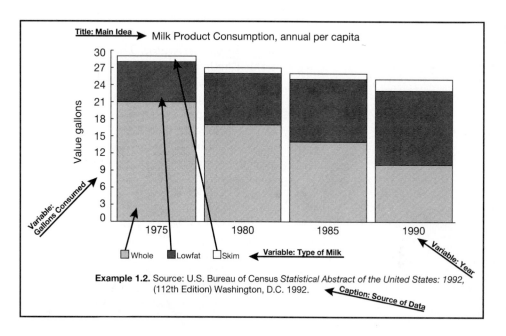

**Example 1.2.** Source: U.S. Bureau of Census *Statistical Abstract of the United States: 1992,* (112th Edition) Washington, D.C. 1992.

## LINE GRAPH

An author uses a line graph to focus your attention on a pattern or an upward or downward trend. See how the line graph in Example 1.3, using the same U.S. Census Bureau data as above, directs your attention to the downward trend in whole milk consumption and the upward trends in lowfat and skim milk consumption.

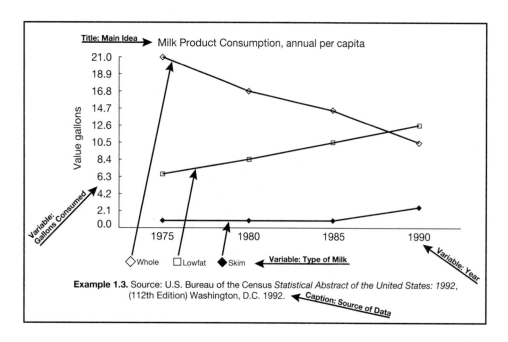

**Example 1.3.** Source: U.S. Bureau of the Census *Statistical Abstract of the United States: 1992,* (112th Edition) Washington, D.C. 1992.

## PRACTICE: READING AND INTEGRATING A GRAPH AND WORDS

In each of the following, read the paragraph, read the graph, integrate the information, and then answer the questions.

1.  Oceans respond very differently than do continents to the arrival of solar radiation. In general, land heats and cools faster and to a greater degree than does water. Therefore, both the hottest and coldest areas of the Earth are found in the interiors of continents, distant from the moderating influence of oceans. In the study of the atmosphere, probably no single geographical relationship is more important than the distinction between continental and maritime climates. A continental climate experiences greater seasonal extremes of temperature—hotter in summer, colder in winter—than does a maritime climate (see Figure 2–1). (Bergman and McKnight, *Introduction to Geography*)

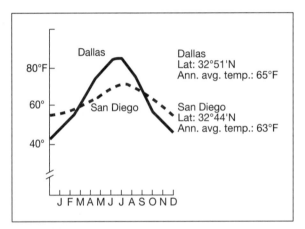

**FIGURE 2–1.** Temperature curves for San Diego and Dallas. San Diego, situated on the coast, experiences milder temperatures in both summer and winter than inland Dallas.

a.  What is the topic of Figure 2–1?

b.  Is the purpose of this line graph to highlight one portion of the paragraph, give an example of the concept, or summarize the paragraph?

c.  If your purpose for reading this selection was to understand why there is a difference between continental and maritime climates, would you need to memorize the details from the graph? Explain.

2.  *Financing the Small Business*  Although determining whether to start from scratch or buy an existing firm is an important decision, it is meaningless unless a small businessperson can obtain the money to set up shop or purchase a business. As Figure 6.5 shows, a bewildering variety of monetary resources—ranging from private to governmental—await the small businessperson. (Griffin and Ebert, *Business*)

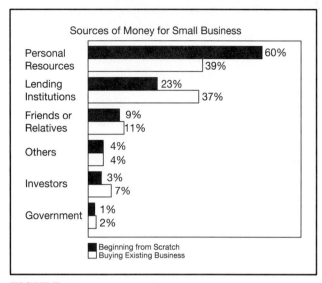

**FIGURE 6.5**

a. What is the topic of Figure 6.5?

b. The paragraph refers to "a bewildering variety of monetary resources." How is the graph more specific?

c. What is the largest source of money for a small businessperson starting a new business?

d. What is the second largest source of money for a small businessperson buying an existing business?

## How Do I Read a Table?

Authors use a table when they want you to have several pieces of specific data rather than a summary. The data, often numbers or statistics, are arranged systematically in rows (horizontal) and columns (vertical). The information in a table often compares qualities or quantities or shows how things change over time (the trend). Tables can be used to display data in almost any subject, from the growth of government spending in an economics text, to the number of calories found in alcoholic beverages in a health text.

When reading a table, use the title or written reference to the table to help predict the main idea. Next, identify the variables by reading the column labels (across the top of the table) and the row labels (down the left side of the table). Clarify the type of data presented for each variable, e.g., raw numbers, percentages. And, as always, check the caption or footnote for the source of the information.

See how the table in Example 1.4 on page 118 displays data from the U.S. Department of Agriculture to show the specific number of calories and grams of fat in average servings of common foods.

Low Fat Foods§   ← Title: Main Idea   Column Labels: Variables →

| | Serving | Calories | Grams of Fat* |
|---|---|---|---|
| *Dairy Products* | | | |
| Cheese: | | | |
| Low-fat cottage (2%) | 1/2 cup | 100 | 2 |
| Mozzarella, part skim | 1 oz. | 80 | 5 |
| Parmesan | 1 Tbs | 25 | 2 |
| Milk: | | | |
| Low-fat (2%) | 1 cup | 125 | 5 |
| Nonfat, skim | 1 cup | 85 | trace |
| Ice Milk | 1 cup | 185 | 6 |
| Yogurt, low-fat, fruit | 1 cup | 230 | 2 |
| *Poultry Products* | | | |
| Chicken, roasted: | | | |
| Dark meat, no skin | 3 oz. | 175 | 8 |
| Light meat, no skin | 3 oz. | 145 | 4 |
| Turkey, roasted: | | | |
| Dark meat, no skin | 3 oz. | 160 | 6 |
| Light meat, no skin | 3 oz. | 135 | 3 |
| Egg, hard cooked | 1 large | 80 | 6 |

Row Labels: Variables → (points to Mozzarella, part skim)

**Example 1.4.** *From Nutritive Value of Foods*, U.S. Department of Agriculture,   ← Source of Fat Data
Home and Garden Bulletin No. 72, 1985.
§From *Diet, Nutrition & Cancer Prevention: The Good News*,   ← Source of Low Fat Data
U.S. Department of Health and Human Services, NIH Publication
No. 87-2878, December 1987.

---

## PRACTICE EXERCISE: READING AND INTEGRATING A TABLE AND WORDS

---

Read the paragraph, read the table on page 119, integrate the information, and then answer the questions.

3. Table 3–1 indicates some changes in attitudes among first-year college students over a single generation: those entering college in 1968 and those entering in 1987. The figures in the table indicate that some things have not changed very much: about the same proportion of students come to college in order to "gain a general education" and to "learn more about things." But students of the late 1980s certainly appear more interested in gaining skills, especially those that will lead to a high-paying job. Moreover, the political activism of the 1960s seems to have declined significantly in favor of pursuing personal success. Note that changes have generally been greater among women than among men. This, no doubt, reflects the fact that the women's movement, concerned with social equality for the two sexes, intensified after 1968. (Macionis, *Sociology*)

a. What is the topic of Table 3–1?

b. Is the purpose of Table 3–1 to highlight one portion of the paragraph, summarize the paragraph, or add details not covered in the paragraph?

c. The paragraph says "students of the late 1980s certainly appear more interested in gaining skills, especially those that will lead to a high-paying job." What specific data from the table supports this statement?

**Table 3–1  ATTITUDES AMONG STUDENTS ENTERING AMERICAN COLLEGES, 1968 AND 1987**

|  |  | 1968 | 1987 | Change |
|---|---|---|---|---|
| ***Reasons to Go to College (Very Important)*** |  |  |  |  |
| Gain a general education | male | 60 | 61 | +1 |
|  | female | 67 | 67 | 0 |
| Learn more about things | male | 69 | 72 | +3 |
|  | female | 74 | 76 | +2 |
| Improve reading and writing skills | male | 22 | 36 | +14 |
|  | female | 23 | 43 | +20 |
| Get a better job | male | 74 | 83 | +9 |
|  | female | 70 | 83 | +13 |
| Prepare for graduate or professional school | male | 39 | 44 | +5 |
|  | female | 29 | 50 | +21 |
| Make more money | male | 57 | 75 | +18 |
|  | female | 42 | 68 | +26 |
| ***Life Objectives (Essential or Very Important)*** |  |  |  |  |
| Develop a philosophy of life | male | 79 | 40 | −39 |
|  | female | 87 | 39 | −48 |
| Keep up with political affairs | male | 52 | 43 | −9 |
|  | female | 52 | 33 | −19 |
| Raise a family | male | 64 | 56 | −8 |
|  | female | 72 | 60 | −12 |
| Help others in difficulty | male | 50 | 50 | 0 |
|  | female | 71 | 67 | −4 |
| Be successful in my own business | male | 55 | 55 | 0 |
|  | female | 32 | 46 | +14 |
| Be well off financially | male | 51 | 80 | +29 |
|  | female | 27 | 72 | +45 |

*Note:* To allow comparisons, data from early 1970s rather than 1968 are used for some items.

*Source:* Richard G. Braungart and Margaret M. Braungart. "From Yippies to Yuppies: Twenty Years of Freshman Attitudes." *Public Opinion,* Vol. 11, No. 3 (September-October 1988):53–56.

# How Do I Read a Pie Chart or Circle Graph?

Authors use pie charts (also called circle graphs) to illustrate the ratio of the values of a category to the total. The whole pie or circle represents 100%, and various segments, or pieces of the pie, show relative magnitude or frequencies. The larger the pie wedge, the larger fraction of the total it represents. Pie charts can be used to illustrate a variety of data. For example, a study skills author might use one to illustrate the percentage of time a student spends in various activities, e.g., studying, working, sleeping; or an accounting text author could use a pie chart to show the relative amounts to budget for household expenses, e.g., rent, food, clothing.

As with other graphics, use the title or the written reference to help predict the main idea. The main idea will tell you what 100% of the pie graph represents. Next, check the key to see how many segments of the whole are included, what they are, and what fill pattern is used to identify each. Check the caption or footnote for the source of the information.

Look at the pie chart in Example 1.5 that displays Social Security benefits data from the U.S. Census Bureau. The whole pie represents all people (100%) who received monthly Social Security benefits in 1990. The pieces of the pie represent the proportion of the total received by each eligible category.

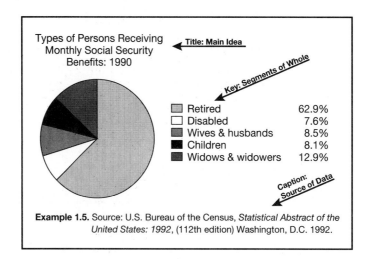

Types of Persons Receiving Monthly Social Security Benefits: 1990 ← Title: Main Idea

Key: Segments of Whole

| | | |
|---|---|---|
| ☐ Retired | 62.9% | |
| ☐ Disabled | 7.6% | |
| ☐ Wives & husbands | 8.5% | |
| ■ Children | 8.1% | |
| ■ Widows & widowers | 12.9% | |

Caption: Source of Data

**Example 1.5.** Source: U.S. Bureau of the Census, *Statistical Abstract of the United States: 1992*, (112th edition) Washington, D.C. 1992.

---

## PRACTICE: READING AND INTEGRATING A PIE CHART AND TEXT

Read the paragraph, read the pie charts, integrate the information, and then answer the questions.

4. Non-direct distribution channels do mean higher prices to the ultimate consumer. The more members involved in the channel, the higher the final price to the purchaser. After all, each link in the distribution chain must charge a markup or commission in order to make a profit. Figure 19.2 shows typical markup growth through the distribution channel. (Griffin and Ebert, *Business*)

a. What is the topic of Figure 19.2?

b. Is the purpose of Figure 19.2 to highlight one portion of the paragraph, give a specific example of the concept, or summarize the paragraph?

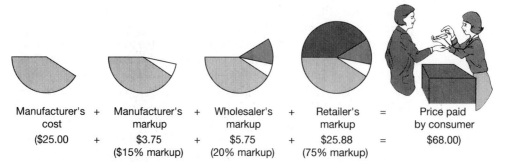

| Manufacturer's cost | + | Manufacturer's markup | + | Wholesaler's markup | + | Retailer's markup | = | Price paid by consumer |
|---|---|---|---|---|---|---|---|---|
| ($25.00 | + | $3.75 | + | $5.75 | + | $25.88 | = | $68.00) |
| | | ($15% markup) | | (20% markup) | | (75% markup) | | |

**FIGURE 19.2** Typical Price Markup: Manufacturer to Consumer

    c. What is the manufacturer's cost for the item? What does the consumer pay for the item?

    d. Why does each member of the distribution chain markup the item? Where did you find that information?

## How Do I Read a Diagram?

Diagram is a general term that refers to any type of drawing an author uses to help you understand ideas, objects, plans, processes, or sequences. Diagrams include everything from a simple labeled line drawing of the parts of a flower in a biology text, to an organizational chart in a management text, to a complex correlation-and-cause diagram in a sociology text.

Begin by identifying the topic and main idea of the diagram. Next, try to establish the purpose of the diagram—what it shows and why the author is using it. In addition, clarify what each portion of the diagram represents.

Look at the diagram in Example 1.6 that I developed for the chapter on "researching information" in my *Magazine Article Writing Basics* text. It shows (with the filled circles) and tells (in words) the differences in the information you will find when you use the three key terms of Boolean logic.

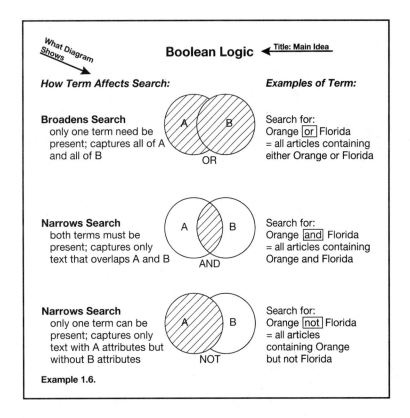

Example 1.6.

### FLOW CHART

A flow chart is a type of diagram that uses boxes, rectangles, diamonds, or circles, with connecting lines or arrows, to show the step-by-step procedure of a complicated process. These sequential diagrams are designed to be read from top to bottom or from left to right. Flow charts can be constructed to show many different kinds of processes—from how a computer program operates in a data processing text, to the procedure for analyzing the elements in a laboratory sample in a chemistry lab manual, to how to write an essay (see Example 1.7 that I developed for students in writing classes).

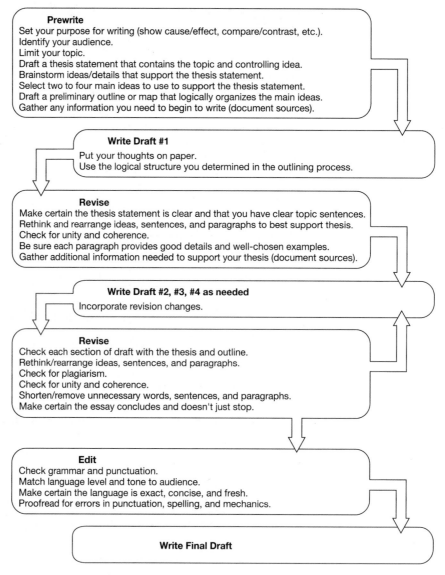

**Prewrite**
Set your purpose for writing (show cause/effect, compare/contrast, etc.).
Identify your audience.
Limit your topic.
Draft a thesis statement that contains the topic and controlling idea.
Brainstorm ideas/details that support the thesis statement.
Select two to four main ideas to use to support the thesis statement.
Draft a preliminary outline or map that logically organizes the main ideas.
Gather any information you need to begin to write (document sources).

**Write Draft #1**
Put your thoughts on paper.
Use the logical structure you determined in the outlining process.

**Revise**
Make certain the thesis statement is clear and that you have clear topic sentences.
Rethink and rearrange ideas, sentences, and paragraphs to best support thesis.
Check for unity and coherence.
Be sure each paragraph provides good details and well-chosen examples.
Gather additional information needed to support your thesis (document sources).

**Write Draft #2, #3, #4 as needed**
Incorporate revision changes.

**Revise**
Check each section of draft with the thesis and outline.
Rethink/rearrange ideas, sentences, and paragraphs.
Check for plagiarism.
Check for unity and coherence.
Shorten/remove unnecessary words, sentences, and paragraphs.
Make certain the essay concludes and doesn't just stop.

**Edit**
Check grammar and punctuation.
Match language level and tone to audience.
Make certain the language is exact, concise, and fresh.
Proofread for errors in punctuation, spelling, and mechanics.

**Write Final Draft**

Example 1.7.

## MAP

A map is a diagram that depicts on a two-dimensional flat surface all or part of the earth's three-dimensional surface. Maps translate data into spatial patterns by using distance, direction, size, and shape. Of course maps are used in geography and history to show the locations of places and events, but they can also be used to show everything from distributions of various religious populations in a philosophy text, to acid rain affected areas in a book on environmental biology.

When reading a map, begin by identifying the topic and the main idea.

Use the words, scale, legend, or other reference points to establish how the information is represented on the map. A scale is a map element that shows the relationship between a length measured on a map and the corresponding distance on the ground. A legend, like a key on a chart, is a reference center that defines the codes being used. As always, consider the source of the data.

Look at the map of Colorado's Indian Peaks Wilderness Area in Example 1.8 on page 124. The map shows the portion of Indian Peaks where a backcountry permit is required. Its scale is in miles and the legend includes an explanation for the nine symbols used on the map.

---

### PRACTICE: READING AND INTEGRATING A DIAGRAM AND WORDS

Read the paragraphs, read the map, integrate the information, and then answer the questions.

5. The Federal Reserve System (the Fed) also serves commercial banks by clearing checks. Imagine you are a photographer living in New Orleans, who wants to participate in a photography workshop in Detroit, Michigan. In order to do so you must send a check for $50 to the Detroit studio. Figure 20.3 traces your check through the clearing process.

   After the studio deposits your check in a Detroit bank (step 1), the bank deposits the check in its own account at the Federal Reserve Bank of Chicago (step 2). The check is sent from Chicago to the Atlanta Federal Reserve bank for collection (step 3) because you, the check writer, are in the Atlanta Federal Reserve Bank district. Your New Orleans bank receives the check from Atlanta and deducts the $50 from your account (step 4). Your bank then has $50 deducted from its deposit account at the Atlanta Federal Reserve Bank (step 5). Finally, the $50 is shifted from Atlanta to the Chicago Federal Reserve Bank (step 6). The studio's Detroit bank gets credited, and the studio's account then gets credited $50, normally within two weeks. Your bank then returns the canceled check to you by mail. (Griffin and Ebert, *Business*)

**FIGURE 20.3**

*(Text and questions continue on page 125.)*

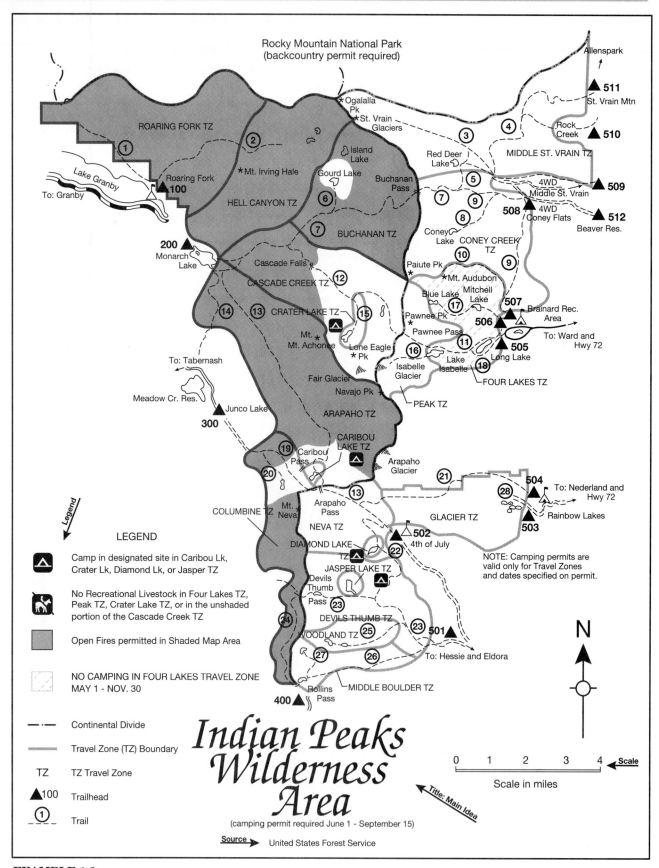

Rocky Mountain National Park
(backcountry permit required)

ROARING FORK TZ

Lake Granby
To: Granby

Roaring Fork
▲100

HELL CANYON TZ

*Mt. Irving Hale

Island Lake

Gourd Lake

Ogalalla Pk
St. Vrain Glaciers

Red Deer Lake

Buchanan Pass

MIDDLE ST. VRAIN TZ

Allenspark

▲ 511
St. Vrain Mtn

Rock Creek

▲ 510

4WD
Middle St. Vrain

▲ 509

Coney Flats 4WD

▲ 512
Beaver Res.

508

200 ▲
Monarch Lake

BUCHANAN TZ

Cascade Falls

CASCADE CREEK TZ

Coney Lake

CONEY CREEK TZ

Paiute Pk

Blue Lake

*Mt. Audubon
Mitchell Lake

Brainard Rec. Area

507
506
505

CRATER LAKE TZ

Mt.
*Mt. Achonee

Lone Eagle
*Pk

Pawnee Pk

Pawnee Pass

Isabelle Glacier

Lake Isabelle

Long Lake

FOUR LAKES TZ

To: Ward and Hwy 72

Fair Glacier

Navajo Pk

PEAK TZ

To: Tabernash

Meadow Cr. Res.

Junco Lake

300 ▲

ARAPAHO TZ

CARIBOU LAKE TZ

Caribou Pass

Arapaho Glacier

To: Nederland and Hwy 72

504

Rainbow Lakes

503

COLUMBINE TZ

Mt. Neva

Arapaho Pass

NEVA TZ

GLACIER TZ

502
4th of July

NOTE: Camping permits are valid only for Travel Zones and dates specified on permit.

DIAMOND LAKE TZ

JASPER LAKE TZ

Devils Thumb Pass

DEVILS THUMB TZ

WOODLAND TZ

501

To: Hessie and Eldora

MIDDLE BOULDER TZ

Rollins Pass

400 ▲

**LEGEND**

Camp in designated site in Caribou Lk, Crater Lk, Diamond Lk, or Jasper TZ

No Recreational Livestock in Four Lakes TZ, Peak TZ, Crater Lake TZ, or in the unshaded portion of the Cascade Creek TZ

Open Fires permitted in Shaded Map Area

NO CAMPING IN FOUR LAKES TRAVEL ZONE MAY 1 - NOV. 30

—·— Continental Divide

——— Travel Zone (TZ) Boundary

TZ      TZ Travel Zone

▲100   Trailhead

①       Trail

Legend

N

0   1   2   3   4  ← Scale
Scale in miles

*Indian Peaks Wilderness Area*

Title: Main Idea

(camping permit required June 1 - September 15)

Source →   United States Forest Service

**EXAMPLE 1.8**

a. Is the purpose of Figure 20.3 to highlight one portion of the paragraph, illustrate what the paragraph says, or add details not covered in the paragraph?

b. What does the map illustrate?

c. Do you think the author wants you to concentrate on remembering the names of the cities? Why or why not?

d. What is the main idea you think the author wants you to remember from the paragraph and graphic?

## How Do I Read a Photograph or Drawing?

Photographs and drawings are also common in expository material. They could be used to show examples of nonverbal communication in a speech communications text, the results of a chemical reaction in a physics text or caste marks of Indian society in a sociology text.

They often lack a title or labels common to other graphics but usually include a caption—a brief description of the contents of the illustration. Like other types of graphics, authors use photographs and drawings to help you visualize the information. Use the caption and words to direct your attention to specific elements.

Look at the photographs in Example 1.9 from Larry McGrath's *Travel Photography Handbook*. Note how the caption points out what to look for in Photo A and Photo B.

**PHOTO A**                    **PHOTO B**

In many cases, selecting a slightly different vantage point and/or using a different lens permits the photographer to exclude distracting elements in a picture. Notice how the distracting wires and light post in Photo A have been eliminated in photo B by moving closer to the chapel and changing from a normal to a wide angle lens.

**EXAMPLE 1.9**

---
**PRACTICE: READING AND INTEGRATING A PHOTOGRAPH
OR ILLUSTRATION AND WORDS**
---

Read the paragraphs and the illustration, integrate the information, and then answer the questions.

6. To see how the mind can shape what we perceive, look at these two pictures:

What do you see? Each would present you with two distinctly different images. When you look at the first one in one way, you see a vase. Look at it differently and you see two faces. The second picture presents either a beautiful young woman facing away from you or an ugly old crone facing you.

How is this possible? The sense data that your eyes take in—the arrangement of lines and shading—remain the same. But you can "shift" the pictures you see. What you "see," then, is the meaning your mind imposes on the data, and your mind can reprocess that data so that they represent something different. (White, *Discovering Philosophy*)

a. What is the purpose of the illustration in this example?

b. What do you think White wants you to remember from the illustration?

---
**REVIEW QUESTIONS**
---

*Review Questions*

1. Why do authors use graphics?

2. List and describe four common types of graphics used with expository writing.

3. How can you identify the source and reliability of the information?

4. Why do you need to integrate information from the words and graphics?

*Think and Connect Questions*

5. Reread the first portion of Chapter 1. What does the "The Plan»Do»Review" flow chart that accompanies the chapter show? What is the purpose of the flowchart? Does it fulfill its purpose? Why or why not?

6. Reread "Sources of Groundwater Pollution," Chapter 1, Exercise 3. What is the purpose of Figure 11-2?

*Application Exercises*

7. Select a text assignment from another class that includes at least one graphic. What is the purpose of the graphic? How do the words help you to understand the graphic? How does the graphic help you to understand the words?

8. From a current newspaper or magazine, select an article that includes at least one graphic. What is the purpose of the graphic? How do the words help you to understand the graphic? How does the graphic help you to understand the words?

---

**USE YOUR STRATEGIES: EXERCISE #1**

# *Five Paragraphs with Graphics*

1. Although America does not have large numbers of people dying from starvation, a condition that characterizes other regions of the world, nutritionists believe that our "diets of affluence" are responsible for many diseases and disabilities, including heart disease, certain types of cancer, hypertension (high blood pressure), cirrhosis of the liver, tooth decay, and chronic obesity. The food choices that Americans make have changed over the past three decades. Some of the changes are outlined in Table 6.1 on page 128. (Donatelle and Davis, *Access to Health*)

   a. What is the topic of Table 6.1?

   b. Is the purpose of Table 6.1 to highlight one portion of the paragraph, summarize the paragraph, or add details not covered in the paragraph?

   c. What quantity do the numbers for red meat, flour, and pasta represent?

   d. Are these trends generally healthy or unhealthy? Which data would you use to support your answer?

**Table 6.1 CHANGES IN ANNUAL FOOD CONSUMPTION OF AMERICANS, 1960–1987**

The following table illustrates changes in annual food consumption per person during the last 3 decades. Unless otherwise indicated, the amounts are presented in pounds. Are these trends generally healthy or unhealthy?

| Food Product | 1960 | 1970 | 1984 | 1987 |
| --- | --- | --- | --- | --- |
| Red meat | 173.7 | 162.8 | 151.9 | 144.0 |
| Fish and shellfish | 10.3 | 11.8 | 13.7 | 15.4 |
| Poultry | 34.0 | 48.2 | 66.5 | 77.8 |
| Eggs (number) | 334. | 309. | 259. | 249. |
| Whole milk | 263.9 | 219.1 | 126.6 | 109.9 |
| Lower-fat milk (1% and 2%) | — | 50.0 | 99.1 | 113.6 |
| Nonfat milk | 10.7 | 11.6 | 11.5 | 14.0 |
| Fats and oils | — | 52.6 | 58.6 | 62.7 |
| Flour (white, whole-wheat) | — | 110.8 | 118.1 | 128.0 |
| Pasta | — | 7.7 | 11.3 | 17.1 |
| Breakfast cereals | — | 10.8 | 14.0 | 15.2 |
| Sugar and corn sweeteners | 111.5 | 121. | 125.1 | 130. |
| Saccharin | — | 5.8 | 10.0 | 5.5 |
| Aspartame | — | — | 5.8 | 13.5 |
| Fruits (fresh) | — | 76.9 | 87.8 | 98.6 |
| Fruits (canned) | — | 14.4 | 8.9 | 8.7 |
| Vegetables (fresh) | — | 64.0 | 78.8 | 78.6 |
| Coffee (gallons) | — | 33.4 | 26.5 | 26.5 |
| Soft drinks (gallons) | — | 20.8 | 27.2 | 30.3 |
| Beer (gallons) | — | 30.6 | 35.0 | 34.4 |
| Wine (gallons) | — | 2.2 | 3.4 | 3.4 |
| Distilled spirits (gallons) | — | 3.0 | 2.6 | 2.3 |

— = data not available

*Source:* U.S. Department of Commerce, Bureau of the Census, *Statistical Abstracts of the United States, 1989.*

2. Several programs have been proposed to provide job opportunities for America's inner-city unskilled. One is to rebuild the blue-collar economies of the central cities by encouraging industry to locate there in urban enterprise zones, where manufacturers receive government subsidies. The federal government has been slow to act, but several states and cities have designated such zones in their poorest communities (see Figure 9-27 on page 129). (Bergman and McKnight, *Introduction to Geography*)

a. Is the purpose of Figure 9-27 to highlight one portion of the paragraph, give an example of a concept, or summarize the paragraph?

b. Which portion of which city is represented on this map?

c. What type of businessperson might be interested in looking at this map? Why?

d. What does urban mean?

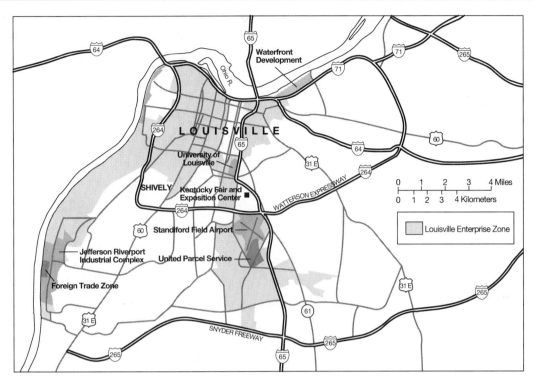

**FIGURE 9–27**

3. From 1965 to 1987, health-care expenses increased 1000 percent: from an average of approximately $176 to $1758 annually for every person in the United States, as shown in Figure 20.2. As of 1989, Americans spent $1.3 billion dollars daily for health care. (Greenberg and Dinti-man, *Exploring Health*)

   a. What is the topic of Figure 20.2?

   b. What does Figure 20.2 show?

   c. What is the source of the data? Do you think this is a reliable source? Why or why not?

   d. In this example, would you use the words or the graphic to deter-mine the percent of increase from 1965 to 1987? Which would you use to determine the dollar amount spent in 1980?

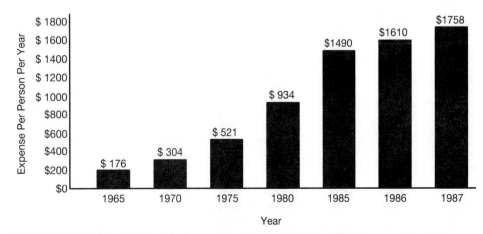

**FIGURE 20.2** Health Care Expenses per Person, 1965 to 1987 (*Source:* Health Insur-ance Association, *1989 Source Book of Health Insurance Data,* Washington, DC: Health Insurance Association of America, 1989).

4. For the purpose of this discussion, we will classify the uses of computers into six general categories: information systems/data processing, personal computing, science and research, process control, education, and artificial intelligence. Figure 1-4 shows how the sum total of existing computer capacity is apportioned to each of these general categories. In the years ahead, look for personal computing, process control, education, and artificial intelligence to grow rapidly and become larger shares of the computer "pie." (Long, *Introduction to Computers and Information Processing*)

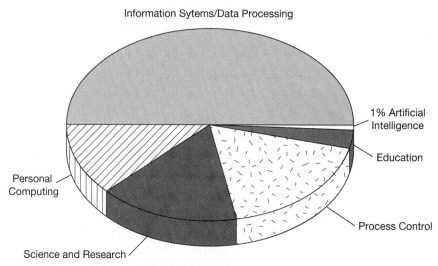

**FIGURE 1–4  The Way We Use Computers** This pie chart is an estimate of how existing computer capacity is distributed among the general categories of computer usage.

   a. What does this pie chart show?

   b. What information is in the pie chart and in the paragraph?

   c. What information is in the pie chart but not in the paragraph?

   d. What information is in the paragraph but not in the pie chart?

5. Management is the process of planning, organizing, leading, and controlling an enterprise's financial, physical, human, and information resources in order to achieve the organization's goals of supplying various products and services. . . . The planning, organizing, leading, and controlling aspects of a manager's job are interrelated, as shown in Figure 5.1. But note that while these activities generally follow one another in a logical sequence, sometimes they are performed simultaneously or in a different sequence altogether. In fact, any given manager is likely to be engaged in all these activities during the course of any given business day. (Griffin and Ebert, *Business*)

   a. What is the topic of Figure 5.1?

   b. Is the purpose of Figure 5.1 to illustrate the concept, or add details not covered in the paragraph?

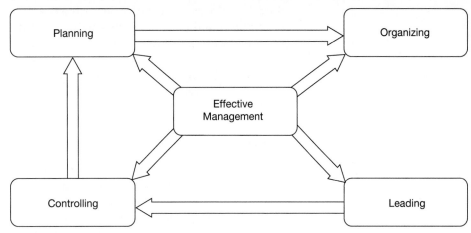

**FIGURE 5.1** The management process

    c. Why do you think Griffin and Ebert chose a flow chart to illustrate the management process?

    d. Assume that you are preparing for a test on the management process. List the information you will need to remember.

---

**USE YOUR STRATEGIES: EXERCISE 2**

# The Health-Illness Continuum

## JERROLD S. GREENBERG AND GEORGE B. DINTIMAN

*Jerrold S. Greenberg teaches at the University of Maryland. George B. Dintiman teaches at Virginia Commonwealth University. This selection is from* Exploring Health.

    It is important to consider health as being separate from illness. You may wonder why, for many people define illness as lack of health, and health as lack of illness. These people might depict health and illness as a straight line and call that line a "health continuum," with ill health at one end and perfect health at the other (see Figure 1.1).

**FIGURE 1.1** The Health Continuum

However, when we consider illness and health as separate entities, the continuum will not show them overlapping. That is, at some point one must stop and the other must begin. Figure 1.2 shows the model for this conceptualization. Illness occupies the right half of the continuum and ends at the midpoint; health begins there and occupies the left half of the continuum.

Perfect
health          Health          Illness          Death

**FIGURE 1.2**  The Health-Illness Continuum

Of course, one may argue that even if someone is ill, that person may have some degree of health. For example, a physically handicapped person who exercises regularly and participates in the Wheelchair Olympics may be healthier than a person who is not ill, but who is not physically fit. For now, though, let's withhold objection until we can explain how we intend to use the health-illness continuum.

## WELLNESS

We'd now like you to look at the health-illness continuum under a microscope. Notice that the line isn't a line at all, but a series of dots. The continuum would then look like Figure 1.3.

Perfect
health          Health          Illness          Death

**FIGURE 1.3**  The Magnified Health-Illness Continuum

If we could get an even more powerful microscope and focus it on just one of the dots on the continuum, you might see something like Figure 1.4. Each dot on the continuum, then, is composed of the five components of health. When we integrate social, mental, emotional, spiritual, and physical health at any level of health or illness, we achieve what we will call wellness. Put another way, you can be well regardless of whether you are ill or healthy. Paraplegics, for example, may not be defined as healthy; but they could have achieved high-level wellness by maximizing and integrating the five components of health so that, within their physical limitations, they are liv-

**FIGURE 1.4**  A Single Health-Illness Continuum Dot

ing a quality life. They may interact well with family and friends (social health); they may succeed at school, on the job, or with a hobby (mental health); they may be able to express their feelings when appropriate (emotional health); they may have a sense of how they fit into the "grand scheme of things" through a set of beliefs (spiritual health); and they may exercise within the boundaries of their capabilities, for example, by finishing a marathon on crutches or in a wheelchair (physical health).

## Questions

1. Define continuum. How do Greenberg and Dintiman use a graphic to represent a continuum?
2. What is the difference between "The Health Continuum" (Figure 1.1) and the "The Health-Illness Continuum" (Figure 1.2)? Did you find the written or the graphic explanation easier to understand? Why?
3. Where is "health" located on the continuum in Figure 1.2? Do you get the same explanation from the written text and the graphic?
4. How is the continuum graphic in Figure 1.3 different from Figure 1.2?
5. What is the relationship of Figure 1.4 to "The Health-Illness Continuum"?
6. What are the five components of health? Where is this information stated?
7. According to Greenberg and Dintiman, you can be well regardless of whether you are ill or healthy. How is this possible?
8. How do Greenberg and Dintiman define wellness?
9. What example do Greenberg and Dintiman use to support and develop their definition of wellness?
10. Name one other topic or subject you could graphically represent on a continuum.

---

### USE YOUR STRATEGIES: EXERCISE 3

# *College Not Worth It?*
# *Think Again*

### THE ASSOCIATED PRESS

*The Associated Press is a national news organization that distributes articles and graphics to news media around the world. This article was written January 28, 1993.*

[1]That college diploma hanging on the wall is worth $1,039 a month in extra pay.

[2]At that rate, it takes the typical four-year graduate just a little less than two years after getting out of school to accumulate enough of the extra pay to cover his or her tuition bill.

[3]On average, people with bachelor's degrees earn $2,116 a month, a Census Bureau study said Wednesday. High-school graduates earn $1,077 a month.

[4]Tuition, books, room and board for four years at a public university averaged $19,880 in 1990, a survey by the College Board found. The cost of education since has risen to more than $23,000 for the four years.

[5]Prestigious private universities cost far more. Is it worth it?

[6]"As my job search threatens—I've gotten four rejections already—it's kind of depressing, especially considering how much education costs today," said Don Modica, 21, a senior who pays more than $18,000 a year to attend Notre Dame.

[7]Despite the cost, Americans increasingly prize a college degree.

[8]In 1990, one American in four had a bachelor's degree or higher, the Census Bureau said. That's up from one in five in 1984.

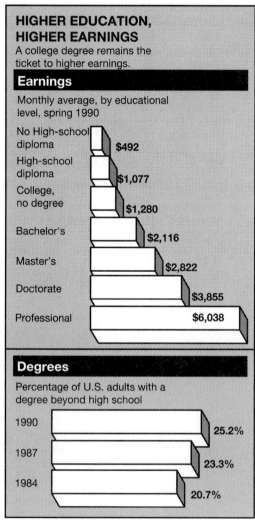

**HIGHER EDUCATION, HIGHER EARNINGS**
A college degree remains the ticket to higher earnings.

**Earnings**

Monthly average, by educational level, spring 1990

| No High-school diploma | $492 |
| High-school diploma | $1,077 |
| College, no degree | $1,280 |
| Bachelor's | $2,116 |
| Master's | $2,822 |
| Doctorate | $3,855 |
| Professional | $6,038 |

**Degrees**

Percentage of U.S. adults with a degree beyond high school

| 1990 | 25.2% |
| 1987 | 23.3% |
| 1984 | 20.7% |

*Source:* Census Bureau

[9]But a diploma doesn't always open the doors to high pay and security.

[10]"It isn't like it used to be," said Susan Miller, president of the Annandale, Va., job-placement firm Susan Miller and Associates Inc. "You have an edge to start, but it's not the guarantee it used to be."

[11]People with degrees in engineering, computer science and other technical fields can get well-paying jobs when they graduate, Miller said. Everyone else is "out there in the job market competing with the high-school grads."

[12]"If someone comes through college and they have no work experience, they're clueless," she said. "We see college grads starting as receptionists."

[13]The universities say the payoff comes several years later, as college graduates are promoted past their less-educated colleagues.

[14]Colleges and universities try to teach their graduates to work smarter, said Pat Riordan, dean of admissions at George Mason University in Fairfax, Va.

[15]"We are teaching them a way to synthesize and communicate at a much higher level than a student that just graduates from high school," Riordan said.

[16]"How is your money better spent? I could have spent the money buying a fancy car and some more vacations . . . but I think, in the long run, spending the money on education is investing in me."

[17]The best-paying bachelor's degree is engineering, worth $2,953 a month, according to the Census figures. Social-sciences graduates trail at $1,841 a month, and a liberal-arts or humanities degree is worth $1,592 a month in earnings.

[18]But the biggest money goes to people with professional degrees, such as law or medicine. On average, those people earn $4,961 a month extra.

## Questions

1. What is the author's thesis?

2. What year was this article written? What year is the "earnings" data from? Why do you think there is a difference?

3. Who is the source of the "earnings" information? Do you think they are a reliable source? Why or why not?

4. Who is the source of the "college expense" information? Do you think they are a reliable source? Why or why not?

5. How did the author calculate the $1,039 figure in paragraph 1?

6. The number/percentage of Americans with a bachelor's degree or higher in 1990 is indicated in both the words and the graphic. How is it listed in words? In the graphic?

7. How did the percentage of U.S. adults with a college degree change between 1984 and 1990? Where did you locate the information?

8. Explain what Riordan means in paragraph 15 by "We are teaching them a way to synthesize and communicate at a much higher level

than a student that just graduates from high school." Do you agree or disagree with the statement? Why?

9. What was the best-paying bachelor's degree in 1990? How much extra a month was it worth?

10. How did the author calculate the $4,961 figure in paragraph 18? Do you find it easier to understand this information in words or in the graphic? Why?

---

**USE YOUR STRATEGIES: EXERCISE 4**

# *The Greying of the Planet*

### JEAN-CLAUDE CHASTELAND

*Jean-Claude Chasteland is a French demographer who was head of the United Nations Population Division in New York until 1990, and is now a consultant with the French National Institute of Demographic Studies in Paris. He has published many articles on the demographic problems of the Third World and on questions of population and development in general. This selection is from* UNESCO Courier.

The world has just experienced three decades of rapid demographic change. In the past thirty years, world population has grown from 2.7 billion to a little over 5 billion. During this period of unprecedented expansion, something occurred, at first unremarked, that, nevertheless, was of great importance for the future—for the first time since the eighteenth century, during the early 1970s, the growth rate of the world population began to decline.

This new trend was an indication that, following the industrialized countries, Third World countries were in their turn entering the phase of demographic transition (see Chart). In other words their fertility was dropping. The speed with which this demographic transition is completed is likely to be the factor which determines not only the future size of the populations concerned but also their age structure. The faster the transition phase is completed the more quickly their populations will age; for, as the French demographer Alfred Sauvy used to say, populations have no other choice than to grow or to grow old.

When all is said and done, the aging of a population, defined here as an increase in the proportion of old people in relation to total population, is striking evidence of the successes achieved in gaining technological mastery over certain aspects of life and death. The sometimes excessive fears expressed about population aging seem, therefore, somewhat paradoxical. Perhaps this rather pessimistic attitude finds its roots in the negative idea that the individual has of his or her own aging—an ineluctable process that ends in death. No one can halt the passage of time and, for the individual, rejuvenation is merely a metaphor. Populations, however, do not stand in the same relationship with time; through the interplay of fertility and mortality rates, they can indeed grow younger or older or maintain a stable age structure. Of course, there are thresholds above which the aging of a population becomes virtually irreversible, but it is possible to achieve a stable state in which the process of aging is, as it were, suspended in time.

**WORLD POPULATION TRENDS BY AGE GROUP BETWEEN 1950 AND 2025 (PERCENT)**

|  | *World Population* | | | | *Industrialized Countries* | | | | *Developing Countries* | | | |
|  | 0–14 | 15–59 | 60 and Over | Total | 0–14 | 15–59 | 60 and Over | Total | 0–14 | 15–59 | 60 and Over | Total |
|---|---|---|---|---|---|---|---|---|---|---|---|---|
| 1950 | 35 | 57 | 8 | 100 | 28 | 61 | 11 | 100 | 38 | 56 | 6 | 100 |
| 1990 | 32 | 59 | 9 | 100 | 21 | 62 | 17 | 100 | 36 | 57 | 7 | 100 |
| 2000 | 31 | 59 | 10 | 100 | 20 | 61 | 19 | 100 | 34 | 58 | 8 | 100 |
| 2025 | 24 | 61 | 15 | 100 | 18 | 57 | 25 | 100 | 26 | 62 | 12 | 100 |

United Nations data, New York, 1988.

## Questions

1. What does the title, "The Greying of the Planet," mean?
2. How much has the world population grown in the past three decades? Is this an unusual amount?
3. What is the "demographic transition" referred to in paragraph 2?
4. How does Chasteland define an "aging population"?
5. To what does Chasteland attribute the aging of the population? Do you agree? Why or why not?
6. What does the chart contain? Which of the entries are actual percentages and which are projected percentages?
7. Describe the membership of the three categories in Figure 1: World population, Industrialized countries, and Developing countries.
8. What is the population expected to look like in the world's industrialized countries in the year 2000?
9. How will that population (described in #8) be alike and/or different than the population in the world's developing countries in the year 2000?
10. What does Chasteland mean by the phrase "an ineluctable process" in paragraph 3?

## CONNECTIONS

A. Do you usually read graphics or skip over them? Do you often read graphics and skip over the words? Are there some types of graphics you find easy to understand? Are there some types of graphics you often have difficulty reading? What makes a graphic difficult for you to understand? What is one thing you will try to do to make reading graphics easier?

B. For the next two days, keep track of the graphics you read in your textbooks, during classes, at work, in newspapers and magazines—everywhere. Then answer these questions. Were you surprised at the number of graphics you had to read—were there more or less than expected? Where did you encounter the largest number of graphics? Describe the graphic that was the hardest for you to read. What did you do to help your understanding? Describe the graphic that was the easiest for you to read. Why do you think it was easy for you?

# 7

## *Organize the Information You Need*

"I've got to get organized!"

How often we hear that phrase. But what do people want to accomplish and how do they go about getting organized?

The dictionary says you organize something by systematically arranging a collection of interdependent parts with relation to the whole. In other words, you introduce an overall order to things. For example, you prioritize a list of tasks you have to get done at work or you arrange the errands you have to run according to your route of travel. You organize, or bring order to things, because it makes your work and life more efficient.

As you develop your plan for this chapter, consider how you organize various tasks and activities in your life. Do you consciously spend part of each day "getting organized" or do you unconsciously order things? Do you have different organization strategies for different kinds of tasks? Does anyone ever say they wish that you were better organized? What do you think they mean?

Highlight definitions for this chapter's key vocabulary:

- annotate
- outline
- information map
- summary and summarize

| Chapter 7 Content Objectives |
| --- |
| • use annotating as a strategy for organizing information |
| • use outlining and mapping as strategies for organizing information |
| • use summarizing as a strategy for organizing information |

## What Is My Basic Strategy for Organizing the Information I Need?

**As You Plan:**

1. Understand the vocabulary.
2. Predict the thesis and/or main idea.
3. Determine how much detail you need to know.

**As You Read:**

4. Actively search for information that helps you clarify and refine your prediction about the thesis and/or main idea.
5. Highlight useful signal words.
6. Determine if the way the author develops the thesis or main idea helps you to understand the details.
7. Use the author's signal words, punctuation, and development as clues to help you identify information and ideas that you need.
8. Integrate graphic and text information.

**As You Review:**

9. Revise and restate the thesis and/or main idea.
10. Restate the supporting details that you need to fulfill your purpose.
11. Organize thesis, main ideas, and supporting details.

## Why Do I Need to Organize Information?

You developed a plan and set your purpose for reading. You read the assignment, found the thesis or main ideas, sorted out the relationships among ideas, and identified the specific information—from all the written text and graphics—that you needed to know. Now you must organize the information so that you can efficiently and effectively review and remember it.

Because you will be reading many different kinds of information for a variety of purposes, you need an assortment of organization strategies. Three common ways to organize the information you need to learn are: annotating the text, creating graphic notes, and summarizing.

# How Can I Effectively Annotate Text?

By annotate I mean write brief, useful information in the margins of your text in your own words. Annotation is an effective strategy whether you need to organize only main ideas or all the information the author gives, down through the minor examples.

For most students, any discussion of marking texts includes how they use their arsenal of highlighting markers. Unfortunately, using highlighters to mark a text is not always a good idea. First, it encourages you to passively mark the author's words rather than restating ideas in your own words. Second, highlighters seem to encourage you to mark too much text without regard to the type or level of information. And finally, page after page of rainbowed lines make it difficult for you to review only the important information.

Annotating, on the other hand, makes you an active participant—you must translate the author's words and ideas into your own. In addition, since you must fit your notes legibly into the text's margins, annotating encourages you to carefully sift and sort ideas. And finally, when it comes time to review, you have already brought order to the information you need.

As with all strategies for organizing information, do not try to annotate, or mark, material the first time you read it. Only after you have read and thought about the material and have a clear understanding of what you need to know, can you begin to annotate.

The better your annotations are, the more organized and effective your review will be. You will have clarified the ideas and concepts that are important to your purpose. Although your annotations will vary depending on your purpose for reading and the content, typically you will:

- restate the thesis and/or main ideas
- mark key words and major details or concepts
- note examples you need to know
- restate information from graphics
- tag confusing ideas you want to clarify
- jot down possible test questions
- cite a useful method of development, e.g., cause/effect, comparison/contrast.

In addition to your marginal summaries, common symbols you might use include: T for thesis; MI for main idea; EX for example; S for summary; DEF for definition; 1, 2, 3, for major points; ? for items to be clarified; and * for important concepts. Underline judiciously. As you practice annotating various texts you will develop additional shorthand, or codes, that make the strategy more effective for you.

I've used some of the common notations on this paragraph from Bergman and McKnight's *Introduction to Geography* "Weather and Climate" section.

*T: Earth different from other planets in many ways*
*MI: major diff.—our atmosphere*

^T The Earth is different from other known planets in a variety of ways. ^MI One of the most notable differences is the presence around our planet of a substantial atmosphere with components and characteristics that are distinctive from those of other planetary atmospheres.

*\* atmosphere makes life possible*
*4 ways:*

\* Our atmosphere makes life possible on this planet. It ①supplies most of the oxygen that animals must have to survive, as well as the carbon dioxide needed by plants. It ②helps maintain a water supply, which is essential to all living things. It serves as an ③insulating blanket to ameliorate temperature extremes and thus provide a livable environment over most of the Earth. It also ④shields the Earth from much of the sun's ultraviolet radiation, which otherwise would be fatal to most life forms.

The annotations reinforce what you established in Chapters 4 and 5: Sentence 1 is the thesis for the section, sentence 2 is the main idea for this paragraph, sentence 3 is a major detail, and sentences 4–7 are minor details.

Consider the annotations on Macionis's paragraph on surveys from *Sociology.*

*MI: survey research: people respond to QS.*

^MI A survey is a research method in which subjects respond to a series of items or questions in a questionnaire or an interview. Perhaps the ①most widely used of all research methods, surveys are particularly ②suited to studying what cannot be observed directly, such as political attitudes, religious beliefs, or the private lives of couples. Like experiments, surveys can be used to ③investigate the relationship among variables. They are also useful for ④descriptive research, in which subject responses help a sociologist to describe a social setting, such as an urban neighborhood or gambling casino.

Annotations are your notes to yourself about what's important to remember.

The excerpt from "Writing About History" by Dr. Robert Weiss in Unger's *These United States,* 5th ed. provides some fundamental principles for reading historical reports and essays. Assume that you are preparing to answer an essay question about how to read history effectively. Annotate it only after you have read and thought about the material and have a clear understanding of what you need to know.

## READING HISTORY

An understanding of the fundamentals of historical writing will make the student of history a more discerning and selective reader. Although no two historical works are identical, most contain the same basic elements and can be approached in a similar manner by the reader. When reading a historical monograph, concentrate on the two basic issues discussed in the preceding section: facts and interpretation.

***Interpretation.*** The first question the reader should ask is: What is the author's argument? What is his theme, his interpretation, his thesis? A theme is not the same as a topic. An author may select the Civil War as a topic, but he then must propose a particular theme or argument regarding some aspect of the war. (The most common, not surprisingly, is why the war occurred.)

Discovering the author's theme is usually easy enough because most writers state their arguments clearly in the preface to their book. Students often make the crucial error of skimming over the preface—if they read it at all—and then moving on to the "meat" of the book. Since the preface indicates the manner in which the author has used his data to develop his arguments, students who ignore it often find themselves overwhelmed with details without understanding what the author is attempting to say. This error should be avoided always.

The more history you read, the more you will appreciate the diversity of opinions and approaches among historians. While each author offers a unique perspective, historical works fall into general categories, or "schools," depending on their thesis and when they were published. The study of the manner in which different historians approach their subjects is referred to as *historiography.* Every historical subject has a historiography, sometimes limited, sometimes extensive. As in the other sciences, new schools of thought supplant existing ones, offering new insights and challenging accepted theories. Below are excerpts from two monographs dealing with the American Revolution. As you read them, note the contrast in the underlying arguments.

1. "Despite its precedent-setting character, however, the American revolt is noteworthy because it made no serious interruption in the smooth flow of American development.

Both in intention and in fact, the American Revolution conserved the past rather than repudiated it. And in preserving the colonial experience, the men of the first quarter century of the Republic's history set the scenery and wrote the script for the drama of American politics for years to come."*

2. "The stream of revolution, once started, could not be confined within narrow banks, but spread abroad upon the land. Many economic desires, many social aspirations were set free by the political struggle, many aspects of colonial society profoundly altered by the forces thus set loose. The relations of social classes to each other, the institution of slavery, the system of landholding, of business, the forms and spirit of the intellectual and religious life, all felt the transforming hand of revolution, all emerged from under it in shapes advanced many degrees nearer to those we know."†

What you have just read is nothing less than two conflicting theories of the fundamental nature of the American Revolution. Professor Jameson portrays the Revolution as a catalyst for major social, economic, and political change, while Professor Degler views it primarily as a war for independence that conserved, rather than transformed, colonial institutions. The existence of such divergent opinions makes it imperative that the reader be aware of the argument of every book and read a variety of books and articles to get different perspectives on a subject.

All historical works contain biases of some sort, but a historical bias is not in itself bad or negative. As long as history books are composed by human beings, they will reflect the perspectives of their authors. This need not diminish the quality of historical writing if historians remain faithful to the facts. Some historians, however, have such strong biases that they distort the evidence to make it fit their preconceived notions. This type of history writing (which is the exception rather than the rule) is of limited value, but when properly treated can contribute to the accumulation of knowledge by providing new insights and challenging the values—and creative abilities—of other historians.

***Evidence.*** Once you are aware of the author's central argument, you can concentrate on his use of evidence—the "facts"—that buttress that argument. There are several types of questions that you should keep in mind as you progress through a book. What types of evidence does the author use? Is his evidence convincing? Which sources does he rely on, and what additional sources might he have consulted? One strategy you might adopt is to imagine that you are writing the monograph. Where would you go for information? What would you look at? Then ask yourself: Did the author consult these sources? Obviously no writer can examine everything. A good historical work, however, offers convincing data extracted from a comprehensive collection of materials.

As you begin to ask these questions, you will develop the skill of critical reading. Used in this sense the word critical does not mean reading to discern what is wrong with the narrative. Rather, it refers to analytic reading, assessing the strengths and weaknesses of the monograph, and determining whether the argument ultimately works. All historical works should be approached with a critical—but open—mind.

One important point to remember is that you need not accept or reject every aspect of a historical monograph. In fact, you most likely will accord a "mixed review" to most of the books you read. You may accept the author's argument but find his evidence inadequate, or you may be impressed by his data but draw different conclusions from it. You may find some chapters tightly argued, but others unconvincing. Even if you like a particular book, almost inevitably you will have some comments, criticisms, or suggestions.

*Carl N. Degler, *Out of Our Past,* rev. ed (New York: Harper & Row, Harper Colophon Books, 1970), p. 73.

†J. Franklin Jameson, *The American Revolution Considered as a Social Movement* (Boston: Beacon Press, 1956), p. 9.

# How Can I Create an Outline or Map to Organize Information I Need?

Another way to organize information is to put your notes on separate paper in a graphic, or picture, format. Graphic organizers are especially effective when you need to order several pieces of information of different levels of importance.

Let's look at two types of graphic organizers—an informal outline and an information map—using Bergman and McKnight's "Weather and Climate" and Macionis's "survey" paragraphs.

## WHAT IS AN INFORMAL OUTLINE?

An informal outline is a type of graphic organizer for information that uses differing amounts of indentation to create a picture of the relationships among ideas. When you create a formal outline, you follow several rules and you designate different levels of information in two primary ways: (1) different letters and numbers at the start of each line and (2) different amounts of indentation, or space, at the start of each line. When you create an informal outline, however, you are not bound by the rules of formal outlining. You are only interested in using different amounts of indentation to draw a picture of the relationships among ideas.

To create an informal outline, identify the thesis, main idea(s), major supporting details, and minor supporting details you need to know. Then, on notebook paper, write down each piece of information indented under the information it supports and explains.

For example, if you were creating an informal outline of a multi-paragraph selection it might look like this:

»*Thesis (of whole selection)*
- Main Idea (of first paragraph)
  —Major Detail
    -Minor Detail
- Main Idea (of second paragraph)
  —Major Detail
  —Major Detail
    -Minor Detail
    -Minor Detail
  —Major Detail

If you were creating an informal outline of a paragraph it might look like this:

»*Main Idea (of whole paragraph)*
- Major Detail
- Major Detail
  —Minor Detail
- Major Detail

If you needed to know all the information, including the examples, in Bergman and McKnight's "Weather and Climate" section, your outline might look like this:

»*The Earth is different from other known planets in a variety of ways.*
- A major difference is the presence around our planet of an atmosphere very different from other planets.
  —Our atmosphere makes life possible on this planet.
    -It supplies most of the oxygen and carbon dioxide.
    -It helps maintain a water supply.
    -It serves as an insulating blanket to lessen temperature extremes.
    -It shields the Earth from much of the sun's ultraviolet radiation.

Now, assume you need to know all the information presented in Macionis's paragraph.

A survey is a research method in which subjects respond to a series of items or questions in a questionnaire or an interview. Perhaps the most widely used of all research methods, surveys are particularly suited to studying what cannot be observed directly, such as political attitudes, religious beliefs, or the private lives of couples. Like experiments, surveys can be used to investigate the relationship among variables. They are also useful for descriptive research, in which subject responses help a sociologist to describe a social setting, such as an urban neighborhood or gambling casino.

Complete this informal outline.

»*A survey is a research method in which subjects respond to a series of items or questions in a questionnaire or an interview.*

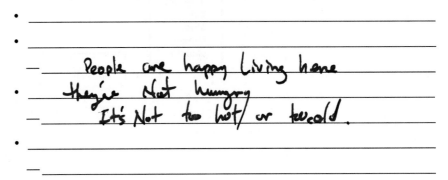

- _____
- _____
  — People are happy Living here
- they're Not hungry
  — It's Not too hot/ or too cold.
- _____
  — _____

## WHAT IS AN INFORMATION MAP?

Another graphic, or visual way you can organize information is to map it. Just like a road map that shows the relationships of small towns, cities, and metropolitan areas with different size dots and different sizes and styles of type, your information map shows the relationships among information with different size boxes or circles and different size type.

Like the process of creating an outline, the first step in creating an information map is to identify the thesis, main idea(s), major supporting details, and minor supporting details you need to know. Then you can begin to construct your map to show the relationships of the different levels of information. Begin by writing the thesis or main idea in a large box or circle. Add the major supporting information as branches off the central idea. Continue adding branches for each level of detail you need to know.

For example, a map of the Macionis paragraph could look like this:

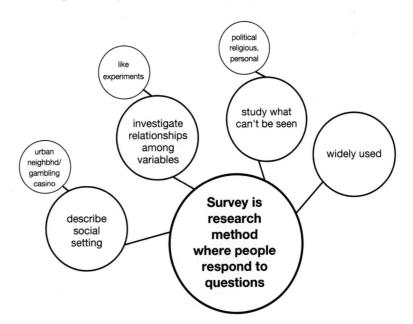

Complete a map of the information from Bergman and McKnight's "Weather and Climate" paragraph. Again, assume you need to know all the information.

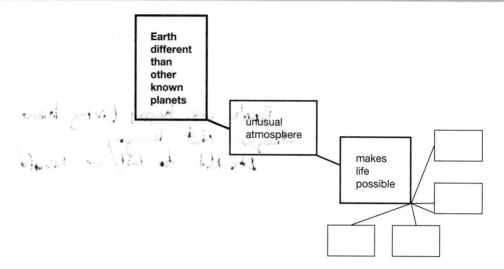

You can also create different types of maps to reinforce the development or organizational clues the author has used.

For example, a map of Long's comparison paragraph from Chapter 5 might look like this.

> A computer system can also be likened to the biological system of the human body. Your brain is the processing component. Your eyes and ears are input components that send signals to the brain. If you see someone approaching, your brain matches the visual image of this person with others in your memory (storage component). If the visual image matches that of a friend, your brain sends signals to your vocal cords and right arm (output components) to greet your friend with a hello and a handshake. Computer system components interact in a similar way. (Long, *Introduction to Computers and Information Processing*)

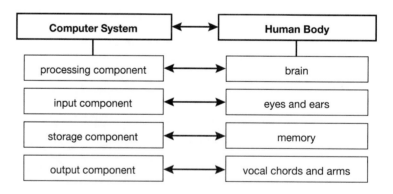

Or, if an author wanted you to understand the steps of a process, like Tocquet does in this paragraph, you might make a simple map like this.

> For the extraction of a square root, the mental calculation broadly follows the normal method: first, you divide the number into groups of two figures, you look for the largest square contained in the first group, you carry the root as the first result and subtract this square from the first group. Next, you mentally add on to the remainder the first figure of the second group and divide the number thus obtained by twice the first figure carried; you retain this quotient as

the second figure of the root required. As can be seen, the process is rather complicated and lengthy. (Tocquet, *The Magic of Numbers*)

To calculate square root mentally:

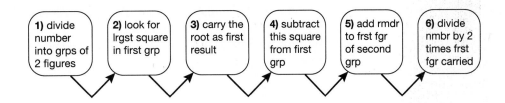

| | | | | | |
|---|---|---|---|---|---|
| **1)** divide number into grps of 2 figures | **2)** look for lrgst square in first grp | **3)** carry the root as first result | **4)** subtract this square from first grp | **5)** add rmdr to frst fgr of second grp | **6)** divide nmbr by 2 times frst fgr carried |

---

### PRACTICE: CREATING AN INFORMAL OUTLINE OR INFORMATION MAP

Create an informal outline or information map using the excerpt from page 141, "Writing About History" by Dr. Robert Weiss from Unger's *These United States,* 5th ed. Again, assume you are preparing to answer an essay question about how to read history effectively. Create your outline or map only after you have read and thought about the material and have a clear understanding of what you need to know.

## How Can I Create a Summary to Organize the Information I Need to Know?

A summary is a paragraph you write that is a condensed version of the original. It begins with a restatement of the thesis or main idea and includes the main ideas or major supporting details in the same order and with the same emphasis as in the original.

When you need to concentrate on just the thesis and main ideas or on the main ideas and major details, writing a summary is a good strategy. A summary does not include examples or minor details that may be included in annotations or graphic organizers.

Your summary must be:

- *in your own words*—do not copy from the original
- *in standard paragraph form*—use good writing techniques, i.e., complete sentences with capital letters, transitions, and punctuation
- *brief*—include only the thesis and main ideas or main idea and major details
- *complete*—do not leave out any main ideas or major details
- *objective*—include only the author's information; do not include your opinion of the information

To write an effective summary:

1. Reread the portion you need to summarize.
2. Write the thesis or main idea in your own words. As with all thesis or main idea statements, do not include your opinion.
3. Identify each main idea and/or major detail in the selection.

4. Write each idea or detail into a sentence.
5. Revise and edit your paragraph.
6. Make certain your summary is an accurate capsule version of the original.

This is a sample summary of Bergman and McKnight's weather and climate paragraph. Because you must use your own words in a summary, yours wouldn't read exactly like this one. The basic content, however, would be the same.

> The Earth differs from other planets in several ways. The biggest difference is the Earth's unique atmosphere. It is the makeup of our atmosphere that makes life possible.

This is a sample summary of Macionis's survey paragraph.

> A survey is a method used in research where people are asked to answer written or oral questions. Surveys are the most common research method and are very useful when studying things that can't be seen. Surveys can also be used to examine the connection among variables and for descriptive research.

## PRACTICE: WRITING A SUMMARY

Write a summary of the excerpt "Writing About History" by Dr. Robert Weiss from Unger's *These United States,* 5th ed. to help you prepare to answer an essay question about how to read history effectively.

## REVIEW QUESTIONS

*Review Questions*

1. Explain how to use annotating as a strategy for organizing information.
2. Explain how to use outlining and mapping as strategies for organizing information.
3. Explain how to use summarizing as a strategy for organizing information.

*Think and Connect Questions*

4. Create an information map for "Theories of Human Behavior," Chapter 4, Exercise 4.
5. Write a summary of "The Health-Illness Continuum," Chapter 6, Exercise 1.

*Application Exercises*

6. Select a one-page reading assignment from another text. Assume your purpose is to prepare for a quiz on the information. Annotate the text selection.

7. Select a five-paragraph reading assignment from another class. Based on your purpose and the content, annotate it, create an informal outline or map, or write a summary of the selection.

---

USE YOUR STRATEGIES: EXERCISE 1

---

# *Feedback*

## KITTIE W. WATSON

*Kittie Watson is an associate professor at Tulane University. The chapter on listening and feedback, from which this is excerpted, was written specifically for the sixth edition of Barker and Barker's text,* Communication.

[1]Communication is a circular process. As a message is transmitted from sender to receiver, a return message, known as feedback, is transmitted in the opposite direction. Feedback is a message that indicates the level of understanding or agreement between two or more people in communication in response to an original message. Feedback represents a listener's verbal or nonverbal commentary on the message being communicated.

[2]Feedback is an ongoing process that usually begins as a reaction to various aspects of the initial message. For example, a definite response is being fed back to the speaker when we shake our heads affirmatively or look quizzically at the speaker. Feedback plays an essential role in helping us to determine whether or not our message has been understood; whether it is being received positively or negatively; and whether our audience is open or defensive, self-controlled or bored. Feedback can warn us that we must alter our communication to achieve the desired effect. If we are not aware of feedback or don't pay any attention to it, there is a strong possibility that our efforts at communicating will be completely ineffective.

[3]To emphasize the importance of the feedback mechanism in communication, you need only imagine yourself growing up for the last 18 years or so, never having received any feedback. No one has praised you as you learned to walk or ride a bike. No one has warned you not to chase a ball into the street or to put your hand on a hot stove. No one has shared your tears or laughter. You probably would not function well at all. How would you appraise your self-concept? What values or morals would you possess? While such an existence is impossible, since a certain amount of feedback comes from you yourself as well as from others in the environment, this example does suggest the various functions and effects of feedback in the communication process.

## TYPES OF FEEDBACK

[4]There are two types of feedback: self-feedback and listener feedback. See Figure 3.5.

[5]Self-feedback applies to the words and actions that are fed

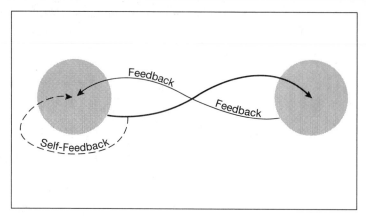

**FIGURE 3–5**  Self-Feedback and Listener Feedback

back into your central nervous system as you perceive your own muscular movements and hear yourself speak. Feeling your tongue twist as you mispronounce a word or, in a library, suddenly realizing that you are speaking too loudly are examples of self-feedback. Another example would be hearing yourself use a word incorrectly, or reversing sounds—for example, asking, "Were you sappy or had?" instead of "happy or sad."

[6]Research indicates that self-feedback plays an important role in the nature and form of our judgmental processes, especially when listener feedback is absent. For example, Hagafors and Brehmer have found that our judgments become more consistent when we are required to justify them to others and when no other form of listener feedback is present. In addition, under these conditions our judgments seem to become more analytical and less intuitive. It seems that self-feedback in the form of justification alters the nature and form of our overall judgmental process.

[7]The other major type of feedback, listener feedback, involves verbal and nonverbal responses. Verbal feedback may take the form of questions or comments. A listener may, for instance, ask a speaker to explain the last point or give praise for making the story so interesting. Nonverbal feedback may be transmitted by applause or laughter, to indicate approval, or by a blank stare, which might indicate disinterest or confusion. Even silence can act as feedback. If a teacher asks a question and no one answers, the silence may indicate understanding, or perhaps dislike of the teacher. If a father asks his son if he has finished his homework and the son doesn't reply, that silence is meaningful.

## FUNCTIONS OF FEEDBACK

[8]Feedback serves various functions in the communication process. The first of these functions is to evaluate what is right or wrong about a particular communication. If you give a speech to the class, your teacher will offer criticism and suggestions for improving your delivery. If someone is watching you hang a painting, he or she will give you feedback as you try various positions, to help you find the right place for it. As will be discussed in Chapter 4, nonverbal

feedback, in the form of nods and hand movements helps to regulate turn taking in conversation.

⁹Secondly, feedback can serve to stimulate change. For example, a popular soft-drink company, after changing its century-old formula, received so much mixed feedback in the form of letters and phone calls that the company not only retained the new formula but brought back the original formula and placed both on grocery-store shelves.

¹⁰A third function of feedback is to reinforce, to give reward or punishment. A father says, "I'm proud of you, son," or "Jim, can't you ever keep quiet!" When used in this way, rewarding feedback encourages certain behaviors, while punishing feedback is intended to discourage certain behaviors. Comedians rely on positive reinforcement from their audience in the form of laughter; their performance may improve if they sense that the audience feedback is positive.

### Questions

Assume that you are going to have a quiz on what feedback is, the types of feedback, and the functions of feedback.

1. Annotate this text selection.
2. Write a sentence that expresses the author's thesis.
3. What is feedback?
4. T/F If we don't pay attention to feedback, we may not communicate effectively.
5. What are the two types of feedback?
6. Identify three major functions of feedback.
7. What is the purpose of Figure 3.5?

---

**USE YOUR STRATEGIES: EXERCISE 2**

---

# *Alcohol in Perspective*

UNIVERSITY OF CALIFORNIA AT BERKELEY WELLNESS LETTER

*The University of California at Berkeley Wellness Letter is published in association with the School of Public Health.*

### DOUBLE MESSAGES

¹Alcohol, a natural product of fermentation, is probably the most widely used of all drugs. It has been a part of human culture since history began and part of American life since Europeans settled on this continent. "The good creature of God," colonial Americans called it—as well as "demon rum." At one time, beer or whiskey

may have been safer to drink than well water, but there have always been many other reasons for drinking: the sociability of drinking, the brief but vivid sense of relaxation alcohol can bring, and the wish to celebrate or participate in religious and family rituals where alcohol is served. In some cultures, abstention is the rule. In others, the occasional use of alcohol is regarded as pleasurable and necessary—but such use is carefully controlled and intoxication frowned upon. Tradition and attitude play a powerful role in the use of this drug.

[2]Some people, unfortunately, drink because of depression and/or addiction to alcohol. Apart from such needs, powerful social and economic forces encourage people to drink. For starters, alcoholic beverages are everywhere—from planes and trains to restaurants and county fairs. Also, drink is cheap. The relative cost of alcohol has declined in the last decades. Since 1967 the cost of soft drinks and milk has quadrupled, and the cost of all consumer goods has tripled, but the cost of alcohol has not even doubled. This is because the excise tax on alcohol is not indexed to inflation. Congress has raised the federal tax on beer and wine only once in 40 years (in 1990). The tax on hard liquor has been increased only twice—small raises in 1985 and 1990. Opinion polls have shown that the public is in favor of raising federal excise taxes on alcohol, but the alcohol industry successfully fights increases. Furthermore, about 20% of all alcohol is sold for business entertainment and is thus tax deductible, making it that much less costly to whoever pays the bar bill.

[3]Finally, the alcohol, advertising, and entertainment industries tirelessly promote the idea that it's normal, desirable, smart, sophisticated, and sexy to drink. In print, on television, and at the movies, we see beautiful, healthy people drinking. Beer ads associate the product with sports events, fast cars, camaraderie, and sex. Hollywood's stars have always imbibed plentifully, on and off camera: "Here's looking at you, kid," echoes down the ages. Among modern American male writers, alcoholism has been a badge of the trade: Hemingway, Fitzgerald, and Faulkner were all alcoholics. In *The Thirsty Muse,* literary historian Tom Dardis cites the deadly effect of alcohol on male American writers, many of whom made a credo of heavy drinking.

[4]Considering all these pro-drinking forces, it is amazing that 35% of us over 18 never drink, and another 35% drink lightly and only occasionally. It's equally amazing that our drinking levels have been declining for the past 10 years. But it's estimated that only 8% of us consume more than half of all the alcohol. Still, out-and-out alcoholism is only one factor in the grief caused by drinking, and alcohol problems are not a simple matter of the drunk versus the rest of us.

## ALCOHOL'S TOLL

[5]It's a rare person in our society whose life goes untouched by alcohol. Alcohol causes, or is associated with, over 100,000 deaths every year, often among the young. In 1990, alcohol-related traffic crashes killed more than 22,000 people—almost the same number as

homicides. Half the pedestrians killed by cars have elevated blood alcohol levels. At some time in their lives, 40% of all Americans will be involved in an alcohol-related traffic crash. Alcoholism creates unhealthy family dynamics, contributing to domestic violence and child abuse. Fetal alcohol syndrome, caused by drinking during pregnancy, is the leading known cause of mental retardation. After tobacco, alcohol is the leading cause of premature death in America. The total cost of alcohol use in America has been estimated at $86 billion annually, a figure so huge as to lose its meaning. But money is a feeble method for measuring the human suffering.

[6]In a free society, banning alcohol is neither desirable nor acceptable. But government, schools, and other institutions could do more than they do to protect the public health, teach the young about the dangers of alcohol, and treat alcoholics. As individuals and as citizens, we could all contribute to reducing the toll alcohol exacts on American life.

### Questions

Assume that you are preparing to answer two essay questions on this selection—one about society's double messages and another about alcohol's toll.

1. Based on your need to prepare to answer two essay questions on this selection, what method would you use to organize the information? Explain.

2. Use the organization strategy of your choice on this selection.

3. What does the subheading "double messages" mean? How does the author develop and support the idea that society sends double messages?

4. Do you agree that society sends double messages about alcohol? Give an example to support your answer.

5. What are four reasons people drink?

6. T/F The relative cost of alcohol to the consumer has dropped over the last several years.

7. T/F The percentage of people who drink has declined over the last ten years.

8. T/F Only 8% of the people consume 50% of all the alcohol.

9. T/F Opinion polls show that Americans do not want an increase in liquor taxes.

10. Who promotes the idea that it's OK to drink? Why do you think these industries promote drinking?

11. What is the main idea of paragraph 5?

12. How does the author develop and support the main idea of paragraph 5?

13. What does the author mean by the phrase "money is a feeble method for measuring the human suffering" in paragraph 5?

14. What is the author's purpose for writing this selection?

# The United States and the Metric System: A Capsule History

NATIONAL INSTITUTE OF STANDARDS AND TECHNOLOGY

[1]The United States is the only industrialized country in the world not officially using the metric system. Because of its many advantages (e.g., easy conversion between units of the same quantity), the metric system has become the internationally accepted system of measurement units.

[2]Most Americans think that our involvement with metric measurement is relatively new. In fact, the United States' increasing use of metric units has been underway for many years, and the pace has accelerated in the past two decades. In the early 1800's the U.S. Coast and Geodetic Survey (the government's surveying and map-making agency) used meter and kilogram standards brought from France. In 1866 Congress authorized the use of the metric system in this country and supplied each state with a set of standard metric weights and measures.

[3]In 1875, the United States reinforced its participation in the development of the internationally recognized metric system by becoming one of the original seventeen signatory nations to the Treaty of the Meter. This agreement established the International Bureau of Weights and Measures (BIPM) in Sèvres, France, to provide standards of measurement for worldwide use.

[4]In 1893, the metric measurement standards, resulting from international cooperation under the auspices of BIPM, were adopted as the fundamental standards for length and mass in the United States. Our "customary" measurements—the foot, pound, quart, etc.,—have been defined in relation to the meter and the kilogram ever since.

[5]In 1960, the General Conference of Weights and Measures, the governing body that has overall responsibility for the metric system, and which is made up of signatory nations to the Treaty of the Meter, approved a modernized version of the metric system. The "modernized" system is called Le Système International d'Unités or the International System of Units, abbreviated SI.

[6]In 1965, Great Britain, as a condition for becoming a member of the European Common Market, began a transition to the metric system in its trade and commerce. The conversion of England and the Commonwealth Nations to SI created a new sense of urgency regarding the use of metric units in the United States. Congress authorized a three-year study of this Nation's systems of measurement, with particular emphasis on the feasibility of adopting SI. Known as the "Metric Study Act of 1968," the study was conducted by the Department of Commerce. As part of the study, an advisory panel of 45 representatives consulted with and took testimony from

hundreds of consumers, business organizations, labor groups, manufacturers, and state and local officials. The panel's report, "A Metric America, A Decision Whose Time Has Come," concluded that measurement in the United States was already based on metric units in many areas and that it was becoming more so every day. The majority of participants in the study believed that conversion to the metric system was in the best interests of the Nation, particularly in view of the increasing importance and influence of technology in American life and our foreign trade.

[7]The study recommended that the United States change to predominant use of the metric system over a ten-year period. Congress passed the Metric Conversion Act in 1975. The stated purpose of the Act was "to coordinate and plan the increasing use of the metric system in the United States." A process of voluntary conversion was initiated with the establishment of the U.S. Metric Board. The Board was charged with "devising and carrying out a broad program of planning, coordination, and public education, consistent with other national policy and interests, with the aim of implementing the policy set forth in this Act." However, the Act did not specify the ten-year conversion period recommended by the study. Further, much of the American public ignored the efforts of the Metric Board. In 1981, the Board reported to Congress that it lacked the necessary clear Congressional mandate to bring about National conversion to predominant use of metric measurements.

[8]Because of the Board's apparent ineffectiveness and efforts to reduce Federal spending, it was disestablished in the fall of 1982.

[9]The Board's demise increased doubts about the United States' commitment to metrication. Public and private sector metric transition slowed at the same time that the very reasons for the United States to adopt the metric system—the increasing competitiveness of other nations and the demands of global marketplaces—made completing United States metric conversion even more important.

[10]Congress, recognizing the criticality of the United States' conformance with international standards for trade, included new strong incentives for United States industrial metrication in the Omnibus Trade and Competitiveness Act of 1988. That legislation designated the metric system as the "preferred system of weights and measures for United States trade and commerce." It also required that all federal agencies use the metric system in their procurement, grants and other business-related activities by a "date certain and to the extent economically feasible, by the end of fiscal year 1992."

[11]The Act's mandates are based on the conclusion that industrial and commercial productivity, effectiveness in mathematics and science education, and competitiveness of American products in world markets, will be enhanced by completing the change to the metric system of units. Failure to do so will increasingly handicap the Nation's industry and economy. The Federal Government's mandate is intended to encourage United States producers to develop their ability to provide goods and services expressed in metric units.

**Questions**

Assume that you are preparing for a quiz on the history of the metric system.

1. Define each of these words or phrases from the selection.
   a. industrialized country (¶1)
   b. pace has accelerated (¶2)
   c. reinforced its participation (¶3)
   d. under the auspices of (¶4)
   e. signatory nations (¶5)
   f. with particular emphasis on the feasibility of adopting SI (¶6)
   g. lacked the necessary clear Congressional mandate to bring about National conversion to predominant use of metric measurements (¶7)
   h. it was disestablished (¶8)
   i. Public and private sector (¶9)
   j. recognizing the criticality of the United States' conformance (¶10)

2. Write a sentence that expresses the author's thesis.

3. Consider the way the author developed the details to support the thesis. What would best organize the major details—a comparison/contrast chart, a cause/effect diagram, or a timeline? Why?

4. Using the method you think is best, map the major details.

5. T/F The United States is the only industrialized country in the world that doesn't officially use the metric system.

6. T/F The United States began using the metric system in the early 1800s.

7. T/F The United States refused to sign the Treaty of the Meter in 1875.

8. T/F Great Britain began its transition to the metric system in 1965.

9. T/F The Omnibus Trade and Competitiveness Act of 1988 is intended to discourage U.S. businesses from using the metric system.

10. Why is the metric system the internationally accepted system of measurement units?

11. When and why was the U.S. Metric Board established?

12. When and why was the U.S. Metric Board disestablished?

13. By what date did the Omnibus Trade and Competitiveness Act of 1988 require federal agencies to use the metric system?

14. The mandates of the Omnibus Trade and Competitiveness Act of 1988 are based on three conclusions. What are they?

15. Do you use the metric system of units at home, at school, or at work? Do you think its use has increased since the end of 1992? Do you think the United States will make a complete transition to the metric system in the next ten years? Why or why not?

---

**USE YOUR STRATEGIES: EXERCISE 4**

---

# *Areas of Computer Applications*

## WILLIAM M. FUORI AND LOUIS V. GIOIA

*William Fuori and Louis Gioia teach in the Mathematics and Computer Processing Department at Nassau Community College in Garden City, New York. This selection is from* Computers and Information Processing, *3rd ed.*

[1]A computer is a very useful tool, but it is certainly not the answer to all of our problems. There are certain types of problems that a computer is equipped to handle more economically and efficiently than other devices or people.

## COMPUTERS DO IT BETTER

[2]Computers are superfast. Because they can perform tasks a lot more quickly than we can, we spend less time waiting. This frees us up to do other things. Computers are capable of performing boring or dangerous tasks (and without complaining). Computers, believe it or not, are extremely dependable. When something goes wrong and service is disrupted or there is an error in your paycheck, statistics reveal that usually it is not the computer's fault; the problem generally lies elsewhere. "Sorry, the computer is down" usually translates into a human error, not a mechanical malfunction.

[3]It should be apparent that computers are ideally suited to handle such primary business functions as payroll, personnel, accounting, and inventory, as each of these functions is justifiable, definable, repetitive, and deals with a large volume of data. New applications of computers are continually being discovered. If we were to attempt to produce a list of all the application areas to which computers are presently being applied, it would be obsolete before it could be completed. Some general areas that extensively employ computers are the following:

[4]**1. General business:** accounts receivable, accounts payable, inventory, personnel accounting, payroll

[5]**2. Banking:** account reconciliation, installment loan accounting, interest calculations, demand deposit accounting, trust services

[6]**3. Education:** attendance and grade-card reports, computer-assisted instruction, research analysis, registration

[7]**4. Government:** income tax return verification, motor vehicle registration, budget analysis, tax billing, property rolls.

[8]Other areas of application include law enforcement, military affairs, sports, transportation, real estate, business forecasting,

medicine, broadcasting, commercial arcade games, publishing, and personal use in the home, to mention but a few. The uses of computers are indeed boundless, and present applications are only a sample of things to come.

**Questions**

Assume that you are preparing to answer an essay question about the effective applications of computers.

1. Write a sentence that expresses the authors' thesis.
2. Based on your need to prepare to answer an essay question about the effective applications of computers, what method would you use to organize the information? Explain.
3. Use the organization strategy of your choice on this selection.
4. Assume that instead of preparing to answer an essay question about the effective uses of computers, you are preparing to take a multiple choice test on the selection. What, if anything, would you do differently? Explain.

## CONNECTIONS

A. When you read a text assignment, what is usually the most difficult part for you, e.g., identifying the main idea, separating levels of details, organizing information? How do you think you can use one or more new strategies to make your reading more successful?

B. Do you consciously spend part of each day "getting organized" or do you unconsciously order things? Do you have different organization strategies for different kinds of tasks? Does anyone ever say they wish you were better organized? What do you think they mean? Do you ever wish other people were more organized? What advice would you give them?

# 8

## *Recognize the Author's Stance*

An important reason to plan before you read is to prime your brain. Planning helps you to start thinking, not just about the tasks you have to do, but about ideas. It gives you the chance to make connections between what you already know and what you are going to learn.

As you prepare to read this chapter, think about your stance, or position, on an issue—for example, "getting older." Consider what kind of words and actions you use when you want to let others know how you feel about your upcoming birthday. How do you communicate that you're delighted about finally getting older or, on the other hand, that you're feeling ancient and need some quiet understanding?

Could you write an essay that equally presents the positive and negative aspects of getting older even if you have strong feelings about the issue? What precautions would you take if you wanted to make sure you were presenting both sides of the issue? Do you think it would be wrong if you wrote only your feelings? Do you think it would be important for someone reading your essay to know if you had personal feelings about aging that influenced what you wrote?

Highlight definitions of this chapter's key vocabulary:

- stance
- reliable
- bias
- point of view
- fact

- opinion
- tone
- irony and ironic
- satire
- sarcasm

**Chapter 8 Content Objectives**

- identify and understand the components of an author's stance
- determine if an author is reliable
- identify and understand an author's point of view
- distinguish between fact and opinion
- define tone and identify strategies for recognizing tone

## What Is My Basic Strategy for Recognizing the Author's Stance?

**As You Plan:**

1. Understand the vocabulary.
2. Predict the thesis and/or main idea.
3. Determine how much detail you need to know.
4. Review the sources of the author's information.
5. Try to determine if the author is reliable as well as knowledgeable.

**As You Read:**

6. Actively search for information that helps to clarify and refine your prediction about the thesis and/or main idea.
7. Highlight words with connotative meanings.
8. Identify the author's point of view.
9. Determine which information is fact and which is opinion.
10. Determine the author's tone.

**As You Review:**

11. Revise and restate the thesis and/or main idea.
12. Confirm the author's reliability and the source of the information.
13. Compare the author's point of view with your own.
14. Review the facts and the opinions given to support the thesis/main idea.
15. Based on your purpose, and considering the author's stance, organize the thesis, main ideas, and supporting details.

## What Is the Author's Stance?

You discovered early that all writing is purposeful; an author wants to communicate information and ideas to you for a reason. In addition, you found that it is important to look at the author's knowledge of the subject and sources of information. Now, you must go beyond the author's expertise and basic reason for writing. You need to determine the author's stance, or position, on the subject—in short, where the author is "coming from."

Much of the time an author does not directly state his or her stance. As you have done when you have made other inferences, you must carefully combine what the author says directly with the author's clues and your own knowledge to infer the author's stance. Uncovering the author's motivation and point of view gives you additional perspective on the author's message.

## Is the Author Reliable?

It is difficult to find out an author's motivation for writing, so it is often hard to know whether he or she is reliable. By reliable, I mean can you trust the author to give you a fair analysis of the topic without undue influence from others.

For example, a professional athlete and a sports medicine doctor could both write knowledgeably on the topic of athletic footwear—from different perspectives, but with knowledge about the topic. It would be difficult, however, to know whether their writing would be reliable—giving a fair analysis of the footwear without undue influence from a sponsor or manufacturer.

To investigate an author's reliability, read other pieces the author has written, read what others have to say about him or her, and ask teachers and librarians for information.

## What Is Point of View?

Another element of the author's stance is point of view—his or her position or opinion. Two broad categories of writing are: objective, meaning without the author's point of view, or neutral and impartial; and biased, reflecting the author's point of view about the topic.

Typically, you expect expository pieces such as encyclopedia entries and scientific reports to be objective, and persuasive works like political brochures and editorials to be biased. What you, as a careful, critical reader must watch for is a biased point of view, even when the primary purpose is exposition.

Writers of academic material strive to write objectively—without displaying their point of view. But all writers are human so even texts and journal articles can reflect the author's point of view.

Writing that reflects the author's point of view is not necessarily bad. Although the connotations of the word "objective" make it seem positive and those of the word "biased" make it seem negative, do not think that only objective writing is good writing or biased writing is bad writing. Writing is not good or bad as long as you identify the author's point of view and factor that into what you will do with the information.

### HOW CAN I IDENTIFY POINT OF VIEW?

To identify point of view in writing, you must use all the available clues, including background information about the author, the title of the selection, and the sources of quotations, references, and illustrations. In addition, watch for words and phrases that have special connotations and emotional effects and a preponderance, or majority, of one-sided information.

The following is the first three paragraphs from "Computers Can't Teach Awareness" by political and environmental columnist Liz Caile. She wrote this column for *The Mountain-Ear,* a small Colorado mountain town weekly newspaper. Read to discover her point of view about computers and humans.

In a recent discussion of careers, young people were told to master computer skills and math if they wanted to "work for the environment." That stuck in my mind the way the limited concept of outdoor education sometimes sticks. It's OK as far as it goes, but are we going to solve global warming or ozone holes with computers, or just diagnose them that way? Are we going to reverse population growth through mathematical models, or just extrapolate the possibilities?

The key to solutions is awareness of what constitutes a healthy environment. You can't get that awareness, staring into a glass tube lit by electricity generated someplace out of sight, out of mind (in our neighborhood by burning coal). You can't feel the complex relationships of air, water, plants and animals. No matter how sophisticated our technology gets, it will never be as intricate as the real thing. Would you like to make love to your computer? They're making great strides in "virtual reality," but . . .

Holly Near has a line in one of her songs, a song both political and environmental, "love disarms." Being disarmed is part of being aware. Disarmed, we become observers. We enlarge our receptiveness to the planet's needs to balance out our active manipulations of it. Awareness requires that we love wild ecosystems as much as ourselves—that we give them life and soul. That kind of awareness can't be taught by a computer.

Based on the questions Caile asks and the words and phrases she uses, we can infer Caile's point of view is that it's up to people, not computers, to help the environment. She appears to view the computer's role as very limited. Do you think Caile is reliable? Why or why not?

Professors Fuori and Gioia in their text *Computers and Information Processing* 3rd ed, conclude their final chapter, "Computers Down the Road," with the following paragraphs. Read to find their point of view about computers and humans.

Whereas some computer experts believe that computers hold the key to great progress for the human race, others feel that computers will eventually lead to depersonalization, unemployment, an invasion of our privacy, and the nuclear destruction of our planet. While some are moving with the flow and striving to acquire computer knowledge and skills, others are laying back and hoping computer technology will not disrupt their lives too much.

As with any powerful scientific advancement, the computer can be a curse or a blessing. Historically, human beings have never reached a new level of technological advancement and deemed it too dangerous to use. Despite its destructive capabilities, there is little chance that we will ever ban the use of nuclear energy; similarly, it looks as though computers are here to stay. But is it the computer we should fear? Or is it the nature of those who would harness its power for good or evil? As always, it is not the *tool* but the *tool user* that must be monitored.

One of the goals of artificial intelligence research is to help us determine how we think, why we interpret as we do, and ultimately, who we are. We humans have been perplexed by our existence since earliest history. By providing us with a clearer understanding of the human mental process, perhaps AI research may eventually lead us to a better understanding of self. As was once said many years ago, "The answer lies within."

Fuori and Gioia present two sides of the controversial technology issue: computers provide the key to success for humanity, versus computers provide the key to destruction of humanity. But because of the questions they ask in paragraph 2 and the words and phrases they use—it's not the tool (computer) but the tool user (human) that needs watching, and that possibly computer research will provide insight to a better humanity—we can infer their point of view is that computers do have a vital role. Do you think Fuori and Gioia are reliable? Why or why not?

## PRACTICE IDENTIFYING POINT OF VIEW

1. Cigarette smoking accelerates artery clogging and greatly increases the risk of death from coronary artery disease, heart attack, and stroke in the adult years. The incidence of cancer, chronic bronchitis, and emphysema also increases. (Greenberg and Dintiman, *Exploring Health*)

   a. What is Greenberg and Dintiman's point of view on smoking?

   b. What point of view might a representative of the tobacco industry have?

   c. You have to write a research paper on the effects of smoking. Why would it be necessary to read more than one source for your research? List three types of sources you would consult.

2. As long as Americans spend more time watching [TV] than reading, educators must address the need for critical viewing as well as critical reading. If readers are trained to read interpretively, so too must viewers be taught to look critically at TV. And if we succeed with this teaching, we'll have changed the present pattern in which 70 percent of what Americans hear in a political campaign consists of thirty- and sixty-second commercials consisting of half-truths and innuendo. . . .

   As E. B. White noted a half century ago, television is "the test of the modern world." Used correctly, it can inform, entertain and inspire. Used incorrectly, television will control families and communities, limiting our language, dreams, and achievements. It is our "test" to pass or fail. (Trelease, "Television")

   a. What is Trelease's point of view on watching television? Do you think Trelease is reliable? Why or why not?

   b. Who might have a different point of view about watching television?

   c. What is your point of view about watching television?

3. New scientific advances promise to multiply future food yields. Biotechnology offers genetically altered crops that can be custom designed to fit the environment, produce bountiful harvests, and resist plant diseases. One bacterial gene eliminates the need for chemicals to kill worms by producing a natural protein that disintegrates the worms' digestive system. Genetically engineered viruses can be used as pesticides. In 1988 scientists mapped the genome of rice—the set of 12 chromosomes that carries all the genetic characteristics of rice. This development could enable geneticists to produce improved strains of rice. Biotechnology can replace chemical pesticides and fertilizers, whose biological or even genetic impact on our own bodies is not fully understood. (Bergman and McKnight, *Introduction to Geography*)

a. What is Bergman and McKnight's point of view about the impact of biotechnology?

b. What point of view might a person who prefers health foods or natural foods have?

c. What point of view might a representative of a pesticide company have?

## Which Information Is Fact and Which Is Opinion?

An author can use facts, opinions, or a combination of facts and opinions to support his or her point of view. A fact is objective information that can be proved to be true. A fact can be verified—no matter where you look or whom you ask, the information is the same. Examples of facts include:

In the mid-1800s the work of Louis Pasteur and others revealed that epidemic diseases were caused by microorganisms.

A lobbyist is a person hired by an individual, interest group, company, or industry to represent its interests with government officials.

An opinion is subjective information that cannot be proved true or false. An opinion cannot be verified; the information can change depending on where you look or whom you ask. An opinion is not true or false, right or wrong, or good or bad. But depending on the amount and type of evidence the author considered before forming the opinion, his or her opinion can be valid or invalid. Sometimes an author will evaluate a significant amount of information and offer an opinion that helps your understanding of the topic. Just remember it is an opinion. Examples of opinions include:

Louis Pasteur made the most significant contributions to the world of medicine of any scientist in history.

Lobbyists are the primary cause of problems in the government today.

As a reader, you can have confidence in facts and valid opinions. You need to be skeptical of invalid opinions.

---

## PRACTICE DISTINGUISHING BETWEEN FACT AND OPINION

Indicate whether a sentence is fact, opinion, or contains both fact and opinion.

1. [1]In managing the planning process, more and more firms have adopted a management by objectives (MBO) approach. [2]MBO is a system of collaborative goal setting that extends from the top of the organization to the bottom. [3]Under this system, managers meet with each of their subordinates individually to discuss goals. [4]This meeting usually occurs annually and focuses on the coming year. [5]The manager and the subordinate agree on a set of goals for the subordinate. [6]The goals are stated in quantitative terms (for example, "I will decrease turnover in my division by 3 percent") and written down. [7]A year later, the subordinate's performance is evaluated in terms of the extent to which the goals were met. [8]MBO has been shown to be quite effective when applied at all levels of the company. [9]Tenneco, Black & Decker, General Motors, General Foods, and Alcoa have all reported success using MBO. [10]However, MBO involves quite a bit of paperwork and is sometimes used too rigidly. (Griffin and Ebert, *Business,* 2nd ed.)

2. [1]A major federal program aimed at identifying and cleaning up existing waste sites was initiated by the Comprehensive Environmental Response, Compensation, and Liability Act of 1980, popularly known as Superfund. [2]Through a tax on chemical raw materials, this legislation provided a fund of 1.6 billion over the period 1980–1985 to identify and clean up sites that posed a threat to groundwater. [3]However, the Environmental Protection Agency's (EPA's) record in administering this program over the first five years was disgraceful. (Nebel, *Environmental Science,* 3rd ed.)

# What Is Tone?

As noted in Chapter 3, words by themselves don't have much meaning. The words "I don't care" can be a simple phrase meaning "I just don't have a preference," or a complex of emotions translated from "you've made me so angry it doesn't matter." If you misunderstand the meaning, you can be in big trouble. But how do you know which meaning to select?

You know the intended meaning when you put the words into a context. Part of that context is the tone—the emotional feeling or attitude we create with our words. Tone is one indication of an author's point of view. When you're talking with someone you identify tone by listening to the pitch and volume of his or her voice, and watching gestures and facial expressions. Using these clues, you can determine if someone is being serious or humorous, straightforward, or ironic. And knowing that helps you understand their meaning.

## WHAT KINDS OF TONE DO AUTHORS USE?

Like a speaker, a writer can create any emotion. In some of your reading assignments you may need to narrowly define the author's tone, e.g., decide whether the tone is funny, witty, whimsical, or comical. However, most of the time you can place the tone of the writing into one of eight general groupings.

### GENERAL TYPES OF TONE

|  | General Description of Tone | Similar Types of Tone |
| --- | --- | --- |
| **straightforward** | objective; without bias | *honest, objective, fair* |
| **ironic** | means opposite of what it says | *contradictory, paradoxical* |
| **serious** | very thoughtful and sincere | *solemn, dignified* |
| **humorous** | intended to be enjoyable | *funny, joking, amusing, comical* |
| **emotional** | subjective; with strong feeling | *passionate, sympathetic, fervent* |
| **positive** | confident and up-beat attitude | *optimistic, enthusiastic, hopeful* |
| **negative** | skeptical and gloomy attitude | *cynical, angry, grim, pessimistic* |
| **sarcastic** | intended to be hurtful | *insulting, cutting, scornful, cruel* |

## HOW DO WORDS AND DETAILS CHANGE TONE?

Although you don't have a speaker's verbal or visual clues available when you are reading, you can understand the author's tone by paying attention to the words and details the author chooses to use or chooses to leave out. Using these clues, along with what the author says directly and your own knowledge, will help you to correctly infer the author's tone.

Read to determine the author's tone for each of these paragraphs. How does the author want you to feel about the person being described? What elements contribute to the differences?

*Description A*: He had apparently not shaved for several days and his face and hands were covered with dirt. His shoes were torn and his coat, which was several sizes too small for him, was spotted with dried mud.

*Description B*: Although his face was bearded and neglected, his eyes were clear and he looked straight ahead as he walked rapidly down the road. He looked very tall; perhaps the fact that his coat was too small for him emphasized that impression. He was carrying two books snugly under his left arm and a small terrier puppy ran at his heels.

Both paragraphs could be describing the same man but the words and details the author has chosen present two very different impressions of the man. Notice how the negatives in Description A (unshaven, coat too small) have been reworded and turned into assets in Description B. Also, leaving out details (like torn shoes) and adding details like the books and the puppy in Description B contributes to the different tone.

## WHAT IS AN IRONIC TONE?

Recognizing tone is especially important when an author doesn't intend for the reader to take his or her words literally. If you don't realize that the author is being ironic—saying the opposite of what he or she means—you will misinterpret the message.

For example, consider this portion of a scientist's presentation to his colleagues. If they take his words literally and follow his principles of good writing, will they be good writers? What clues does he provide to let you know that he is deliberately saying the opposite of his real message?

# *The Principles of Good Writing*

Write hurriedly, preferably when tired. Have no plans; write down items as they occur to you. The article will thus be spontaneous and poor. Hand in your manuscript the moment it is finished. Rereading a few days later might lead to revision—which seldom, if ever, makes the writing worse. If you submit your manuscript to colleagues (a bad practice), pay no attention to their criticisms or comments. Later resist any editorial suggestions. Be strong and infallible; don't let anyone break down your personality. The critic may be trying to help you or he may have an ulterior motive, but the chance of his causing improvement in your writing is so great that you must be on guard.

The title tells us that his purpose is to give information on techniques for good writing. But, when his first details, e.g., writing hurriedly, when tired, and without plans, seem to contradict what you know about good writing practices, you begin to question his real meaning. Then, in his third sentence where he actually says his advice will lead to a poor article—the opposite of his stated purpose—you know that he's being ironic. Rather than just list the practices of good writing, he used a bit of ironic humor to make his point.

## WHAT KIND OF TONE ARE SATIRE AND SARCASM?

Satire and the more caustic sarcasm often use ironic statements to poke fun at people and deride foolish or dishonest human behaviors. Satire and sarcasm make use of ridicule, mockery, exaggeration, and understatement. This type of biting humor is used by cartoonists like Doonsberry's Gary Trudeau and comedians on shows like *Saturday Night Live*. When you're reading a cartoon or watching one of these comedy shows and you understand the words but don't understand that they are making fun of the politician or the movie star, you miss the point and the humor. You also miss the point when you don't understand that an author is using satire or sarcasm. Analyze the words and details an author uses as clues to tone.

Veteran Chicago columnist Mike Royko is known for his acerbic style. He begins his jab at trendy public television viewing habits this way in a 1985 column. Look for words and details Royko uses as clues to his sarcasm.

# *Work the Bugs Out,*
# *Channel 11*

A friend of mine asked if I had seen some wonderful television show recently presented on the public channel.

When I told him that I hardly ever watch that channel, he looked amazed.

"You don't watch public TV?" he said, "But that's the only station that shows anything of *quality.*"

That's what everybody always says. If you want to see thoughtful drama or fine music shows with deep social significance, you are supposed to watch public TV.

Well, maybe they have such shows, but they're never on there when I turn my set on.

No matter when I turn my set on, all I ever see is one of four shows:

1. Insects making love. Or maybe they are murdering each other. With insects it's hard to tell the difference. But after a day's work, my idea of fun isn't watching a couple of bugs with six furry legs and one eye trying to give each other hickies.

2. A lion walking along with a dead antelope in its jaws. I don't know how many times I've seen that same mangy lion dragging that poor antelope into a bush. The tourist bureau in Africa must bring him out every time a TV crew shows up. But the question is, why do they keep showing it? Does somebody at the channel think that we must be taught that lions don't eat pizza?

3. Some spiffily dressed, elderly Englishman sitting in a tall-backed chair in a room that is paneled in dark wood. He is speaking to a younger Englishman who wears a WWI uniform and stands before a crackling fire. The older bloke says things like: "Well Ralph, see you're back from the front. Jolly good you weren't killed. Sorry to hear about your brother. Bloody bad luck, that. Shell took his head clean off. Oh, well, we must go on. Will you be joining us for dinner?" And the younger man says: "Thank you, Father."

4. The station announcer, talking about what great shows they have on Channel 11. The last time I tuned in, he talked about it for so long that I dozed off. When I awoke, he was talking about how great the show had been. Before I could get to the dial, two insects started making love again.

That's it. That's all I ever see on public TV.

Wait, I forgot. There are a couple of others.

Some skinny, bearded, squeaky-voiced, wimpy guy from Seattle does a cooking show. . . .

If you read only the words written by Royko, you miss the message; you must infer—read between the lines—to determine what he means by what he says. For any form of wit or humor like irony, satire, or sarcasm to be effective, the reader must clearly understand the author's intended message, not just the words he or she uses.

## PRACTICE IDENTIFYING TONE

1. **Reaching the Point of No Return.** There are those who believe that a rapidly advancing computer technology exhibits little regard for the future of the human race. They contend that computers are overused, misused, and generally detrimental to society. This group argues that the computer is dehumanizing and is slowly forcing society into a pattern of mass conformity. To be sure, the computer revolution is presenting society with complex problems, but they can be overcome. (Long, *Introduction to Computers and Information Processing*)

   a. What is Dr. Long's point of view about computers?

   b. Would you describe Dr. Long's tone as optimistic or cynical? Why?

2. Donald Trump had not granted an interview or smirked into a camera in nearly a month. It was his longest media dry spell since 1986—when he started taking reporters on grand tours aboard his black Puma helicopter, laying claim to the Manhattan-to-Atlantic City landscape with a lordly wave of his hand. At forty-four, despite almost daily, banner-headlined catastrophes since the beginning of 1990, he was still willing to play posterboy, and a birthday was a great photo opportunity. So, after weeks of hiding from a suddenly carnivorous press, he decided to surface at a birthday blast organized by his casino dependents. With his golden hair backing up beneath his starched collar, a wounded half smile on his silent lips, and perfectly protected by his ever-present blue pinstriped suit, the icon of the eighties—slowed in the first six months of the new decade to an uncertain pace—worked his way out onto a Boardwalk blanketed by a mid-June haze. (Barrett, *Trump: The Deals and the Downfall*)

   a. What is Barrett's point of view about Trump?

   b. How would you describe Barrett's tone? Why?

3. One of the strongest barriers to good thinking, then, is fear. Fear may show itself as anger, envy, selfishness, or hatred, but these are just expressions of our fear. And don't underrate the power of such emotions. History has shown what devastation fear and hatred among nations can wreak. Our personal fears can be just as damaging to our inner world, blinding our critical faculties with their dark energies. When we argue, then, we must be aware of what we feel as well as what we think. A good critical thinker may have to scrutinize not only the intellectual character of an argument, but its emotional temperature as well. (White, *Discovering Philosophy*)

   a. What is White's point of view about the impact of fear?

   b. How would you describe White's tone? Why?

## REVIEW QUESTIONS

*Review Questions*

1. What is the author's stance?

2. What does the word reliable mean? Why is it difficult to determine if an author is reliable?

3. What is point of view? How can you recognize an author's point of view?

4. What is a fact? What is an opinion?

5. What is tone?

6. What are strategies for recognizing tone?

*Think and Connect Questions*

7. Reread "Alcohol in Perspective," Chapter 7, Exercise 2.

   a. Do you consider the author to be knowledgeable and reliable? Why or why not?

   b. What is the author's point of view and tone?

   c. Does the author use mostly facts or opinions? Give examples to support your answer.

   d. Does this analysis change your view of the author's message? Why or why not?

8. Make a list of:

   • things you have bought recently (like shoes, jeans, cereal, a car)

   • things you have done recently (such as gone to a movie, drunk a soft drink, voted)

   • views you have adopted (such as for or against abortion, for or against nuclear energy, for or against affirmative action)

   Can you identify what you saw or read that influenced what you buy, do, or believe? Did you realize you were being influenced? What types of things will you watch for in the future?

*Application Exercises*

9. Using the topic "getting older," write a humorous paragraph and then a serious paragraph. Notice how you can make the change easily by the type of words, details, and punctuation that you use.

10. Using the primary reading materials (texts, journals, etc.) in each of your classes, determine the authors' general tone and point of view. Also, investigate their background and evaluate their expertise and reliability.

---

**USE YOUR STRATEGIES: EXERCISE 1**

---

# Execution Has Benefits— Doesn't It?

### E. J. MONTINI

*E. J. Montini's column appears daily in* The Arizona Republic. *He writes on social and political issues and their effect on people. This selection is from* The Arizona Republic.

[1]Now that Don Harding is dead, now that we've killed him, it's time to reap the rewards, to count up the ways we're benefiting from his death. There must be plenty.

[2]Two days ago, the convicted murderer was alive and in prison. Today, he's dead. He was killed at our expense. In our name. By us. Which means we must have thought it was important to kill him. We must have believed there were benefits in it for us.

[3]Like, for instance, safety.

[4]Maybe we're safer today than we were Sunday, when Harding was still alive.

[5]No, that's not it.

[6]Harding was in a maximum-security prison cell Sunday, as he had been every day for the past 10 years. We were as safe from him then, while he was alive, as we are from him now.

[7]It must be something else. There must be some other benefit to having strapped Harding into a chair in a tiny room and filled the space with poison gas. It took him about 10 minutes to die.

## $16,000 TO KEEP HIM ALIVE

[8]How about money?

[9]Some people say that killing Harding saved us a lot of money. It was costing us $16,000 a year to keep him alive, and we no longer have to spend the cash. That's the benefit, right?

[10]Wrong.

[11]Our efforts to kill Harding (and anyone else on death row) probably cost us more than it would have cost to keep him in prison for life. In fact, several states have abolished the death penalty partly because it costs so much.

[12]It must be something else.

[13]There must be some other extremely beneficial reason for standing by calmly as the tiny capillaries in Harding's lungs were exploded by the cyanide gas, filling his chest with blood. Drowning him from the inside.

[14]Maybe we figured that, if we execute Harding, others will think twice before killing. That would be nice.

[15]Too bad it's not true. Not even those who foam at the mouth at the thought of executing people, like high-profile proponent Arizona Attorney General Grant Woods, believe the death penalty is a deterrent. Studies in states that execute people—as we now do—show that it's not, that murder rates don't go down.

[16]It must be something else.

## WE DON'T KILL ALL MURDERERS

[17]I know. Everyone says there's a benefit to the families of the victims. We kill people like Harding for them. So the families can get revenge.

[18]What about other cases, though?

[19]There are hundreds of inmates in Arizona prisons who have killed people. Yet there are only 99 on death row. We don't kill all murderers, even though the families of all victims suffer the same loss.

[20]We're willing to kill 100 but not 1,000. Killing 1,000 would be considered too barbaric, wouldn't it? A little death goes a long way.

[21]Still, the fact that we don't kill all murderers proves we're really not interested in satisfying the revenge of all victims' families.

[22]If there's a benefit to having killed Harding, it must be something else.

[23]Like the fact that it freed up a prison cell. That's something. We might say there's now room for one more criminal in Arizona prisons.

[24]Except, unfortunately, there isn't. The prisons already contain about 1,000 more inmates than they're designed to handle. Killing one or two people won't help. We'd have to kill a thousand or so, and, like I said, we don't have the stomach for that.

[25]So, it must be something else.

[26]Maybe the benefit we got from killing Harding is less tangible. Maybe we killed him only to prove, as Attorney General Woods likes to say, that "justice is being served."

[27]In other words, to send a message. To teach a lesson.

[28]That must be it. The execution was a lesson. Our children, I figure, will learn something by it. They'll find out we're willing to strap a man down, poison him, then stand around and watch him slowly and painfully die.

[29]That's the benefit.

[30]The boys and girls we sent to bed Sunday night, before the killing, eventually will learn something very important from what we did. They'll learn what type of people their parents really are.

## Questions

1. What is Montini's purpose?
2. What is his thesis?
3. What is Montini's point of view on the death penalty?
4. What is his tone?

5. How does his tone relate to his point of view and/or bias?

6. Do you think he has the knowledge to write this article? Why or why not?

7. Do you think he is reliable? Why or why not?

8. Do you think anything could cause him to change his point of view?

9. Define these words or phrases as used by Montini:

  a. reap (¶1)

  b. abolished (¶11)

  c. extremely beneficial (¶13)

  d. high-profile proponent (¶15)

  e. deterrent (¶15)

  f. too barbaric (¶20)

  g. less tangible (¶26)

10. What event happened to make Montini write this column?

11. How and where was Harding killed?

12. Montini lists and discounts five "benefits" of Harding's execution. List them.

13. What is the "benefit" that Montini decides "must be it"? Does he really think it is a benefit?

14. Montini says that children will "learn what type of people their parents really are." What does he mean?

15. Do you agree or disagree with Montini? Why or why not?

16. If you wanted to get more information on the death penalty, list three places you would be likely to find more information.

---

**USE YOUR STRATEGIES: EXERCISE 2**

# *U.S. Kids Need More School Time*

### ELLEN GOODMAN

*Ellen Goodman is a nationally syndicated columnist known for her writings on American social and political issues. This column was written in the summer of 1990. This selection is from the* Boston Globe.

¹The kids are hanging out. I pass small bands of once-and-future students on my way to work these mornings. They have become a familiar part of the summer landscape.

²These kids are not old enough for jobs. Nor are they rich enough for camp. They are school children without school. The calendar called the school year ran out on them a few weeks ago. Once supervised by teachers and principals, they now appear to be in "self care." Like others who fall through the cracks of their parents'

makeshift plans—a week with relatives, a day at the playground—they hang out.

[3]Passing them is like passing through a time zone. For much of our history, after all, Americans framed the school year around the needs of work and family. In 19th-century cities, schools were open seven or eight hours a day, 11 months a year. In rural America, the year was arranged around the growing season. Now, only 3 percent of families follow the agricultural model, but nearly all schools are scheduled as if our children went home early to milk the cows and took months off to work the crops. Now, three-quarters of the mothers of school-age children work, but the calendar is written as if they were home waiting for the school bus.

[4]The six-hour day, the 180-day school year is regarded as somehow sacrosanct. But when parents work an eight-hour day and a 240-day year, it means something different. It means that many kids go home to empty houses. It means that, in the summer, they hang out.

[5]"We have a huge mismatch between the school calendar and the realities of family life," says Dr. Ernest Boyer, head of the Carnegie Foundation for the Advancement of Teaching.

[6]Dr. Boyer is one of many who believe that a radical revision of the school calendar is inevitable. "School, whether we like it or not, is custodial and educational. It always has been."

[7]His is not a popular idea. Schools are routinely burdened with the job of solving all our social problems. Can they be asked now to synchronize our work and family lives?

[8]It may be easier to promote a longer school year on its educational merits and, indeed, the educational case is compelling. Despite the complaints and studies about our kids' lack of learning, the United States still has a shorter school year than any industrial nation. In most of Europe, the school year is 220 days. In Japan, it is 240 days long. While classroom time alone doesn't produce a well-educated child, learning takes time and more learning takes more time. The long summers of forgetting take a toll.

[9]The opposition to a longer school year comes from families that want to and can provide other experiences for their children. It comes from teachers. It comes from tradition. And surely from kids. But the crux of the conflict has been over money.

[10]But we can, as Boyer suggests, begin to turn the hands of the school clock forward. The first step is to extend an optional after-school program of education and recreation to every district. The second step is a summer program with its own staff, paid for by fees for those who can pay and vouchers for those who can't.

[11]The third step will be the hardest: a true overhaul of the school year. Once, school was carefully calibrated to arrange children's schedules around the edges of family needs. Now, working parents, especially mothers, even teachers, try and blend their work lives around the edges of the school day.

[12]So it's back to the future. Today there are too many school doors locked and too many kids hanging out. It's time to get our calendars updated.

**Questions**

1. Who is the author?
2. What is Goodman's purpose?
3. What is her thesis?
4. What major reasons does Goodman use to support her thesis?
5. What is Goodman's tone?
6. What is her point of view?
7. Do you feel she has the knowledge to write this article? Why or why not?
8. Do you feel she is reliable? Why or why not?
9. Define these words or phrases as used by Goodman:

    a. self care (¶2)
    b. rural America (¶3)
    c. sacrosanct (¶4)
    d. mismatch (¶5)
    e. radical revision (¶6)
    f. inevitable (¶6)
    g. custodial (¶6)
    h. synchronize (¶7)
    i. compelling (¶8)
    j. crux of the conflict (¶9)
    k. vouchers (¶10)
    l. calibrated (¶11)

10. Around what has the school year been built for much of our history?
11. How long was the typical school year of 19th-century cities?
12. Why is there a mismatch between the school calendar and the realities of 20th-century family life?
13. Which industrialized nation has the shortest school year?
14. Which three groups or things, according to Goodman, are against a longer school year?
15. What does she say is the biggest obstacle to a longer school year?
16. Who is Dr. Ernest Boyer? What is his point of view?
17. What are Boyer's three steps to changing the school calendar?
18. What do you think is one major advantage of a longer school year? What do you think is one major disadvantage of a longer school year?
19. Do you agree or disagree with Goodman? Why?
20. If you wanted to get more information on changing the school calendar, list three places you would be likely to find more information.

# Will Grammar Survive?

## WILLIAM SAFIRE

*William Safire is a journalist, novelist, and former White House speech writer. He won the Pulitzer Prize for distinguished commentary in 1978 and his famous "On Language" column has appeared in* The New York Times *and more than 300 newspapers for 15 years. This selection is from* Coming to Terms.

¹Who gives a hoot if a noun that modifies another noun is called *attributive?* Can't you get through life speaking clearly and writing in happy syntax without that information? Those are questions that percolate in the minds of those of us who are, late in life, studying grammar.

²"Are you aware that teaching grammar is considered *outré* in the world of education?" writes Dianne Ravitch, professor of history at Teachers College, Columbia University. "It is now dogma among teachers of writing that student papers should never, never be corrected for minor details like grammar, spelling, punctuation and syntax; to do so, goes the predominant wisdom, is to inhibit the student's ego and interest in self-expression."

³Professor Ravitch is concerned that the advent of high-tech in schools will make matters worse, because the coming availability of spell-checkers and grammar-fixers in word-processing programs removes the need for a knowledge of the way letters and words come together. In other words, correctness of form is not important, say our strawmen-educators, and if and when it is, let the machine do it for you. Let's chew that over.

⁴Divide all knowledge into knowledge for survival, knowledge for achievement, knowledge for pleasure. The first lets us move around in the jungle, the second gives us a sense of satisfaction, the third offers us intellectual and physical kicks.

⁵Some of the knowledge for achievement—arithmetic, spreadsheeting, grammar—can be relegated to machines. One of my kids resisted learning the multiplication tables, now has a handy-dandy calculator that does it all and wants to know why I knocked myself out memorizing nine times seven. The philosophical question is a reprise of the spook's query: do we learn only what we have a need to know?

⁶I think we have a need to know what we do not need to know. What we don't need to know for achievement, we need to know for our pleasure. Knowing how things work is the basis for appreciation, and is thus a source of civilized delight.

⁷That's why I am not worried at the prospect of knowledge for achievement becoming available by easy purchase rather than by hard learning. The whole thing will move over into the next category of mental need. We'll break our heads over abstract art, and try to learn about the intricacies of music, and plow the fields of

grammar not to show the damn machines we're smarter than they are, but to satisfy our human yearning for the pleasure of understanding.

**Questions**

1. What is Safire's purpose?
2. What is his thesis?
3. What is Safire's point of view on learning?
4. What is his tone?
5. How does his tone relate to his point of view and/or bias?
6. Do you think he has the knowledge to write this article? Why or why not?
7. Do you think he is reliable? Why or why not?
8. Do you think anything could cause him to change his point of view?
9. Define these words or phrases as used by Safire:

    a. attributive (¶1)

    b. syntax (¶1)

    c. outré (¶2)

    d. dogma (¶2)

    e. predominant wisdom (¶2)

    f. strawmen-educators (¶3)

    g. reprise (¶5)

10. How does Safire divide knowledge?
11. What type of knowledge, according to Safire, can be done by machines?
12. Why does Safire think we have a need to know what we do not need to know?
13. Why isn't Safire worried about the prospect of knowledge for achievement becoming available by easy purchase?
14. Do you agree with Safire's view? Why or why not?

---

**USE YOUR STRATEGIES: EXERCISE 4**

---

# Endorsements Just a Shell Game

### MIKE ROYKO

*The funny, acerbic syndicated columnist Mike Royko takes on any and all social and political issues in his daily column that appears in hundreds of newspapers daily. This selection is from* Dr. Kookie You're Right.

[1]The man from an advertising agency had an unusual proposition.

[2]His agency does the TV commercials for a well-known chain of Mexican restaurants in Chicago.

[3]"You may have seen our commercials," he said. "They include a cameo appearance by Lee Smith and Leon Durham of the Cubs. It shows them crunching into a tortilla."

[4]No, I somehow missed seeing that.

[5]"Well, anyway, we'd like to have you in a commercial."

[6]Doing what?

[7]"Crunching into a tortilla."

[8]I thought tortillas were soft. I may be wrong, but I don't think you can crunch into a tortilla. Maybe you mean a taco.

[9]"Well, you'd be biting into some kind of Mexican food."

[10]What else would I have to do?

[11]"That's it. It would be a cameo appearance. You'd be seen for about four seconds. You wouldn't have to say anything."

[12]I'd just bite into a piece of Mexican food?

[13]"Right. For a fee, of course."

[14]How big a fee?

[15]He named a figure. It was not a king's ransom, but it was more than walking-around money.

[16]"It would take about forty-five minutes to film," he said.

[17]Amazing. In my first newspaper job almost thirty years ago, I had to work twelve weeks to earn the figure he had mentioned.

[18]It was a small, twice-a-week paper, and I was the only police reporter, the only sports reporter, the only investigative reporter and the assistant political writer, and on Saturday I would edit the stories going into the entertainment page. The publisher believed in a day's work for an hour's pay.

[19]Now I could make the same amount just for spending forty-five minutes biting into a taco in front of a TV camera.

[20]And when I was in the military, it would have taken eight monthly paychecks to equal this one taco-crunching fee. Of course, I also got a bunk and meals and could attend free VD lectures.

[21]"Well, what do you think?" he asked.

[22]I told him I would think about it and get back to him.

[23]So I asked Slats Grobnik, who has sound judgment, what he thought of the deal.

[24]"That's a lot of money just to bite a taco on TV. For that kind of scratch, I'd bite a dog. Grab the deal."

[25]But there is a question of ethics.

[26]"Ethics? What's the ethics in biting a taco? Millions of people bite tacos every day. Mexicans have been biting them for hundreds of years. Are you saying that Mexicans are unethical? Careful, some of my best friends are Mexicans."

[27]No, I'm not saying that at all. I like Mexicans, though I'm opposed to bullfighting.

[28]"Then what's unethical?"

[29]The truth is, I can't stand tacos.

[30]"What has that got to do with it? I can't stand work, but I do it for the money."

[31]It has everything to do with it. If I go on TV and bite into a taco, won't I be endorsing that taco?

[32]"So what? You've endorsed politicians and I've never met a politician that I liked better than a taco."

[33]But endorsing a taco I didn't like would be dishonest.

[34]"Hey, that's the American way. Turn on your TV and look at all the people who endorse junk. Do you think they really believe what they're saying?"

[35]Then it's wrong. Nobody should endorse a taco if they don't like a taco.

[36]"Then tell them you'll bite something else. A tortilla or an enchilada."

[37]But I don't like them either. The truth is, I can't stand most Mexican food. The only thing I really like is the salt on the edge of a margarita glass. Oh, and I do like tamales.

[38]"Good, then bite a tamale."

[39]No, because the only tamales I like are the kind that used to be sold by the little Greeks who had hot dog pushcarts on the streets. They were factory-produced tamales about the size and weight of a lead pipe. But I don't think anybody would want me to do a TV commercial for hot dog stand tamales.

[40]"Can't you just bite the taco and spit it out when the camera is turned off?"

[41]That would be a sham. Besides, even if I liked tacos or tortillas, what does it matter? Why should somebody eat in a restaurant because they see me biting into that restaurant's taco? Am I a taco expert? What are my credentials to tell millions of people what taco they should eat? I'm not even Mexican.

[42]"Well, you're a sucker to turn it down. Why, it's almost un-American. Do you think that in Russia any newsman would ever have an opportunity to make that much money by biting into a pirogi?"

[43]That may be so. But maybe someday a food product will come along that I can lend my name to, something I can truly believe in.

[44]"I doubt it. Not unless they start letting taverns advertise shots and beers on TV."

## Questions

1. What is Royko's purpose?

2. What is his thesis?

3. What is Royko's point of view on endorsements?

4. What is his tone?

5. How does his tone relate to his point of view and/or bias?

6. Do you think he has the knowledge to write this article? Why or why not?

7. Do you think he is reliable? Why or why not?

8. Do you think anything could cause him to change his point of view?

9. Explain these phrases or figures of speech used by Royko.

   a. cameo appearance (¶3)

   b. king's ransom (¶15)

   c. walking-around money (¶15)

   d. that kind of scratch (¶24)

   e. a sham (¶41)

10. What did the advertising agency want Royko to do?

11. Do you think Royko made the commercial? Why or why not?

12. How much of a factor do you think money was in Royko's decision?

13. How does Royko's thesis match or contradict your concept of reliability? Explain.

14. If you were in Royko's position, what would you have decided to do? Why?

15. This type of situation is often referred to as a moral dilemma. Have you ever had a moral dilemma? How did you resolve the dilemma?

---

**USE YOUR STRATEGIES: EXERCISE 5**

# *The Future*

### EDWARD F. BERGMAN AND TOM L. McKNIGHT

*Edward Bergman is chairman of the geography department at Lehman College of the City University of New York. He has taught widely in Europe, and he has written about New York City, U.S. history, political geography, and international affairs.*

*Tom McKnight teaches geography at the University of California, Los Angeles. Most of his professional life has been based at UCLA, but he has also taught at other schools in the U.S., Canada, and Australia.*

*This selection is from* Introduction to Geography.

[1]Until now all the factors just discussed have held off the specter of worldwide starvation. Is it possible that humankind is now, at last, at the end of its ability to increase food supplies?

[2]The answer to this question is no. There is no reason to fear that humankind is, technologically, in danger. If demographers are correct in their projections of the Earth's future population, the population can be fed. Although farmers now utilize almost all potential cropland, and the amount of cropland per capita is declining, humankind has scarcely begun to maximize productivity even with present-day technology. The leading contemporary technology has been applied to only a small portion of the Earth, and newly emerging technology offers still greater possibilities.

[3]A 1983 study by the Food and Agriculture Organization (FAO, a UN agency) of the world's soil and climate determined that with

basic fertilizers and pesticides, all cultivable land under food crops, and the most productive crops grown on at least half the land, the world in the year 2000 could feed four times its projected 2000 population. (That study discounted any possible technological breakthroughs between 1983 and 2000.) If average farm yields rose just from the present 2 tons of grain equivalent per hectare (2.47 acres) to 5 tons, the world could support about 11.5 billion people. Each person could enjoy "plant energy"—food, seed, and animal feed—of 6,000 calories per day, the current global average. (North America currently uses about 15,000 calories per person per day, but most of that is consumed by animals, which are then eaten by people.)

[4]In addition, humankind could improve its diet by concentrating on raising those domesticated animals that most efficiently transform grain into meat. Chickens are the most efficient. They yield 1 pound (0.46 kg) of edible meat for every 4 pounds (1.8 kg) of grain they consume. Pigs produce 1 pound for every 7 pounds of grain, and beef cattle 1 pound for every 15 pounds (6.8 kg) of grain. In addition, chickens reach maturity—and therefore can be consumed—much faster than do pigs and cattle. Therefore, a greater emphasis placed on raising chickens could immensely improve the human diet. China is widely replacing swine with chicken farming, and several other countries have established programs to multiply their chicken populations. In many societies, however, cattle are viewed as a status symbol, and this preference delays the switch into more productive livestock.

[5]***Biotechnology in Agriculture.*** New scientific advances promise to multiply future food yields. Biotechnology offers *genetically altered crops* that can be custom designed to fit the environment, produce bountiful harvests, and resist plant diseases. One bacterial gene eliminates the need for chemicals to kill worms by producing a natural protein that disintegrates the worms' digestive system. Genetically engineered viruses can be used as pesticides. In 1988 scientists mapped the genome of rice—the set of 12 chromosomes that carries all the genetic characteristics of rice. This development could enable geneticists to produce improved strains of rice. Biotechnology can replace chemical pesticides and fertilizers, whose biological or even genetic impact on our own bodies is not fully understood.

[6]Scientists have also conducted research on *halophytes,* plants that thrive in salt water. Interbreeding halophytes with conventional crops has made these crops more salt-resistant, which means that they can grow in more diverse environments. Farmers are today harvesting lands in Egypt, Israel, India, and Pakistan once thought too salt-soaked to support crops. Conventional crops may someday be grown in salt water.

[7]Mechanized fishing on technologically advanced ships has already multiplied yields from the sea, but humankind has scarcely begun the shift from hunting and gathering seafood (fishing and gathering a few aquatic plants) to aquaculture, which involves herding or domesticating aquatic animals and farming aquatic plants. Humankind took this step with agriculture and livestock herding on land thousands of years ago. Presumably this food frontier will be expanded.

⁸All these possibilities justify optimism. The economist Henry George (1839–1897) succinctly contrasted the rules of nature with the multiplication of resources through the application of human ingenuity. He said, "Both the jayhawk and the man eat chickens, but the more jayhawks, the fewer chickens, while the more men, the more chickens."

⁹This principle is key to understanding and counting all resources, but technological solutions to problems can still trigger unexpected new problems. Overreliance on insecticides, for example, can lead to the poisoning of farm workers or the contamination of water supplies. The debate between the optimists and the pessimists continues.

### Questions

1. What is Bergman and McKnight's purpose?
2. What is their thesis?
3. What is their point of view on the ability of the world to provide food for its population in the future?
4. What is their point of view on the promise of genetically altered crops?
5. What is their general tone?
6. How does their tone relate to their point of view and/or bias?
7. Do you think Bergman and McKnight have the knowledge to write this article? Why or why not?
8. Do you think they are reliable? Why or why not?
9. What, if anything, do you think could cause them to change their point of view?
10. Explain these words or phrases:

    a. specter of worldwide starvation (¶1)

    b. newly emerging technology (¶2)

    c. per hectare (¶3)

    d. genetically altered crops (¶5)

    e. halophytes (¶6)

11. If farmers are currently using almost all available cropland and the amount of available cropland is diminishing, how do Bergman and McKnight suggest food yields can be increased to meet future demands?
12. Why do the authors suggest that raising a greater percentage of chickens could improve the human diet?
13. Name three advantages of genetically altered crops.
14. Why do Bergman and McKnight compare aquaculture to agriculture and livestock herding? Do you think it is a useful comparison? Explain.
15. Explain, in your own words, the meaning of economist Henry George's quote in paragraph 8, "Both the jayhawk and the man eat chickens, but the more jayhawks, the fewer chickens, while the more men, the more chickens." Do you agree or disagree with George? Why?

## CONNECTIONS

A. Reread the paragraphs by Caile and those by Fuori and Gioia about computers. Which piece most closely matches your point of view about the use and impact of computers? Why? Did either Caile or Fuori and Gioia spark an idea you hadn't thought about? Did either author change your mind?

B. Dr. Robert Weiss states in "Writing About History," quoted in Chapter 7, "As long as history books are composed by human beings, they will reflect the perspectives of their authors." Do you think it's acceptable for textbook authors, most of whom are scholars in their field, to include their personal point of view within the text? Why or why not?

# Decide What to Do with the Author's Information

As you worked through the first eight chapters you discovered that reading for learning requires more than just reporting what an author says. To be successful, you must become involved with the author's thoughts and ideas. Now you must decide what to do with those thoughts and ideas. As Edgar Dale says,

> Reading, we must remember, is a process of getting meaning from the printed page by putting meaning into the printed page. Reading taste and ability are always tethered to past experience. But reading itself is one way of increasing this capital fund of past experience. Reading, therefore, must be seen as more than saying the word, more than seeing the sentences and paragraphs. Good reading is the way a person brings his whole life to bear on the new ideas which he finds on the printed page. It is reading the lines, reading between the lines, and reading beyond the lines. It is an active, not a passive process. The good reader becomes involved with the writing and the writer. He agrees, he argues back. He asks: Is it true? Is it pertinent? What, if anything, should I or could I do about it?

How did you decide whom to vote for during the last election? If you had to vote on "English Only" legislation what sources would you read? Among all the organizations that ask for contributions, how do you decide whom to give your time and money? As you plan for reading this chapter, think about how you reach decisions such as these and the impact that reading has on your life.

Highlight definitions of this chapter's key vocabulary:

- critical reader
- objectively analyze
- argument
- evidence

---

**Chapter 9 Content Objectives**

- identify the strategies of a responsible reader
- understand what it means to be a critical reader
- understand the need to make a conscious decision to accept, reject, or suspend judgment on the author's information

---

## What Is My Basic Strategy for Deciding What to Do with What I Read?

**As You Plan:**

1. Think about how you form opinions and how you decide what to do.
2. Think about what makes you believe or disbelieve an author.
3. Understand the vocabulary.
4. Predict the thesis/argument and main ideas.
5. Determine how much detail you need to know.

**As You Read:**

6. Actively search for information that helps to clarify and refine your prediction about the thesis/argument and main ideas.
7. Consider what you know about the topic; how does the new information agree and/or disagree with what you know.
8. Keep an open mind; do not unquestioningly accept or reject what you read.

**As You Review:**

9. Revise and restate the thesis/argument and main ideas.
10. Organize the thesis/argument, main ideas and supporting details.
11. Make a conscious decision to accept, reject, or suspend judgment on the author's ideas and information. If you have suspended judgment, plan where you will gather more information on the topic.

## What Are My Strategies as a Responsible Reader?

### INITIAL STRATEGIES

***Use a Plan»Do»Review Cycle*** (review Chapter 1). You begin with a systematic approach to reading because it promotes objectivity and decreases opportunities for impulsive or emotional reactions to an author's ideas and information.

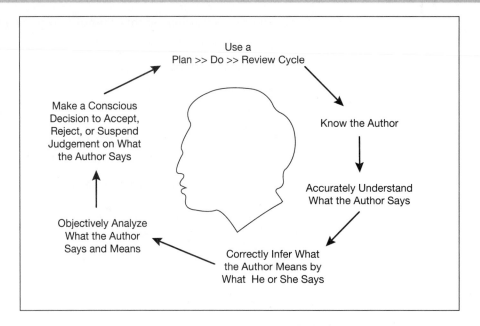

When you develop and implement a plan based on an assignment's two critical factors—your purpose for reading the assignment and the difficulty of the material—you are more likely to be an active, thinking participant in the process. And, as you have discovered, reading requires thinking.

By viewing reading as a continuing, or cyclic, activity you have time to integrate new information with what you know, and are able to link ideas into the larger perspective.

***Know the author*** (review Chapters 2 and 8). Reading without knowing the writer, like talking with someone you don't know, makes communication difficult.

First, recognizing why an author wants to communicate information and ideas to you—to explain or make clear facts, events, and ideas; paint a picture in words; tell a story; influence you to believe or feel a certain way or take a particular action—helps you understand what the author writes.

Then, staying aware of the author's knowledge, reliability, and stance provides additional insight into what the author means by what she or he says.

***Accurately understand what the author says*** (review Chapters 1–8). Your purpose when you are reading for learning always requires that you accurately understand the author's thesis—or argument as it is called when the author's purpose is to persuade—and main ideas. This is because the thesis or argument and main ideas are the framework that holds the author's information together. As Weiss said in his "Reading History" excerpt in Chapter 7, "The first question the reader should ask is: What is the author's argument? What is his theme, his interpretation, his thesis?"

Next, turn your attention to how the author supports and develops the thesis or argument and main ideas. Investigate the kinds of details or evidence provided. Remember what Veit, Gould, and Clifford said about writing: "If stating an idea were enough, there would be no books or essays. Each piece of writing would consist of only a topic sentence. Of course more is needed. Writers must explain, expand and support their ideas. Sometimes facts or logic are called for, sometimes the narration of events, and sometimes examples, illustrations, and reasons. . . . The way that an author chooses to develop a main idea depends on the work's purpose and its intended audience."

In addition, it is useful to determine the structure, or method of development, because it provides a clue to locating and sorting out the relationships among details you need for good comprehension.

***Correctly infer what the author means by what he or she says*** (review Chapters 2, 3, 4, 5, 8).  In your reading assignments you have discovered instances in which an author doesn't directly state what she or he wants you to know. In these situations you have had to infer what the author meant. You have logically developed your best reasoned conclusion based on the information the author provided.

Because inferences are perceptive thoughts about the author's information, not just reckless guesses or opinions, your knowledge of the author and an accurate understanding of what he or she does say is critical.

Revisit the inferences you've made in previous chapters: in Chapter 2 you connected information from all the sentences and inferred the author's reason for writing, in Chapter 3 you carefully combined the author's information to identify the denotative and connotative meanings of a word from context, in Chapter 4 you added together information from all the sentences to determine an unstated main idea, in Chapter 5 you used all of the author's clues to establish how ideas were developed, and in Chapter 8 you linked together a variety of clues and information to determine the author's stance.

## USE THOSE STRATEGIES AS A BASIS TO:

***Objectively analyze what the author says and means.***  Contrary to the common connotation, a critical reader's goal is *not* to find fault or criticize. Quite the opposite, a critical reader comprehends, questions, clarifies, and analyzes to reach objective, responsible judgments.

The most difficult aspect of analysis for most readers is trying to separate their personal opinions and biases from the author's ideas and information. Our first inclination is to agree with authors who provide information that supports our views, and to discount authors who provide information that contradicts our views. One of the best defenses against opinionated or impulsive reactions to an author's ideas and information is to maintain an honest awareness of your own ideas and views.

You should not unquestioningly accept what an author says just because it is in print. Likewise, you should not automatically reject what an author says just because it differs from your point of view.

Once you have an accurate understanding of what the author says and means, you examine it objectively. By objectively, I mean without being influenced by your own biases. You must thoughtfully and impartially analyze the soundness and significance of the author's information. These strategies for analyzing the support, or evidence, the author provides for the thesis or argument and main ideas will provide a solid base for the more sophisticated analysis techniques you will encounter in advanced course work.

First, determine if the author is using facts, opinions, or a combination of facts and opinions to develop and support his or her thesis or argument. In your analysis you can have confidence in facts and valid opinions but you should be skeptical of unsubstantiated opinions. Also review the sources the author used—are they sufficient and reputable?

Other criteria to consider in evaluating the author's information and ideas include the relevance, logic, and clarity of the support or evidence. Relevant evidence directly supports the author's thesis or argument. The relationship between relevant evidence and the thesis or argument is obvious. It includes pertinent and specific details that advance the author's position. Logical evidence provides reasonable and rational support for the author's thesis or argument. Logical evidence makes sense to you. Evidence clarifies; it seeks to simplify and make clear the author's thesis or argument.

Try to locate other information, ideas, or points of view and compare them with the author's.

***Make a conscious decision to accept, reject, or suspend judgment on what the author says.*** The most important point to remember is that you need not accept or reject every aspect of what an author says. In fact, you will likely give a "mixed review" on most of what you read. You may accept an author's argument but find the evidence inadequate, or you may be impressed by the data but draw different conclusions from it. Even if you like a particular author or book, you will probably have some comments, criticisms, or suggestions. I have liberally paraphrased Dr. Weiss' comments about reading history to focus attention on your complex and difficult task as a critical reader.

Also remember that your decision to accept, reject, or suspend judgment on an author's thesis or argument is not irreversible. As a critical reader, you are open-minded; new information, changing facts, and fresh material give you the opportunity to review, rethink, and grow.

---

## PRACTICE: USE YOUR CRITICAL READING STRATEGIES

Consider again these two paragraphs from "Writing About History" by Dr. Robert Weiss in Unger's *These United States,* 5th ed.

1. "Despite its precedent-setting character, however, the American revolt is noteworthy because it made no serious interruption in the smooth flow of American development. Both in intention and in fact, the American Revolution conserved the past rather than repudiated it. And in preserving the colonial experience, the men of the first quarter century of the Republic's history set the scenery and wrote the script for the drama of American politics for years to come." (Carl N. Degler, *Out of Our Past,* rev. ed. (New York: Harper & Row, Harper Colophon Books, 1970), p. 73.)

2. "The stream of revolution, once started, could not be confined within narrow banks, but spread abroad upon the land. Many economic desires, many social aspirations were set free by the political struggle, many aspects of colonial society profoundly altered by the forces thus set loose. The relations of social classes to each other, the institution of slavery, the system of landholding, of business, the forms and spirit of the intellectual and religious life, all felt the transforming hand of revolution, all emerged from under it in shapes advanced many degrees nearer to those we know." (J. Franklin Jameson, *The American Revolution Considered as a Social Movement* (Boston: Beacon Press, 1956), p. 9.)

Because these authors present two conflicting theories of the fundamental nature of the American Revolution, you cannot accept both of them. Using your strategies as a responsible, critical reader, what do you do?

    a. Do you accept one thesis or argument and reject the other? Explain why you accepted or rejected each author's thesis or argument.

    b. Do you reject them both? Explain why you rejected each author's thesis or argument.

    c. Do you suspend judgment on both? If you suspend judgment, indicate where you would look for additional clarifying information.

## REVIEW QUESTIONS

*Review Questions*

1. What are the strategies of a responsible reader?

2. What does it mean to be a critical reader?

3. What are your personal guidelines for accepting or rejecting an author's information, and seeking additional information?

*Think and Connect Questions*

4. Reread "Food Irradiation: A Scary Word" by Blumenthal, Chapter 3, Exercise 3. Read "Irradiated Food: Some Facts to Consider" by Greene, Exercise 1 on page 192. In what ways do the two authors agree and/or disagree? Based on the information provided by Blumenthal and Greene, what is your point of view on irradiated food? Will you buy irradiated food? Why or why not? Where could you look for more information?

5. Reread the selection "Can Interpersonal Skills Be Taught?" by Robbins in Chapter 2, Exercise 2. Do you accept or reject that interpersonal skills can be taught or do you suspend judgment until you have more information? What is the basis for your decision? Where could you look for information with a different point of view?

*Application*

6. From recent newspapers and magazines, identify one article in which you accept the author's thesis or argument, one article in which you reject the author's thesis or argument, and one article where you are suspending judgment until you gather more information. In each case, explain why you reached the conclusion you did.

7. From any of your textbooks, identify a section in which you accept the author's thesis or argument, a section where you reject the author's thesis or argument, and a section in which you are suspending judgment until you gather more information. In each case, explain why you reached the conclusion you did.

---

**USE YOUR STRATEGIES: EXERCISE 1**

---

# Irradiated Food: Some Facts to Consider

### LINDA GREENE

*Linda Greene is a feature writer for* Vitality, *from which this selection is taken.*

[1]The idea of irradiated food may conjure up images of glowing vegetables that would send a Geiger counter reading through the ceiling. But does irradiation make food radioactive?

[2]When food is irradiated, it is sent on a conveyor belt into a room containing cobalt 60 rods (a radioactive isotope). The room is then flooded with gamma rays. After treatment, the food looks and tastes the same as before.

[3]According to Edward Josephson, professor of food science and nutrition at the University of Rhode Island in West Kingston, irradiated food is no more radioactive than luggage is after it passes through an airport X-ray machine. The gamma rays used to irradiate food pass right through without leaving waste products behind.

[4]However, Michael F. Jacobson, Ph.D., executive director of the Center for Science in the Public Interest in Washington, D.C., explains that just because the food isn't radioactive doesn't mean it is safe to eat. Research indicates that irradiated food contains tiny amounts of a few unsavory chemicals. And the amount of nutrients in the food are reduced by the process.

## IRRADIATED FOOD—THE PROS

[5]The reasons to treat foods with radiation sound reasonable in theory. Radiation can kill bacteria (such as salmonella) that cause food poisoning and parasites that cause disease. It can destroy insects in produce, lengthen the shelf life of fruits and vegetables and offer an alternative to the use of certain fumigants and chemicals that have been linked to cancer. Irradiation holds the promise of dramatically reducing food-related disease and expanding the world food supply.

[6]Currently, the FDA has approved the use of radiation to treat fruit, vegetables, grains, pork, poultry, wheat and wheat flour, white potatoes, spices and dry or dehydrated enzyme preparations used in many processed foods.

## IRRADIATED FOOD—THE CONS

[7]Irradiation eliminates some problems with food but has the potential to create others. The process causes molecules to break down, and a few stray parts called free radicals may recombine into

new derivatives called radiolytic products (such as benzene and formaldehyde), some of which have been linked to cancer.

[8]With low doses of radiation, the number of radiolytic products produced is minimal. Moreover, some radiolytic products also occur naturally in foods and are sometimes created during cooking or processing. But no tests exist that can detect food that has received abnormally high doses of radiation and that could contain many radiolytic products. Also, some scientific research indicates irradiated foods have a degree of toxicity.

[9]An additional concern is irradiation's effect on food nutrients. Studies have shown that irradiation reduces levels of vitamin C, thiamin, vitamin E and polyunsaturated fats. This may prove to be a critical problem because the FDA estimates that, eventually, as much as 40% of the food we eat could be irradiated.

## THE BOTTOM LINE

[10]Much of the food we eat will never undergo irradiation. Some foods, such as dairy products and water-based vegetables, aren't suitable for the process. And because U.S. food distribution and hygiene systems are good, irradiation is not cost-effective for most products. If you don't want to eat irradiated food until more research has been completed, pay attention to packaging in the grocery store: All radiation-treated foods must bear a special green symbol. Avoiding them when eating out is more of a challenge because restaurants aren't required to identify dishes made with irradiated ingredients. Each of us, weighing the pros and cons, will have to make our own decision about eating irradiated food. Irradiated food can lower our risk of food poisoning, but its long-range cancer-causing potential is still largely unknown.

### Questions

1. What is Greene's purpose?
2. What is Greene's thesis or argument?
3. What is Greene's point of view on irradiated foods?
4. Would you characterize Greene's article as biased or objective: Give a specific example to support your answer.
5. Do you accept, reject, or suspend judgment on Greene's thesis or argument?
6. Explain your decision and what, if any, next steps you would take.

# *"Is the School Year Too Short?" Part 1*

## TOM MCCOY

*Tom McCoy, a media specialist at Nicollet Junior High School in Burnsville, Minnesota, is a 25-year teaching veteran. He was Burnsville's 1989 Teacher of the Year. Over the years, McCoy has served as president, chief negotiator, and newsletter editor for the Burnsville Education Association. This selection is from* NEA Today.

¹Our school year is an artifact of simpler times. When our nation was agricultural, families needed help with their summer farm work. It made sense then to suspend school during the summer so children could stay home and help.

²But today education must coexist with technology, global competition, increasing social problems, and a tremendously expanding knowledge base—and we're locked into a school year that doesn't serve these needs.

³Proponents of the 180-day school year say teachers and students need a break. Well, who doesn't? Most folks get much less time to recharge themselves than do students and teachers.

⁴By persisting in the pattern we now have, we admit to the world that education isn't as important as endeavors that continue year round.

⁵Churches don't close their doors in the summer. Hardware stores stay open all year. The start-stop-start mentality of the school year postpones true improvement of the system because it enables lots of teachers and students to "endure" until summer. If we all knew we were in for the long haul, we might get serious about school reform.

⁶Proponents of the current school calendar say kids should spend time with their families during the summer. I say: What time? What families?

⁷Today's parents and children spend very little time together under the best of circumstances. In fact, studies reveal that parents and children spend almost no time in meaningful dialogue, whether school is in session or not.

⁸If there are two parents at home, most likely both hold jobs. Often there's only one parent—typically a harried, overworked mother trying to hold things together.

⁹A very few lucky kids spend summers with their parents doing fun and worthwhile activities that add to their development. Are we making national education policy for those few?

¹⁰What happens to the rest of the kids during the long, hot, unproductive summer? Are they dreaming dreams, fishing, reading, using their imaginations? No, they're watching low-quality TV, playing video games, running in the streets, wasting time, forgetting

what they learned in school, and—all too often—taking care of themselves.

[11]School isn't perfect, but we do better than that.

[12]The most discouraging reason for a longer school year is that—try as we may—we're unable to bring our students up to world standards. The only choice we have is to try to improve education 20 percent by adding 20 percent to the time we spend in the classroom.

[13]You say we're already doing things that will turn education around? That national attention is focused on the problem? That business wants to help? That political leaders are becoming more aware? That we're getting computers and special programs and outcome-based education and parent involvement and site-based management?

[14]Well, all these things are nice. They represent progress. But when will they make our students do as well in math as Swedish kids? When will they make most, if not all, kids graduate from high school? When will a diploma mean that you can speak, spell, and write your mother tongue—and perhaps another language—as, say, Irish kids can?

[15]Will it be when I'm an old man? When my son is an old man? Will the rest of the world stand still while we make hopelessly slow improvements?

[16]We can have a 20 percent improvement next year by extending the school year by 20 percent. It will cost more. We won't want to pay for it. Nobody will like it. Students and school staff will have to make big changes.

[17]But the alternative is to struggle along, falling behind and waiting for the next headline about low math scores or the next study analyzing the sorry state of education in our country.

[18]If we want our nation to be on the move, doing great things, we have to devote more time to preparing our next generation to create such a society and to partcipate in it.

(Questions for this exercise follow Exercise 2B.)

---

**USE YOUR STRATEGIES: EXERCISE 2B**

---

# *Is the School Year Too Short? Part 2*

### LORNA HOCKETT

*Lorna Hockett, a fifth-grade teacher at Waldport (Oregon) Elementary School, has taught for 14 years. She is treasurer of the Lincoln County Education Association and a certified trainer in drug and alcohol abuse prevention and personal development programs. This selection is from NEA Today.*

[1]Despite popular opinion, today's classrooms are very different from what they were 20, or even 10, years ago. I've never met a teacher who wasn't constantly seeking to grow and improve. The current public rhetoric for restructuring the schools merely gives validity to what teachers want.

[2]But would lengthening the school year improve education? Like any proposal involving major change, the concept deserves calm consideration. In weighing the pros and cons, we must ask some questions.

[3]*What would be the benefits?* A frequent answer is that more time in the classroom would produce more student learning. I challenge that.

[4]True, many private corporations have found that running their computers 24 hours a day, 365 days a year, allows them to process more data. But we work with human beings, not computers.

[5]Humans need time to do things other than process information. They must eat, sleep, integrate skills, and use parts of their bodies other than the brain. Increasing school time would decrease time available for individual development.

[6]Recently, corporations like Nike and Saturn have come to recognize that increased work time doesn't automatically improve production or quality. These corporations understand the value of providing for all employee needs by offering on-site programs for physical fitness, medical care, child day care, and recreation.

[7]Many developmental needs of children can't—and shouldn't—be met in school. For example, learning to perceive oneself as capable, influential, and significant isn't possible in a classroom with 20 or 30 other children the same age. Kids need time to experience the real world, where people typically work in small multiaged groups.

[8]*Would an increased school year yield any negative results?* From a practical standpoint alone, costs would increase, adding to our school funding crisis. Cutting programs or increasing class size to compensate for this extra cost would cancel any benefits.

[9]We're still feeling the negative effects of class size increases that took place when the baby boomers entered school. Teachers with classes of 30 or more students spend most of their day dealing with paperwork. They have little time or energy left to give youngsters the individual attention they need. Let's not make it worse.

[10]Most likely, a longer school year would also mean increased student stress. Japanese studies show that the level of student stress relates directly to the student suicide rate.

[11]*Can projected benefits be realized in another way?* If we're adding days to the school calendar to allow more time for learning, it would be prudent to look at how we're using time now. In many districts—mine included—we devote about 10 days a year to achievement testing.

[12]I challenge this use of time. There are more convincing ways to let the public know we're doing our job and more valid ways of assessing student growth. In fact, many students—and parents, too—develop fears about schools and their own worth based on the results of these tests.

[13]The proposal for a longer school year raises other issues, too. Will teachers have the time for professional development and

growth? Will students who have to work to help support themselves and their families be forced out of the system?

[14]How will student enrichment and extension programs—athletic and academic camps, foreign student exchanges, and extended field trips, including family vacations—fit into the picture?

[15]We must also keep in mind certain basics, like a child's attention span; assimilation rate; need for self-initiated learning; and physical, vocational, and social or emotional needs.

[16]Sure, the current school year was created for a rural, agrarian economy. But before we discard this system in the name of progress and a "more is better" philosophy, we should carefully consider who it is that we serve and how the change would affect those persons.

### Questions

1. What is McCoy's purpose?
2. What is Hockett's purpose?
3. What is McCoy's thesis or argument?
4. What is Hockett's thesis or argument?
5. Does McCoy use mostly facts or opinions to support his thesis or argument? Give two examples.
6. Does Hockett use mostly facts or opinions to support her thesis or argument? Give two examples.
7. Do you accept, reject, or suspend judgment on McCoy's thesis or argument?
8. Explain your decision and what, if any, next steps you would take.
9. Do you accept, reject, or suspend judgment on Hockett's thesis or argument?
10. Explain your decision and what, if any, next steps you would take.

---

**USE YOUR STRATEGIES: EXERCISE 3**

# In Perspective: Nature's Corporations

## BERNARD J. NEBEL AND RICHARD T. WRIGHT

*Dr. Nebel is a biology professor at Catonsville Community College in Maryland where he has taught environmental science for 21 years. He is a member of several professional associations and actively supports a number of environmental organizations. Dr. Richard T. Wright is chairman of the Division of Natural Sciences, Mathematics, and Computer Science at Gordon College in Massachusetts, where he has taught environmental science for 22 years. He has received research grants from the National Science Foundation for his work in aquatic microbiology, and works on many professional and environmental endeavors. This selection is from* Environmental Science, *4th ed.*

[1]The Spotted Owl controversy pits jobs against the preservation of the old-growth forests of the West. Timber interests maintain that preservation will result in 20,000 lost jobs. In their view, the controversy comes down to this: We should continue to cut the old-growth forests for the sake of keeping loggers employed.

[2]General Motors and other major businesses facing hard times lay off thousands of workers, and no one questions their need or right to do so. Clearly, the survival of General Motors is more important than keeping all their workers employed. It is assumed that those laid off will find other employment. According to conventional wisdom, corporate America must survive if the economy is to have a chance of recovering from economic bad times.

[3]In a real sense, ecosystems are the corporations that sustain the economy of the biosphere. If we want those ecosystems to survive and recover, we may have to tighten our belt and withdraw some of the work force engaged in exploiting them. The maintenance of these systems is obviously more important than some jobs. Why can't laid-off loggers seek other employment the way laid-off autoworkers, steelworkers, or computer engineers do? Why should a natural ecosystem be "bankrupted" just to maintain the temporary employment of a few (temporary because the loggers will be out of a job in a few years when the old-growth forests are finally all cut)?

[4]Clearly, it is short-sighted to assume that ecosystems are there just to provide jobs and that the jobs are more important than the ecosystems. When the old-growth forests are gone, we shall have lost more than just loggers' jobs—we shall have lost a priceless heritage and a major part of the natural world that provides us with vital services.

### Questions

1. What is Nebel and Wright's purpose?
2. What is Nebel and Wright's thesis or argument?
3. What do Nebel and Wright compare ecosystems to? Do you think this is a valid comparison? Why or why not?
4. Do Nebel and Wright use mostly facts or opinions to support their thesis or argument? Give two examples.
5. Do you accept, reject, or suspend judgment on Nebel and Wright's thesis or argument?
6. Explain your decision and what, if any, next steps you would take.

# Problems in American Education—Bureaucracy and Student Passivity

## JOHN J. MACIONIS

*Dr. Macionis is an associate professor of sociology at Kenyon College in Gambier, Ohio. He teaches a wide range of upper-level courses, but his favorite course is Introduction to Sociology. His doctorate is in sociology and he is the author of several articles and papers on topics such as community life in the United States, interpersonal relationships in families, effective teaching, and humor. This selection is from* Sociology, *3rd ed.*

[1]A problem more specific to schools themselves is pervasive student passivity—a lack of active participation in learning. This problem is not confined to any particular type of school: it is commonly found in both public and private schools and at all grade levels (Coleman, Hotter, & Kilgore, 1981).

[2]Schooling would seem a wonderful opportunity. In medieval Europe, children assumed many adult responsibilities before they were teenagers; a century ago, American children worked long hours in factories, on farms, and in coal mines—for little pay. Today, however, the major responsibility faced by youths is to study their human heritage, learn the effective use of language, master the manipulation of numbers, and acquire knowledge and skills that will empower them and enhance their comprehension, enjoyment, and mastery of the surrounding world.

[3]Yet the startling fact is that many students do not perceive the opportunities provided by schooling as a privilege, but rather as a series of hurdles that are mechanically cleared in pursuit of credentials that may open doors later in life. Students are, in short, bored. Some of the blame must be placed on students themselves, and on other factors such as television, which now takes up more of young people's time than school does. Even so, much of the pervasive passivity of American students is caused by the educational system.

[4]In the nineteenth century, American children were typically taught in one-room schoolhouses: small and highly personal settings in their local communities. During this century, with rising costs, many local schools were dissolved; at the same time, expanding state and federal governments favored large regional schools as a more efficient means of supervising educational curricula and ensuring uniformity. Schools today, therefore, reflect the high level of bureaucratic organization found throughout American society. As Chapter 7 ("Groups and Organizations") explained, such rigid and impersonal organization can negatively affect administrators, teachers, and students.

[5]After studying high schools across the United States, Theodore Sizer (1984) acknowledged that the bureaucratic structure of Amer-

ican schools is necessary to meet the massive educational demands of our vast and complex society. Yet he found that a bureaucratic educational system fosters five serious problems (1984:207–209).

[6]First, bureaucratic uniformity ignores the cultural variation within countless local communities. It takes schools out of the local community and places them under the control of outside "specialists" who may have little understanding of the everyday lives of students.

[7]Second, bureaucratic schools define success by numerical ratings of performance. School officials focus on attendance rates, dropout rates, and achievement test scores. In doing so, they overlook dimensions of schooling that are difficult to quantify, such as the creativity of students and the energy and enthusiasm of teachers. Such bureaucratic school systems tend to define an adequate education in terms of the number of days (or even minutes) per year that students are inside a school building rather than the school's contribution to students' personal development.

[8]Third, bureaucratic schools have rigid expectations of all students. For example, fifteen-year-olds are expected to be in the tenth grade, and eleventh-grade students are expected to score at a certain level on a standardized verbal achievement test. The high-school diploma thus rewards a student for going through the proper sequence of educational activities in the proper amount of time. Rarely are exceptionally bright and motivated students allowed to graduate early. Likewise, the system demands that students who have learned little in school graduate with their class.

[9]Fourth, the school's bureaucratic division of labor requires specialized personnel. High-school students learn English from one teacher, receive guidance from another, and are coached in sports by others. No school official comes to know the "full" student as a complex human being. Students experience this division of labor as a continual shuffling among rigidly divided fifty-minute periods throughout the school day.

[10]Fifth, the highly bureaucratic school system gives students little responsibility for their own learning. Similarly, teachers have little latitude in what and how they teach their classes; they dare not accelerate learning for fear of disrupting "the system." Standardized policies dictating what is to be taught and how long the teaching should take render many teachers as passive and unimaginative as their students.

[11]Several factors have enhanced bureaucracy in American schools. Bureaucratic schools, Sizer claims, were needed to effectively process the rapid influx of immigrant children during the last century; since then, the student population of New York City alone has grown larger than that of all of America in 1900. Cultural values are also at work: Americans tend to believe that the most effective way to accomplish any task is to formulate a system, and for better or worse, that is precisely what formal education in the United States has become.

[12]Since bureaucracy discourages initiative and creativity, students become passive. The solution, drawing on the discussion in Chapter 7 ("Groups and Organizations"), is to "humanize" bureaucracy, or in this instance, Sizer claims, to humanize schools. He recommends eliminating rigid class schedules, reducing class size, and training teachers more broadly to enable them to become more fully

involved in the lives of their students. Perhaps his most radical suggestion is that graduation from high school should depend on what a student has learned rather than simply on the length of time spent in school.

**Questions**

1. What Macionis's purpose?

2. What is Macionis's thesis or argument?

3. Define these words or phrases:

   a. student passivity (¶1)

   b. empower and enhance (¶2)

   c. series of hurdles that are mechanically cleared (¶3)

   d. pervasive (¶3)

   e. ensuring uniformity (¶4)

   f. high level of bureaucratic organization (¶4)

   g. fosters (¶5)

   h. cultural variations (¶6)

   i. difficult to quantify (¶7)

   j. teachers have little latitude (¶10)

   k. several factors have enhanced bureaucracy (¶11)

4. What is the primary cause of student passivity according to Macionis?

5. What are the five ways bureaucracy encourages student passivity?

6. What does Macionis say is Sizer's "most radical" suggestion? Do you think that it is a radical suggestion?

7. Give one reason why you think Sizer's "radical suggestion" would work and one reason why it would not work.

8. What is Macionis's point of view on bureaucracy? Explain your answer.

---

### CONNECTIONS

A. What tasks or situations at school, work, and home require you to make inferences? What kinds of clues do you use to help you make valid inferences? What tasks or situations are easiest for you to make inferences? What are the most difficult? What strategies do you use to check the validity of your inferences?

B. During most of your prior school experience you have probably been taught to accept the information in textbooks without question. What are the advantages of accepting text information without question? What are the disadvantages? What changes in this approach, if any, would you suggest to elementary and high school teachers?

# Theme 1
# Staying Healthy in America

"The first wealth is health." Emerson—*The Conduct of Life*

How do you define "health"? Being able to play in sports? Not missing a day of work? Feeling good about yourself? Leading a balanced life?

Good health may be difficult for us to define in just a few words but I suspect we all agree that being healthy means more than just being free of a disease. Being healthy involves a combination of physical, psychological, social, environmental, and spiritual elements.

This unit looks at health and the activities, behaviors, and attitudes that affect health and the quality of life.

The textbook chapter that opens this theme, "Promoting Your Health," from *Access To Health* by Dr. Rebecca Donatelle and Dr. Lorraine Davis, defines both health and wellness. It describes the benefits of achieving optimal health and presents a framework for developing behaviors that promote health and wellness.

Next, in "Fitness for Every Body," Mary-Lane Kamberg says you don't have to be a world-class athlete to enjoy the benefits of fitness. She analyzes three major components of fitness—strength, endurance, and flexibility—as they apply to "regular" people.

"Fruits and Vegetables" from the *Mayo Clinic Health Letter* reports on the research surrounding the current focus on increasing fruits, vegetables and grains in the diet and reviews the USDA's food guide pyramid. Then, Maureen Callahan attempts to solve just one food mystery by investigating the facts on fat in "Heartening News."

"Growing older isn't what it used to be," says Carl Sherman. So, in "The New Aging," he looks at what you can do to "head off the effects of time." Next, "Good Friends Are Good Medicine" by the *Prevention* magazine staff provides a sampling of research findings on the relationship between personal friendships and good health. "Jest for the Health of It" is Susan Goodman's prescription for a good giggle.

And finally, experts debate the links between mind and body in "Think Right. Stay Well?" by Denise Grady.

Each of the readings is by a different author(s), of a different length, and requires different tasks.

---

**Strategies for Success**

- Develop a plan for each of the readings.
- Determine who the author is and why he or she is writing.
- Know the vocabulary the author uses.
- Identify what the author is writing about.
- Establish how the author develops the writing.
- Integrate graphic and text information.
- Organize the information you need.
- Recognize the author's stance.
- Decide what you can do with the author's information.

---

# *Promoting Your Health*

## REBECCA J. DONATELLE AND LORRAINE DAVIS

*Rebecca J. Donatelle, Ph.D., CHES, is an associate professor and Coordinator of Graduate Studies in the Department of Public Health at Oregon State University. A nationally recognized health educator, Dr. Donatelle has taught thousands of students over the years in a wide range of health promotion and disease prevention areas that are directly related to, or serve as the basis for, chapters in this text. In addition to her teaching experience, her research areas have focused on health behaviors and those factors that serve to reduce risk and promote health in social and political environments.*

*Lorraine Davis, Ph.D., CHES, is a professor of health education and Vice Provost for Academic Personnel at the University of Oregon. Dr. Davis has taught a variety of classes to scores of undergraduate and graduate students focusing on the multi-faceted areas of health promotion and education, disease prevention, and analysis of health data. She has been awarded the Ersted Award for excellence in teaching and was inducted into the Hall of Excellence at the University of Wisconsin for professional excellence in health education.*

*This selection is from* Access to Health, *3rd ed.*

# Promoting Your Health

## THE KEYS TO

### CHAPTER OBJECTIVES

- Provide a definition of health, including the physical, social, mental, emotional, environmental, and spiritual components.
- Define wellness and characterize the continuum from illness to wellness.
- Provide examples of primary, secondary, and tertiary prevention.
- Discuss the health status of Americans in terms of life expectancy, chronic disease, risk factors, the environment, violence and abusive behaviors, mental health, and access to health care.
- Contrast quantity of life and quality of life.
- Identify factors that influence health status and provide examples of each.
- List the benefits of achieving optimal health.
- Discuss the role of beliefs, values, self-efficacy, and locus of control in making decisions about health.

# PERSONAL WELLNESS

## WHAT DO YOU THINK?

• Jennifer is an active college sophomore who watches her weight, tries to eat healthful foods and limits her alcohol consumption. She also claims to be an adult child of an alcoholic, dysfunctional family and has seen a counselor twice a week for the last four years. She goes to numerous support groups and likes to associate with people who have had similar experiences. Whenever she talks with someone, she always refers to her therapist or what her therapist or support group has said. She prefaces many of her conversations with new people with: "I'm an adult codependent child of an alcoholic and am recovering from a dysfunctional family." Whenever she has a problem, she blames her abusive father and codependent mother.

• John is 100 pounds overweight and does not like to work up a sweat exercising. He is a sensitive, caring young man with many close friends and a volunteer for many health-related agencies, helping people in need. He likes to be out enjoying nature and likes the inner peace he derives from a walk on the beach or a quiet night by

the campfire in the wilderness. Recently he was arrested for spiking trees in the Pacific Northwest, which promotes the preservation of old growth forests, but endangers the lives of loggers.

• Martha is a college freshman who has been a paraplegic since she was in a car accident at the age of 10. She is bright and extremely funny, and she gets along well with people around her. Martha spends her free time at the local homeless shelter, talking to people who she feels are much worse off than she is. She eats a diet extremely high in fat and cholesterol and says that if she's going to die, she might as well exit after eating what she wants.

Which of these people is the healthiest? Which is the most unhealthy? Based on your own definition of health, in what areas are they most "unhealthy"? What factors may have contributed to these problems? Among the people you know, who would you consider to be the most "healthy"? Why?

If someone were to ask you and your close friends to list the most important things in your lives, you might be surprised at the differences in the responses. Some of you would probably list family, love, financial security, significant others, and happiness. Others, including yourself, also might view health as one of the most important factors. Raised on a steady diet of clichés—"If you have your health, you have everything," "Be all that you can be," "Use it or lose it," "Just do it"—many people readily acknowledge that health is a desirable goal. But what does it really mean to be healthy? How healthy are *you?* What can you do to influence your own health? Why bother trying to change or improve your health status? Why all this fuss over health, anyway?

In this book, we attempt to answer these questions and many more in ways that are relevant for you. We will also help you to attain the basic knowledge and skills necessary to make the best health-related decisions in an area laden with conflicting research reports, deliberate attempts by some to mislead you into purchasing worthless products and services for their own financial gain, and an ever-changing, often overwhelming, mass of new information.

Attaining good health is no easy task. Each of us is a unique product of our genetic history, our family interactions, our experiences with friends and significant others, our sex, culture, race, socioeconomic status, and a host of other subtle and not-so-subtle influences. We are also influenced by the environment we navigate through and live in and by all the external political, economic, and social forces that help or hinder us along the way. Some of us may discover very few obstacles in our quest for optimum health and wellness. Others may come upon significant barriers, many of which may be difficult to overcome. There is no one recipe for obtaining health. As a unique individual with a unique blend of attitudes, beliefs, values, knowledge, and experiences, you must find your own best way to achieve health goals within your own special set of environmental conditions.

This text is designed to offer fundamental information that will provide an *Access to Health* that is consistent with who you are and what you want to become. Health is not an all-or-none proposition that is always totally within your control. But, there are many major and minor changes and adaptations that you can make in your behavior that may significantly impact on your risk factors. For those risk factors beyond your control, you must learn to react, adapt, and make optimum use of your existing resources to create the

*Your health status is the result of many influences, some of which are immediate, such as what you ate during the last week and how much you exercised. But other influences extend back to your family environment when you were a child. Warm and loving families contribute positively to the mental and emotional health of members not only when they are children but throughout their lives.*

best situation for yourself. By making informed, rational decisions, you will be able to improve both the quality and the quantity of your life.

# Finding the Right Health Vocabulary

## *Defining Health*

Definitions of the term **health** have changed dramatically over the years, evolving from its earliest definitions as synonymous with hygiene and sanitation, to the widely accepted definition by the World Health Organization (WHO) in the 1940s: "Health is the state of complete physical, mental and social well-being, not merely the absence of disease or infirmity."[1]

René Dubos later clarified the WHO definition of health by stating, "Health is a quality of life, involving social, emotional, mental, spiritual and biological fitness on the part of the individual, which results from adaptations to the environment."[2] Each of these definitions describes health as being multidimensional, including many different components and encompassing many different aspects of life. These components typically include the following:

- *Physical Health*—Includes such characteristics as body size and shape, sensory acuity, susceptibility to disease and disorders, body functioning, recuperative ability, and ability to perform certain tasks.
- *Social Health*—Refers to our interactions with others, our ability to adapt to various social situations, and our daily behaviors—the ability to have satisfying interpersonal relationships.
- *Mental Health*—Includes the ability to learn—our rational thinking component and intellectual capabilities.
- *Emotional Health*—Includes the ability to control emotions so that we feel comfortable expressing them when appropriate as well as expressing them appropriately—our feeling component; the ability to *not* express emotions either when it is inappropriate to do so or in an inappropriate manner.
- *Environmental Health*—An appreciation of our external environment and the role we play in preserving, protecting, and improving environmental conditions.
- *Spiritual Health*—May involve a belief in a higher form of being or a specified way of living prescribed by a particular religion, but it also extends to the feeling of being part of some wider form of existence—a sense of unity with the larger environment or a guiding sense of meaning or value. It includes a feeling of oneness with others, with nature, and with the larger environment. It also may include our ability to understand and express our own basic purpose in life, to feel that we are part of the greater spectrum of existence, to experience love, joy, pain,

*Health is neither static nor single dimensional. Healthy people understand that their health is not based merely on the absence of illness, but on an optimal level of physical, emotional, social, spiritual, and environmental responsiveness.*

sorrow, peace, contentment, and wonder over life's experiences, and to care about and respect all living things.

The current definition of health proposes a positive view that focuses on individual attempts to achieve optimum well-being within a realistic framework of individual potential. In Figure 1.1, health is described as a continuum from illness to optimum well-being. Where you are on this continuum may vary from day to day as you are buffeted by life's ups and downs. But if you persist in your attempts to change behaviors and reduce risk, the likelihood of remaining on the positive end of the continuum will be greatly improved. "Keeping Track of Yourself" will help you locate your own health status within the continuum.

Health relates to who we are as individuals, how we respond to others and the environment, what we value and perceive as important in our lives, and how we respond to the daily challenges of life. Health is an ever-changing dimension of our lives, in which we strive to be the best possible physical, emotional, social, spiritual, and environmentally sensitive beings we can. The current definition of health acknowledges that each of us must attempt to achieve this optimum level of being in a "sometimes hostile environment." Each of us must come to terms with the adversity and obstacles obstructing the way to optimal health in our own special way, focusing on our positive attributes whenever possible, changing those things about ourselves that we can change, and learning to recognize and deal with those that we cannot change.

---

**health** A quality of life, involving social, emotional, mental, and spiritual, biological fitness on the part of the individual, which results from adaptations to the environment.

Lifespan  ⟶

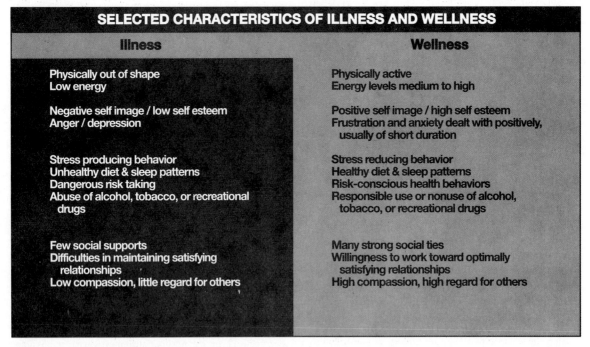

**SELECTED CHARACTERISTICS OF ILLNESS AND WELLNESS**

| Illness | Wellness |
|---|---|
| Physically out of shape<br>Low energy | Physically active<br>Energy levels medium to high |
| Negative self image / low self esteem<br>Anger / depression | Positive self image / high self esteem<br>Frustration and anxiety dealt with positively, usually of short duration |
| Stress producing behavior<br>Unhealthy diet & sleep patterns<br>Dangerous risk taking<br>Abuse of alcohol, tobacco, or recreational drugs | Stress reducing behavior<br>Healthy diet & sleep patterns<br>Risk-conscious health behaviors<br>Responsible use or nonuse of alcohol, tobacco, or recreational drugs |
| Few social supports<br>Difficulties in maintaining satisfying relationships<br>Low compassion, little regard for others | Many strong social ties<br>Willingness to work toward optimally satisfying relationships<br>High compassion, high regard for others |

*Figure 1.1    The continuum from illness to wellness.*

## Defining Wellness

**Wellness** is a term that has been popularized in the last decade. Like the modern definitions of health, *wellness* refers to an ever-changing movement toward optimum well-being. The two terms are not mutually exclusive. In fact, most health professionals agree that the term *health* no longer implies the mere absence of disease, but is instead a dynamic, lifelong process in which the physical, psychological, social, environmental, and spiritual dimensions are all considered essential. The closer we get to achieving the ideal level of functioning in and balance between each of the

# Promoting Your Health

## KEEPING TRACK OF YOURSELF

1. How would you define being healthy? Whom do you know who you think is very healthy? What criteria have you used to make this assessment?

2. How do you rate yourself on the wellness continuum shown in Figure 1.1? How many characteristics do you have that are listed on

the "Illness" side of the continuum? The "Wellness" side of the continuum?

3. What areas are your major weaknesses in terms of achieving optimal health? What things could you change now that might improve your health? Are there any barriers that might stop you from changing?

above dimensions, the closer we are to achieving **high-level wellness.**

The wellness continuum described in Figure 1.1 also illustrates the various dimensions of wellness. "Well" individuals take an honest look at their personal capabilities and limitations and make an effort to change those factors that are within their control. They try to achieve a *balance* in each of the wellness dimensions while trying to achieve a *positive wellness position* on an imaginary continuum. Many people believe that, like health, wellness can best be achieved by adopting a *holistic* approach in which the interaction and positive balance between mind, body, and spirit are emphasized. Persons on the illness and disability end of the continuum have failed to achieve this integration and balance and may be seriously deficient in one or more of the wellness dimensions. But the disability component of the wellness continuum does not imply that a physically handicapped person cannot achieve wellness. A handicapped person may in fact be very "healthy" in terms of relationships with others, level of self-confidence, environmental sensitivity, and overall attitude toward life. In contrast, a person who spends hours in front of a mirror lifting weights to perfect the size and shape of each muscle may be "unhealthy" in interactions with others, level of self-esteem, and attitude toward life. Although we often place a premium on physical attractiveness and external trappings, appearance is actually only one indicator of a person's overall health. Typically, the closer you get to your potential in the five components of health, the more "well" you will be. Both health and wellness are ongoing *active* processes, including those positive attitudes and behaviors that continually improve the quality of your life.

## Health Promotion: A New Focus

In discussions of health and wellness, terms such as **health promotion** are often used. Health promotion has been de-

fined as "any combination of educational, organizational, economic, and environmental supports for behaviors that are conducive to health." More recently, health promotion has also been viewed as the "science and art of helping people change their lifestyles to move toward a state of optimal health." Regardless of how it is defined, health promotion identifies healthy people who are at a certain risk for disease and attempts to motivate them to improve their health status. It encourages those whose health and wellness behaviors are already sound to maintain and improve them. But health promotion goes one step further by attempting to modify behaviors, attitudes, and values and introduce health-enhancing activities.

Whether we use the term *health* or *wellness,* it is commonly understood that we are talking about a person's overall reactions or responses to the nuances of living. Occasional dips into the ice cream bucket and other dietary slips, failure to exercise every day, flare-ups of anger, and other deviations from optimal behavior should not be viewed as major failures. Actually, our ability to recognize that we are imperfect beings, attempting to adapt in an imperfect world, is considered an indicator of individual well-being.

We must also remember to be tolerant of others who are attempting to improve their health. Rather than being "warriors against pleasure" in our zeal to reform or transform the health behaviors of others, we need to be supportive, under-

---

**wellness** An ever-changing movement toward optimum well-being, involving multiple dimensions of health.

**high-level wellness** The ideal level of functioning in and balance between each of the health and wellness dimensions.

**health promotion** Any combination of educational, organizational, economic, and environmental supports for behaviors that are conducive to health. Includes the science and art of helping people change their lifestyles to move to a state of optimal health.

standing, nonjudgmental, and positive in our interactions with others. **Health bashing**—intolerance or negative feelings, words, or actions toward people who fail to meet our own expectations of health—may indicate our own deficiencies in the psychological, social, and/or spiritual dimensions of the health continuum.

## *Prevention: The Key to Future Health*

Although a great deal can be done to promote healthy behaviors, a key goal of Americans today is the **prevention** of premature death and disability. Instead of relying on medical professionals to fix you when you're broken, the focus of prevention is on taking positive actions now, making the best health decisions to avoid even becoming sick. Getting immunized against diseases such as polio, never starting to smoke cigarettes, using condoms during sexual intercourse, and similar measures constitute **primary prevention**: taking actions to stop a health problem *before* it starts. Another form of prevention focuses on **secondary prevention,** or recognizing a health problem early in its development and intervening (also referred to as *intervention*) in the process to eliminate the underlying causes before serious illness develops. Attending health education seminars to help you cut down or stop cigarette intake is an example of secondary prevention.

Because so many deaths and illnesses are directly related to aspects of lifestyle such as tobacco use, obesity, alcohol abuse, sedentary activities, overeating (particularly fats), and so forth, primary and secondary prevention are essential to reducing the **incidence** (numbers of new cases) and **prevalence** (number of existing cases) of a disease or disability. (For a comparison of health indicators between blacks and whites, see "Disparities in Health: Real or Imagined?")

Unfortunately, health education and health promotion activities have historically been seriously underfunded by governmental officials, with less than 5 percent of the total health care expenditures in the United States focusing on these areas. Instead, governmental monies have been primarily allocated for research and **tertiary prevention,** treatment and/or rehabilitation efforts after a person has gotten sick. This form of prevention is not only the most costly; it is also less effective in promoting health than is any other prevention method.

If the government and the health care system are primarily interested in taking care of you only *after* you are sick, who is responsible for helping you remain well? Although many health agencies, programs, and public health prevention specialists are available to assist you, much of the responsibility for your health rests with you. As costs for treatment rise in the years ahead, people will have increasing difficulty in paying for them. What are your options? Clearly, the best option is for you to take action now that will help you to achieve your optimal health level and to make responsible and informed decisions so that you stay well in the future.

*Since the connection between a healthy lifestyle and the prevention of disease is clear, choosing an exercise or sports activity you enjoy is not only fun, but is also a positive step toward good health.*

---

**health bashing** Intolerance, negative feelings, and a general placing of total blame on the victim that is expressed in terms of feelings, words, or actions toward people who fail to meet our own expectations of health.

**prevention** Taking positive actions now to avoid even becoming sick.

**primary prevention** Taking prevention steps that stop a health problem before it starts. Getting vaccinations, using condoms during intercourse, and so forth are common examples.

**secondary prevention** Form of prevention that recognizes a health problem early in its development and intervenes early to address the underlying cause before serious illness develops.

**incidence** Numbers of new cases of a disease or disability.

**prevalence** Number of existing cases of a disease or disability.

**tertiary prevention** Prevention efforts that occur after a person has become sick or disabled. Efforts aimed at treatment (medical model) and/or rehabilitation.

# Multicultural Perspectives

## DISPARITIES IN HEALTH: REAL OR IMAGINED?

While current arguments rage over the best system of health care in the United States, it is useful to remember the vast differences between the haves and the have-nots when it comes to certain health indicators. Achieving a healthier America depends on significant improvements in the health of population groups now at higher risk of premature death, disease, and disability. For example:

| INDICATOR OF HEALTH | WHITE MALE | BLACK MALE | WHITE FEMALE | BLACK FEMALE |
|---|---|---|---|---|
| 1. Death rates for suicide* | 19.6 | 12.5 | 4.8 | 2.4 |
| 2. Death rate for homicide and legal intervention* | 8.1 | 61.5 | 2.8 | 12.5 |
| 3. Maternal mortality rates for complications during pregnancy and childbirth* | NA | NA | 5.4 | 18.6 |
| 4. Death rates for breast cancer* | NA | NA | 22.9 | 26.0 |
| 5. Life expectancy at birth | 72.6 | 66.0 | 79.3 | 74.5 |
| 6. Infant mortality rates** | 8.2 | 17.7 | 8.2 | 17.7 |
| 7. Years of potential life lost*** (Before age 65—all causes) | 6,525.1 | 14,186.5 | 3,403.8 | 7,431.5 |
| 8. Persons under 65 years of age without health care | 14% | 22% | 14% | 22% |
| 9. Death rates for human immunodeficiency* virus | 13.1 | 40.3 | 0.9 | 8.1 |
| 10. Death rates for heart disease* | 205.9 | 272.6 | 106.6 | 172.9 |
| 11. Death rates for cancer* | 157.2 | 230.6 | 110.7 | 130.9 |
| 12. Death rates for stroke* | 28.0 | 54.1 | 24.1 | 44.9 |
| 13. Self-reported poor/fair health status | 8.1% | 15.1% | 8.1% | 15.1% |
| 14. Age-adjusted percentage who are regular cigarette smokers | 27.6% | 32.2% | 23.9% | 20.4% |

*Age-adjusted rates per 100,000.

**Per 1,000 live births.

***Years of potential life lost are calculated by multiplying the number of deaths for each age group by the years of life lost (the difference between age 65, which is used as the standard, and the midpoint of the age group). For example, the death of a person aged 15–24 years counts as 45 years of potential life lost.

## WHAT DO YOU THINK?

1. Of all the factors listed, where do there appear to be the greatest disparities between whites and blacks? Which factors are worse for whites than for blacks? For females than for males? Why do you think these differences occur?

2. What factors do you believe have contributed to these disparities?

3. What actions might be taken to improve each of the above health indicators? Which ones may be modified through individual actions? Which ones must be modified through community (legislative, economic, environmental, health care system) measures? By both individual and community actions?

SOURCES: C. Hogue and M. Hargraves (1993), "Class, Race, and Infant Mortality in the United States," *American Journal of Public Health, 83*(1): 9–13. U.S. Department of Health and Human Services (1992), *Health: United States 1991 and Prevention Profile*, DHHS Publication No. (PHS) 92: 1232.

# HEALTH STATUS INDICATORS

## *How Healthy Are We?*

The health status of a group of people, a community, a state, a nation, or the world is often reduced to statistical data for descriptive and comparative purposes. In 1979, the surgeon-general of the United States observed that "the health of the people has never been better." In his assessment, he looked at statistical data on death rates from disease (particularly the childhood diseases), injuries, life expectancy, and other criteria. This information helped lay the foundation for *Healthy People 2000: The National Health Promotion and Disease Prevention Objectives for the United States.* (See Table 1.1.)

Although this and other documents provide an important source of information for health planners, they typically do not offer a complete assessment of our current health status. Data used in developing documents such as these typically do not assess levels of human suffering, emotional health, spiritual health, and other *quality-of-life* measures. Instead they often focus on *quantity-of-life* variables.

*Life Expectancy* By 1993, the average life expectancy (number of years a person is expected to live) was over 79.3 years for white females, 72.6 for white males, 74.5 for black females, and 66.0 for black males. Life expectancy for a white female born in 1990 exceeds 83.4 years, and a white male born in 1990 can expect to live to over 76 years.[3]

*Chronic Disease* During the 1980s, death rates for three of the leading causes of death among Americans declined: heart disease, stroke, and unintentional injuries. Infant mortality also decreased, and some childhood infectious diseases were nearly eliminated. These gains provide hope that the 1990s will see progress against other diseases. Heart disease continues to kill more people than all other diseases combined. Lung cancer deaths have increased steadily since the 1960s, and breast cancer deaths remain stubbornly high.

*Risk Factors* Since the 1970s we made dramatic improvements in high blood pressure detection and control, experienced declines in cigarette consumption, increased our awareness of cholesterol and dietary fats as risk factors, and reduced alcohol consumption and use of alcohol when driving.

## TABLE 1.1   HEALTHY PEOPLE 2000: SELECTED OBJECTIVES OF THE NATION FOR CHILDREN AND YOUNG ADULTS

1.  Reduce overweight to a prevalence of no more than 20 percent among people aged 20 and older.
2.  Reduce dietary-fat intake to an average of 30 percent of calories or less and average saturated-fat intake to less than 10 percent of calories. (Now nearly 40 percent for both.)
3.  Increase complex carbohydrate and fiber-containing foods in the diets of adults to 5 or more daily servings for vegetables (including legumes) and fruits, and to 6 or more daily servings for grain products. (Now slightly over 2 1/2 servings of vegetables and fruits and 3 of grains.)
4.  Reduce alcohol consumption by people aged 14 and older to an annual average of no more than 2 gallons of ethanol per person. (Was 2.50 gallons in 1989.)
5.  Reduce to no more than 30 percent the proportion of all pregnancies that are unintended. (During past 5 years, 56 percent of pregnancies were unintended, unwanted, or earlier than desired.)
6.  Reduce coronary heart disease deaths to no more than 100 per 100,000. (Now over 135 per 100,000.)
7.  Reduce the prevalence of mental disorders (exclusive of substance abuse) among adults to less than 10.7 percent. (Now over 12 percent.)
8.  Reduce homicides to no more than 7.2 per 100,000. (Now over 8.5 per 100,000.)
9.  Reduce deaths from work-related injuries to no more than 4 per 100,000. (Now more than 6 per 100,000.)
10. Reduce destructive periodontal disease to a prevalence of no more than 15 percent among people aged 35–44. (Now 24 percent or more.)
11. Reverse the rise in cancer deaths to achieve a rate of no more than 130 per 100,000. (Now over 133 per 100,000.)
12. Reduce rape and attempted rape of women aged 12–34 to no more than 225 per 100,000. (Now in excess of 400 per 100,000.)
13. Increase to at least 30 percent the proportion of people aged 6 and older who engage regularly, preferably daily, in light-to-moderate physical activity for at least 30 minutes per day. (Only 22 percent of people aged 18 and older are active 30 minutes or more 5 times per week; only 12 percent are active 7 days per week.)
14. Increase to at least 20 percent the proportion of people aged 18 and older who engage in vigorous physical activity that promotes the development and maintenance of cardiorespiratory fitness. (Now only about 12 percent.)
15. Reduce the proportion of college students engaging in recent occasions of heavy drinking of alcoholic beverages to no more than 32 percent. (Now over 42 percent.)
16. Increase to at least 50 percent the proportion of people with high blood pressure whose blood pressure is under control. (Now an estimated 26 percent for persons 18 and older.)
17. Reduce the mean serum cholesterol among adults to no more than 200 mg/dL. (Now over 215 mg/dL.)
18. Increase to at least 20 percent the proportion of people aged 18 and older who seek professional help in coping with personal and emotional problems. (Now slightly over 13 percent.)
19. Increase to at least 60 percent the proportion of sexually active, unmarried women aged 15–19 whose partners used a condom at last sexual intercourse. (Now approximately 30 percent.)

SOURCE: *Healthy People 2000: The National Health Promotion and Disease Prevention Objectives for the United States*

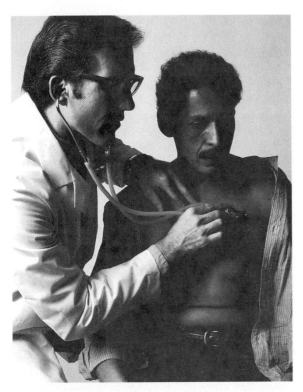

*Healthy people in our society feel committed to increasing access to good health care for themselves and also for all Americans.*

***The Environment*** During the last decade, there has been increasing concern about toxic substances, solid waste, acid rain, the ozone level, dying oceans, global warming, polluted water supplies, food supplies, and many other life-threatening conditions.

***Violence and Abusive Behaviors*** Child abuse, spouse abuse, and other forms of intrafamilial violence threaten millions of Americans each year. The United States ranks first among industrialized nations in violent deaths. Taken together, suicides and homicides constitute the fourth leading cause of potential years of life lost. Suicide is the third leading cause of death among people aged 15–24, and homicide is the leading cause of death for African Americans aged 15–34.

***Mental Health*** Depression has been described as the "common cold of mental illness," affecting at least 5 percent of the population at any given time.

- Between 10 and 12 percent of children and adolescents suffer from mental disorders, including autism, attention-deficit disorder, hyperactivity, and depression.
- Over 23 million adults are severely incapacitated by mental disorders, not including substance abuse, and more than twice that number have experienced at least one diagnosable mental problem.

***Access to Health Care*** Nearly 25 percent of the American public is uninsured or underinsured, and these numbers are increasing daily. Millions of Americans need medical care or will need it in the near future and will be shut out of the system. The number of homeless, undernourished, and mentally ill persons continues to grow in direct proportion to economic and social service problems. Some critics argue that we are moving toward a society of haves and have-nots when it comes to health and well-being. While one group focuses on whether to join a health club, another group wonders if they will be safe sleeping under the bushes in the park. While one group fastidiously reads labels on food products to ensure that they don't consume too much saturated fat, another group wonders where their next meal may come from. The dichotomy between a middle-class perspective on health and the "survival" health status of many other Americans and people throughout the world is reason for growing concern.

By definition, a truly healthy person possesses a sense of both individual and social responsibility. Rather than focusing on their own personal health, genuinely healthy people are concerned about others and the greater environment. This concern translates into taking actions designed to help them live a high-quantity and high-quality life, as well as to help others who are less fortunate.

# IMPROVING YOUR HEALTH STYLE

## *Benefits of Achieving Optimal Health*

Table 1.2 provides an overview of the leading causes of death in the United States today. Risks for each of these leading killers have been reduced significantly by practicing specific lifestyle patterns—for example, consuming a diet low in saturated fat and cholesterol, exercising regularly, reducing sodium, managing stress, and other practices. Lifestyle and individual behavior are believed to account for over 58 percent of good health (see Figure 1.2). Heredity, access to health care, and the environment are other factors that influence health status. While you can't change your genetic history, and improving your environment and the health care system is difficult, you can influence your future health status by the behaviors you choose today.

Reduction in risk for major diseases is just one of the benefits that you can hope to achieve. Among the others are:

- Improved quality of life, in addition to increased longevity
- Increased capacity for pleasure
- Greater zest for living
- Greater energy levels, improved productivity, more interest in having fun
- Improved self-image

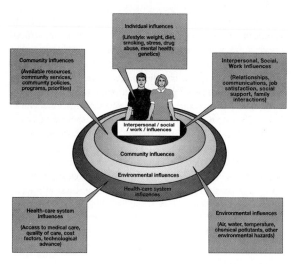

**Figure 1.2** *Factors that influence your health status.*

- Improved immunological functioning with enhanced ability to fight off infections
- Enhanced relationships with others due to better communication and "quality" time spent with others
- Improved ability to control and manage stress
- Enhanced levels of self-efficacy, more personal control of your life

- Reduced reliance on the health-care system, increased ability to engage in self-care, health-enhancing behaviors, lower health-care costs
- Adding life to years, as well as adding years to life
- Improved cardiovascular functioning
- Increased muscle tone, strength, flexibility, and endurance, resulting in improved physical appearance, performance, and self-esteem
- More positive outlook on life, fewer negative thoughts, ability to view life as challenging and negative events as a potential for growth
- Improved self-confidence and ability to understand and reach out to others
- Improved environmental sensitivity, responsibility, and behaviors
- Greater appreciation for nature and our place in the larger frame of existence.
- Enhanced levels of spiritual health, awareness, and feelings of oneness with self, others, and the greater environment

Although mounting evidence indicates that there are significant benefits to being healthy, many people find it difficult to become and stay healthy. Rather than realistically assessing their lifestyles, they tend to make excuses for their behavior.

| TABLE 1.2 LEADING CAUSES OF DEATH IN THE UNITED STATES FOR ALL RACES BY AGE | | | |
|---|---|---|---|
| **All Ages and Races Combined** | **1–4 Years** | **5–14 Years** | **15–24 Years** |
| 1. Diseases of the heart | 1. Accidents and adverse effects | 1. Accidents and adverse effects | 1. Accidents and adverse effects |
| 2. Malignant neoplasms | 2. Congenital anomalies | 2. Malignant neoplasms | 2. Homicide & legal intervention |
| 3. Cerebrovascular diseases | 3. Malignant neoplasms | 3. Homicide and legal intervention | 3. Suicide |
| 4. Accidents and adverse effects (includes motor vehicle and other accidents and adverse effects) | 4. Homicide and legal intervention | 4. Congenital anomalies | 4. Malignant neoplasms |
| | 5. Diseases of the heart | 5. Diseases of the heart | 5. Diseases of the heart |
| 5. Chronic obstructive pulmonary diseases and allied conditions (COPD) | 6. Pneumonia and influenza | 6. Suicide | 6. Human immunodeficiency virus |
| 6. Pneumonia and influenza | 7. Certain conditions originating in the perinatal period | 7. Pneumonia and influenza | 7. Congenital anomalies |
| 7. Diabetes mellitus | | 8. Chronic obstructive pulmonary disease | 8. Pneumonia and influenza |
| 8. Suicide | 8. Human immunodeficiency syndrome | 9. Benign neoplasms, carcinoma in situ, and neoplasms of uncertain nature | 9. Cerebrovascular disease |
| 9. Chronic liver disease and cirrhosis | 9. Meningitis | | 10. Chronic obstructive pulmonary disease |
| 10. Homicide and legal intervention | 10. Septicemia | 10. Cerebrovascular disease | |
| 11. Human immunodeficiency virus infection | | | |
| 12. Nephritis, nephrotic syndrome, and nephrosis | | | |
| 13. Atherosclerosis | | | |
| 14. Septicemia | | | |
| 15. Certain conditions originating in the perinatal period. | | | |

SOURCE: National Center for Health Statistics (January 7, 1992), *Monthly Vital Statistics Report: Final Mortality, 40,* (8), 1–51.

*By the simple act of choosing to eat nutritious and attractively served foods in a relaxing environment, people increase their chances for a long and healthy life.*

Typically, sleeping seven to eight hours a day, eating a nutritious breakfast, not eating between meals, maintaining proper weight, not smoking cigarettes, limiting intake of alcohol, and exercising regularly are recognized as essential components of a long and healthy life. These commonsense recommendations have withstood the test of time, remaining unsurpassed as sound health advice. How close do we come to meeting these goals? Table 1.3 offers an overview of how

well we are doing in several of these key areas. This information indicates many areas in which people can make changes to improve the quality of their lives.

Change is not easy. In our culture, it is normal to eat when we're not hungry, to be overweight, to take the elevator instead of the stairs, and to drive around the parking lot for five minutes to avoid a one-minute walk. We don't relax because we don't know how. We eat high-fat foods because they were a part of our upbringing. We don't exercise because exercise is often equated with work. Health behaviors are learned behaviors that are encouraged by both peers and family. Decisions to change old, negative thinking patterns or behaviors take conscious effort, planning, and an awareness of individual barriers to success.

## Factors Influencing Health Changes

Mark Twain once said that "habit is habit, and not to be flung out the window by anyone, but coaxed downstairs a step at a time." Changing negative behavior patterns into healthy ones is often a time-consuming and difficult process. The chances of success are better when people make gradual changes that give them time to unlearn negative patterns and substitute positive ones. We have not yet developed a foolproof method for effectively changing people's behavior, but we do know that certain behaviors can benefit both individu-

| TABLE 1.2 LEADING CAUSES OF DEATH IN THE UNITED STATES FOR ALL RACES BY AGE | | |
|---|---|---|
| **25–44 Years** | **45–64 Years** | **65 Years +** |
| 1. Accidents and adverse effects | 1. Malignant neoplasms | 1. Diseases of the heart |
| 2. Malignant neoplasms | 2. Diseases of the heart | 2. Malignant neoplasms |
| 3. Human immunodeficiency virus | 3. Cerebrovascular diseases | 3. Cerebrovascular accidents |
| 4. Diseases of the heart | 4. Accidents and adverse effects | 4. Chronic obstructive pulmonary disease |
| 5. Suicide | 5. Chronic obstructive pulmonary disease | 5. Pneumonia and influenza |
| 6. Homicide and legal intervention | 6. Chronic liver disease and cirrhosis | 6. Diabetes melioidosis |
| 7. Chronic liver disease and cirrhosis | 7. Diabetes mellitus | 7. Accidents and adverse effects |
| 8. Cerebrovascular diseases | 8. Suicide | 8. Atherosclerosis |
| 9. Pneumonia and influenza | 9. Pneumonia and influenza | 9. Nephritis, nephrotic syndrome, and nephrosis |
| | 10. Human immunodeficiency virus | 10. Septicemia |

**TABLE 1.3**
**SELECTED PERSONAL HEALTH BEHAVIORS IN THE UNITED STATES, 1989 (BY PERCENTAGE)**

| Health Behavior | Sleeps 6 Hours or Less | Never Eats Breakfast | Snacks Every Day | Less Physically Active | 5 or More Alcoholic Drinks a Day | Current Smoker | 30% or More Above Ideal Weight |
|---|---|---|---|---|---|---|---|
| All persons | 22.0 | 24.3 | 39.0 | 16.4 | 37.5 | 30.1 | 13.1 |
| **Age** | | | | | | | |
| 18–29 | 19.8 | 30.4 | 42.2 | 17.1 | 54.4 | 31.9 | 7.5 |
| 30–44 | 24.3 | 30.1 | 41.4 | 18.3 | 39.0 | 34.5 | 13.6 |
| 45–64 | 22.7 | 21.4 | 37.9 | 15.3 | 24.6 | 31.6 | 18.1 |
| 65 + | 20.4 | 7.5 | 30.7 | 13.5 | 12.2 | 16.0 | 13.2 |
| **Gender** | | | | | | | |
| Male | 22.7 | 25.2 | 40.7 | 16.5 | 49.3 | 32.6 | 12.1 |
| Female | 21.4 | 23.6 | 37.5 | 16.3 | 23.3 | 27.8 | 13.7 |
| **Race** | | | | | | | |
| White | 21.3 | 24.5 | 39.4 | 16.7 | 38.3 | 29.6 | 12.4 |
| Black | 27.8 | 23.6 | 37.2 | 13.9 | 29.3 | 34.9 | 18.7 |
| Other | 21.4 | 21.5 | 32.6 | 16.5 | 33.3 | 24.8 | 6.7 |

SOURCE: *Statistical Abstract of the United States 1989,* 109th ed. (Washington, DC: U.S. Government Printing Office, 1989).

als and society as a whole. To understand how the process of behavior change works, we must first identify specific behavior patterns and attempt to understand the reasons for them.

Unfortunately, the development or maintenance of health behaviors is not necessarily a linear model in which we can assume that if we have knowledge, our attitudes and behaviors will automatically change. Knowledgeable people would not then behave in ways detrimental to their health. The reasons people behave in unhealthy ways, despite known risks, are complex and not easily understood. Health researchers have studied health behaviors for decades and continue to analyze the reasons that one person chooses to act responsibly while another ignores obvious health risks.

Figure 1.3 identifies the major factors that influence behavior and behavior-change decisions. These factors can be divided into three general categories: predisposing, enabling, and reinforcing factors.

- *Predisposing factors* are those things we bring to the situation, such as our life experiences, knowledge, cultural and ethnic inheritance, and current beliefs and values.
- *Enabling factors* are factors such as skills or abilities, physical, emotional, and mental capabilities, resources and accessible facilities that make our health decisions more convenient or more difficult. For example, if you like to

swim for exercise but the only available pool is inaccessible, you might be less likely to go swimming than if the pool were located nearby. Although it is easy to use negative enabling factors as excuses for not behaving in a positive manner, it is often possible to devise strategies for dealing with difficult circumstances.

- *Reinforcing factors* relate to the presence or absence of support, encouragement, or discouragement that significant people in your life bring to a situation. For example, if you decide to stop smoking and members of your family smoke in your presence, you might be tempted to start smoking again. Internal reinforcement that comes from the *self-talk* you give yourself is another key reinforcing factor.

The manner in which you reward or punish yourself for your own successes and failures may affect your chances of adopting healthy behaviors. Learning to accept small failures and to concentrate on your successes may foster further successes. Berating yourself because you binged on ice cream, argued with a friend, or didn't jog because it was raining might create an internal environment in which failure becomes almost inevitable. Telling yourself that you're worth the extra time and effort and giving yourself a pat on the back for small accomplishments is an often overlooked aspect in positive behavioral change.

Although a variety of factors influence our decisions, each of us decides either consciously or unconsciously to behave in a particular manner. Our decision-making process is motivated by a complex interaction between our values, beliefs, and selected factors in our social environment, as discussed earlier.

When we make decisions about our health, our underlying beliefs play a role. Proponents of the *Health Belief Model* note that people are more likely to alter a given behavior if several conditions are met (see Chapter 2).

An example of the Health Belief Model would be a college student who is extremely overweight but, although he has suffered several episodes of chest pain, does not believe that he is old enough to be at risk. After a brief jog he passes out, only to wake up in the emergency room. The doctor tells him that he has had a mild heart attack and that some blockage has been detected in his coronary arteries. He is warned that unless he loses 80 pounds, lowers his intake of saturated fat, and begins to exercise regularly, he faces major coronary bypass surgery or death in the months ahead. The student goes on a medically supervised diet, loses weight, and starts an aerobic exercise program. Clearly, he responded to the risk, realized the consequences, and saw the benefits of changing his behavior.

*Mentally stimulating activities like collecting stamps or watching baseball or going to the movies can contribute to mental and emotional health at any age.*

**Figure 1.3**
*Influences on your health decisions and behaviors.*

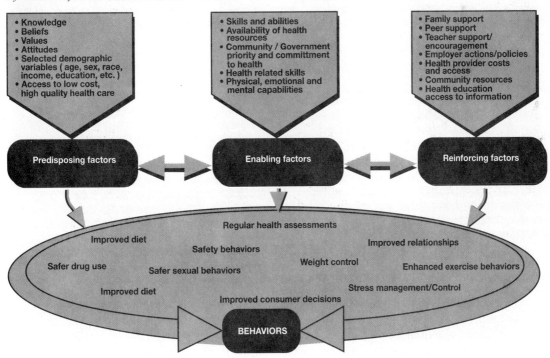

# Promoting Your Health

## FACT OR FALLACY? MAKING SENSE OF HEALTH REPORTS

One of the most difficult problems you may have when trying to *inform* yourself about health issues is in determining what to believe and what not to believe out of all the conflicting claims about various health risks. Is oat bran really of any help in warding off cardiovascular disease? Is sodium as bad as we once thought it was? Does a glass of wine a day keep the doctor away? If you're puzzled by it all, you are not alone. Although no 100 percent foolproof methods exist for determining the merits of all health claims, there are some basic questions you can ask when reading reports of new findings about foods, products, services, or behaviors. Acquiring the analytical skills necessary to critique such claims and make prudent behavioral changes will help ensure that the actions you take are the best ones for you.

**1.**  *What is the source of the information?* **Finding out where the study was done and who paid for the research will often uncover possible unreliable or biased research objectives. Data supplied by independent investigators working for agencies that do not have a vested interest in the outcome may reduce the potential threat of error.**

**2.**  *Who are the authors of the study? Who conducted the research?* **If possible, try to discover who the researchers themselves were. What were their credentials for doing the research? Are they working at a reputable institution or agency? Have they done similar research in these areas previously?**

**3.**  *What research methods were used in the study?* **Familiarity with basic research terms and principles of sound research methods may help you determine the merit of a study. You should consider the following:**
*Sample size:* **Always look at the numbers of people involved in the study that supposedly proved a health effect. Studying 100 people in one geographical area may provide some interesting preliminary data on a particular subject, but it would not be enough to**

generalize the findings to everyone. Obviously, the more people participating in the study, the better, particularly if the researchers are generalizing their findings to the population. While some studies using small numbers of subjects may be valid, certain research protocols must be followed before this is true.
*Subjects:* **How were the subjects selected? From volunteers, by random selection into groups, and so forth? Were both men and women in the group? What were the ages of participants? Were persons from different races, regions, and so forth, represented in the study group?**
*Study design:* **Does the study have a** *control group* **(a group of people with similar characteristics but who did not receive the treatment being used to study a given effect)? Were adequate controls for inherent differences in race, age, gender, socioeconomic factors, and so forth, taken into consideration? Were subjects from different groups** *matched* **to try to equalize potential confounding effects? Did all subjects think that they were receiving a scientifically tested treatment? (The** *placebo effect* **is the subject's tendency to experience a desired effect because he or she thinks that a certain medical or other treatment will help.)**
*Source of information:* **Although you may not have access to all of the preceding information, try to note where the article or report was published. Consider the following sources:**
*Tabloids.* **These news headlines are usually found at the checkout lines in grocery stores. Typical headlines might include: "Man mates with alien woman and produces new race," "Baby raised by dinosaur found in the jungles of Africa." Suffice to say, you should be skeptical of health "facts" found in these formats.**
*News Magazines/Newspapers.* **Weekly or daily news magazines or newspapers may have a "sensational" twist in their news reporting. Often, they have interesting articles written by health writers who are not necessarily**

**FACT OR FALLACY? MAKING SENSE OF HEALTH REPORTS** *(cont.)*

knowledgeable about the subject. They may have a one-sided approach to an issue, or provide inaccurate or incomplete information. Although you may find out some very good information in these formats, it is best to dig deeper before coming to any health conclusions.

*Self-Help Books.* Reader beware. In the effort to "make a buck" in the health arena, many self-made authorities have been successful in getting people to buy their books. Keep in mind that the key factor here is "selling" and that publishers often do not verify facts in these books. Just because something is published in a book doesn't make it accurate or reliable! Stick to reputable authors with degrees or academic training in the area and be critical of what is said. Check their statements against textbooks in the field, or call health professionals in your area to verify particular points.

*Professional Journals.* Although sometimes more difficult to read, *refereed journals (peer-reviewed)* are perhaps the most reliable sources of information. A refereed article is reviewed very carefully by at least three experts in the field before it is accepted for publication. Peer reviewing helps to ensure reliability and credibility. Do not confuse an *edited* journal with a peer-reviewed journal. Edited journals have paid editors who review the work for style, and so forth, but they may have no background to deal with content. Most peer-reviewed journals publish guidelines for submitting manuscripts to their journal. These guidelines typically give information about the peer review process. Most college and university journals are probably peer-reviewed.

*Values* are also significant factors in determining behavior change. People may be more likely to engage in a weight-training or fitness program if they believe that these activities will improve other aspects of their social lives or interpersonal relationships. Selected *cues to action* may provide those underlying stimuli that motivate people to take aggressive, firm action to change a given behavior. Finding out that her total cholesterol level is over 300 may be a cue that influences one person to reduce her saturated-fat intake. Another person may read an article about the harmful effects of high cholesterol levels and reduce cholesterol intake. Remember that each person's cue to action may be different. Determining which ones work for you is a key aspect of any behavior change strategy.

If you believe health to be a result of factors beyond your control, you will not take personal responsibility for your health. A certain sense of internal control over your health coupled with a high degree of confidence in your ability is the ideal situation for positive health-behavior change. If you believe that you can change negative health behavior (self-efficacy) and that your actions will make a difference in your health (health locus of control), positive change becomes much more likely.

**Readiness** is the state of being that precedes behavioral change. People who are ready to change (see Figure 1.4) possess the attitudes, skills, and internal and external resources that make change a likely reality. To be ready for change, certain basic steps and adjustments in thinking must occur.

## CHOICES FOR CHANGE

Various behavioral theories have been studied as they relate to health. Ideas and concepts such as self-efficacy, locus of control, and health locus of control are becoming more widely understood. **Self-efficacy** refers to a person's appraisal of his or her own ability to change or to accomplish a particular task or behavior. **Locus of control** refers to a person's perceptions of forces or factors that control individual destiny. **Health locus of control** focuses specifically on those factors that relate to health actions and activities. These constructs influence how we view ourselves and also how we behave or seek to change behaviors.

**self-efficacy** Refers to a person's appraisal of his or her own ability to change or accomplish a particular task or behavior.

**locus of control** Personal perceptions of forces or factors that control individual destiny. Some people are more internally controlled and believe that they are powerful instruments for change in their situation. Others are more externally controlled and believe that external forces beyond their control dictate their behaviors.

**health locus of control** Locus-of-control factors relating specifically to health-related actions/activities.

**readiness** State of being that precedes a behavioral change.

*Being able to express feelings and talk through problems with friends is part of good health.*

## What Do You Need to Know to Change?

- *Facts and information about topics and issues in health.* You may have many questions about various issues regarding your health status. How much and what types of fat are O.K. in your diet? What are the best body-toning exercises you can do to achieve a given result? How can you improve your weak interpersonal communication skills? How can you have an intimate sexual relationship and avoid STDs? Knowing where to go for accurate information and how to make good decisions based on sometimes conflicting reports are important first steps in being ready to change. The box "Fact or Fallacy" will help you become a more cautious, skilled reader of health materials. Although there is a tremendous amount of information available, using the best resources and thinking critically will permit you to make the best choices.

- *Important information about your own health.* People seldom change their behaviors until they believe that they are really at risk or that the perceived benefits are worth their efforts. Self-awareness is usually created by the process of *self-assessment* or *self-appraisal.* One method used extensively by individuals, organizations, health-care professionals, and educational institutions is the *Health Risk Appraisal (HRA).* The U.S. Department of Health and Human Services questionnaire gives you a basic indicator of your overall health status and the areas in which you may need improvement (see box on pages 17 to 19). Some HRAs are much more complex and use actual physical tests of blood chemistry, cholesterol counts, urinalysis, and other measures of health status combined with pencil-and-paper-questions to determine health. Regardless of the type of instrument used, such analyses provide a starting point. If you have high cholesterol or high blood pressure, or if you have a family risk for breast cancer, these may be key

areas to focus on. Once you understand the health facts and they become personally relevant, you may value change more. Valuing change and seeing it as beneficial may encourage you to believe that change is good, right, and important. In addition, such information may strengthen your own beliefs in your ability to change (self-efficacy).

- *Knowing how to choose from options.* Understanding the facts, valuing the facts, and believing in the importance and likelihood of change are essential elements of basic change. But, unless you know *how* to go about change, your efforts may be futile. Knowing what your resources are, practicing certain optional health-related skills and behaviors, and developing the ability to continue a behavior are the next steps in initiating and continuing change. If you start jogging and you don't like it or can't stick to it, try swimming or another activity rather than giving up.

- *Making the commitment to change.* Because behaviors are learned responses that often develop into subconscious rituals and procedures, they become a significant part of a person's identity. Changing these behaviors is difficult. In general, the younger you are, the less likely that these behavioral patterns will have become deeply ingrained and the better your chances for change.

*Figure 1.4*
*The steps and stages in becoming ready for behavioral change.*

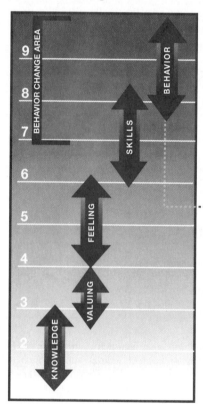

# Promoting Your Health

## U.S. DEPARTMENT OF HEALTH AND HUMAN SERVICES HEALTH BEHAVIOR QUESTIONNAIRE

This is not a pass-fail test. Its purpose is simply to tell you how likely your behavior is to keep you healthy. The behaviors covered in the test are recommended for most Americans. Some of them may not apply to persons with certain chronic diseases or handicaps. Such persons may require special instructions from their physicians or other health professionals.

You will find that the test has six sections: smoking, alcohol and drugs, eating habits, exercise and fitness, stress control, and safety. Complete one section at a time by circling the number corresponding to the answer that best describes your behavior (2, 3, or 4 for "Almost Always," 1 for "Sometimes," and 0 for "Almost Never"). Then add the numbers you have circled to determine your score for that section. Write the score on the line provided at the end of each section. The highest score you can get for each section is 10.

### CIGARETTE SMOKING

If you never smoke, enter a score of 10 for this section and go to the next section, "Alcohol and Drugs."

| | Almost Always | Sometimes | Almost Never |
|---|---|---|---|
| 1. I avoid smoking cigarettes. | 2 | 1 | 0 |
| 2. I smoke only low-tar and low-nicotine cigarettes, *or* I smoke a pipe or cigars only. | 2 | 1 | 0 |

Cigarette Smoking Score: _____

### ALCOHOL AND DRUGS

| | Almost Always | Sometimes | Almost Never |
|---|---|---|---|
| 1. I avoid drinking alcoholic beverages, *or* I drink no more than one or two drinks a day. | 4 | 1 | 0 |
| 2. I avoid using alcohol or other drugs (especially illegal drugs) as a way of handling stressful situations or the problems in my life. | 2 | 1 | 0 |
| 3. I am careful not to drink alcohol when taking certain medicines (for example, medicine for sleeping, pain, colds, and allergies). | 2 | 1 | 0 |
| 4. I read and follow the label directions when using prescribed and over-the-counter drugs. | 2 | 1 | 0 |

Alcohol and Drugs Score: _____

### EATING HABITS

| | Almost Always | Sometimes | Almost Never |
|---|---|---|---|
| 1. I eat a variety of foods each day, such as fruits and vegetables, whole grain breads and cereals, lean meats, dairy products, dry peas and beans, and nuts and seeds. | 4 | 1 | 0 |
| 2. I limit the amount of fat, saturated fat, and cholesterol I eat (including fat on meats, eggs, butter, cream, shortenings, and organ meats such as liver). | 2 | 1 | 0 |
| 3. I limit the amount of salt I eat by cooking with only small amounts, not adding salt at the table, and avoiding salty snacks. | 2 | 1 | 0 |
| 4. I avoid eating too much sugar (especially frequent snacks of sticky candy or soft drinks). | 2 | 1 | 0 |

Eating Habits Score: _____

## HEALTH BEHAVIOR QUESTIONNAIRE

| EXERCISE AND FITNESS | Almost Always | Sometimes | Almost Never |
|---|---|---|---|
| 1. I maintain a desired weight, avoiding overweight and underweight. | 3 | 1 | 0 |
| 2. I do vigorous exercises for fifteen to thirty minutes at least three times a week (examples include running, swimming, brisk walking). | 3 | 1 | 0 |
| 3. I do exercises that enhance my muscle tone for fifteen to thirty minutes at least three times a week (examples include yoga and calisthenics). | 2 | 1 | 0 |
| 4. I use part of my leisure time participating in individual, family, or team activities that increase my level of fitness (such as gardening, bowling, golf, and baseball). | 2 | 1 | 0 |

Exercise and Fitness Score: _____

| STRESS CONTROL | | | |
|---|---|---|---|
| 1. I have a job or do other work that I enjoy. | 2 | 1 | 0 |
| 2. I find it easy to relax and express my feelings freely. | 2 | 1 | 0 |
| 3. I recognize early, and prepare for, events or situations likely to be stressful for me. | 2 | 1 | 0 |
| 4. I have close friends, relatives, or others whom I can talk to about personal matters and call on for help when needed. | 2 | 1 | 0 |
| 5. I participate in group activities (such as church and community organizations) or hobbies that I enjoy. | 2 | 1 | 0 |

Stress Control Score: _____

| SAFETY | | | |
|---|---|---|---|
| 1. I wear a seat belt while riding in a car. | 2 | 1 | 0 |
| 2. I avoid driving while under the influence of alcohol and other drugs. | 2 | 1 | 0 |
| 3. I obey traffic rules and the speed limit when driving. | 2 | 1 | 0 |
| 4. I am careful when using potentially harmful products or substances (such as household cleaners, poisons, and electrical devices). | 2 | 1 | 0 |
| 5. I avoid smoking in bed. | 2 | 1 | 0 |

Safety Score: _____

## HEALTH BEHAVIOR QUESTIONNAIRE

### YOUR HEALTH STYLE SCORES

After you have figured your score for each of the six sections, circle the number in each column that matches your score for that section of the test.

| Cigarette Smoking | Alcohol and Drugs | Eating Habits | Exercise and Fitness | Stress Control | Safety |
|---|---|---|---|---|---|
| 10 | 10 | 10 | 10 | 10 | 10 |
| 9 | 9 | 9 | 9 | 9 | 9 |
| 8 | 8 | 8 | 8 | 8 | 8 |
| 7 | 7 | 7 | 7 | 7 | 7 |
| 6 | 6 | 6 | 6 | 6 | 6 |
| 5 | 5 | 5 | 5 | 5 | 5 |
| 4 | 4 | 4 | 4 | 4 | 4 |
| 3 | 3 | 3 | 3 | 3 | 3 |
| 2 | 2 | 2 | 2 | 2 | 2 |
| 1 | 1 | 1 | 1 | 1 | 1 |
| 0 | 0 | 0 | 0 | 0 | 0 |

Remember, there is no total score for this test. Consider each section separately. You are trying to identify aspects of your lifestyle that you can improve in order to be healthier and to reduce the risk of illness. So let's see what your scores reveal.

### WHAT YOUR SCORES MEAN TO YOU

*Scores of 9 and 10* Excellent! Your answers show that you are aware of the importance of this area to your health. More important, you are putting your knowledge to work for you by practicing good health habits. As long as you continue to do so, this area should not pose a serious health risk. It's likely that you are setting an example for your family and friends to follow. Although you received a very high score on this part of the test, you may want to consider other areas where your scores could be improved.

*Scores of 6 to 8* Your health practices in this area are good, but there is room for improvement. Look again at the items you answered with a "Sometimes" or an "Almost Never." What changes can you make to improve your score? Even a small change can often help you achieve better health.

*Scores of 3 to 5* Your health risks are showing! Would you like more information about the risks you are facing and about why it is important for you to change these behaviors? Perhaps you need help in deciding how to make the changes you desire. In either case, help is available in this book.

*Scores of 0 to 2* You may be taking serious and unnecessary risks with your health. Perhaps you are not aware of the risks and what to do about them. In this book you will find the information and help you need to improve your scores and, thereby, your health.

SOURCE: U.S. Department of Health and Human Services, *Health Style: A Self Test* (Washington, D.C.: Public Health Service, 1981).

# T A K I N G   C H A R G E
## P E R S O N A L   A N D   C O M M U N I T Y   A C T I O N

Although people are more concerned today about health issues than at any time in our nation's history, many of us feel that we can do little to reduce our own risk. We find it even more difficult to bring about change at the community level. Following are suggestions that may improve your own health status and that of those around you.

### MANAGING YOUR PERSONAL HEALTH BEHAVIORS

- *Are you really ready to do whatever it takes to change?* Assess your readiness by analyzing where you are in terms of a readiness scale.

- Complete a personal health history, including individual risks from your genetics, inheritance, lifestyle, environment, and health care system. Prioritize those that *your behavior* can have an impact on, either short- or long-term.

- Develop a short-term plan of action to reduce your immediate risks, and begin to control your long-term risks. Improve your diet, increase your fitness levels, avoid harmful substances, improve your social skills, help others, consider spiritual issues more often, take time to control stress, get adequate amounts of sleep, practice self-care activities, use the health care system wisely, practice responsible sexual behaviors, etc.

- *Decide how things will improve or be different in your life as a result of the change.* What will really be different if you succeed? How much will the ultimate change matter to your relationships? Your health? Your self-concept? How important are these things to you?

- *Listen to the things that you are telling yourself (self-talk) that are affecting your emotional response to change.* Are your past experiences, values, and attitudes causing you to make unrealistic excuses or to defend your past behaviors? Are you making this change because you really want to, or are you being pressured by others?

- *Assess your resources.* What things will help you achieve your goals? Will friends, community support groups, or other networks help you in your efforts to change?

- *Determine what things have previously stood in the way of reaching your goals.* What are the barriers or blocking agents? Which of these can you avoid?

- *Establish priorities for change.* Determine what things are most important for you to change now. Which is *the* most important factor? The *next* most important?

- *Develop a plan of action.* Break the parts of your action into small components or objectives. Tackle each component one at a time, being careful not to try too many changes at a time.

- *Determine how you will know when you have satisfactorily met your goal.* How will you evaluate success? Will you evaluate success by a series of small objectives to be met or only in terms of the ultimate goal? For example, people who begin an exercise program often find it helpful to start with a graduated program that will enable them to reach their goal after a specified period of time (say, one month). This is often easier than saying "By this time next year, I will be running the Boston Marathon."

- *Determine what things will keep you going.* What will help you maintain the behavior change? The most difficult part of any behavior change strategy is to be able to continue for prolonged periods of time.

- If you have already tried several of the items on this list and failed, don't be discouraged. The problems you have encountered may be due to influences you've never really thought about, or to a lack of support or encouragement. Sometimes people will even help you fail—by sabotaging your diet, for example, or encouraging you to take another drink. Positive reinforcement is essential.

### MANAGING YOUR COMMUNITY HEALTH BEHAVIORS

- Act responsibly to preserve the environment. Consume fewer resources, use fewer prepackaged products, *reuse, recycle, and reduce consumption* whenever possible. Water, air, natural resources, and animals are important legacies, and each of us can play a significant role in protecting them.

- Analyze what is going on in your school, your community, your state, and the nation. *Read, discuss, and develop opinions* about the critical health issues likely to have an impact on you, your parents, your friends, and society in general.

- Listen to the opinions of your school administrators, your state elected officials, and your national elected representatives. If an important health issue is being considered, *write or call* these officials and let them know how you feel about the issues. *Become involved* in city government and in social services, particularly when the health of others is likely to be affected.

- *Vote* for elected officials whose policies, rhetoric, and past histories have indicated that they support improvements in health care, environmental issues, education, minority health, and other critical issues facing the nation.

- *Purchase* products and services from companies that have proven records of protecting the environment, providing safe foods and products, and supporting the health and well-being of others through their organizational practices.

# SUMMARY

- There are no simple definitions of what it means to be healthy.

- Health can be defined as the ability of an organism to achieve optimal well-being within a realistic framework of individual potential and in a sometimes hostile environment.

- Total health or wellness involves physical, mental, emotional, environmental, spiritual, and social components in addition to the absence of physical infirmity.

- Overemphasizing one component of the wellness continuum and ignoring other components can lead to serious health deficiencies.

- Health promotion can be defined as any combination of educational, organizational, economic, and environmental supports for behaviors conducive to health.

- The benefits of good health include improved self-image, life satisfaction, enhanced creativity, increased energy levels, and reduced medical costs.

- Lifestyle, environment, biology and heredity, health care, and other factors are major influences in individual health and longevity.

- Disease prevention refers to a variety of techniques used to prevent worsening of health conditions. In general, there are three types of prevention: primary, secondary, and tertiary.

- Health status can be measured by analysis of such factors as incidence, prevalence, morbidity, mortality, and infant mortality rates. However, many nonstatistical factors must be considered as well. Disparities in health are important future considerations.

- Behavior change is a complex task, and a deliberate plan is required. Logical steps include identifying a behavior change, listening to yourself, determining why it's important that you change, developing a plan of action, evaluating your progress, and maintaining the behavior change.

- Predisposing, enabling, and reinforcing factors affect our ability to change our behaviors.

- Our beliefs, values, and readiness for change may significantly affect our ability to change.

- We must each accept personal responsibility for keeping current, evaluating priorities, and choosing viable options regarding health.

# FURTHER READINGS

U.S. Department of Health and Human Services. *Health United States: 1991.* Washington, DC: Government Printing Office.

> Contains the 1991 *Prevention Profile,* submitted by the secretary of the Department of Health and Human Services to the president and the congress of the United States. This is the sixteenth report on the health status of the nation and provides vital health statistics.

U.S. Department of Health and Human Services. (1993) *Monthly Vital Statistics Report,* vol. 41 no. 7. Washington, DC: Centers for Disease Control and Prevention, National Center for Health Statistics.

> This publication includes the final data from the CDC/National Center for Health Statistics. Includes statistics on deaths and death rates, causes of death, infant mortality, and other important data.

U.S. Department of Health and Human Services. (1992) *Healthy People 2000: National Health Promotion and Disease Objectives.* Boston, MA: Jones and Bartlett.

> This document contains a national strategy for significantly improving the health of the nation over the coming decade. It addresses the prevention of major chronic illnesses, injuries, and infectious diseases.

# Fitness for Every Body

## MARY-LANE KAMBERG

*Mary-Lane Kamberg is a frequent contributor to* Current Health 2, *from which this selection is taken.*

[1]The starting gun fires. The track star propels himself from the starting block. He sprints around the track. He breaks the tape with his chest as he crosses the finish line.

[2]No argument here: Everyone agrees that sports celebrities are physically fit. What you may not know is that you don't have to be a world-class athlete to enjoy the benefits of fitness.

[3]Forty years ago, fitness tests measured only athletic skills. Participants were scored in such events as the 50-yard dash and the standing long jump. If you weren't a star athlete, you wouldn't rate well—but you might have been fit by today's more accurate standards.

## THE BIG THREE

[4]Today, experts test fitness levels by looking at three major components that contribute to good health: strength, endurance, and flexibility.

[5]*Strength* is the amount of force the muscles can exert. Strength is what lets you lift a barbell or do a pull-up. However, you don't have to do weight training to build strength. Any weight-bearing activity—walking, gymnastics, or exercises such as push-ups, for example—will make you stronger.

[6]*Endurance* is the ability to exercise over a period of time. Endurance keeps you going in a cross-country run; it lets you swim another lap after you've already done 10. Aerobic exercise—exercise that increases the body's consumption of oxygen and improves both the respiratory and circulatory systems' functioning—develops endurance. Swimming, walking, and bicycling are examples of aerobic activities. So are dancing, jumping rope, and running. Aerobic exercise makes the heart and lungs work harder, which, in turn, improves the capacity to work longer and harder. Experts say that you need about 20 minutes of aerobic exercise three times per week to be physically fit.

[7]*Flexibility* is the ability to stretch. People with good flexibility have full use of the muscles and joints through what experts call the range of motion. A baseball pitcher, for example, must be able to use the entire range of motion of his shoulder to be able to throw well. Stretching before and after exercise improves flexibility, but be careful not to stretch cold muscles. Warm up first with some easy running, rope jumping, or a similar activity. Activities such as dance and gymnastics require lots of stretching, so they are good ways to improve flexibility.

## TESTING, ONE, TWO, THREE!

[8]Fitness tests measure a person's strength, endurance, and flexibility. They can also measure a person's percentage of body fat compared with his or her lean muscle tissue. Body-fat measurement tells more about a person's fitness level than weight, because muscle weighs three times more than fat. Someone who weighs more than another person might be more physically fit if the weight is muscle tissue. Excess fat is associated with risk factors for disease.

[9]Just how is body fat measured? A doctor or other health professional measures body fat percentage with an instrument called a skin-fold caliper. The caliper takes a "pinch" of flesh and measures its thickness.

[10]The person being tested is usually checked in the abdomen, the front of the thigh, the back of the arm, and the angle of the shoulder blade. Boys between the ages of 5 and 17 should have between 10 percent and 20 percent body fat. Girls in that age group should have body fat between 20 percent and 25 percent.

[11]Other tests that tell how fit someone is include blood pressure and heart rate screenings and tests that measure how well the heart is pumping blood past your lungs. Another test measures how much air you can hold in your lungs and breathe out in one second. Healthy habits—eating nutritious food, exercising, and not smoking—improve scores on these tests.

## FITNESS AND FATNESS

[12]Most athletes, to be sure, qualify as being fit using these criteria. So do many people who aren't interested in competitive sports, but who do care about their well-being. Unfortunately, even by today's standards, many adults and children are not fit.

[13]A 1989 study by the Amateur Athletic Union found that 68 percent of 9 million Americans between the ages of 6 and 17 couldn't pass tests of strength, endurance, and flexibility. The research also documented a steady decline in fitness in this age group between 1980 and 1989. The number of students who scored satisfactory on the tests declined from 43 percent in 1980 to 32 percent in 1989.

[14]In another study, the U.S. Department of Health and Human Services compared school-age children of today with those of 20 years ago. Researchers found that today's children have a higher percentage of body fat than children had 20 years ago. Obesity is a growing problem for Americans between the ages of 6 and 17. (Obesity is defined as weighing 20 percent or more over ideal weight, which is based on a combination of individual and statistical factors.) A study reported in the *American Journal of Diseases of Children* found that during the last 15 years, obesity in 6- to 11-year-old children went up 54 percent, and increased 39 percent in children aged 12 to 17. This information, however, must also be seen in the light of the increasing incidence of eating disorders in young people. Fear of fatness has its own set of serious problems.

## FIT FAMILIES

[15]Generally, fit children have fit parents. In many families, fitness is a way of life, with parents and their children frequently participating together in sports and other physical activities. On the other hand, children who are obese usually have obese parents. Research has shown that a tendency to be overweight may be inherited.

[16]Heredity is only part of the story, however. Too much fast food, as well as more television viewing and avid interest in home video games have all been blamed for playing a part in the decline in fitness among children and adolescents. It's obvious: The more time you sit in front of the tube, the less time you spend riding your bike, walking, or playing sports.

## FITNESS FACTS

[17]Why do we care about fitness? The fact is, people who are physically fit stay healthy longer.

[18]Five years ago, a study of 17,000 Harvard University graduates that was reported in the *New England Journal of Medicine* found that people who stayed active lived longer than their classmates who didn't exercise.

[19]But good health is only one benefit of regular exercise. Here's another fact: Being physically fit improves self-esteem, helps relieve stress, and can improve appearance. And some educators think fitness is linked to better grades!

[20]A fifth-grade teacher in California had his students run 20 minutes to 40 minutes every morning. The teacher found that the students were more ready to learn after they ran. He also compared his runners to other students who didn't run. The runners not only scored better than nonrunners on academic tests, the runners also missed fewer days of school because of illness. Runners missed about two days per year; nonrunners missed an average of 17 days per year. Another study that linked exercise with academic achievement kept track of more than 500 Canadian children for more than six years. Researchers found a connection between fitness and how well students learned math and writing skills.

[21]A third benefit of physical fitness is social adjustment. Young children relate to other children through movement. As people grow up, movement plays an important part in social development. During physical activity, children learn to get along with each other. Sports and physical play activities offer opportunities to learn to share, negotiate, and work together to solve problems. It worked that way when you were young; it works today now that you're in your teens.

[22]If you want to improve your fitness level, consider asking your school physical education instructor for advice. Explain your plans and ask about a fitness screening. A screening helps identify areas in which you need improvement. Your instructor may tell you to modify your program, avoid certain exercises, or increase others to strengthen weak muscles or stabilize joints to prevent injury. For

instance, the instructor may say you have good strength and endurance, but need to work for more flexibility.

## FITNESS FUN-DAMENTALS

[23]Teens with certain medical conditions may need to discuss their fitness plans with their parents and physician. Your fitness plan will include some form of exercise, but how can you tell which exercise or sport is best for you? One fitness expert says that the best exercise is the one you actually do. Try different activities until you find something you like. If exercise isn't fun, you probably won't do it for long.

[24]Organized sports teams are good because they offer social contact as well as exercise. But what if you're not a great athlete? Try recreational sports classes or leagues. Many community youth groups sponsor co-ed volleyball games, for example. Your local parks and recreation department may offer tennis lessons or basketball clinics.

[25]You can also exercise on your own or with just a couple of friends. Meet a few times a week for a group walk. Or use an exercise videotape to work out together. Walking, running, bicycling, and other aerobic activities offer fitness benefits and don't require athletic prowess.

[26]While you're trying new activities, don't forget that exercise is not always sports-related. Ballet lessons or a square dance club can give you plenty of exercise. You might want to try bench stepping or water walking. Because water increases resistance and reduces the effect of gravity, 15 minutes of walking in water equals an hour on land. (Get in the water about chest deep, and walk as if you were on land. Swing your arms for better results.)

[27]Some high schools are setting up on-site fitness centers that students and teachers alike may use. If you can afford it, look for a fitness center nearby. Many health clubs allow only adults, but some have programs designed especially for children and teens. And don't forget that cleanliness is an important finale to a fitness program. Shower and put on clean clothes (including socks) after you're finished.

## STUMBLING BLOCKS

[28]If getting exercise is as simple as taking a brisk walk, why don't more people get fit? Fears and misconceptions get in the way.

[29]Some people think they can't become physically fit. Or they don't want to exercise. Teens who are overweight, for instance, might be uncomfortable with the way they look in a leotard or sports uniform, so they'd rather not participate. Those who are small for their age may feel the same way. Also, teens who have never been good at competitive sports sometimes don't want to try anything that involves exercise. The battle is even tougher for teens whose family is inactive.

[30]Misconceptions also keep some people from exercising. Many girls mistakenly believe that they will build bulky, unattractive muscles if they do too much exercise. The truth is, even the most muscular women body-builders don't look like Arnold Schwarzenegger. That's because female hormones don't allow the same muscle development as male hormones do.

[31]Boys who build muscles through weight lifting may look good, but if that's their only exercise, they may be neglecting the endurance and flexibility components of true fitness. Big biceps have little or no effect on the efficiency of the heart. Girls who care about the way they look most often think in terms of eating for an attractive body shape instead of exercising. If they are underweight, they may fear exercise will make them lose weight. The truth is exercise will tone their muscles and make a skinny body more attractive.

## FOOD FOR FITNESS

[32]A last component in the fitness equation is food. Food gives your body the energy it needs to perform the physical activities that lead to fitness. The important thing to remember is that the right kinds of food really do make a difference in how fit you are. A healthy diet includes the correct proportions of carbohydrates, proteins, and fats. And within those categories some food choices are better than others.

[33]Limit fat intake to 30 percent of your daily calories. You can limit fat by choosing protein sources with less fat. Choose lean meats. Trim the visible fat. Remove the skin from chicken before cooking. Eat more fish. Some beans are good protein sources without fat. When you cook use polyunsaturated oils. Substitute salads (beware of the dressing!) and frozen yogurt for french fries and ice cream.

[34]Remember that complex carbohydrates—apples, broccoli, and carrot sticks, for example—are better for you than simple sugars because they provide more nutritional value. Have fruit for dessert. Try whole grain bread. These foods also provide more fiber and more fiber is more healthful.

## SOLVING THE DIET DILEMMA

[35]Changing your attitudes about food choices will make a better contribution to your overall fitness than dieting to lose weight. Some experts believe that dieting doesn't work without exercise. Their theory is that when someone diets, his or her body thinks it is starving. It reacts by slowing the metabolism, the chemical and physical processes involved in living. The body then tries to store fat—just when the dieter is hoping to lose that fat.

[36]Still, health experts are concerned about the 40 percent of high school students who say they have been on diets. Life-threatening eating disorders often follow periods of extended and/or fad dieting. If you want to lose weight, change your food choices and increase your activity level. That will prove to be the best route to physical fitness.

## WHAT'S IN IT FOR YOU

[37]The most important steps you ever take may well turn out to be those you take to become physically fit. You'll be healthier and feel better if you watch what you eat and set aside time each week for physical activity—even if you never reach the ranks of the superstars.

### Content Questions

*True or False*

If the statement is false, rewrite it to make it true.

1. Today's fitness tests are much the same as they were 40–50 years ago.
2. Strength is the amount of force that the muscles can exert.
3. Exercise means playing an organized sport.
4. Today's children have a higher percentage of body fat than children 20 years ago.
5. You should limit fat intake to 30 percent of your daily calories.

*Completion*

6. Experts test fitness levels by looking at three major components. Name them.
7. Why does a body-fat measurement tell more about a person's fitness level than their weight?
8. Why do some people resist participating in a fitness program?
9. A healthy diet includes the correct proportions of what three elements?
10. If you want to lose weight, what two major things should you do?

### Vocabulary

1. propels (¶1)
2. components (¶4)
3. aerobic exercise (¶6)
4. caliper (¶9)
5. tendency (¶15)
6. modify (¶22)
7. stabilize (¶22)
8. prowess (¶25)
9. finale (¶27)
10. misconceptions (¶28)
11. visible (¶33)
12. metabolism (¶35)

### Content Analysis Questions

1. State Kamberg's thesis.
2. Compare and contrast strength, endurance, and flexibility.

3. What reasons does Kamberg give for the growing problem of obesity in Americans between the ages of 6 and 17?

4. What age was this article's primary target audience? What specific clues did you use?

5. What are the major benefits of regular exercise? Do you see any disadvantages?

**Application Questions**

1. How do you define being physically fit? Do you feel you are physically fit? Why or why not? Do you think most of you family and friends are physically fit? Why or why not? What do you think are the major factors that keep you, your family, and your friends physically fit? What do you think would improve your fitness level and the fitness level of others?

2. Assume you have been assigned to a college committee charged with recommending general fitness guidelines for students, faculty, and staff. What would you recommend as the major components of such a program? Why?

# *Fruits and Vegetables*

MAYO CLINIC HEALTH LETTER EDITORIAL STAFF

*The* Mayo Clinic Health Letter *is written and published by the Mayo Foundation for Medical Education and Research, a subsidiary of the Mayo Foundation.*

## EAT FIVE A DAY EVERY DAY

[1]How many fruits and vegetables did you eat today? One? Two? Even if you can say three, there's room for improvement.

[2]The Food and Nutrition Board of the National Academy of Sciences recommends that you eat five servings of fruits and vegetables daily. The reason: Fruits and vegetables can help you control your weight and reduce your risk of coronary heart disease and cancer.

## WHY MORE IS BETTER

[3]At the forefront of research into the relationship between diet and disease is a new focus on fruits and vegetables. These foods are a natural fit for diets aimed at reducing the risk of obesity and heart disease.

[4]Fruits and vegetables contain virtually no fat and most have fiber. They also are rich in a variety of vitamins, minerals and other chemicals that scientists suspect may be related to disease prevention, particularly cancer protection.

[5]Although research has given no clear-cut answers, health and

government agencies are calling for Americans to eat five servings from a variety of fruits and vegetables every day. One serving equals one-half cup of cooked vegetables, canned fruit or juice. Count one cup of chopped vegetables or fruit, or a medium whole fruit, as one serving.

[6]Here's a closer look into how eating fruits and vegetables may protect your health:

[7]•***Beta Carotene***—Deep-yellow and dark-green vegetables are rich sources of beta carotene—a substance that your body uses to make vitamin A.

[8]Low blood levels of beta carotene are linked with the development of lung cancer.

[9]Good sources of beta carotene are carrots, spinach, tomatoes, winter squash, sweet potatoes, pumpkin, papaya, cantaloupe, mango, apricots and watermelon.

[10]In addition to beta carotene, fruits and vegetables contain other carotenoids that may be involved in cancer prevention.

[11]•***Vitamins C and E***—These nutrients act as antioxidants. They fight free radicals—molecules that may cause disease by injuring cells or harming your body's natural healing ability. (See *Mayo Clinic Health Letter,* January 1992.)

[12]Look for vitamin C in broccoli, broccoflower, oranges, brussels sprouts, grapefruit, strawberries, cantaloupe, cauliflower and baked potatoes. Vegetable oils, nuts, leafy greens and whole grains contain vitamin E.

[13]•***Phytochemicals***—These chemicals are contained naturally in fruits, vegetables and grains.

[14]Scientists used to believe phytochemicals were not essential to human nutrition. Yet new studies suggest substances in cruciferous vegetables may be related to cancer protection.

[15]Cruciferous vegetables include brussels sprouts, cauliflower, broccoli, broccoflower, kale, mustard greens, cabbage (bok choy, green, red and savoy), turnips, rutabaga and kohlrabi. Many of these vegetables also contain vitamin C.

[16]The National Cancer Institute (NCI) began a five-year project in 1990 to study how foods rich in phytochemicals may prevent cancer or slow its progress. The first year of the Designer Foods program focused on garlic, licorice root, flax-seed, citrus fruits and a group of vegetables that includes parsley, carrots and celery.

[17]•***Fiber***—The NCI recommends that you eat 20 to 30 grams of fiber daily. The recommendation stems from evidence suggesting that a high-fiber, low-fat diet lowers your risk of colon and rectal cancer. (See *Mayo Clinic Health Letter,* May 1992.)

[18]Fruits and vegetables, especially legumes, are good sources of fiber. One-half cup of cooked legumes provides an average of 5 grams of fiber and less than 1 gram of fat. Legumes include split peas, blackeyed peas and lentils, as well as kidney, pinto, black, navy and garbanzo beans.

[19]Data from a national food consumption survey show that diets with five servings of fruits and vegetables contained about 17 grams of fiber. Adding just two slices of whole-wheat bread brings the total to at least 20 grams of fiber—and meets the NCI daily goal for fiber.

[20]•*Low Fat*—The same food consumption survey found that eating fruits and vegetables can help you control fat.

[21]In diets with no fruits and vegetables, fat contributed about 38 percent of daily calories. Eating two servings of vegetables and at least three servings of fruits lowered daily calories from fat to around 34 percent.

[22]Limiting fat to no more than 30 percent of daily calories may reduce your risk of obesity, coronary heart disease and cancer.

## LIMIT FAT AND BOOST FIBER

[23]Eating more fruits and vegetables is not a panacea. The relationship of diet to disease is overwhelmingly complex, influenced by many lifestyle and environmental factors. No one food is perfect. It's your overall diet that counts.

[24]Yet, at a minimum, eating five servings of fruits and vegetables every day can improve your diet by helping control fat and boosting fiber.

## HERE ARE WAYS TO EAT FIVE A DAY

[25]Does eating five servings of fruits and vegetables a day sound like a lot? If so, try these ideas:

[26]• *Serve soup*—Use vegetables and legumes as a base for soups or as added ingredients.

[27]• *Moisturize lean ground meats*—Add raw, grated carrot, potato or apple to lean ground beef or turkey to make meat loaf or meatballs.

[28]• *Thicken sauces without fat*—Substitute cooked and pureed vegetables for cream or whole milk.

[29]• *Be creative*—Pasta and stir-fry dishes are ideal ways to serve lots of different vegetables and small portions of meat.

[30]• *Enhance old standbys*—Add fruit to your breakfast cereal and raw, grated vegetables or fruit to muffins and cookies.

[31]• *Try new and unusual vegetables*—The genetically engineered broccoflower is a good example. A cross between broccoli and cauliflower, this vegetable looks like a light green head of cauliflower with a milder, sweeter taste.

[32]• *Don't let lettuce limit salads*—Choose a wider variety of greens, including arugula, chicory, collards, dandelion greens, kale, mustard greens, spinach and watercress.

## NEW GUIDE TO HEALTHY EATING
## FOCUS IS ON FRUITS, VEGETABLES,
## AND GRAINS

[33]On April 28, 1992, the U.S. Department of Agriculture (USDA) gave a fresh, new look to its guide for healthy eating. The federal agency unveiled its new "food guide pyramid"—a change in geometry that offers updated advice on nutrition.

[34]The pyramid conveys three essential elements of a healthy diet:

[35]• *Proportion*—Eat different amounts every day from the basic food groups.

[36]• The shape of the pyramid tells you at a glance that grains, vegetables and fruits should make up the bulk of your diet.

[37]• *Moderation*—Use fats and sugars sparingly. Although this point is reflected in the 1990 Dietary Guidelines for Americans, the food guide pyramid adds visual impact to the message.

[38]• *Variety*—Choose different foods from each major food group every day. The pyramid doesn't claim that any food is better or worse than another.

[39]As you look at the pyramid, keep this important point in mind:

[40]The USDA groups foods according to the most important nutrients they contain and how they're used. That's why you see legumes grouped with meat, poultry, fish, eggs and nuts.

[41]Legumes contain protein in amounts comparable to these

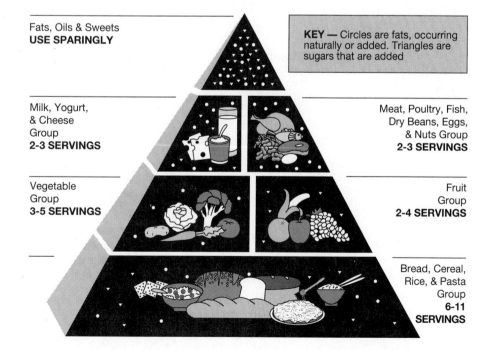

Fats, Oils & Sweets
**USE SPARINGLY**

KEY — Circles are fats, occurring naturally or added. Triangles are sugars that are added

Milk, Yogurt,
& Cheese
Group
**2-3 SERVINGS**

Meat, Poultry, Fish,
Dry Beans, Eggs,
& Nuts Group
**2-3 SERVINGS**

Vegetable
Group
**3-5 SERVINGS**

Fruit
Group
**2-4 SERVINGS**

Bread, Cereal,
Rice, & Pasta
Group
**6-11
SERVINGS**

other protein-rich foods. But they also provide fiber with virtually no fat—healthful qualities none of the other foods in this group have.

[42]Don't worry about where legumes are grouped—with meats or with fruits and vegetables. Just remember to eat them.

## Content Questions

*True or False*

If the statement is false, rewrite it to make it true.

1. It is recommended that you eat five servings of fruits and vegetables daily.
2. Fruits and vegetables contain very little fat.
3. It is thought that beta carotene causes lung cancer.
4. A high-fiber, low-fat diet may lower your risk of colon cancer.
5. Eating more fruits and vegetables is all you need to do for a perfect diet.

*Completion*

6. List two reasons you should eat five servings of fruits and vegetables daily.
7. List three essential elements of a healthy diet according to the USDA.
8. Name three health risks that can be reduced by limiting your fat intake to no more than 30 percent of daily calories.
9. Name two ways in which eating five servings of fruits and vegetables every day can improve your diet.
10. What is the advantage of legumes over other protein-rich foods?

## Vocabulary

1. virtually (¶4)
2. beta carotene (¶7)
3. cruciferous (¶14)
4. legumes (¶18)
5. panacea (¶23)
6. enhance (¶30)
7. genetically engineered (¶31)

## Content Analysis Questions

1. What is the source of the food guide pyramid? Do you think this is a reliable source? Why or why not?
2. Why are legumes grouped with meat, poultry, fish, eggs and nuts? Explain your answer.
3. What do the writer's mean by "no one food is perfect"?

4. Why do you think scientists are engineering food genetically? What do you see as the positive aspects of such food experiments? What do you see as negative aspects? *Note:* If you are not familiar enough with the concept of genetically engineered food to state any positive or negative aspects, where could you find more information?

**Application Questions**

1. Make a list of what you have eaten during the last three days (or keep a record for the next three days). How closely does your diet match the USDA Food Guide Pyramid? Is one of the food groups consistently under- or over-represented in your diet? How could you change your diet to include more fruits and vegetables?

2. Assume that you belong to a community service group on campus that has been asked to develop a "healthy eating" campaign for a local primary school. What would you stress in your campaign? Why? How would you present the information to the youngsters?

# *Heartening News: Just the Facts on Fat, Ma'am*

## MAUREEN CALLAHAN

*Maureen Callahan is a registered dietitian and a writer in Brookline, Massachusetts. This selection is from* Mature Outlook.

[1]Sorting through the information available about fat and healthy diets can leave you feeling more like a private investigator than a consumer. Take a clue from detectives in the movies: To solve a mystery, start by looking at the facts.

[2]• *Fact:* A high-fat diet contributes to a wide variety of illnesses, including heart disease and some forms of cancer.

[3]• *Fact:* More than 35 percent of the daily calorie intake for the average person in the United States comes from fat.

[4]• *Fact:* Reducing your fat intake to 30 percent or less of total calorie intake is recommended for good health.

[5]• *Fact:* Reducing fat intake helps many people keep their cholesterol level within acceptable limits.

[6]• *Fact:* You can choose from a variety of ways to reduce the fat in your diet.

## 100 PERCENT CONFUSING

[7]To help you reduce fat consumption, many health experts espouse the seemingly simple solution that healthy adults should limit their calories from fat to 30 percent of their total calorie intake.

[8]However, most folks don't know how to use this figure to make smart dietary decisions. Does it mean you should eat only those foods that contain no more than 30 percent of their calories from fat?

[9]No, says Liz Diemand, R.D., a representative of the American Dietetic Association. The idea is to balance your high- and low-fat food choices so the daily or weekly calories from fat total no more than 30 percent of all calories.

[10]Using a fat budget is one way to keep track. For example, a woman who needs 1,500 calories a day would have a daily fat budget of 50 grams. (Thirty percent of 1,500 is 450. Fat has 9 calories per gram, so divide 450 by 9 to get 50 grams.)

[11]For that individual, consuming no more than 50 grams of fat each day could be accomplished with an almost limitless number of food combinations. And it allows for personal taste. A slice of apple pie (12 grams of fat) at lunch doesn't have to be rejected if it is balanced out the rest of the day with other low-fat food choices.

## THE EZ APPROACH

[12]If that's still too much math, an even simpler method for cutting back on fat is endorsed by Penny Kris-Etherton, R.D., Ph.D., a professor of nutrition at Pennsylvania State University. Start by concentrating on the major sources of fat: whole-milk dairy products and meat.

[13]"People tend to adopt an all-or-nothing attitude toward fat," Kris-Etherton says. "It's easy to just go overboard and translate advice to limit fat into a need to eliminate fat," she says. Simple changes in eating habits are the most effective because you're most likely to stay with them.

[14]Kris-Etherton and her colleague Madeleine Sigman-Grant, R.D., Ph.D., used a computer model to determine the simplest ways to reduce fat in a variety of typical diets. The computer made only minor adjustments in meals to achieve the desired fat level. Often, substituting lean meats for fatty cuts and skim-milk dairy products for whole-milk products was sufficient to bring fat content down to 30 percent.

## LOW-FAT SHOPPING

[15]Even though you needn't eat only low-fat foods, you still need to make smart choices, especially when selecting foods that you eat regularly. Keep your personal eating habits in mind. If you like dessert, choose a low-fat item that you can enjoy regularly, such as fig bars, gingersnaps or vanilla wafers.

[16]And if you sometimes find yourself standing in the store having a mental debate over whether a food is high or low in fat, use the 3-gram rule to resolve the issue. Any food that contains 3 grams of fat or less per each 100 calories is considered low in fat.

## WHAT FAT-FREE REALLY MEANS

[17]The plethora of low- and no-fat foods on grocery store shelves gives you plenty of choices, but you still will need to consider the overall healthfulness of an item. Don't let the jargon on the label override your common sense. Anything that sounds too good to be true, probably is.

[18]"The definition of good nutrition is not 'fat free,'" Diemand stresses. Fat is only one thing to consider. You need to look at the total nutritional picture to make smart choices. For example, a fat-free coffee cake may sound like an acceptable choice, but one way manufacturers keep fat content low is by using more sugar, so the calorie count goes up—and coffee cake isn't exactly full of nutrients, explains Diemand.

## FAKE FATS

[19]The new fat substitutes are helping food manufacturers develop reduced-fat foods with taste and texture most folks find acceptable, says Diemand.

[20]Kris-Etherton applauds the arrival of fat substitutes. "I think they're a wonderful invention that help consumers make the recommended changes in diet," she says. However, it's important to realize that fat substitutes aren't the complete answer. That's because fat substitutes are used mostly in desserts. Few are used in the foods that make up the bulk of a healthy diet.

[21]Fat-free does not mean calorie-free. Fat substitutes often are made from modified sugars and starches that can be high in calories. (The synthetic, no-calorie fat substitutes are not yet approved by the Food and Drug Administration.)

[22]But, for some people, substitutes just don't cut it. Diemand notes that for most folks, nothing is wrong with using regular foods that have the full quota of fat as long as you keep portion sizes small and use these foods less frequently. That, in fact, is her personal preference. "I would rather have just a little of the real thing," she says.

## FREEDOM OF CHOICE

[23]A clear understanding of the facts about fat leaves you free to make smart choices.

[24]As Kris-Etherton notes, having choices is what fat budgeting is all about. "People can use a variety of strategies," she says. And now that you've got the facts on fat, you can devise your own strategy to solve the mystery.

### Truth in Labeling

[25]The good news: Laws have been passed that require the wording on food packages to accurately describe fat and cholesterol content for realistic portions of a food.

[26]The bad news: These laws didn't go into effect until May 1994.

[27]Here's a look at the approved wording for labels that should help end some of the confusion.

28• Low fat contains three grams of fat or less per serving and per 100 grams.

29• Reduced fat contains 50 percent or less fat than the original version of the same food.

30• Fat free contains less than $\frac{1}{2}$ gram of fat per serving and no added fat or oil.

31• *X* percent fat free can be used only if the food meets the low-fat definition.

32• Low in saturated fat contains one gram or less of saturated fat per serving and less than 15 percent of total calories come from saturated fat.

33• Reduced saturated fat contains 50 percent or less saturated fat and a minimum reduction of more than one gram per serving than the original variety.

34• Low in cholesterol contains a maximum of 20 milligrams cholesterol per serving and no more than two grams of saturated fat.

35• Reduced cholesterol has a minimum reduction of 20 milligrams per serving from the original version.

**Content Questions**

*True or False*

If the statement is false, rewrite it to make it true.

1. The average person in the United States consumes more than 35 percent of their daily calories from fat.
2. Eating a low-fat diet means you must eliminate foods like apple pie and ice cream from your diet.
3. An acceptable definition of good nutrition is fat-free.
4. Fat-free means calorie-free.
5. People should use a variety of strategies to reduce fat in their diet.

*Completion*

6. Your daily/weekly calories from fat should total no more than _____ % of all calories.
7. What are the two major sources of fat in our diet?
8. What is the "3-gram rule"?
9. Under the new labeling requirements, "low fat" means the food contains:

    a. 50 percent or less of fat per serving

    b. 3 grams or less of fat per serving

    c. $\frac{1}{2}$ gram or less of fat per serving

    d. 20 milligrams or less of *fat* per serving

10. Under the new labeling requirements, what does "low in cholesterol" mean?

**Vocabulary**

1. espouse (¶7)
2. plethora (¶17)
3. jargon (¶17)
4. synthetic (¶21)

**Content Analysis Questions**

1. What do the initials R.D. and Ph.D., following Kris-Etherton's name in paragraph 21, mean? Why is this information important?
2. Callahan lists the information in paragraphs 2–6 as facts. Do you agree that they are facts? Why or why not? If you're not sure, what resource could you consult to find out?
3. How can you use the "3-gram rule" in daily life for healthier eating?
4. What is the purpose of a fat substitute? What kinds of foods currently use fat substitutes?
5. Using the basic formula in paragraph 10 for determining a daily budget, calculate a fat budget for yourself. List four ways that you could reduce your fat intake.

**Application Questions**

1. Callahan states that the average person in the U.S. consumes more than 35 percent of his or her daily calories from fat. In what countries do you think people consume more fat? In what countries do you think they consume less fat? Explain your reasoning. *Note:* If you are not familiar enough with what people in other countries eat to answer this question, how and where could you find the information?
2. Collect the labels, or nutritional information, from five foods that you eat often. How do they fit into your fat budget? If any of them are especially high in fat, identify a lower-fat alternative you could enjoy or describe how you could adjust your diet to enjoy them without guilt.

# *The New Aging*

## *The research is in: How we grow older is being redefined*

### CARL SHERMAN

*Carl Sherman is a freelance health and psychology writer trying to survive in Brooklyn. This selection is from* Working Woman.

[1]Growing older isn't what it used to be. Today's 40-year-old looks, acts and feels like yesterday's 30-year-old, says trend-spotter Faith Popcorn, and 50 now is like 40 was a generation ago. Popcorn calls it "down-aging," a culturewide revision of life's timetable.

[2]Has an obsession with youth turned into a national inability to act our age? Not quite. Science is in fact validating our new youthful lifestyle and outlook. As Americans live longer—about 30 million are over 65, compared with 17 million 25 years ago—research on aging has boomed. For example, the Baltimore Longitudinal Study of Aging, conducted by the National Institute on Aging (NIA), has tracked over 2,000 men and women, ranging from their 20s through their 90s, with thorough physiological and psychological tests every two years. One major finding: Much of the slowing and breakdown that a decade ago was considered the inevitable result of time is actually due to disease, lifestyle and environmental wear and tear. Most symptoms of age can be postponed, and in some cases prevented.

[3]"To an extent, you can take control of your own aging," says James Fozard, who directs the Baltimore study. If you eat right, stay active and avoid health-sapping habits, you're likely to be younger—physically, mentally and in spirit—than your 40-, 50- or 60-year-old counterpart was a generation ago. Here's what you can do to head off the effects of time.

## THE SENSES

[4]Vision generally remains unchanged through the 30s, but as the lens of the eye loses flexibility, it becomes harder for it to bend to bring close objects into focus. Farsightedness will almost certainly force you to hold the newspaper at arm's length sometime in your 40s and to keep trading up to ever-stronger glasses.

[5]But beneath the surface, a far graver threat to vision may be slowly progressing, beginning in your teens. Cataracts, the clouding of the lens that often dims vision in the 60s, are the result of lifelong oxidation damage, a by-product of normal body chemistry, says Paul Jacques, research associate at the USDA Human Nutrition Research Center on Aging at Tufts University. Jacques's study found that people without cataracts had higher levels of antioxidant nutrients—vitamins E and C and beta carotene—in their blood and got them more from natural sources (fruits and vegetables) than from supplements. Studies done at Johns Hopkins University have linked cataracts to smoking and sun exposure, both avoidable.

[6]By your 20s, you also begin to lose your ability to hear high tones, according to James Jerger, a professor of audiology at Baylor College of Medicine in Houston. Most people don't notice the slow, progressive muffling until their 60s, when they start to find speech hard to follow, although women are less likely to go deaf than men. Jerger also points out that some people still have perfectly good hearing into their 90s.

[7]Maybe it's not just luck. A high-fat diet can clog the blood vessels that nourish the delicate hearing organs, and years of rock concerts can cause cumulative trauma. Tribes in the deserts of the Sudan, who subsist largely on fruits and berries, keep acute hearing all their life, while Scandinavians ("They put a little coffee in their cream," says Jerger) suffer hearing loss early.

[8]Our sense of smell remains practically unchanged as we age, but our voice box tissue becomes less elastic, leading to a slightly deeper voice for women (men's voices actually get higher).

## THE BODY

[9]A gradual decline in organ efficiency occurs throughout adulthood. The kidneys filter waste a little more slowly each decade. By your 40s, kidney stones will have appeared if you're predisposed to them. Women who've had children may find by their 40s that they leak a few drops of urine when they cough or sneeze, but simple exercises are very effective in strengthening stretched pelvic muscles. It won't be until your 60s that your liver will metabolize toxin more slowly, but barring heavy drinking and/or chronic hepatitis, it will function perfectly well for a lifetime. Between your early 20s and age 80, it's natural to lose 40 percent of your pulmonary function. Yet nature gave us lung power to spare: If you're healthy, you won't notice the difference.

[10]Blood pressure goes up every decade after 40 among Americans; overall, fewer women suffer from hypertension than men, but it still strikes 32 percent of women between 25 and 74. Coronary heart disease is uncommon in premenopausal women; estrogen seems to work as a kind of special protector, possibly by affecting the level of HDLs, the "good" cholesterol that keeps the bad cholesterol in check. The benefits of estrogen seem to last for 10 years after menopause, but by age 65 women's death rate from heart disease is almost as high as men's. According to statistics from the NIA, one out of every four women over 65 suffers from some form of cardiovascular disease. Yet despite these statistics, abundant research shows that a lifelong low-fat diet and an ongoing exercise program can help protect against heart disease, even during the most vulnerable later years.

[11]As for the more visible shape we're in, the decades do leave their mark. At 20, the average woman's body is 26.5 percent fat; by her 40s, it's 33 percent; and by her 50s, 42 percent. By 70, she'll have lost 30 percent of the muscle she had at 20. Flabbiness in the thighs, tummy and upper arms can show up as early as the 30s. But in fact, changes in muscle tone and body composition—the ratio of fat to muscle—can be minimal until close to 50 for women who keep up a good fitness program, says Everett Smith, director of the biogerontology laboratory at the University of Wisconsin. "I have a lot of staffers in their mid-30s who have better muscle tone now than in their 20s." (Breasts have no muscle tissue, and with age the ligaments above them stretch, especially after nursing.)

[12]Your functional capacity—the ability to generate energy for work and play—will drop 7.5 percent per decade, after a peak in the early 30s. At 40, many women find that stairs seem steeper and that they run out of steam earlier in the day. Much of this outgo may be accounted for by the fact that most women in their 40s are under more pressure than they were at 20, and they devote less time to exercise, says Smith. Those who exercise regularly cope better with business and family stresses, and exercise can dramatically slow or even reverse the energy drop. In one study, sedentary women from 35 to 65 were enrolled in a program of aerobic exercise. "After 10 years their functional capacity was 6 percent higher than when they started," says Smith.

[13]Training can build muscle at any age. In one program, a group of men and women with an average age of 90 worked with weights,

increasing muscle size by 10 percent and nearly tripling their strength. Since lean tissue burns more calories than fat, muscle maintenance also makes it easier to stay slim.

[14]Creaky knees and stiff shoulders may creep into your life between 35 and 50. The health of your joints depends on the strength of the muscles supporting them, so again, regular exercise, especially weight lifting, running or walking, is important. Stress and physical changes make lower-back pain more common in the 30s, 40s and 50s (the disks that cushion the vertebrae in your spine gradually degenerate), but pain can often be prevented by strengthening lower-body and abdominal muscles.

[15]Healthy bones are crucial for heading off osteoporosis, one of the major health problems suffered by older women. This disease, which causes bones to become thin and porous enough to fracture easily, accelerates at menopause and strikes one out of four white women past age 65 (black women tend to have denser bones and so are less susceptible). The stronger your bones are before menopause, the less affected you'll be, so it's important to "bank bone" when you're young, says Sheryl Sherman, project director for osteoporosis at the NIA. Adequate calcium in your diet, about 1,000 milligrams a day (8 ounces of skim milk has 302 milligrams), and regular weight-bearing exercise (walking or running) will help build strong bones while you're young, then slow the drain.

## THE MIND

[16]Brain tissue begins to deteriorate in your 20s, but it will take 50 years or more before there's a noticeable change in your mental functions. Although some people feel they've already lost some of their edge by their 30s—they forget names and don't concentrate as well—there's no evidence at all to tie this to aging, according to Dr. Gene Cohen, acting director of the NIA.

[17]If you do tend to forget more, it may be that remembering some facts just isn't as important to you as it was when you were a student, and you have more years of information and names to sort through. The stress of business and family life can also lead to lapses. Still, scientific tests show that, for most people, true memory doesn't change until the 70s.

[18]From the 30s onward there is a slight mental slowdown, such as in reaction time, which determines how quickly you step on the brake and how fast you come up with the answers in "Jeopardy." But other functions, like vocabulary, get better through your 50s and 60s.

[19]Biologically, the brain actually continues to develop throughout your adult life. Although a number of brain cells die each year, the connecting branches between them—pathways for the nerve impulses that create thought, feeling and memory—keep on sprouting and spreading, compensating for the loss of cells, says Cohen. Studies show that intellectual challenge can enhance this growth. Mice that were put in a complex maze (the rodent equivalent of an adult-education class) sprouted extra intercell bridges.

[20]Physical exercise can help brain function, too. Robert Dustman, chief of the neuropsychology laboratory at the Salt Lake City, Utah, V.A. Hospital, found that aerobically fit individuals in their 50s, as well as those in their 20s, had more mental flexibility, adjust-

ing more quickly to changing tasks, than same-age couch potatoes. "Fitness seems to slow mental decline, perhaps by bringing more oxygen to the brain," Dustman says. In fact, says Fozard of the Baltimore study, "a physically fit 60-year-old may have the same reaction time as a sedentary 20-year-old."

[21]The bottom line is that the passing years should leave mental powers pretty much unscathed. The deterioration we used to blame on age, it seems, can often be due to illnesses such as thyroid disease, lung disease and depression, which are more common in middle age and later. Alzheimer's disease strikes more women than men, primarily because more women live to be old enough to suffer from it. The disease occurs most commonly in people over age 85 who, it is suspected, have a genetic predisposition to it, coupled with some environmental trigger. More controllable is a condition called multi-infarct dementia, caused by ministrokes that block blood flow to the brain, killing tissue. Improving your circulation through a low-fat, low-cholesterol diet and exercise can help prevent strokes. "In healthy people," says Cohen, "intellectual performance remains robust throughout life." When the Social Security Administration surveyed centenarians some years ago, it found no lack of creativity and intellectual activity; one still wrote a daily newspaper column.

## SEXUALITY

[22]If you're already enjoying a satisfying sex life in your 30s and 40s, you have even more to look forward to. "Woman tend to report that sex is better as they get older—much better," says Patricia Schreiner-Engel, director of psychological services at the obstetrics-and-gynecology department at Mount Sinai Medical Center in New York. "They become more sexually responsive and comfortable with sex." The longer a woman has been orgasmic, the more easily she will achieve orgasm.

[23]For most women, the hormone shifts of menopause have little impact on desire or responsiveness. Although it's true that the drying and thinning of vaginal tissues at menopause can make intercourse painful, a topical estrogen cream can usually help. Regular sex is actually the best treatment for the problem.

[24]There's no age limit on the joy of sex. Schreiner-Engel describes a conference in which a group of doctors, all women, were discussing this issue: "At what point does sexual desire really start to go down?" they asked one doctor, who was 75 years old. "I'll let you know," she said.

[25]At any age, a drop in desire or sexual interest is probably due to depression, physical illness, relationship difficulties or the lack of a partner. All treatable.

## ILLNESS

[26]The risk of heart disease, the biggest killer of women as well as men, accelerates with menopause because of the loss of estrogen. The risk of cancer, the number two killer, rises sharply each decade after 30. Lung cancer has become the leading cause of cancer death for women as the number of female smokers has risen. Of course, it

is highly preventable. The incidence of breast cancer has risen dramatically, although survival rates have also increased. Meanwhile, researchers are accumulating more information about possible causes of this disease (a high-fat diet is clearly one culprit), and thus potential preventive measures.

[27]Adult-onset diabetes is 10 times more likely at 60, when it strikes 20 out of 1,000 women, than it is at 30. Immune function starts to drop off in your 40s, but the change isn't significant until your 60s, when infections become more frequent.

[28]How well we can fight off illnesses, from cancer to colds, is one of the biggest health issues of the last 20 years. It's now known that a low-fat diet can lower the risk of heart disease, as well as a range of cancers. Recent research suggests that antioxidant nutrients help, too. Exercise seems to protect against heart disease, cancer and diabetes.

[29]Even the decline in immune defense may be negotiable. Dr. Ranjit Chandra, a research professor at Memorial University of Newfoundland, recently found that nearly one third of people over 65 have deficiencies of nutrients like iron, zinc, vitamin C and beta carotene, probably due to a poor diet. When a group of older men and women were given multivitamin supplements, they had 40 percent fewer colds, flus and other illnesses than a control group who had not taken vitamin supplements.

## LONGEVITY

[30]Life expectancy has risen dramatically, from 47 at the turn of the century to nearly 80 today. But optimum life span is still about 116 years, says Huber Warner, deputy associate director of the biology of aging program at the NIA. Some scientists believe that sooner or later we must run into a brick-wall genetic program for death.

[31]The future may revise this, too. Studies of animals have shown that drastically limiting food intake can vastly extend the maximum life span. Rats given a very low calorie diet live to 50 months, compared with their normal 32. Whether the same thing can be done with humans, creating a race of 170-year-old Methuselahs, is far from certain. "It's not a goal of modern research," says Warner. "Extending the healthy life span is."

### Content Questions

*True or False*

If the statement is false, rewrite it to make it true.

1. Americans have a longer life span than they did in past centuries.
2. Men are less likely to go deaf than women.
3. A high-fat diet can contribute to hearing problems.
4. We have no control over the aging process.
5. Biologically, the brain continues to develop throughout adult life.

*Completion*

6. What are three possible contributors to the formation of cataracts?

7. List three general things you can do to take control of your own aging.

8. What is the biggest killer of women and men? What is the number two killer?

9. We used to think that growing older meant an inevitable physical and mental slowing and breakdown. What is the current thinking?

10. What is the goal of modern health research?

## Vocabulary

1. down-aging (¶1)

2. validating (¶2)

3. longitudinal study (¶2)

4. inevitable (¶2)

5. a far graver threat (¶5)

6. cumulative trauma (¶7)

7. subsist (¶7)

8. predisposed (¶9)

9. vulnerable (¶10)

10. biogerontology laboratory (¶11)

11. sedentary (¶12)

12. compensating (¶19)

13. unscathed (¶21)

14. optimum life span (¶30)

## Content Analysis Questions

1. What is Sherman's thesis?

2. How does Sherman develop and support his thesis? Give examples to support your answer.

3. In paragraph 29 Sherman writes, "Even the decline in immune defense may be negotiable." What does he mean?

4. Based on Sherman's information, what are four positive steps you can take to keep your mind alert?

5. Do you believe we are "down-aging?" To explain and support your answer: compare and contrast your attitudes and behavior today with the attitudes and behavior of someone older when he or she was your age; and compare and contrast the attitudes and behaviors you had when you were younger with the attitudes and behaviors of today's young teens.

## Application Questions

1. Members of your campus community service group are going to be working with a group of folks in their 70s at a neighborhood senior adult center for five hours a week. Design two activities or projects you think would be enjoyable and beneficial for the seniors.

2. You've decided to "head off the effects of time." Outline the changes you are going to make in your life.

# Good Friends Are Good Medicine

PREVENTION STAFF

[1]Exercise is great for health. And so are vitamins, steam baths, SmokeEnders and the "Richard Simmons Show." But something else is great for health, and it doesn't take running shoes. It's called friendship.

[2]"More and more, research is teaching us that healthy, long lives depend on deepening our bonds with other human beings."

[3]That's Richard Grossman talking, who's director of the Center for Health in Medicine at the Montefiore Hospital and Medical Center in the Bronx, New York. What he's talking about is something that should come as especially good news: Good friends can be good medicine.

[4]Grossman isn't saying party till you drop, but he is saying get out and "make meaningful contacts with people. An active social life can nourish the mind, the feelings and the spirit, and it's clear that good physical health depends as much on these parts of ourselves as it does on a strong and well-functioning body."

[5]Grossman isn't saying that regular exercise and a healthy diet aren't important. But he is saying that the fitness buff who does all the right things—but does them alone—might be missing out on what new research suggests could be the greatest health protector of all. He's missing out on the peace of mind in knowing he's got people he can turn to in times of need.

[6]It may, in short, be as important to talk heart to heart with a good friend each week as to go to the spa.

[7]Sound like your kind of fitness program?

[8]Good, because the evidence looks quite convincing. Here's just a sampling of what research has come up with.

[9]• A study of 7,000 residents of Alameda County, California, by researchers from Yale University found that people with good social-support systems were two to five times more likely to outlive people with fewer social involvements.

[10]• An investigation by researchers reporting in the *Journal of Health and Social Behavior* found that a strong social support system was a powerful protector of both physical and mental health in 100 men who had been laid off from their jobs.

[11]• A study of 170 pregnant women reported in the *American Journal of Epidemiology* recalled that pregnancy complications were three times more likely in women with weak social-support systems as compared with women with strong ones.

[12]• No surprise, kids need meaningful companionship, too. A report in the *Journal of Youth and Adolescence* showed sig-

nificantly greater rates of illnesses of all kinds in children lacking close contact with their folks. Like the saying goes, people need people. And not just for emotional health, but for physical health, too.

## Content Analysis Questions

1. What is the writers' purpose?
2. What is the writers' thesis?
3. What type of details do the writers use to support and develop the thesis?
4. Is the information presented in paragraphs 9–12 primarily fact or opinion? Explain your answer.
5. Did the writers achieve their purpose? Why or why not?

# *Jest for the Health of It*

### Susan Goodman

*Susan Goodman is a staff writer for* Current Health 2 *magazine, from which this selection is taken.*

¹Your friend comes up to you and asks if you've heard what Tom replied to the English teacher when she asked him the meaning of "derange." You haven't, but you want to. He delivers his funny line, and you groan—but then together you have a big laugh.

²It isn't just your mouth or vocal cords that are getting a humorous workout. When you laugh, your chest, thorax, and abdominal muscles contract along with your diaphragm, heart, and lungs. When you really let go and howl, your blood pressure soars from an average of 120 to about 200. Your pulse rate doubles from 60 to 120 beats per minute. Laughter pumps more adrenaline into your bloodstream. It may also cause endorphins, the body's natural painkillers, to flood through your body.

## GOOD EXERCISE

³People always knew that a good giggle could brighten any day, but now science tells us it can do much more than that. For one thing, laughter is good exercise. When you just read about what happens when you laugh, you might have thought it resembled your body's efforts when playing tennis or going up for a jump shot. If so, you were not far from wrong.

⁴Even mild laughter is good exercise, explains William F. Fry Jr., M.D., a professor of psychiatry at Stanford University. A hearty laugh stimulates almost every system in your body. It helps you

breathe more deeply, bringing oxygen to the blood and expelling carbon dioxide. Laughing has even been called a form of internal jogging.

[5]All these benefits seem reason enough to run to the circus or to a Pee Wee Herman movie. Yet laughter improves health in additional ways that can't easily be measured by a blood pressure cuff. The amazing story of Norman Cousins is an example.

## MIND OVER MATTER

[6]In 1964, Cousins, an editor of *Saturday Review,* was told he had a crippling spinal disease and a one-in-500 chance for survival. Cousins rejected the traditional medical approach in favor of his own laugh-yourself-to-health cure. He checked into a hotel with lots of funny books, tapes of Marx Brothers' movies, and reruns of the old television show "Candid Camera." Regular laughter not only gave him some pain-free time to sleep, it also helped him beat the odds and make a full recovery.

[7]At first medical science put cases like Cousins' in the same category as faith healing and wearing copper bracelets to cure arthritis. Now, they are putting humor where it belongs—in places that help sick people get well. St. Joseph's Hospital in Houston, for instance, created a "Living Room" complete with funny books and magazines and live performances by comics and magicians. Patients are welcome to come to the room for a little comic relief. Other hospitals wheel carts of funny stuff—from video tapes to comic books—around to patients.

## STRESS REDUCING

[8]Just like jogging and other forms of exercise, laughing helps reduce stress. You see, once laughing stops, your muscles are much more relaxed than they were before you started. Your heartbeat and blood pressure also fall to lower levels. With all these bodily functions running at a low and easy pace, you can feel a little slower and easier yourself. Researchers now know that laughter can relieve certain types of headaches, even help lessen hypertension. Psychologist Jeffrey Goldstein of Temple University even believes laughter, with its reduction of stress and hypertension, helps people with a good sense of humor live longer.

## LAUGHTER AND LEARNING

[9]Before you get set to snicker, wait! Let us stretch laughter's list of good points even further. Does the idea of chortling your way to better grades tickle your fancy? A study conducted by Dr. Dolf Zillmann at Indiana University found that children learn better and remember more when lessons are mixed with laughter. For one thing, humor keeps their attention focused upon the material. Also, everybody is more willing to enter into an activity wholeheartedly if they think they are going to have a good time.

[10]People with a full-blown funnybone reap its rewards long after they graduate from school. Studies have shown that a sense of humor is the most consistent characteristic among executives promoted in major companies. Scientists have found that if you smile, you are more likely to be hired for a job. You are also more likely to be trusted once in that job.

## PRESCRIPTION FOR MIRTH

[11]Sounds like it's time to put a little more humor in your life, doesn't it? *Mad Magazine,* funny movies, and the daily newspaper comics will help, but it's also important to develop your own internal resources. Here are a few suggestions:

[12]1. *Adopt a playful attitude.* Keep your mind open to silly thoughts. If you're too worried about being cool to appear silly, remember that the word silly itself comes from the Old English word "saelig" meaning "happy, prosperous, and blessed."

[13]2. *Think funny.* Try to see the amusing side of every situation, especially ones that could otherwise be difficult. So when you discover you left your homework at home after you're already late for school because you stained your brand new white shirt which you only put on because you ripped your favorite sweater, make a joke out of the whole thing. It sure beats crying.

[14]3. *Laugh at yourself and take yourself lightly, but don't make jokes that put yourself or others down.* And make sure to take important responsibilities seriously. After that, a dose of humor makes all of life's worries and burdens a little lighter.

[15]4. *Make others laugh.* Laughter is contagious; making others happy often makes you feel happy. So pass on a good joke when you hear one. Some people say that health and happiness aren't laughing matters—but maybe they should be.

[16]Oh, yes, how did Tom define that word? "A place where de cowboys ride."

## Content Questions

*True or False*

If the statement is false, rewrite it to make it true.

1. Laughter is good exercise.
2. A good laugh primarily benefits your lungs.
3. During a hearty laugh, your blood pressure drops.

4. Norman Cousins used traditional medicine in addition to his laugh-cure.

5. Traditional medical science does not believe there are any real benefits to humor and laughter.

*Completion*

6. List four benefits of laughing.

7. Goodman talks about big laughs, mild laughs, and hearty laughs but also uses four synonyms for laugh. List them.

8. What is the most consistent characteristic among executives promoted in major companies?

9. What are endorphins?

10. List two reasons children learn better and remember more when their studies are mixed with laughter.

**Content Analysis Questions**

1. Explain the title "Jest for the Health of it."

2. Why is laughing called a form of internal jogging?

3. State Goodman's thesis.

4. What does the phrase "mind over matter" mean?

5. Write yourself a prescription for mirth.

**Application Questions**

1. List four adjectives that describe a person you know who has a good sense of humor and smiles often. List four adjectives that describe a person you know who doesn't laugh or smile very often. Which list has more words with positive than negative connotations? If someone were describing you, what kind of words would they use?

2. Design a plan that one of your instructors could use to appropriately mix humor into his or her course. Your plan should include a minimum of three specific suggestions.

# *Think Right, Stay Well?*

## *Experts debate whether you can really rev up your immune system*

### DENISE GRADY

*Denise Grady, an* American Health *contributing editor, lives in Albuquerque, NM. This selection is from* American Health.

[1]Whatever happened to the good old days, when people got sick because of germs, bad genes or just plain bad luck? In this era of empowerment, there are no innocent victims. If you've got a sore throat, it's your own fault. Illness reflects your emotional failings: not managing your stress, letting life get you down, having a bad

attitude, repressing your feelings. Anybody can tell you those things are bad for your immune system. Get your act together or you'll wind up with cancer. But is it really so? Have 2 million years of evolution molded the human body to self-destruct when its owner gets the blues? Studies of links between body and mind have demonstrated that states such as tension and hostility can influence the course of heart disease. But efforts to determine whether emotions contribute to cancer, infections and other illnesses that involve the immune system have yet conclusively to prove a connection. Nonetheless, tantalizing bits of evidence have captured the popular imagination, to the dismay of some scientists, who fear that research findings are being exaggerated or oversimplified, then used to berate sick people for failing to think medically correct, happy thoughts.

[2]"There is far too much blaming of people for getting their illnesses in the first place and then for not getting better," says Dr. Bruce Naliboff, chief of psychophysiology research at the Veterans Administration Medical Center in Sepulveda, Calif. "A lot has to do with not understanding an illness and blaming it on emotional factors. There's not nearly the level of scientific understanding relating emotions to cancer that there is connecting smoking to cancer."

[3]The underlying idea that the mind can affect the body is as old as medicine itself. Hippocrates observed that even the sickest patients sometimes got well simply through "their contentment with the goodness of the physician." More than 2,000 years later common sense also argues that if good feelings can help, bad ones can hurt. But only during the past 25 years have medical scientists begun to look systematically for physical and chemical links between emotional states, such as stress and depression, and the body's susceptibility to infections, cancer and so-called auto-immune diseases, such as rheumatoid arthritis and lupus, in which the body attacks itself.

[4]A new field of research called psychoneuroimmunology (PNI) is devoted to the connections among emotions and the nervous and immune systems. (The immune system, the body's disease-fighting network, includes the thymus [a gland under the breastbone], bone marrow, spleen and lymph nodes, as well as the infection fighting cells and antibodies that originate in these tissues.) Underlying the new discipline is physical evidence that the nervous and immune systems exchange signals: A dense collection of nerve fibers, for instance, reaches into the immune system organs. It has also become clear that stress and depression can hamper certain important immune system activities, at least as measured in the laboratory.

[5]According to the simplest theory of this interaction, the brain of a person who feels stressed sends signals to the adrenal glands, which respond by secreting cortisol and epinephrine (adrenaline), the hormones that activate the body's "fight or flight" responses. These chemicals can also suppress immune system function.

[6]A critical link is missing, however. Unhappy mental states may lead to immune system changes, but it's not known whether those changes, which are small, affect health. There is no definitive proof that emotional distress actually makes people prone to illness. In actuality, we may be more able to tolerate life's ups and downs than we think.

[7]The work thus far on emotions and immunity adds up to little more than "findings in search of meaning," concluded a team headed

by Dr. Marvin Stein, a professor of psychiatry at the Mount Sinai School of Medicine in New York City, in an article in *The Archives of General Psychiatry.* Stein emphasizes that he's not denying a link between emotions, immunity and health. "It may be there," he says, "but we just haven't been able to demonstrate it. We need to know more about how the brain, the immune system and the endocrine system [glands that release hormones into the blood stream] talk to one another." Until that mysterious language is deciphered, doctors won't really know what to tell patients about the healing power of the mind.

[8]For that matter, dispensing mind-body advice may even be risky, because research sometimes contradicts common sense. Most people, for example, would assume that relaxation training would help ease tension for surgery patients. But when British psychologists put it to the test in a study, they found that even though hospital patients said they felt more relaxed, they had potentially dangerous increases in epinephrine and cortisol during and after surgery. These very high readings weren't found among surgical patients left to worry and fret, the researchers reported in *Psychosomatic Medicine.* Though the hormonal surges didn't seem to do any physical harm, epinephrine and cortisol can suppress the immune system, increasing the risk of infection after surgery. The study thus led the researchers to conclude that moderate anxiety might actually be good for surgical patients.

[9]And yet it has become an article of faith in American society that tension, sadness and misfortune are physically harmful. As a nation, we seem at times to be tyrannized by cheer. The notion that laughter can even save your life gained wide acceptance with the 1979 publication of *Anatomy of an Illness,* the late magazine editor Norman Cousins' account of his recovery from a rheumatic disease of the spine—ankylosing spondylitis—with the aid of Candid Camera videos and Marx Brothers movies. And in his 1988 best seller, *Love, Medicine and Miracles,* surgeon Bernie Siegel argued that a fighting spirit and the determination to survive are vital adjuncts to standard cancer therapy.

[10]The 1970s and '80s also saw a series of provocative and widely publicized studies on the health of widowed or divorced people. Their rates of illness and death are higher than those among married people, with divorce producing the greater risk. Moreover, lab tests showed immune cell function was also below par in both groups; the same is true for people who score high on measures of loneliness. In addition, several studies have found unusually high cancer rates among people suffering from depression.

[11]At first glance, these would seem to be convincing cases. But there are factors the studies don't account for. For example, some researchers suggest that people who are divorced, widowed or depressed are more likely to drink, use drugs, eat and sleep poorly and fail to exercise, all of which may affect the immune system. Emotionally, such people may also be less tolerant of illness and more likely to report their problems. Then there's the fact that a high proportion of depressed patients smoke, skewing statistics relating to depression and cancer. It's even possible that some types of cancer, even before they're diagnosed, cause depression—not the other way around.

[12]Moreover, the immune system changes measured in all these studies are relatively small (nowhere near the size of the disruptions that occur in people with AIDS, for example). "The actual health consequences of these less extreme alterations are unknown," says Dr. Janice Kiecolt-Glaser, a professor of psychology and psychiatry at Ohio State University College of Medicine in Columbus, and a leading researcher in the field.

[13]Kiecolt-Glaser notes that the body may be able to tolerate some reduction in immune function without risk of illness. How much, though, is not known. She suggests that people whose immunity is already compromised—the elderly, say, or people with AIDS—are those most likely to be harmed by any further loss. But she and other researchers also note that there's no evidence that psychotherapy or treatment for depression enhances a patient's immune function.

[14]Other, more basic difficulties complicate research in this field. For one thing, people respond to stress in different ways. And long-term stress may have different effects than short-term stress. Depression too takes different forms and varies greatly in its degree of severity. So supposedly similar patients lumped together in studies may actually be very different—with different organic problems at the root of their mental conditions. No wonder findings on depression and immune function have been "inconsistent and inconclusive," in the words of Marvin Stein.

[15]Among the work most widely cited as proof that psychological treatment can help patients fight disease is an experiment involving women with advanced breast cancer. Dr. David Spiegel, a professor of psychiatry at Stanford University Medical Center, reported in 1989 that 50 women randomly assigned to a weekly support group lived an average of 18 months longer than 36 similar patients not in support groups. It's inviting to assume that the women cheered each other up and thus enhanced their immune function. But that is only an assumption: Spiegel didn't measure immune function, though he plans to in a new study. Stein speculates that group members helped one another endure grueling therapy. Perhaps they also "slept and ate better, and took their medications more faithfully," he adds.

[16]In a study praised for being more scientifically rigorous than most in the field, a team of British and American researchers reported in *The New England Journal of Medicine* in 1991 that people under stress were more likely than others to catch colds. In the study, 94 volunteers took nasal drops containing cold viruses and then waited to see whether they became ill. Those who revealed themselves in a questionnaire to be highly stressed were more than five times as likely as low-stress subjects to become infected, and twice as likely to develop cold symptoms (lab tests show a person can become infected without getting sick).

[17]A pretty compelling indictment of stress, it might seem. But at least one researcher, Dr. Morton Swartz, a professor of medicine at Harvard University Medical School, was cautious in interpreting the results. "The observed effects of stress were relatively small," he wrote in a critique of the report, concluding that they probably were of limited importance in triggering colds. He also wondered whether the authors had really taken sufficient account of other factors that

might have affected the subjects' health, such as smoking, alcohol consumption and quality of sleep.

[18]Possibly the boldest theory in mind-body research is the notion that certain behavior patterns can leave people especially vulnerable to cancer. In her book on the mind-cancer link, *The Type C Connection* (Random House, $23), psychologist Lydia Temoshok reports that among the patients she studied who had malignant melanoma, a potentially deadly skin cancer, 75% shared certain behavioral traits: They were unfailingly pleasant, repressed negative feelings such as anger, fear and sadness, constantly put other people's needs ahead of their own and went to extraordinary lengths to please others.

[19]Dr. Temoshok describes this "Type C" behavior as "a modest but important risk factor for cancer progression." She believes that repressing emotions for years and years inhibits the immune system and that breaking loose from the Type C pattern might help some patients recover from cancer or even help prevent it from developing in the first place. But Temoshok acknowledges the lack of studies to measure the prevalence of Type C behavior or to track healthy Type C's to determine how many eventually develop cancer.

[20]And she condemns what she calls "a New Age version of mind over matter": the dangerous myth that we have complete mental control over sickness and health. Temoshok thinks we have some influence at best; expecting too much sets the stage for failure, guilt and discouragement.

[21]Dr. George Solomon, a UCLA professor of psychiatry and biobehavioral sciences who has collaborated with Temoshok on her research, is exploring the idea of an "immunodysregulation-prone personality characterized by self-sacrifice and unassertiveness even to the point of wimpiness." But he adds, "I'm just saying these kinds of people are too nice. These are personality styles, not pathologies. In many ways they're much lovelier people than most." Solomon hopes to find out whether assertiveness training can change their behavior and consequently their immune function. Asked whether his characterization of them offends his subjects, Solomon says, "I don't think so, but if that's how they take it, maybe they should get some therapy to deal with having their feelings hurt too easily."

[22]But not everyone sees it that way. "I think it's terrible, calling cancer patients wimps," says Dr. Marcia Angell, executive editor of *The New England Journal of Medicine.* Angell has been an outspoken critic of mind-body theories since 1985, when she wrote that attaching "credit to patients for controlling their disease also implies blame for the progression of the disease." When people are sick, Angell went on, "they should not be further burdened by having to accept responsibility for the outcome."

[23]Today, Angell remains unconvinced of the mind's ability to fight disease: "I don't think there's much good research," she says. "There's a little more information about tiny postulated links. But a lot of small links do not a chain make. If it were true that you really could cure yourself by meditating or whatever, it would be worth it. But with no proof, it's cruel." She calls her journal's report on colds "one of the few well-done studies," but one in which "the clinical implications are probably very small." Her stance, she notes, has drawn vituperative attacks from legions of positive thinkers. "I've

been their target for many years," she says. "I can't help feeling that what I tapped into was a religious movement."

[24]Some self-help manuals do strike an accusatory tone. In *Heal Your Body,* for example, best-selling author Louise Hay lists "the mental causes" of several hundred physical illnesses. Birth defects, for instance, are "karmic. You selected to come that way. We choose our parents and our children." Cancer, she says, comes from "deep hurt," resentment and "carrying hatreds." Blackheads result from "small outbursts of anger," and multiple sclerosis from "mental hardness." Bladder infections? "Anxiety. Holding on to old ideas. Fear of letting go. Being pissed off." As for AIDS, it's related to "sexual guilt." Hay's nonsensical remedies consist of substituting "new thought patterns" for old, such as "I express love and joy and I am at peace."

[25]Surely there must be some way to take advantage of PNI's potential without chanting platitudes or, more importantly, putting one's self-esteem on the line. Perhaps the answer lies in allowing that meditation, or assertiveness training, or picturing our immune cells gobbling up enemy cells is worth a try. But if those approaches don't work, blame the method, not yourself.

## Content Questions

*True or False*

If the statement is false, rewrite it to make it true.

1. Research studies have proven a connection between tension/hostility and heart disease.
2. Research studies have conclusively proven tension/hostility cause illness.
3. Most scientists are concerned that mind-body research findings are being minimized.
4. The idea that the mind can affect the body is a new concept.
5. In actuality, we may be more able to tolerate life's ups and downs than we think.

## Vocabulary

Define each of these words or phrases:

1. era of empowerment (¶1)
2. conclusively (¶1)
3. berate (¶1)
4. provocative (¶10)
5. enhances (¶13)
6. scientifically rigorous (¶16)
7. critique (¶17)
8. postulated links (¶23)
9. stance (¶23)
10. vituperative attacks (¶23)

Explain the meaning and then indicate whether the phrase has a positive or negative connotation. Explain your reasoning.

1. tantalizing bits of evidence (¶1)
2. tyrannized by cheer (¶9)
3. skewing statistics (¶11)
4. compelling indictment (¶17)
5. a New Age version (¶20)
6. to the point of wimpiness (¶21)
7. nonsensical remedies (¶24)
8. chanting platitudes (¶25)

**Content Analysis Questions**

1. What is Grady's purpose?
2. State Grady's thesis.
3. State Dr. Naliboff's point of view on the mind-body connection.
4. State Dr. Stein's point of view of the mind-body connection.
5. State Dr. Kiecolt-Glaser's point of view of the mind-body connection.
6. State Dr. Swartz's point of view of the mind-body connection.
7. State Ms. Temoshok's point of view of the mind-body connection.
8. State Dr. Angell's point of view of the mind-body connection.
9. What is Grady's point of view? Justify your answer.
10. Did Grady fulfill her purpose? Why or why not?

**Application Questions**

1. Assume a close friend has been diagnosed with a painful but non-life threatening auto-immune disease. Her doctor has offered a wide range of traditional and nontraditional treatments. She has asked your advice. What would you recommend? Why?
2. What is your current point of view about the mind-body connection? Has your view changed recently?

# Theme 2
# Living in a
# Throwaway Society

Trend forecaster Faith Popcorn says that things don't always have to go from bad to worse; it's possible, she says, that they can go from bad to better. Consider these two scenarios.

It's 2010.

Try to open your door and you can't, because there's too much garbage piled up outside. While you once spent about 10% of your salary to buy nonessential items, now it costs about 10% more of your salary to get rid of these nonessentials. You'll know who has money and who doesn't by who gets his or her garbage picked up. The newly rich of 2010 will have made their money not by creating new products, but by making the garbage go away—these are the garbage barons. And the owners of any remaining landfills will have a stranglehold on the community.

Or:

We will adopt a consume/replenish approach to living. Replenish and consume. Consumers and corporations alike will have learned that production and consumption aren't the end of the line. The cycle ends with replenishing, giving back.

If you, like Ms. Popcorn, see the future optimistically, have you considered the changes we must enact to ensure that future?

This theme begins with an excerpt from Vice President Albert Gore's best-selling book, *Earth in the Balance—Ecology and the Human Spirit*. In this essay he calls on Americans to confront "one of the clearest signs that our relationship to the global environment is in severe crisis—the floodtide of garbage spilling out of our cities and factories."

Next, environmental science Professors Bernard J. Nebel and Richard T. Wright overview the solid waste crisis and potential solutions in their textbook chapter, "Converting Trash to Resources." They look at the problems, costs and limitations of landfills, and discuss the pros and cons of incineration. They not only examine ways to reuse and recycle materials but how to reduce the amount of source waste.

In "The History of Garbage," archaeologist and garbologist Bill Rathje discusses an "important truth" about garbage—there are no ways of dealing with garbage that haven't been known for thousands of years: dumping it, burning it, turning it into something that can be used again, and minimizing the volume produced in the first place. He also challenges us to look at all aspects of the garbage crisis, including our personal attitudes and behaviors.

Then, in "A Perverse Law of Garbage," Rathje reveals Parkinson's Law of Garbage: "Garbage expands so as to fill the receptacles available for its containment."

France Bequette, a Franco-American journalist specializing in environmental questions, provides a look at the waste problem around the world in "Living with Waste." "Cleaning Up Your Act," by Susan Goodman briefly reviews the available "solutions" to the garbage problem with an emphasis on what individuals can do to help. And finally, Bruce VanVoorst tackles "the dirty little secret" of recycling in "The Recycling Bottleneck."

Each of the readings is by a different author(s), of a different length, and requires different tasks.

---

### Strategies for Success

- Develop a plan for each of the readings.
- Determine who the author is and why he or she is writing.
- Know the vocabulary the author uses.
- Identify what the author is writing about.
- Establish how the author develops the writing.
- Integrate graphic and text information.
- Organize the information you need.
- Recognize the author's stance.
- Decide what you can do with the author's information.

---

# The Wasteland

## ALBERT GORE

*Written in 1992 by Al Gore, then Democratic senator from Tennessee,* Earth in the Balance—Ecology and the Human Spirit *was hailed as a brave and powerful book on the environment. Vice President Gore was a journalist for seven years before winning a seat in the House of Representatives in 1976. He was elected to the Senate in 1984, the vice presidency in 1992, and is considered a leader in the fight to save the global environment. This selection is from* Earth in the Balance.

[1]One of the clearest signs that our relationship to the global environment is in severe crisis is the floodtide of garbage spilling out of our cities and factories. What some have called the "throwaway society" has been based on the assumptions that endless resources will allow us to produce an endless supply of goods and that bottomless receptacles (i.e., landfills and ocean dumping sites) will allow us to dispose of an endless stream of waste. But now we are beginning to drown in that stream. Having relied for too long on the old strat-

egy of "out of sight, out of mind," we are now running out of ways to dispose of our waste in a manner that keeps it out of either sight or mind.

[2]In an earlier era, when the human population and the quantities of waste generated were much smaller and when highly toxic forms of waste were uncommon, it was possible to believe that the world's absorption of our waste meant that we need not think about it again. Now, however, all that has changed. Suddenly, we are disconcerted—even offended—when the huge quantities of waste we thought we had thrown away suddenly demand our attention as landfills overflow, incinerators foul the air, and neighboring communities and states attempt to dump their overflow problems on us.

[3]The American people have, in recent years, become embroiled in debates about the relative merits of various waste disposal schemes, from dumping it in the ocean to burying it in a landfill to burning it or taking it elsewhere, anywhere, as long as it is somewhere else. Now, however, we must confront a strategic threat to our capacity to dispose of—or even recycle—the enormous quantities of waste now being produced. Simply put, the way we think about waste is leading to the production of so much of it that no method for handling it can escape being completely overwhelmed. There is only one way out: we have to change our production processes and dramatically reduce the amount of waste we create in the first place and ensure that we consider thoroughly, ahead of time, just how we intend to recycle or isolate that which unavoidably remains. But first we have to think clearly about the complexities of the predicament.

[4]Waste is a multifaceted problem. We think of waste as whatever is useless, or unprofitable according to our transitory methods of calculating value, or sufficiently degraded so that the cost of reclamation seems higher than the cost of disposal. But anything produced in excess—nuclear weapons, for example, or junk mail—also represents waste. And in modern civilization, we have come to think of almost any natural resource as "going to waste" if we have failed to develop it, which usually means exploiting it for commercial use. Ironically, however, when we do transform natural resources into something useful, we create waste twice—once when we generate waste as part of the production process and a second time when we tire of the thing itself and throw it away.

[5]Perhaps the most visible evidence of the waste crisis is the problem of how to dispose of our mountains of municipal solid waste, which is being generated at the rate of more than five pounds a day for every citizen of this country, or approximately one ton per person per year. But two other kinds of waste pose equally difficult challenges. The first is the physically dangerous and politically volatile material known as hazardous waste, which accompanied the chemical revolution of the 1930s and which the United States now produces in roughly the same quantities as municipal solid waste. (This is a conservative estimate, one that would double if we counted all the hazardous waste that is currently exempted from regulation for a variety of administrative and political reasons.) Second, one ton of industrial solid waste is created each week for every man, woman, and child—and this does not even count the gaseous waste steadily being vented into the atmosphere. (For example, each person in the United States also produces an average of twenty tons of $CO_2$ each year.) Incredibly, taking into account all three of these conserva-

tively defined categories of waste, every person in the United States produces more than twice his or her weight in waste every day.

[6]It's easy to discount the importance of such a statistic, but we can no longer consider ourselves completely separate from the waste we help to produce at work or the waste that is generated in the process of supplying us with the things we buy and use.

[7]Our cavalier attitude toward this problem is an indication of how hard it will be to solve. Even the words we use to describe our behavior reveal the pattern of self-deception. Take, for example, the word consumption, which implies an almost mechanical efficiency, suggesting that all traces of whatever we consume magically vanish after we use it. In fact, when we consume something, it doesn't go away at all. Rather, it is transformed into two very different kinds of things: something "useful" and the stuff left over, which we call "waste." Moreover, anything we think of as useful becomes waste as soon as we are finished with it, so our perception of the things we consume must be considered when deciding what is and isn't waste. Until recently, none of these issues has seemed terribly important; indeed, a high rate of consumption has often been cited as a distinguishing characteristic of an advanced society. Now, however, this attitude can no longer be considered in any way healthy, desirable, or acceptable. . . .

## Content Questions

*True or False*

If the statement is false, rewrite it to make it true.

1. We are running out of ways to dispose of our garbage.
2. Most people agree that the best way to dispose of garbage is to burn it.
3. The most visible evidence of the waste problem is our cities' garbage.
4. Every person in the United States produces more than twice his or her weight in waste every day.
5. Even when we consume something, we create some waste.

*Completion*

6. What is happening, according to Gore, because of the way we think about waste?
7. What does Gore think is "our only way out"?
8. How does Gore define "waste"?
9. List the three types of waste that pose the most difficult disposal challenge.
10. When we consume something, what actually happens?

## Vocabulary

Explain each of these words or phrases:

1. global environment (¶1)
2. disconcerted (¶2)

3. embroiled (¶3)
4. strategic threat (¶3)
5. complexities of the predicament (¶3)
6. transitory (¶4)
7. sufficiently degraded (¶4)
8. physically dangerous and politically volatile material (¶5)
9. cavalier attitude (¶7)
10. pattern of self-deception (¶7)

## Content Analysis Questions

1. State Gore's thesis.
2. What does Gore mean by "waste is a multi-faceted problem?"
3. In paragraph 4, Gore writes, "Ironically, however, when we do transform natural resources into something useful, we create waste twice—once when we generate waste as part of the production process and a second time when we tire of the thing itself and throw it away." What is the irony?
4. Why do you think some have called us a "throwaway society"? Give an example that illustrates this concept.
5. How do you define "useful" and "waste?" How do your definitions agree or disagree with Gore?

## Application Questions

1. Think about everything you have bought, used, eaten, done, and produced during the last two days. Identify three types of waste you have created. How did you dispose of the waste? Who then disposed of that waste? Can you identify one thing you could do differently to reduce that waste?
2. Identify four items that you currently consider "waste," e.g., used computer paper, plastic grocery bags, egg cartons, and devise a way to make them "useful" again. How would you convince your family and friends to "use" the item?

# Converting Trash to Resources

## Bernard J. Nebel and Richard T. Wright

*Dr. Nebel is a biology professor at Catonsville Community College in Maryland where he has taught environmental science for 21 years. He is a member of several professional associations and actively supports a number of environmental organizations.*

*Dr. Wright is chairman of the division of natural sciences, mathematics, and computer science at Gordon College in Massachusetts, where he has taught environmental science for 22 years. He has received research grants from the National Science Foundation for his work in aquatic microbiology and works with many professional and environmental endeavors.*

*This selection is from* Environmental Science, *4th ed.*

# 20

# Converting Trash to Resources

## LEARNING OBJECTIVES

**When you have finished studying this chapter, you should be able to:**

1. Sketch the historical background of refuse disposal.

2. Name the main components of municipal solid waste today and describe how each is disposed of.

3. Describe four problems that stem from landfilling with refuse.

4. Describe the features that new landfills must have in order to prevent problems.

5. Discuss the pros and cons of incineration.

6. Describe some of the costs and limitations of landfills.

7. Describe ways in which the total volume of refuse might be reduced.

8. Name six factors that make it difficult to recycle refuse and describe how each can be overcome.

9. Give examples of laws that might be passed to promote recycling.

10. Explain what composting is and describe the components of refuse that might be composted.

11. Describe how refuse may be converted to energy.

12. Discuss the concept of integrated waste management.

On your next trip to the mall, take a good look at all the products piled high on the shelves and hanging from the racks of the scores of retailers there. Everything you see will eventually end up as trash. These goods are there to be purchased, used, and then thrown away; the economy depends on it. Little of the materials used to make all these products is ever reused, a clear violation of the first principle of sustainability: that ecosystems dispose of wastes and replenish nutrients by recycling all elements. Common sense dictates that a throwaway society is not sustainable, but it appears that we have had to prove this fact experimentally. The results: We are on the brink of a crisis as we produce more trash than ever before and are rapidly running out of places to put it. Yet, solutions that might avert a full-blown crisis are available and are being implemented. In this chapter, we look at the dimensions of the crisis and discuss some potential solutions.

## The Solid Waste Crisis

So far in this book we have talked about animal feedlot wastes (Chapter 12), sewage wastes (Chapter 13), and industrial wastes (Chapters 14 and 15). A fourth category of wastes, the focus of this chapter, is **municipal solid waste** (MSW), defined as the total of all the materials thrown away from homes and commercial establishments (commonly called trash, refuse, or garbage).

Over the years, the amount of municipal solid waste generated in the United States has grown steadily, in part because of increasing population but more so because of changing lifestyles and the increasing use of disposable materials and excessive packaging (Fig. 20–1). It now amounts to somewhat over 4 pounds (2 kg) per person per day. At the current U.S. population of 250 million, that is enough waste to fill 75 000 garbage trucks each day, a total of 185 million tons (166 million metric tons) per year.

Studies show that the refuse generated by municipalities is roughly composed of:

| | | | |
|---|---|---|---|
| Paper, paperboard | 41% | Food wastes | 8% |
| Yard waste | 18% | Glass | 8% |
| Metals | 9% | Other | 7% |
| Plastics | 9% | | |

However, the proportions vary greatly depending on the generator (commercial versus residential), the neighborhood (affluent versus poor), and the time of year (during certain seasons, yard wastes, such as grass clippings and raked leaves, add to the solid waste burden, often equaling all the other categories combined).

Traditionally, local governments have assumed

**FIGURE 20–1**
Output of solid wastes in the United States. While the population increased by 22 percent between 1970 and 1990, the amount of MSW collected increased by 60 percent and the per capita waste output increased by 30 percent. (Data from J. E. Young, "Discarding the Throwaway Society," Worldwatch Paper 101. © 1991 by Worldwatch Institute.)

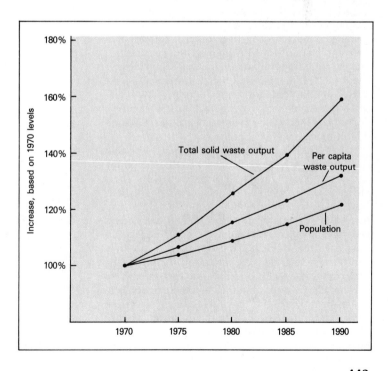

the responsibility for collecting and disposing of MSW. The local jurisdiction may own the trucks and employ workers, or it may contract with a private firm to provide the collection service. Collected MSW is then disposed of in a variety of ways, as discussed below. Alternatively, some municipalities have opted for putting all trash collection and disposal in the private sector. The collectors bill each home by volume of trash. This system allows competition between collectors and gives homeowners a strong incentive to reduce trash volume.

Until the 1960s most MSW was disposed of in open, burning dumps. The waste was burned to reduce volume and lengthen the life span of the dump site, but refuse does not burn well. Smoldering dumps produced clouds of smoke that could be seen from miles away, smelled bad, and created a breeding ground for flies and rats. Some cities turned to incinerators, which are huge furnaces in which high temperatures allow the waste to burn more completely than in open dumps. Without air pollution controls, however, incinerators were also prime sources of air pollution. Public objection and air pollution laws forced the phaseout of open dumps and many incinerators during the 1960s and early 1970s. Open dumps were then converted to *landfills*.

## CURRENT DISPOSAL PROCESSES

At present in the United States, three-fourths of municipal solid waste is disposed of in landfills and the remaining one-fourth is equally divided between incineration and recycling (Fig. 20–2). The pattern is different in countries where population densities are higher. High-density Japan, for instance, incinerates about half of its trash and recycles over half of the rest. Many Western European nations (also high-density areas unable to devote valuable land to landfills) deposit less than half of their municipal waste in landfills and incinerate most of the rest.

In a **landfill,** the waste is put on or in the ground and covered with earth. Because there is no burning and because each day's fill is covered with a few inches of earth, air pollution and vermin populations are kept down. Unfortunately, aside from those concerns and the minimizing of cost, no other factors were given real consideration when the first landfills were opened. Municipal waste managers generally had no understanding of or interest in ecology, the water cycle, or what products would be generated by decomposing wastes, and they had no regulations to guide them. Therefore, in general, any cheap, conveniently located piece of land on the outskirts of town became the site for a landfill. This site was frequently a natural gully or ravine, an abandoned stone

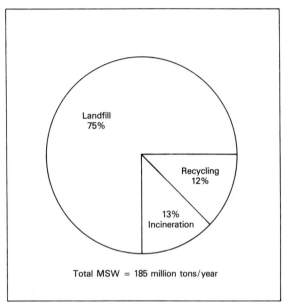

Total MSW = 185 million tons/year

**FIGURE 20–2**
Current processes of MSW disposal in the United States.

quarry, a section of wetlands, or a previous dump. Once the municipality acquired the land, dumping commenced with no precautions taken. The plan usually was that after the site was full, it would be covered with earth and converted to a park or playground. Thus, landfilling was originally thought of as a means of upgrading "wasteland" to a higher use as well as a means of disposing of trash.

## PROBLEMS OF LANDFILLS

With the understanding you have gained from previous chapters, you should be able to predict the consequences of landfilling:

○ Leachate generation and groundwater contamination
○ Methane production
○ Incomplete decomposition
○ Settling

### Leachate Generation and Groundwater Contamination

The most serious problem by far is groundwater contamination. Recall that as water percolates through any material, various chemicals in the material may dissolve in the water and get carried along, a process called leaching. The water with various pollutants in it is called **leachate.** As water percolates through MSW, a noxious leachate is generated, which consists of residues of decomposing organic matter combined with iron, mercury, lead, zinc, and other metals from rusting cans, discarded batteries, and appliances—generously spiced with paints, pesticides, cleaning fluids, newspaper inks, and other chemicals. The nature of the landfill site and the absence of precautionary measures noted above funnel this ''witch's brew'' directly into groundwater aquifers.

All states have some municipal landfills that either are or soon will be contaminating groundwater, but Florida is in a real crisis. The state is topographically flat and hence has vast areas of wetlands. Most of the land is only a few feet above sea level and rests on water-saturated limestone. No matter where Florida's landfills were located, they were either in wetlands or just a few feet above the water table. Since residents rely on groundwater for 92 percent of their fresh water, you can guess the result: more than 200 municipal landfill sites on the Superfund list. Recall from Chapter 14 that Superfund is the federal program to clean up sites that are in imminent danger of jeopardizing human health through groundwater contamination. It will cost between $10 million and $100 million to clean up each site. So much for cheap waste disposal!

### Methane Production

Because 67 percent of MSW is organic materials, it is potentially subject to natural decomposition. However, buried wastes do not have access to oxygen. Therefore, their decomposition is anaerobic, and a major byproduct of this process is biogas, which is about two-thirds methane, a highly flammable gas (p. 303). Produced deep in a landfill, methane may seep horizontally through the earth, enter basements, and cause explosions as it accumulates and is ignited. Over 20 homes at distances up to 1000 feet from landfills have been destroyed, and some deaths have occurred as a result of such explosions. Also, methane seeping to the surface kills vegetation by poisoning the roots. Without vegetation, erosion occurs, exposing the unsightly waste. A number of cities have exploited the problem by installing ''gas wells'' in landfills. The wells tap the biogas, and the methane is purified and used as fuel. There are now 70 commercial landfill gas facilities in the United States; the largest, in Sunnyvale, California, generates enough electricity to power 100 000 homes.

### Incomplete Decomposition

The plastic components of MSW cannot be decomposed because of their chemical composition. For this reason, much emphasis has been placed on developing biodegradable plastics. There are serious questions about the degradability of these plastics, however. The term *biodegradation* refers to the complete breakdown of carbon compounds to carbon dioxide and water. All the purported biodegradable plastics do is disintegrate into a fine polymer powder that still resists microbial breakdown.

Recent research on landfills has shown that even materials always assumed to be biodegradable—newspapers, wood, and so on—are degraded only slowly if at all. Newspapers 30 years old were recovered in a readable state; layers of telephone directories were found marking each year, practically intact. Since paper materials are 40 percent of MSW, this is a serious matter. The reason paper and other organics decompose so slowly is the lack of suitable amounts of moisture; the more water percolating through a landfill, the better the biodegradation of paper materials. However, the more percolation there is, the more toxic leachate is produced!

### Settling

Finally, waste settles as it compacts. Luckily, this eventuality was recognized from the beginning, and so buildings have never been put on landfills. Settling presents a problem where landfills have been converted to playgrounds and golf courses, though, because it creates shallow depressions that collect and hold water. This process converts some of the land back to a ''wetland,'' albeit usually one with noxious leachate seeping to the surface.

## IMPROVING LANDFILLS: TRYING TO FIX A WRONG ANSWER

Recognizing the above problems, the Environmental Protection Agency has upgraded siting and construction requirements for new landfills. Under current regulations:

○ New landfills are sited on high ground well above the water table. Often the top of an existing hill is bulldozed off to supply a source of cover dirt and at the same time create a floor that is above the water table.

○ The floor is first contoured so that water will drain into a tile leachate-collection system. The floor is then covered with at least 12 inches of impervious clay or a plastic liner or both. On top of this is a layer of coarse gravel and a layer of porous earth. With this design, any leachate percolating through the fill will encounter the gravel layer and then move through that layer into the leachate collection system. The clay layer or plastic liner prevents leachate from ever entering the groundwater. Collected leachate can be treated as necessary.

○ Layer upon layer of refuse is positioned such that the fill is built up in the shape of a pyramid. Finally it is capped with a layer of clay and a layer of topsoil and then seeded. This clay-topsoil cap and the pyramidal shape help the landfill to shed water. In this way, water infiltration into the fill is minimized, and so less leachate is formed.

○ Finally, the entire site is surrounded by a series of groundwater monitoring wells that are checked periodically, and such checking must go on indefinitely.

These design features are summarized in Figure 20–3.

The regulations do protect groundwater, but the landfill pyramids may well last as long as the Egyptian pyramids (though they are not likely to become tour-

ist attractions!). And if they do break down, they become a threat to the groundwater—therefore, the need for monitoring remains. As trash keeps coming, more and more landfills are created, leading only to more problems in the future. It is clear that we are "fixing a wrong answer."

## INCINERATION: ANOTHER WRONG ANSWER

Currently, 128 incinerators are operating in the United States, burning about 25 million tons of waste annually—13 percent of the waste stream. Incineration of municipal solid waste has some advantages over landfilling. Its primary appeal is reduction of volume; incinerators can reduce trash volume by 80 to 90 percent, and thus greatly extend the life of a landfill (which is still required to receive the ash). Also, most newer incinerators are designed to generate electricity, which is sold to offset some of the costs of disposal.

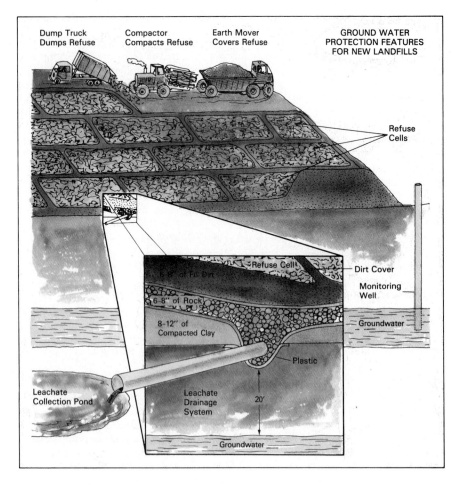

**FIGURE 20–3**
Features of a modern landfill with environmental safeguards. The landfill is sited on a high location well above the water table. The bottom is sealed with compacted clay or a plastic liner or both overlaid by a rock or gravel layer with pipes to drain the leachate. Refuse is built up in layers as each day's refuse is covered with earth so that the completed fill has a pyramid-shape that sheds water. The fill is provided with groundwater monitoring wells.

Incineration has some serious drawbacks, however. Trash does not burn cleanly. Despite being equipped with air pollution control devices, incinerator stacks emit toxic fumes into the air as burning oxidizes and vaporizes the assortment of metals, plastics, and hazardous materials that inevitably end up as municipal waste. Incinerators are very expensive to build, and their siting has the same problem as the landfills: No one wants to live near one. Incinerator ash is loaded with metals and other hazardous substances and must be disposed of in secure landfills. The worst criticism of the incineration option is that, even if the incinerator generates electricity, the process wastes both energy and materials when compared with recycling. Indeed, incinerators compete directly with recycling for burnable materials such as newspapers and represent a major impediment to recycling in many municipalities. For these reasons, incineration represents a wrong direction in waste management.

## COSTS OF MUNICIPAL SOLID WASTE DISPOSAL

The costs of disposing of MSW are becoming prohibitive. Increasing costs are not just a result of the new design features of landfills. More and more, they reflect the expenses of acquiring a site and providing transportation. **Tipping fees**—the costs assessed at the disposal site—now exceed $100 a ton at some landfills, and the waste collector must recover this cost as well as transportation costs to the site. Tipping fees at incinerators are no better; one trash-to-energy incinerator in Saugus, Massachusetts, recently had to increase its tipping fee from $22 to $80 per ton to cover the cost of adding a mandated stack scrubber.

No one wants a landfill in her or his backyard, and with spreading urbanization there are few areas near cities not already dotted with high-priced suburban homes. Any site selection, then, is met with protests and often legal suits declaring, "Anywhere

---

## IN PERSPECTIVE
### *Trash on the Move*

Long Island, New York, achieved a certain notoriety in 1987 when a garbage barge piled high with Long Island trash cruised the Atlantic Ocean for 4 months looking for a place to dump the load. Now some Long Island villages are adding to this dubious reputation as their trash is trucked 900 miles to a landfill in Taylorville, Illinois. In Tonawanda, New York, trash from Canada has become the newest item of economic exchange between Canada and the United States. Some 500 000 tons of garbage was exported into the United States from Ontario province in 1991. This may be Canada's most effective rebuttal to acid rain from the United States! And the small town of Welch, West Virginia, is poised to become the nation's largest recipient of out-of-state trash if a developer's plan to set up a huge landfill 3 miles from town is approved.

The underlying reason for this traffic in trash is market economics.

Cities and towns are looking for the least expensive way to get rid of their municipal solid waste, and it sometimes happens that trucking the trash out of state or even out of the country is less expensive than taking it to a local incinerator or landfill. It would cost $87 a ton to dump trash from Westbury, Long Island, at an incinerator 10 miles away in Hempstead, but Westbury can hire Star Recycling Inc. of Brooklyn to take the trash all the way to Illinois for $69 a ton. Since the 13 000 citizens of Westbury already pay $2.1 million to get rid of their trash, they're looking for ways to keep down their costs.

In Ontario, the provincial government raised tipping fees to $136 a ton (from $18 just 4 years ago), in order to push a new recycling program. Much lower fees in neighboring New York landfills have "drawn haulers to American dumps like sea gulls," in the words of a *New York Times* reporter. New York legisla-

tors, unhappy about the flood of Canadian garbage, are exploring the imposition of a hefty "inspection fee" of $150 a ton at the border in order to stem the tide. However, some observers fear the possibility of retaliatory action by Canada that would hurt another waste exchange: the movement of hazardous waste from the United States to Canada!

The lessons here are obvious. We are indeed in a crisis mode, and waste *management*, not simply waste *removal*, must become a high priority on the national agenda. Trucking trash long distances to save a few dollars makes no economic sense when the total costs of lost energy and environmental impact at the final dump sites are calculated. And it certainly makes no ecological sense. *Trash on the move* is the final, ridiculous consequence—and let us hope, the death throes—of the lack of coherent public policy for managing municipal solid waste.

---

but here!'' The legal costs incurred in overcoming these objections, if they are overcome, are often as expensive as all other costs combined. Or, the process leads to selection of a very distant site, which involves inordinate hauling expenses. There are also limits of state lines; no state wants to act as the dump site for another state (see In Perspective Box, p. 447).

With new landfills being held back by costs and legal objections, the sad fact is that most MSW is still going into old landfills with inadequate safeguards. Of the 6000 municipal landfills in the United States, which receive 75 percent (over 130 million tons per year) of our MSW per year, 75 percent are unlined, 95 percent do not have leachate collection systems, and 75 percent do not monitor groundwater.

About 1200 old landfills are scheduled to close by 1997 either because they have reached capacity or because of environmental problems. New landfills are being constructed at less than half this rate, however. In the 1960s, many environmentalists thought that our throwaway society would meet limits in the form of shortages of resource materials. It is ironic to note that the actual limit is turning out to be space to dump the garbage.

Running out of space is beside the point, however, since even if new sites could be obtained, the system is not sustainable. Fortunately, there is a better way.

## Solutions

### REDUCING WASTE VOLUME

The best strategy of all is to reduce waste at its source. We noted earlier that the increased amount of waste produced over the years is largely a result of changing lifestyles, notably the growing use of disposable products and excessive packaging. This may be changing. To mention just two recent developments, concerned over the mass of disposable diapers in MSW, many families are switching to cloth diapers, and environmentally concerned consumers have successfully pressured some producers to reduce packaging. The manufacturers of compact discs have agreed to downsize their unnecessarily large packages, for example.

An option that thus far has received too little attention is the potential for reducing waste volume by keeping products in use longer. Reusing items in their existing capacity is the most efficient form of recycling. The use of returnable versus nonreturnable beverage containers is a prime case in point.

### Returnable versus Nonreturnable Bottles

Before the 1960s, most soft drinks and beer were marketed by local bottlers and breweries in returnable bottles that required a deposit. Trucks delivered filled bottles to retailers and picked up empties to be cleaned and refilled. This procedure is efficient when the distance between producer and retailer is relatively short. As the distance increases, however, transportation costs become prohibitive because the consumer pays for hauling the bottles as well as for the beverage. In the late 1950s, distributors, bent on expanding markets and growth, observed that transportation costs could be greatly reduced if they used lightweight containers that could be thrown out rather than shipped back. Thus, no-deposit, nonreturnable bottles and cans were introduced. The throwaway container is also an obvious winner for its manufacturers, who profit by each bottle or can they produce.

Through massive advertising campaigns promoting national brands and the convenience of throwaways, a handful of national distributors gained dominance during the 1950s and 1960s, and countless local breweries and bottlers were driven out of business. At the same time, bottle and can manufacturing grew into a multibillion-dollar industry.

The average person drinks about a quart of liquid each day. For 250 million Americans, this daily consumption amounts to some 1.3 million barrels of liquid. That a significant portion of this volume should be packaged in single-serving containers that are used once and then thrown away is bizarre. It is difficult to imagine a more costly, wasteful way to distribute fluids.

Beverages in nonreturnable containers and those in returnable containers appear to be priced competitively on the market shelf, but this equality evaporates when you look at the hidden costs of single-use containers. Nonreturnable containers constitute 6 percent of the solid waste stream in the United States and about 50 percent of the nonburnable portion; they also constitute about 90 percent of the nonbiodegradable portion of roadside litter. Broken bottles along the road are responsible for innumerable cuts and other injuries, not to mention flat tires. Both the mining of the materials they are composed of and the manufacturing process create pollution. All of these are hidden costs that do not appear on the price tag, but we pay them with taxes for litter cleanup, our injuries, flat tires, environmental degradation, and so on.

In an attempt to reverse the trend, environmental and consumer groups have promoted **bottle bills**—laws that facilitate the recycling or reuse of beverage containers. Such bills generally call for a deposit on all beverage containers—both returnables and throwaways. Retailers are required to accept the used containers and pass them along for recycling or reuse.

Bottle bills have been proposed in virtually every state legislature over the last decade. In every case, however, the proposals have met with fierce opposition from the beverage and container industries and certain other special interest groups. The reason for their opposition is obvious—economic loss—but the arguments they put forth are more subtle. The container industry contends that bottle bills will result in loss of jobs and higher beverage costs for the consumer. They also claim that consumers will not return the bottles and litter will not decline.

In most cases, the industry's well-financed lobbying efforts have successfully defeated bottle bills. However, some states—10 as of 1992—have adopted bottle bills despite industry opposition (Table 20–1). Their experience has proved the beverage and bottle industry's arguments false. More jobs are gained than lost, costs to the consumer have not risen, a high percentage of bottles are returned, and there is a marked reduction in can and bottle litter. In some cases, local breweries and bottlers are making a comeback, thus improving the local economy.

A final measure of the success of bottle bills is continued public approval. Despite industry efforts to repeal bottle bills, no state that has one has repealed it. As this text goes to press, a national bottle

**TABLE 20–1**

**States That Have Bottle Bills**

| State | Year Passed | State | Year Passed |
|---|---|---|---|
| Oregon | 1972 | Iowa | 1978 |
| Vermont | 1973 | Massachusetts | 1978 |
| Maine | 1976 | Delaware | 1982 |
| Michigan | 1976 | New York | 1983 |
| Connecticut | 1978 | California | 1991 |

bill has been introduced in Congress. Opponents are arguing that the bill will threaten the newly won successes in curbside recycling, with some justification. Beverage containers represent the most important source of revenue in curbside recycling. However, as curbside recycling currently reaches only 15 percent of the U.S. population, a national bottle bill will recover a much greater proportion of beverage containers (states with bottle bills report 80 to 97 percent rates of return of containers).

## Other Measures

Whenever items are reused rather than thrown away, the effect is a reduction in waste and better conservation of resources. In this respect, it is encouraging to see the growing popularity of yard sales, flea markets, and other "not new" markets (Fig. 20–4).

**FIGURE 20–4**
One way to recycle. The yard sale has become a Saturday morning staple in communities all over the country. (George E. Jones III/Photo Research.)

Consideration of our domestic wastes and their disposal emphasizes what a mammoth stream of materials flows in one direction from our resource base to disposal sites. Just as natural ecosystems depend on recycling nutrients, the continuance of a technological society will ultimately depend on our learning to recycle or reuse not only nutrients but virtually all other kinds of materials as well.

## THE RECYCLING SOLUTION

In addition to reuse, recycling is another obvious solution to the solid waste crisis. More than 75 percent of MSW is recyclable material. Of course, many people have been advocating recycling for a long time now, and various groups and individuals have been recycling paper, glass, and aluminum cans on a small scale for decades. What has prevented recycling from

being implemented on a large scale? There are some real impediments to large-scale recycling that must be overcome. However, once these problems are recognized and understood, they can be and are being solved. Indeed, recycling is now a tremendous growth industry with prospects for a bright future.

### Impediments to Recycling

The problems that must be overcome are:

*Sorting* We are used to the convenience of throwing all our refuse into a single container and handling it in one bulk mass. For recycling, the various constituents must be separated either in the home or after collection.

*Lack of Standards* Sorting is made even more difficult by lack of standards. That is, several kinds of plastic

---

### ETHICS
*Recycling—The Right Thing to Do?*

The town meeting is an institution in Massachusetts. Held once a year, it is a forum for decision making on the town's budget and all sorts of ancillary business (such as deciding on a leash law, changing the zoning requirements, or accepting new streets). Originally, the whole town was expected to attend; nowadays, 10 percent of the voting population is considered a good turnout. Microphones are set up in the auditorium, and anyone in the town can express her or his opinion on matters on the docket.

In recent years, Massachusetts towns have taken a strong turn toward fiscal stringency, a symptom of the larger economic recession in the United States. Many school programs have been radically cut, town personnel have been let go, and many items on town budgets have been voted down. In the face of such stringency, it is encouraging that recycling programs have gone against the cutback trend in almost every town and city in Boston's Northshore area. By 1992, most Northshore towns had some kind of recycling program. Very often, the

program was proposed by a nonpaid town official acting on behalf of grass roots citizens' groups. Arguments pro and con were aired at the town meeting, and, in town after town, recycling was adopted by overwhelming votes even though the programs do not pay for themselves; it still costs money to recycle.

The city of Beverly is one example. Beverly has curbside recycling, and the town picks up 50 tons of recyclables a week, at a cost of $30 a ton. This compares unfavorably with the current tipping fee of $22 a ton at a regional trash-to-energy incinerator. When asked why the townspeople were in favor of recycling, one Beverly town official stated that they're doing it because "it's the right thing to do!"

One town—Topsfield—recently celebrated its twentieth year of a recycling program, clearly a leader in the trend. Not all towns have jumped on the bandwagon, however. Danvers, for example, has held back because "it's just not cost-effective," according to the town public works director.

However, the handwriting is not only on the wall, it's now a matter of a state **solid waste master plan** issued in 1990. Leaf waste, large appliances, and tires were phased out of landfill dumping statewide in 1991; the ban extended to other yard waste, metals, and glass in 1992, and by 1994, recyclable paper and plastics will be banned from landfills. Obviously, the recycling trend is not simply a matter of virtuous decision making on the part of the townspeople; they see the state mandates coming and are acting wisely. However, it should be noted that recycling in Massachusetts began as a grass roots movement. It has reached the state level and is now working back down to the grass roots to catch those towns that have been dragging their feet.

Recycling is one of the most obvious ways for people to demonstrate their concern for the environment. And perhaps the reason it got started is the most basic one: Because it's the right thing to do. Do you agree?

or grades of paper may be used in similar products or even in the same product.

*Reprocessing* There must be companies capable of receiving the materials collected and converting them into salable materials. Otherwise it is off to the landfill after sorting.

*Marketing* There must be industrial or consumer markets to buy the products made from recycled material. Otherwise the manufacturing company goes bankrupt, and the products become refuse before they are even sold.

*Separation between Government and Private Enterprise* In general, refuse collection is done by local governments, and governments are reluctant to (and probably shouldn't) get into the business of producing and marketing materials, which is the realm of private enterprise. Conversely, companies engaged in production like to deal with clean, uniform raw materials, which trash is not. Therefore, with few exceptions, they have been less than eager to deal with refuse. Lack of cooperation between local governments and the private sector frequently impedes recycling.

*Vested Interests in the Status Quo* Tremendous profits can be maintained indefinitely in manufacturing and selling bottles, cans, and other items that are used only once and then discarded. The vested interests who profit from the throwaway habit have been a potent force against implementing any form of recycling.

*Hidden Costs* Since refuse disposal is usually financed out of tax revenues, people generally do not realize how much they are paying. The costs of cleaning up a hazardous site or monitoring such a site forever to check for groundwater contamination are not tallied into the costs of disposal. With costs thus hidden, refuse disposal may seem like a free (and carefree) service. The costs of alternatives seem expensive by comparison, even though the long-term costs would be less.

### Addressing the Problems

Problems should not be taken as an excuse for inaction, however; rather, they should be taken as an opportunity to develop creative solutions. Thousands of communities in the United States (15 percent of the population) are overcoming the aforementioned obstacles in one way or another and entering into curbside recycling. Let us look at a few of the basic ideas being tried.

*Government-Business Partnerships* Companies that will provide full-service recycling—that is, collection through processing, including production of certain products from recycled materials—are forming and growing rapidly. Governments are forming partnerships with such companies. Basically the company is contracted to collect and recycle a certain minimum percentage of the municipality's waste stream. In return, the government gives the company certain guarantees such as exclusive collection and marketing rights of certain recycled materials in their area. Further, the government may agree to purchase certain amounts of recycled paper, compost, and plastic. Finally the government agrees to continue to dispose of a certain quantity of material that cannot be recycled at the present time. Can you see the need for these guarantees? Without them the company could be forced out of business, to the detriment of both parties.

*Sorting* Sorting is best done at the source (homes), although it may be done after collection. Sorting at the source requires the cooperation of a large portion of the population, but it is relatively inexpensive since the work is "volunteer." A system that is gaining acceptance in a number of communities is the issuance of color-coded containers for plastic, metals, glass, paper, yard wastes, and "other." A trailer with colored bins is drawn behind the regular trash truck, and workers dump containers in the respective bins. Unsorted refuse continues to go into the regular trash truck for traditional disposal. The sorted refuse is then transported to a facility that processes it for further distribution to businesses that deal in recycled materials (see In Perspective Box, p. 453).

Alternatively, unsorted trash can be picked up by regular trucks and separated after collection. Refuse separation facilities have been built and are in operation. The general scheme for one such facility is shown in Figure 20–5. However, such equipment is very costly to purchase, and operation and maintenance costs are also high. The payback from the sale of recycled materials comes nowhere close to offsetting these costs. The major savings comes from not having to pay tipping fees at landfills or incinerators. When the savings in fees are added to proceeds from the sale of recycled materials, the total can more than offset the maintenance costs.

In Third World countries many poor people make their living by picking through dumps and reselling "garbage" (Fig. 6–6). This is a sign of their desperate poverty, however, not a recommended solution to the garbage problem.

*Reprocessing and Profits* There is an abundance of alternatives for reprocessing various components of

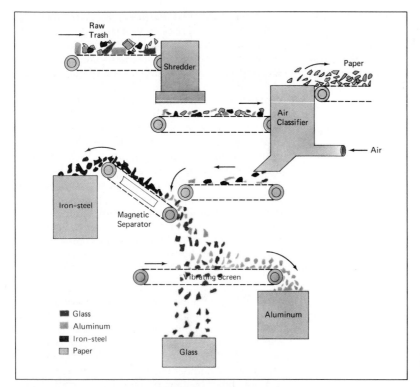

**FIGURE 20–5**
Schematic flow diagram for the separation of MSW after collection. Separation can be achieved, but is it superior to separation at the source, as in curbside recycling? Does the value of the separated materials justify the costs of separation?

refuse, and people are coming up with new ideas and techniques all the time. A few of the major established techniques follow.

○ Paper can be repulped and reprocessed into recycled paper, cardboard, and other paper products; finely ground and sold as cellulose insulation; or shredded and composted (see below).

○ Glass can be crushed, remelted, and made into new containers or crushed and used as a substitute for gravel or sand in construction materials such as concrete and asphalt.

○ Some forms of plastic can be remelted and fabricated into "synthetic lumber" (Fig. 20–6). Such lumber, since it is not biodegradable, has potential for use in fence, sign, and guardrail posts, docks, decks, and other outdoor uses.

**FIGURE 20–6**
Waste plastics can be fabricated into "synthetic lumber," which has great potential for outdoor uses, such as the deck boards of this dock, because it is nonbiodegradable. This deck was provided by the Chicago Park District as part of a 1988 Pilot Recycling Program. The deck material was manufactured from approximately 84 500 plastic milk bottles by Eaglebrook Profiles, Chicago, IL. (Photograph by BJN.)

## IN PERSPECTIVE
### *Regionalized Recycling*

Currently, most recycling is on a town-by-town basis. Either the towns or their waste contractors must find markets for the recycled goods: cans, bottles, newspapers, and plastics. This problem has kept many municipalities from getting into recycling. The solution? A regionalized materials recycling facility (MRF), referred to in the trade as a "murf." Here's how the state-owned MRF in Springfield, Massachusetts, works:

Basic sorting takes place when waste is collected, either by curbside collection or by town recycling stations (sites where townspeople can bring wastes to be recycled). The waste is then trucked to the MRF and handled on three tracks—one for metal cans and glass containers, another for paper products, and a third for plastics. The materials are moved through the facility by escalators and conveyor belts, tended by workers who inspect and do further sorting. The objective of the process is to prepare materials for the recycled goods market. Glass is sorted by color, cleaned, crushed into small pebbles, and then shipped to glass companies, where it replaces the raw materials that go into glass manufacture—sand and

soda ash—and saves substantially on energy costs. Cans are sorted, flattened, and sent either to de-tinning plants or to aluminum processing facilities. Paper is sorted, baled, and sent to reprocessing mills. Plastics are sorted into four categories, depending on color and type of plastic polymer, and then sold.

The facility's clear advantages are its economy of scale and its ability to produce a high-quality end product for the recycled materials market. Towns know where to bring their waste, and they quickly become familiar with the requirements for initial sorting during collection and transfer.

Currently, there is only one MRF in Massachusetts, built with state funds at a cost of $5 million and operated by the state Department of Environmental Protection. Several more are on the drawing board. After one year of operation, the Springfield MRF was declared a success. It took in 42 886 tons of materials from 91 towns representing a population of 750 000. The process has diverted 22 to 50 percent of the waste stream (depending on the community) from landfills and incinerators, and saved the towns millions of dollars in disposal costs.

The facility has attracted recycled wastes from Connecticut and New York while those states are setting up their own regional recycling centers.

There have been some unanticipated problems at the Springfield facility during its first year of operation. Several towns have reduced their trash so much that they are not fulfilling their contractural obligations to a regional incinerator. Landfill revenues have declined, forcing landfill operators to lower their fees in order to attract more haulers. These appear to be temporary problems that will be worked out in time, however. The state is committed to recycling almost half of municipal solid waste, and incinerating most of the rest, by the year 2000. In theory, landfills will operate mainly as recipients of incinerator ash and materials that can't be either recycled or burned.

Very likely, the future of regional recycling will be in the private sector. In order for this to work, the recycling market will have to be substantially strengthened. However, all indications point to such facilities as the wave of the future.

○ Metals can be remelted and refabricated. Making aluminum from scrap aluminum saves up to 90 percent of the energy required to make aluminum from virgin ore.

○ Food wastes and yard wastes (leaves, grass, and plant trimmings) can be composted to produce a humus soil conditioner.

○ Textiles can be shredded and used to strengthen recycled paper products.

○ Old tires can be remelted or shredded and made into a number of other products.

In addition, literally hundreds of new processes are being developed and commercialized to make refuse components into more valuable end products.

Thus recycling is becoming increasingly profitable. Consequently, the profit potential of recycling is bringing many new companies into the field despite the vested interests of some old established companies in maintaining the status quo.

### Promoting Recycling through Mandate

A number of measures are being adopted by various state and local governments that mandate or at least support recycling. These include:

*Mandatory Recycling Laws* A number of states have passed mandatory recycling laws. Such laws require that each county, under threat of loss of state funds, recycle a certain percentage of its refuse by a certain

**FIGURE 20–7**
Composting refuse. Keeping material moist but well aerated results in odor-free decomposition of paper, food, yard, and other organic wastes into humuslike material. Photograph shows windrow of refuse being turned and fluffed by machinery to aid decomposition. (Courtesy Wildcat Manufacturing Co., Inc. Freeman, SD.)

date. Massachusetts, for example, has adopted a goal of recycling 46 percent of all of its MSW by 2000.

***Banning the Disposal of Certain Items in Landfills***
Yard wastes are a good first candidate here because they take up considerable volume and can easily be collected separately, composted into humus, and applied to park lands. To date, Florida, Illinois, Minnesota, New Jersey, Pennsylvania, and Wisconsin have banned yard wastes from landfills. Of course, items that present a toxic or explosive hazard, such as car batteries, are already generally banned.

***Mandating Government Purchase of Recycled Materials*** A state can require that all its agencies buy a certain percentage of recycled paper. Requiring highway departments to use plastic signposts and parks departments to use compost can extend recycling beyond paper.

***Mandating the Use of Recycled and Reusable Materials in Packaging*** One-third of landfill space is taken up by packaging materials. Great savings—at the source and by recycling—can come from requiring that all packaging be reusable or made (at least partly) of recycled materials. A bill to that effect has been introduced in the Massachusetts legislature, calculated to triple recycling rates in the state by the year

2000 if enacted. The province of Ontario has already passed a similar initiative aimed at soft drink packaging.

## COMPOSTING

One way of treating some forms of refuse that is rapidly growing in popularity is composting. Recall that composting involves the natural biological decomposition (rotting) of organic matter in the presence of air (see Chapter 9, In Perspective Box, p. 195). The end product is a residue of humuslike material, which can be used as an organic fertilizer. Composting was one method of treating sewage sludge described in Chapter 13. Likewise, since refuse is usually 60 to 80 percent organic matter (paper and food wastes)—or more when yard wastes are added—it may be treated by composting (Fig. 20–7).

A number of companies have entered into the business of selling equipment or of building and running facilities for composting refuse. Glass, metals, and plastics may be removed either before or after composting and recycled as desired. Also, raw sewage sludge may be mixed with the refuse to achieve a synergistic composting of both simultaneously. Paper helps to dewater the sewage sludge and provides better aeration, and the sludge supports better decomposition. There is a good market for compost from landscaping firms, and it may be used on city parks or agricultural fields. It is important, however, that wastes to be composted be free of toxic household products and heavy metals. Otherwise, the compost is unacceptable for agricultural use.

## REFUSE-TO-ENERGY CONVERSION

Because it has a high organic content, refuse, including the plastics portion, can be burned. When burned, unsorted MSW releases about half as much energy as coal, pound for pound. We noted earlier in this chapter that incineration of MSW releases toxic fumes into the air and keeps recyclable materials (75 percent of MSW) from being recycled. Despite these serious drawbacks, a number of municipalities across the United States have built plants to incinerate MSW and generate electricity at the same time—almost three-fourths of the currently operating incinerators. Sale of the electricity offsets some of the costs of MSW

disposal, and the incinerators are usually able to compete successfully with landfills for MSW.

Incinerator ash must be landfilled, but because ash makes up only about 10 to 20 percent of the original volume, the life of the landfill will be extended about five- to tenfold. More important, since the incinerated material is not subject to further decomposition and settling, it can sometimes be used as fill dirt in construction sites, road beds, and so forth. However, the heavy metals in the ash may preclude this kind of use in many areas.

A refuse-to-energy plant that went into operation in Baltimore, Maryland, in 1984 is shown in Figure 20–8. This plant is capable of consuming 2000 tons of unsorted MSW per day. Steam produced in boilers drives a 60 000-kilowatt generator that produces enough power to service about 60 000 homes. Exhaust gases from the combustion are processed through electrostatic precipitators to remove some of the objectionable air pollutants.

The major drawback of converting refuse to energy is that it largely precludes future options for recycling and composting.

**FIGURE 20–8**
Conversion of municipal solid waste to energy. This diagram represents a refuse-to-energy plant in Baltimore, Maryland. The facility can incinerate 2000 tons of unseparated MSW per day to generate 60 megawatts of on-line power, enough to supply 60 000 homes.

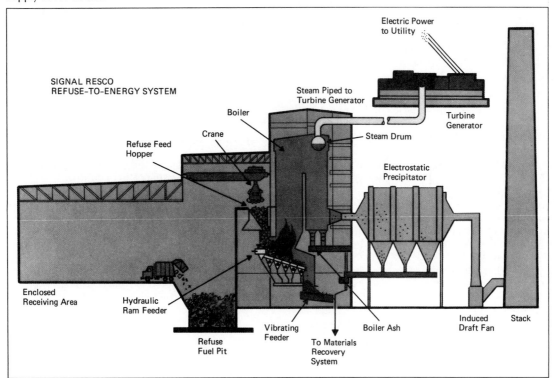

## INTEGRATED WASTE MANAGEMENT

It is important to remember that it is not necessary to fasten on a single method of waste handling. Almost any combination of recycling, composting, and reducing waste volume may be used. Further, recycling can be introduced gradually, pursuing a number of options while phasing out landfilling. This system of having several alternatives in operation at the same time is called **integrated waste management.** Balancing the interests of all parties involved obviously requires skilled managers. However, the days where each town could go its own way are in the past; regional and state management of solid waste is becoming the rule. Public policy is moving in the direction of integrated waste management under regulations at the state and even the federal level. Given the dimensions of the solid waste crisis, this increased attention to management is a welcome development.

It is also important to remember, however, that true management of MSW begins in the home. Lifestyle changes have been responsible for the increase in per capita MSW; it would be entirely possible to bring about a decrease in per capita MSW through lifestyle changes. The growing use of recycling will undoubtedly draw the attention of consumers to choices they make in the purchase and use of materials. Those who want to be part of the solution to the solid waste crisis will find many ways to reduce the waste they generate. Our society can make real progress toward sustainability in the MSW arena only through a combination of public policy and personal lifestyle changes that reject the throwaway mentality.

 *Review Questions* _____

1. List six components and their percent composition in MSW. What level of government is responsible for disposal of these wastes?
2. Trace the historical development of refuse disposal. What method of disposal is now most common?
3. What are the major costs and limitations of landfilling?
4. Outline the EPA's latest regulations for the construction of new landfills.
5. What are the advantages and disadvantages of incineration?
6. Why is landfilling not a sustainable option for solid waste disposal?
7. How can waste volume be reduced?
8. What seven impediments to recycling have prevented its large-scale implementation?
9. How are communities overcoming these obstacles to recycling?
10. What laws have been adopted by state and local governments to support recycling?
11. Which waste materials may be composted?
12. Discuss the pros and cons of converting refuse to energy.
13. What is integrated waste management?

 *Thinking Environmentally* _____

1. Compile a list of all the plastic items you used and threw away this week. Consider how you could reduce the length of this list.
2. If you live near the ocean or a large lake, walk along the beach for 20 minutes and collect all of the items that are clearly not natural. Where did these come from? What is their volume per 100 yards of beach?
3. How and where does your school dispose of solid waste? Is a recycling program in place? How well does it work?
4. Why do you suppose the United States creates so much more waste than other countries?
5. Does your state have a bottle bill? Is it effective? If you live in a state without such a bill, explore the politics that have prevented the bill from being adopted.
6. Suppose your town planned to build an incinerator near your home. You are concerned about your family's health but also about the rising costs of solid waste disposal. Explain your decision for or against the incinerator.

# The History of Garbage

## *Archaeologists bust myths about solid waste and society*

### BILL RATHJE

*Archaeologist and garbologist Bill Rathje, founder and director of The Garbage Project, is a professor in the department of anthropology at the University of Arizona. His widely read articles have appeared in such diverse publications as* The Journal of Resource Management and Technology, American Behavioral Scientist, *and* The Atlantic. *This selection is from* Garbage.

[1]GARBAGE IS NOT MATHEMATICS. To understand garbage you have to touch it, feel it, sort it, smell it. You have to pick through hundreds of tons of it, counting and weighing all the daily newspapers, the telephone books, the soiled diapers, the Styrofoam clamshells that briefly held hamburgers, the lipstick cylinders coated with grease, the medicine vials still encasing brightly colored pills, the empty bottles of scotch, the cans of paint and turpentine, the forsaken toys, the cigarette butts. You have to count and weigh all the organic matter, the discards from thousands of plates: the noodles and the Cheerios and the tortillas; the hardened jelly doughnuts bleeding from their wounds; the pieces of pet food which have made their own gravy; the half-eaten bananas, mostly still with their peels, black and incomparably sweet in the embrace of final decay. You have to confront sticky green mountains of yard waste and slippery brown hills of potato peels and brittle ossuaries of chicken bones and T-bones. And then finally there are the "fines," the vast connecting soup of indeterminable former nutrients, laced with bits of paper and metal, glass and plastic, which suffuse every landfill like a kind of lymph. The fines, too, must be gathered and weighed.

[2]To an archaeologist like myself, garbage trails mankind in an unbroken line from the first flakes of flint left by tool-makers a million years ago to the urine bags left by astronauts in outer space.

[3]For most of the last two million years, human beings left their garbage where it fell. This disposal scheme functioned adequately because hunters and gatherers frequently abandoned their campgrounds. When modern hunter-gatherers, like the aborigines of the Australian outback, are provided with government housing, one of the immediate problems they face is that of garbage disposal. Aborigines typically begin their settled lives by trashing their houses, leaving debris in all the rooms and throwing it out the windows and doors. As such behavior suggests, man faced his first garbage crisis when he became a sedentary animal.

[4]That brings us to the first important truth about garbage: There are no ways of dealing with it which haven't been known for many thousands of years. As the species has advanced, people have introduced refinements, but the old ways are fundamentally still the only ways, and they are four: dumping garbage, burning garbage, turning garbage into something that can be used again, and mini-

mizing the volume of material goods (future garbage) produced in the first place ("source reduction" it's called).

[5]Given the choice, a human being's first inclination is always to dump. From prehistory through the present day, dumping has been the means of disposal favored everywhere, including the cities. Archaeological excavations of hard-packed dirt and clay floors usually recover a multitude of small finds, suggesting that a great deal of garbage was just left on the floor where it fell, or was brushed into a corner. In 1973 a civil engineer with the Department of Commerce, Charles Gunnerson, calculated that the rate of uplift due to debris accumulation in the ancient city of Troy was about 4.7 feet per century. If the idea of a city rising above its garbage at this rate seems quaint, it may be worth considering that "street level" on the island of Manhattan is fully fourteen feet higher today than it was when Peter Minuit lived there.

[6]At Troy and elsewhere, of course, not all trash was kept indoors. The larger pieces of garbage and debris were thrown into the streets where semi-domesticated animals (usually pigs) ate up the food scraps while human scavengers, in exchange for the right to sell anything useful they might find, carried what was left to vacant lots or to the outskirts of town, where it was sometimes burned but more often simply left. The image of sulfurous "garbage mountains" in the Third World is repelling and almost a cliché, but the people who work these dumps, herding their pigs even as they sort paper from plastic from metal, are performing the most thorough job of garbage recycling and resource recovery in the world. What's an enlightened, right-thinking environmentalist to say? The garbage mountains point up another important truth about garbage: Efficient disposal is not always completely compatible with other desirable social ends—due process, human dignity, economic modernization. In a liberal democracy, these other ends compete for priority. In the United States, a garbage problem is in some respects just the modest price we pay for having done many things right. It was the threat of disease, finally, that made garbage removal at least partially a public responsibility in Europe and the U.S. In the United States, the path was pioneered by Colonel George E. Waring, Jr., the "Apostle of Cleanliness," who became the Street Cleaning Commissioner of the City of New York in 1895 and set up the first comprehensive system of refuse management in the country. Col. Waring and his 2,000 uniformed White Wings cleared the streets of rubbish and offal and carted off the refuse to dumps, incinerators, and, until the affluent owners of shorefront property in New Jersey complained, the Atlantic Ocean. Waring's powerful image as protector of the public health influenced communities everywhere. Taking the long view reminds us of one more important fact about garbage: Ever since governments began facing up to their responsibilities, the story of the garbage problem in the West has been one of steady amelioration, of bad giving way to less bad and eventually to not quite so bad.

## HOW MUCH GARBAGE?

[7]It stands to reason that something for which professionals have a technical term of long standing—solid waste stream—should also have a precisely calibrated volume attached to it. But the fact is

that estimates of the amount of garbage produced in the United States vary widely.

[8]During the past 15 years, The Garbage Project has handsorted and recorded modern household refuse in Tucson, Phoenix, Milwaukee, New Orleans, and Marin County (Calif.). By some happenstance, our sample neighborhoods—white, Hispanic, black, low income, middle income, upper income—all discarded less than the prevailing national averages for residential refuse. As a result, I became interested in the way national averages are calculated. I found that there are limits on the accuracy of material measurements because of the biases of the researchers and the logistical constraints involved in data collection, analysis, and reporting.

[9]Since there is no way to measure or weigh more than a fraction of what is actually discarded, all studies take short cuts. Some have tried to measure refuse in ten or 20 cities and then extrapolate findings to the nation as a whole. These studies suffer from acknowledged biases in data collection: Their informants were garbage haulers who had a vested interest in high figures. And sample sizes were small.

[10]Another estimation technique, the "materials-flow" method, doesn't examine garbage at all. Instead, it looks at industrial production, distribution, and sales records and applies assumptions about discard patterns to determine the rate at which materials enter the solid waste stream. The problem here is that the assumptions are largely untested. The study most quoted for current generation rates, for example, assumed that the maximum uselife of major household appliances is no more than 20 years, after which time the appliances are discarded. That assumption ignores the substantial trade in used durables, which supplies many low-income households with appliances and is a source of parts no longer carried by standard dealers. Such untested assumptions abound.

[11]Perhaps it should not have been a surprise that hands-on sorts produced figures consistently below accepted estimates. Nor should it be shocking that over the past two decades many incinerators were over-sized beyond their actual refuse intake, or that a 1981 column in Public Works asked, "Where has all the refuse gone?"

[12]Even though today most of us believe we are in the midst of a "Garbage Crisis," we don't really know how much garbage we actually generate every day or every year. We don't even seem to know if the quantities discarded are growing or shrinking. My own view is that the higher estimates of garbage generation (frequently reported as five to eight pounds per person per day) significantly overstate the problem. Garbage Project studies of actual refuse reveal that even three pounds of garbage per person per day may be too high an estimate for many parts of the country. A weight sort of garbage in Milwaukee in 1978–79 yielded a weight of one-and-a-half pounds per person per day, a result that has been roughly corroborated by weight sorts in other communities. Americans are wasteful, but to some degree we have been conditioned to think of ourselves as more wasteful than we truly are—and certainly as more wasteful than we used to be. The evidence of our senses reinforces such perceptions. Fast-food packaging is ubiquitous and conspicuous. Planned obsolescence is a cliché. Our society is filled with symbolic reminders of waste. What we miss is what is no longer there to see. We do not see the 1,200 pounds per annum of coal ash which every American gen-

erated at home at the turn of the century and which was dumped usually on the poor side of town. We do not see the hundreds of thousands of dead horses which once had to be disposed of by American cities every year. No, Americans are not suddenly producing more garbage. On a per capita basis, our record is, at worst, one of relative stability.

## THE ROLE OF BEHAVIORS

[13]The root problem in assessing the true magnitude of garbage accumulation is in the nature of garbage itself. Unlike the evidence of other social problems, be it a human one such as poverty or an aesthetic one such as bad architecture, the evidence of specific pieces of garbage disappears from one day to the next. People put their garbage in the can under the sink and then someone TAKES IT OUT. The garbage that is taken out is eventually left at the curb and then IT IS GONE. Garbage passes under our noses virtually unnoticed, the constant turnover inhibiting perception.

[14]With the permission of the sanitation division of the city of Tucson, my students and I have during the past 15 years examined the garbage of thousands of households. The Project has conducted studies designed to compare how people say they behave with how the garbage they discard says they behave; or, to put it another way, to compare what people say they throw away with what they actually throw away. Such detailed studies require that the interview responses of any household be matched against its garbage over a period of several weeks.

[15]As you might suspect, people are an utterly unreliable source of information. What people claim in interviews to have purchased and used, eaten and drunk, recycled and wasted, almost never corresponds directly to the packaging and debris in their garbage bags.

[16]If a behavior has a generally positive public image, it is over-reported. People report eating far higher quantities of high-fiber cereals, vegetable soups, and skim milk than the boxes, cans, and cartons they throw out would suggest. By the same token, if a behavior is seen in a negative light, it is under-reported. Informants drastically deflate the volume of alcoholic beverages, breakfast pastries and desserts, and high-fat foods they consume. One common form of distortion results from what might be called the Good Provider Syndrome: Heads of households usually estimate that their families go through a great deal more food and other goods than one can actually find evidence for in the family's garbage. On the other hand, when asked to report their own diets, most people succumb to the Lean Cuisine Syndrome and report smaller portions and fewer fats and sweets than their garbage indicates. If you want to know how much alcohol people drink at home, don't ask them. They will typically under-report by 40 to 60 percent.

[17]People's unpredictable behavior can have a direct impact on any attempt to change their discard patterns. For example, in California's Marin County, 88,000 households produce about 64,700 tons of hazardous materials each year. The county began sponsoring "collection days" when residents are encouraged to bring household hazardous wastes to a centralized location. To determine the efficacy of

the Toxics Away! Day held in 1986, The Garbage Project sorted Marin household refuse for one month before and two months after the event. The results were not at all what we (or the County) expected. The refuse discarded after the collection day contained more than twice the quantity of hazardous materials which we had found discarded in refuse samples examined before the collection day. Why? The collection was held on only one day with no future collections announced. Most likely some citizens, who had been made aware of their household toxic products through publicity—but had missed the actual collection, decided to get rid of their hazardous wastes through normal channels—at the curb. Or let's look at the realities of changing behaviors that would facilitate, say, recycling. Let's say that the demand for recycled paper, plastic, aluminum, and glass was insatiable. How much garbage would Americans be prepared to recycle? If Americans were Germans or Japanese, the answer might be a lot. Germans are furnished by local governments with three different trash containers, and they "source separate" their garbage to make recycling easier. In Japan, citizens are required to separate their garbage into at least seven and in some places as many as twenty categories to expedite re-use. In America, the only factor that could conceivably drive a systematic recycling effort is money. Money is the reason why junk dealers pay attention to some kinds of garbage and not to others, and it is the reason why most people return bottles and cans to supermarkets, and newspapers to recycling centers, instead of just throwing them away. If recycling does not make economic sense to the actors at every link along the great garbage chain, it simply won't happen.

[18]I belabor this point because it is so often overlooked, and because there are studies that seem to suggest—erroneously, I think—that for noble motives alone people would go to considerable lengths to make recycling an integral part of American life. Barry Commoner, the biologist and environmentalist, recently conducted a study of a hundred households in Easthampton, Long Island, in which participants were asked to separate their garbage into four containers: one for food debris and soiled paper (to be made into fertilizer), one for clean paper, one for metal cans and glass bottles, and one for all the rest. Mr. Commoner found that, because it was rationally discarded, a stunning 84 percent of the garbage from these households could be sold or recycled. Only 16 percent had to be deposited in a landfill. Of course, this experiment lasted only a few weeks, and the households surveyed had actively volunteered to take part. Recognizing that his results were perhaps a little skewed, Mr. Commoner conducted a telephone survey in Buffalo, New York, and ascertained that a reassuring 78 percent of all respondents said sure, they'd be willing to separate their garbage into four containers. However, only 25 percent of the respondents said that they thought their neighbors would be willing to do so. This "What would the neighbors do?" question has a special resonance for Garbage Project researchers. We have found over the years by comparing interview data with actual trash that the most accurate description of the behavior of any household lies in that household's description of the behavior of a neighboring household. Americans have a pretty firm understanding of human nature; they just don't want to admit that it applies to themselves.

[19]There have been studies that claimed that the people most likely to recycle are those with the most money and the most education, but all of these studies are based on people's "self-reports." A look through household garbage yields a different picture. Between 1973 and 1980, the Project examined some 9,000 refuse pickups in Tucson from a variety of sample neighborhoods chosen for their socioeconomic characteristics. The contents were carefully sorted for newspapers, aluminum cans, glass bottles, and tinned-steel cans (evidence that a household is not recycling), and for bottle caps, aluminum pop-tops, and plastic six-pack yokes (possible evidence, in the absence of bottles or cans, that a household is recycling). A lot of statistical adjustments and cross-referencing had to be done, but in the end we made three discoveries. First, nobody recycles as much as they say they do (but they do recycle just about as much as they say their neighbors do). Second, patterns of recycling by household vary over time; recycling is not a consistent habit. Third, high income and education and even a measure of environmental concern did not predict household recycling rates. The only reliable predictor was the price paid for various commodities at buyback centers. When prices rose for, say, newsprint, the number of newspapers found in local garbage suddenly declined as service groups and charities found it worth their time to collect and recycle.

[20]Every Garbage Project study seems to prompt the same conclusion: Our world is composed of two realities, one mental and one material. I personally believe that today's "Garbage Crisis" is largely the result of significant differences between the real world and the mental worlds which revolve around common household refuse. On one side there are still very few quantitative studies that physically measure the constituents of refuse. On the other side are all of the unique experiences each of us has had and the resulting set of personalized attitudes, beliefs, and ideas stored in our minds about garbage. These two sets of information—material measurements and mental perceptions—are equally "real," and both are constantly summoned by government officials, businessmen, environmentalists, and concerned laymen into evaluations of our solid-waste dilemma. As an archaeologist, I further believe that an even bigger problem with what our society recognizes as a garbage problem is that human behavior is systematically ignored. Today, garbage is perceived as a kind of primordial ooze, spontaneously generated. The material view usually reports "x" percent of plastic by weight, while the mental view often depicts plastics as materials to be eliminated from refuse because they are "unnatural" and "harmful to the environment" (usually in some unspecified way). But neither view identifies the role of specific plastics in our lifestyles or social order. As a bathroom products company, would you rather transport your product in glass containers or in much lighter, unbreakable plastic? As a consumer, would you purchase a glass container for the tiled bathroom or a lighter, safer container that won't shatter and cut? Because of the consistency of business and consumer choices, it is now difficult to find bathroom commodities in glass.

[21]For good, for bad, or for ugly, garbage cannot be successfully understood or managed or legislated separate from the behaviors that produce it.

## THE FUTURE OF CRISIS

[22]The garbage problem in the United States today is indeed serious, but I believe that the most critical issue is not landfill closings or incinerator emissions, collecting recyclables or mandating source reduction. To me, the central issue is obtaining accurate, objective, scientific data on each of these issues in all three of their dimensions—material, mental, and behavioral. Politicians, city officials, municipal and private haulers, the municipal engineering industry, environmental groups, and more all have elegant plans to reduce, collect, recycle, reuse, and dispose of solid wastes by means both efficient and environmentally appropriate. In contrast, the physical reality is a mess of immense proportions and complexity. At present, our knowledge and attitudes are out of sync with both behaviors and material realities. *That* is the real garbage crisis.

### Content Questions

*True or False*

If the statement is false, rewrite it to make it true.

1. We don't really know how much garbage we generate every day.
2. Americans are suddenly producing more garbage than ever before.
3. People always accurately report what they have purchased, used, eaten, and drunk.
4. In the United States, people are interested in recycling primarily for environmental reasons.
5. Rathje feels that tougher recycling laws would eliminate most of our garbage.

*Completion*

6. What are the only four ways of dealing with garbage.
7. Explain the phrase "the rate of uplift due to debris accumulation."
8. Name three discoveries that the Project made, based on its work in Tucson between 1973 and 1980.
9. "Every Garbage Project study seems to prompt the same conclusion." What is that conclusion? Explain what that means.
10. What does Rathje believe to be the most critical issue in the garbage problem?

### Vocabulary

Explain each of these words or phrases:

1. when he became a sedentary animal (¶3)
2. first inclination (¶5)
3. amelioration (¶6)
4. solid waste stream (¶7)

5. logistical constraints (¶8)
6. extrapolated findings (¶9)
7. a result that has been roughly corroborated (¶12)
8. fast-food packaging is ubiquitous and conspicuous (¶12)
9. planned obsolescence is a cliché (¶12)
10. most people succumb to (¶16)
11. determine the efficacy of (¶17)
12. garbage is perceived as a kind of primordial ooze, spontaneously generated (¶20)

Explain each of these figurative phrases from paragraph 1.

1. hardened jelly doughnuts bleeding from their wounds.
2. the "fines," the vast connecting soup
3. which suffuse every landfill like a kind of lymph

### Content Analysis Questions

1. What is Rathje's purpose for writing? What is the purpose of paragraph 1?
2. What is Rathje's thesis?
3. List four main ideas that Rathje uses to support and develop his thesis.
4. Do you think Rathje is both knowledgeable and reliable? Why or why not?
5. In general, do you think Rathje and Nebel and Wright have a similar or divergent point of view about the garbage problem and its solutions?
6. Compare and contrast your point of view on the garbage problem and its solutions with Rathje's.

### Application Questions

1. Assume that you have been asked to work with a group to develop a trash-reduction and recycling program for your campus. What would be your top two priorities? Why? What factors do you think would be critical to the success of your program? Why?
2. Why do you think there is such a different view of recycling between Americans and people in Germany or Japan? How could you find out more information about trash reduction and recycling programs in other countries?

# A Perverse Law of Garbage

## BILL RATHJE

[1]Only two refuse realities can reduce stalwart Garbage Project sorters to fear and loathing: one is raw, rancid chicken (as bad as any smell stinks); the other is Parkinson's Law of Garbage (as unintentionally perverse as any human behavior becomes). Anyone in the

vicinity immediately recognizes rancid chicken; Parkinson's Law of Garbage was exposed only after thousands of Garbage Project sorts of household refuse pick-ups.

²The original Parkinson's Law was formulated in 1957 by C. Northcote Parkinson, a British bureaucrat who concluded: "Work expands so as to fill the time available for its completion." Parkinson's Law of Garbage similarly states: "Garbage expands so as to fill the receptacles available for its containment." While the evidence for this refuse law is not yet conclusive, its implications go to the heart of every city's solid waste-management strategy.

³During the past decade, many municipalities have switched from a system whereby homeowners provided their own garbage cans, and sanitation workers emptied them by hand, to a system whereby the city provides special containers that trucks empty mechanically. The object is to save labor costs and to reduce worker injuries. Mechanized trucks can handle only a limited number of sizes of bins. Since large households must be accommodated, most city residents therefore receive a very large—90 gallon, in most cases—wheeled container.

⁴In 1980 the city of Phoenix adopted such an automated system, with 90-gallon containers, and a subsequent Garbage Project study (in 1988) revealed that the per-capita generation of garbage seemed to have become abnormally high, at least as compared to Tucson, a mere 100 miles away.

⁵Nothing more was made of this finding until researchers began analyzing data from areas of Tucson that had recently converted to mechanized collection. We realized that garbage-generation rates of sample households had shot up about a third, comparable to the apparent increase in Phoenix.

⁶Other cities that have mechanized are also registering significant increases. In Sacramento, for example, the annual per-capita haul has risen from about 1.4 tons before mechanization to more than 1.8 tons afterward, even as tipping fees (money paid by the hauler to the landfill) have more than doubled. A Dodge City, Kansas, sanitation official expressed surprise at the results of a pilot program in which households were given 120-gallon garbage bins: "People filled the suckers up!" In Beverly Hills, neighborhoods have been given 300-gallon containers, and one can only wonder what effect such encouragement will have on a community whose discard patterns are already excessive (Beverly Hills is the kind of place, according to sanitation officials there, where some homeowners regularly pick up the sod and throw out their entire lawns twice a year, switching grass type to keep it green year 'round.)

⁷Parkinson's Law, with respect to garbage, is quite simple. When people have small garbage cans, larger garbage—old cans of paint, broken furniture perpetually awaiting repair, bags of old clothing—do not typically get thrown away. Rather, these items sit in basements and in garages, often until a residence changes hands.

⁸But when homeowners are provided with plastic mini-dumpsters, they are presented with a new option. Before long what was once an instinctive "I'll just stick this in the cellar" becomes an equally instinctive "I'll bet this will fit in the dumpster."

⁹The Garbage Project has compared the contents of Tucson garbage collected before and after mechanization. Solid-waste dis-

cards went from an average of less than 14 pounds per biweekly pick-up to an average of more than 23 pounds. The largest increase was in the yard-waste category, followed by "other" (broken odds-and-ends), food waste, newspapers, and textiles. The first pick-up of the week was substantially heavier than the second, reflecting the accomplishment of weekend chores, and the discards in that pick-up contained consistently larger amounts of hazardous waste than we had come to expect in a typical load. These findings suggest that the introduction of 90-gallon containers should be of concern for three reasons.

### 3 UH-OHS

[10]First, the increase in discarded newspapers suggest that one counter-productive result of larger containers may be a lower participation rate in any form of recycling. For those who find separating out recyclables a bother, the 90-gallon bin is a no-penalty means to circumvent the issue. Likewise, the increase in "other" and textiles could mean an alternative to the "donation avenue," which leads unwanted resources to the Salvation Army and other charities.

[11]Second, the substantial increase of hazardous wastes indicates that the large bins are a convenient alternative to storing toxic items until used up at home or until the next household hazardous waste collection day.

[12]Third, at the same time massive, all-out recycling programs are being implemented to *decrease* the flow of garbage, collection techniques are being installed which unwittingly may be *increasing* the overall flow of garbage to an even higher rate.

### Content Questions

*True or False*

If the statement is false, rewrite it to make it true.

1. Switching from small trash containers that could be hand emptied to large containers for mechanical dumping was designed to save labor costs and reduce worker injuries.
2. Most cities that have switched to large containers for mechanized pickup are collecting more garbage.
3. Parkinson's Law of Garbage appears to apply only to the Southwest United States.
4. The large trash containers help recycling efforts.
5. The Garbage Project does the majority of their work with business and industrial garbage.

*Completion*

6. What is Parkinson's Law of Garbage? Explain it's meaning in your own words.
7. List three reasons that Rathje thinks we should be concerned about the use of large trash containers.

8. What effect have the large containers had on the disposal of hazardous waste? Is this good or bad?

9. What two categories of solid-waste increased the most once people had larger containers?

10. What effect will the large trash containers likely have on charitable donations? Explain.

### Vocabulary

1. stalwart (¶1)
2. loathing (¶1)
3. rancid (¶1)
4. unintentionally perverse (¶1)
5. refuse (¶1)
6. subsequent (¶4)
7. per capita (¶4)
8. biweekly (¶9)
9. circumvent (¶10)

### Content Analysis Questions

1. What is Rathje's purpose?
2. What is Rathje's thesis?
3. How does Rathje develop and support his thesis? Give at least two examples.
4. Do you agree or disagree with Rathje's thesis? Explain your answer.
5. How is this article alike and/or different than "The History of Garbage," by Rathje?

### Application Question

1. The city sanitation director has asked your campus recycling club to recommend some ways to encourage trash reduction and recycling in your city. What are two recommendations you would make? Would you recommend the use of large trash containers? Why or why not?

# *Living with Waste*

### FRANCE BEQUETTE

*France Bequette is a Franco-American journalist specializing in environmental questions. Since 1985 she has been associated with the WANAD-UNESCO training program. This selection is from* UNESCO Courier.

¹Our ancestors used objects made of wood, which rotted, and iron, which rusted. Today we produce durable materials like stainless steel and plastic, but instead of being delighted at how tough they are and holding on to them as long as possible, we throw them away at the earliest opportunity, egged on by manufacturers. In his book *The Waste Makers* the American writer Vance Packard quotes

the industrial designer Brook Stevens as saying: "Our whole economy is based on planned obsolescence. . . . It isn't organized waste. It's a sound contribution to the American economy."

[2]The more developed a country is, the more waste it produces. Waste is an excellent standard-of-living indicator. Because we are generating a rising tide of it and because it is a significant source of pollution, it has also become a major cause for concern to governments all over the planet.

[3]The Organization for Economic Cooperation and Development (OECD) has drawn up the following categories for waste classification: municipal (mainly household) waste; industrial waste; residue from the production of energy, hospital and agricultural waste, mining spoil and demolition debris; dredge spoil, and sewage sludge. (Nuclear wastes are generally dealt with separately.)

[4]We don't all throw away the same amount of garbage. The average person gets rid of 300 kg of waste per year in Italy, 400 kg in Japan, 600 kg in Finland, 860 kg in the United States, and only 180 kg in Yaoundé, Cameroon. (1 kg = 2.2 pounds) But all of these figures are constantly rising.

[5]The results of a survey conducted in France by CREDOC, the French centre for the study and observation of living conditions, give some idea of the kind of things that are thrown out: 34 per cent is organic matter, 30 per cent paper and cardboard, 13 per cent glass, 10 per cent plastic, 7 per cent metal, 4 per cent wood and 2 percent textiles.

[6]In the industrialized member countries of OECD, where 90 to 100 per cent of garbage collection is carried out by municipal authorities, people tend not to worry about what happens to their household waste. Either it ends up in an official dump, or landfill, or it is taken to an incineration plant. Storage and treatment capacities, however, are under increasing pressure because of the amounts involved—423 million tonnes for the OECD countries alone in 1989. With the spread of the NIMBY ("Not in My Back Yard") syndrome people are refusing to live in the vicinity of landfills and incineration plants, and it is becoming virtually impossible to build new plants. The odours from landfills, and the endless procession of trucks going to and fro unquestionably represent a serious disamenity to residents in the immediate vicinity, not to mention potential health hazards, which are only now becoming the subject of epidemiological studies. Solutions must be found.

[7]The first solution is to sort out waste at source. Several garbage bins in the kitchen, special containers in the street, and a well-organized selective collection system are keys to efficient recycling and to the conservation of energy and raw materials. Paper, glass and metal can easily be sorted in this way. Plastic, which is totally non-biodegradable, is very difficult to recycle. Organic substances, as anyone who has a garden knows, can be allowed to decay for use as compost to fertilize the soil.

[8]Such an attitude to recycling implies that we should all be aware of the problem and make a daily effort to solve it. This can only become a habit if there is considerable educational backup. We can do our marketing with our own bags or baskets and refuse to accept plastic bags, which are not a negligible source of pollution. Another solution would be to make it compulsory for stores to take back car-

tons and other forms of packaging, to encourage the charging of a deposit on glass and even plastic bottles, the re-use of metal and plastic containers and the sale of unpackaged goods.

[9]We have to act now, before we are submerged in our own waste. . . .

## Content Questions

*True or False*

If the statement is false, rewrite it to make it true.

1. The more developed a country is, the less waste it produces.
2. Waste, as pollution, is a concern around the world.
3. The amount of waste generated is slowly decreasing.
4. Paper, glass, and metal can easily be sorted for recycling.
5. Plastic is biodegradable and can be easily recycled.

*Completion*

6. Of all the countries mentioned, which one throws away the most?
7. According to CREDOC's study, what are the top four categories of waste?
8. Explain the NIMBY syndrome.
9. What is Bequette's "first solution" to the waste problem?
10. What does she propose as another solution?

## Vocabulary

1. durable materials (¶1)
2. egged on (¶1)
3. planned obsolescence (¶1)
4. municipal authorities (¶6)
5. represent a serious disamenity (¶6)

## Content Analysis Questions

1. What is Bequette's thesis?
2. In paragraph 4, kg is used as the measurement instead of pounds. In paragraph 5, the word "center" is spelled "centre." In paragraph 6, the word "tons" is spelled "tonnes" and "odors" is spelled "odours." Why?
3. What does Bequette mean by "Waste is an excellent standard-of-living indicator." Do you agree or disagree? Explain.
4. Why do you think Bequette and OECD separate "industrialized countries" from other nations when discussing waste problems? Do you think it is a valid way to classify nations in this context? Explain.
5. Which of Bequette's "solutions" do you think has the greatest chance of success in your city? Which one do you think is least likely to succeed? Explain your answers.

**Application Questions**

1. Identify two items you consider to be examples of "planned obsolescence." What can you suggest to increase their usefulness? Do you think most people would be willing to follow your suggestions? Why or why not? Would you be willing to follow your suggestions? Why or why not?

2. Assume that through Internet you participate in an electronic forum with college students in Germany and Italy. A question is posted: "What is the greatest advance that you, your city, and your state have taken to reduce waste?" How would you answer? What question would you like to ask the German and/or Italian students?

# *Cleaning Up Your Act*

### Susan Goodman

*Susan Goodman is a staff writer for* Current Health 2 *magazine, from which this selection is taken.*

[1]As a typical American, you create about 4 pounds of trash a day. All those milk cartons and paper bags and apple cores and used-up plastic pens add up to 1,500 pounds of garbage a year.

[2]You can just dump it in the trash can and forget about it. But your city or town has a much harder time getting rid of it. Most communities cart their garbage off to landfills or burn it in incinerators. These solutions, however, create their own problems.

[3]Landfills (huge garbage dumps) can poison the earth and groundwater as some of the garbage leaks dangerous chemicals into the ground. The world's biggest landfill, Fresh Kills near New York City, leaches about 2 million gallons of toxic ooze a day. The methane gas released from decomposing landfills contributes, some experts believe, to global warming.

[4]Incineration spews fine particles of toxic substances into the air that can enter human lungs and contribute to many problems, according to some scientists, from learning disabilities to cancer. The gases released in the burning process contribute to acid rain. This process also destroys only two-thirds of the trash. It leaves behind the last third as dangerous, toxic ash to be disposed of.

[5]Clearly, dumping and burning all these materials doesn't really make sense. After all, we always need bottles and paper and cans. And we can always reuse other materials in new products. When we toss these things away, we use more of the earth's limited resources to make these products all over again. Recent figures indicate that American cities and towns recycle about 11 percent of their trash. Experts think we could recycle up to 80 percent of our solid waste if we worked at it.

[6]True, recycling has some problems of its own. But let's take a look at some currently recyclable materials to see how they could help us reduce our garbage:

[7]•***Glass.*** Returnable bottles can be used on average 19 times before they must be melted down to use again. Imagine how many

bottles that reuse would keep out of the garbage can. And if everyone recycled all their nonreturnable glass—those empty mayonnaise and applesauce jars and ketchup bottles—we could reduce our nation's garbage by 7 percent. Furthermore, making new glass from old takes about 30 percent less energy than making glass from scratch. Some states—such as Oregon and Washington—have put a ban on nonreturnable bottles.

## A Ton of Recycled Paper . . .

- **Saves about 17 trees**
- **Saves enough energy to provide power to the average home for six months**
- **Keeps almost 60 pounds of air pollution effluents out of the air**
- **Is made from a cleaner, less toxic process than nonrecycled paper**
- **Eliminates 3 cubic yards of landfill material and reduces the need for more landfill**
- **Saves 7,000 gallons of water**

[8]•*Paper.* Paper represents a whopping 41 percent of our garbage, but, sadly, at present only about 25 percent is recoverable for recycling.

[9]We are pretty good at recycling newspaper. Although newspaper is only about one-tenth of our noncommercial solid waste, it represents one-quarter of all our recycled waste. Although some newspapers are recycled into newsprint, most become cardboard, insulation, animal bedding, and cat litter. But the demand for old newspapers is expected to soon explode. Some experts predict that by the end of the '90s a shortage of old newspaper may actually occur.

[10]•*Yard Waste.* Leaves, Christmas trees, grass clippings. Although yard waste takes up a huge 18 percent of our landfills, it may be the easiest type of waste to do something about. Many families and communities are *composting:* piling up these organic materials so they can decompose into mulch. Mulch is an invaluable product that can prevent erosion and supply nutrients or fertilizers to gardens everywhere.

[11]•*Aluminum.* Refunds on beverage cans have helped push our recycling rate of these cans to 65.5 percent. Aluminum is a recycling success story. Making new cans from bauxite is 10 times more expensive and uses 19 times more energy than turning old into new. In fact, the energy you save by recycling one aluminum can will operate a TV for 3 hours.

[12]Despite its obvious improvements, recycling is only a partial solution to waste. To change tires into asphalt or newspapers into greeting cards or cat litter, a new production process is needed. Our present process uses up a great deal of energy and materials. And, sometimes, the materials include chemicals that can be dangerous.

### WASTE NOT, WANT NOT

[13]The best—and easiest—solution of all? Waste reduction: not producing so much garbage in the first place. This is something to consider as you watch the store clerk put a single can of soda or one paperback book into a plastic bag. That plastic can clutter the environment for the next 500 years because it does not decompose.

[14]It's easy to reduce the amount of garbage you produce each day when you start thinking about it. Thirty-two percent of America's garbage is packaging. We may get so caught up in these fancy packages that we forget that plastic wrappers and bright-colored cardboard have little to do with the product inside them. Juice boxes, for instance, might be an easy way to carry a drink around. But once those few sips are through, you're left with a cardboard box and plastic straw. Think about putting a vacuum bottle in your lunch bag.

[15]While you're at it, how about putting your lunch in reusable plastic containers or cloth bags, instead of paper bags and boxes you throw away? How about bringing your own tote bag or knapsack or bookbag to the store instead of getting a new bag each time to take your purchases home?

[16]Of course, consumers aren't the only ones who have to clean up their acts. Industries and businesses have even more to learn. Even here you can make a difference. Every time you buy something, you are giving the people who manufacture it your vote of confidence. You are saying, "I like what you do. Keep doing it." Use this vote wisely. When you buy notebooks or napkins made out of recycled paper, for example, you're telling all companies you like the idea of recycling paper. You're also helping create a way for recycling to become profitable.

[17]Every time you refuse to buy something, you are also sending a message. Manufacturers will not keep making a product that does not make money. If, for example, enough people refuse to buy juice boxes, companies won't make them. If enough people say they will not buy an item until the manufacturer becomes more environmentally aware, the message will be sent—and received.

[18]It's easy to feel a little helpless in the face of our current environmental problems. But you can make a difference. And your involvement can start the very next time you put your soda can in the recycling bin.

### Content Questions

*True or False*

If the statement is false, rewrite it to make it true.

1. We currently recycle only about half of what experts think we could.
2. If everyone recycled all nonreturnable glass, we could reduce our nation's garbage by seven percent.

3. Yard waste is probably the most difficult waste to dispose of.
4. Recycling is only a partial solution to the waste problem.
5. Thirty-two percent of America's garbage is packaging.

*Completion*

6. What does Goodman say is the best and easiest solution to the garbage problem?
7. What are two environmental problems created by dumping trash in landfills?
8. What are three environmental problems created by burning trash?
9. Why is aluminum a recycling success story?
10. Name four reasons to recycle paper.

## Vocabulary

Explain each of these words or phrases:

1. leaches (¶3)
2. spews (¶4)
3. noncommercial solid waste (¶9)
4. decompose (¶10)
5. invaluable product (¶10)
6. environmentally aware (¶17)

## Content Analysis Questions

1. What is Goodman's purpose?
2. State Goodman's thesis.
3. What is the main idea of paragraph 2? What is the relationship of paragraphs 3 and 4 to paragraph 2?
4. What is the main idea of paragraphs 5 and 6? What is the relationship of paragraphs 7–11 to paragraphs 5 and 6?
5. What is the main idea of paragraph 13? What is the relationship of paragraphs 14–17 to paragraph 13?

## Application Questions

1. Assume you are working with a group to start a recycling program on your campus. How would you decide which materials to recycle? Who would you ask for help? What would be your campaign slogan to convince people to recycle?
2. Assume Goodman convinced you that waste reduction makes sense. List two things you can do to reduce waste at home. List three things you can do to reduce waste at school and work. List two ways your campus could reduce waste.

# The Recycling Bottleneck

*Everybody's doing it. But where
do all those cans and bottles
go from here?*

BRUCE VAN VOORST WITH RHEA SCHOENTHAL
AND JANE VAN TASSEL

*Bruce Van Voorst reports for* Time *magazine from Washington, Rhea Schoenthal from Bonn, and Jane Van Tassel from New York.*

[1]It's a self-congratulatory ritual, repeated every day, every
week, all over America. Separate the clear glass bottles from the
green and amber ones. Place the newsprint in one basket, mixed
white paper in another, the reams of used computer paper in a third.
Haul the whole lot out to the curb. There. You've just done your bit
for humanity: you've recycled. It's Miller time.

[2]Not so fast.

[3]To be sure recycling is in vogue. Citizen participation is at
an all-time high; curbside collection programs have exploded from
600 in 1989 to 4,000 today. But the dirty secret, and it's not a little
one, is that major quantities of the material being collected never
actually get recycled. More than 10,000 tons of old newspapers have
piled up in waterfront warehouses in New Jersey, and a congressional committee has heard testimony that the nationwide figure
tops 100 million tons. At the Pentagon, employees looking out over
the parking lot can watch paper they've carefully segregated in the
office being tossed into a single Dumpster, destined for an incinerator. The used-glass market has been so soft that Waste Management of Seattle, Inc. is stuck with a mini-mountain of 6,000 tons
of bottles from neighborhood collections. In the Minneapolis-St.
Paul area, haulers have run out of storage space and are incinerating some recyclable goods. "It's like having your suitcase all
packed with no place to go," laments Amy Perry, solid-waste program director for the nonprofit Massachusetts Public Interest
Research Group.

[4]The problem is that the economics of recycling are out of
whack. Enthusiasm for collecting recyclables has raced ahead of the
capacity in many areas to process and market them. Right now, says
Victor Bell, a veteran Rhode Island recycling expert, "the market
can't keep up with the recycling binge." In recent years many states
and municipalities have passed laws mandating the collection of
newspapers, plastics, glass and paper. But arranging for processing—and finding a profit in it—has proved tricky. As trucks loaded
with recyclable materials arrive at processors, backlogs develop.
Worse, the glut has depressed already soft prices for used paper and
plastics.

[5]"Long term, our members recognize that if you're not in recycling, you'll be out of business in 10 years," says Allen Blakey, public relations director for the National Solid Wastes Management
Association, the nation's trash collectors. Yet government-mandated

recycling laws, by requiring haulers in some instances to pick up unmarketable items, are actually forcing some into bankruptcy. The danger in this short-term failure of recyclonomics, warns William Rathje, author of the recently published book *Rubbish! The Archaeology of Garbage,* "is that, in the interim, recycling enthusiasts will become disillusioned at reports of difficulties." If there's money in trash, entrepreneurs will find it. And in many instances they have. Processors are turning a profit by recycling high-value steel and aluminum cans and, in general, paper cartons and cardboard. A Shearson Lehman analysis concludes that recycling is now attracting "the attention of the solid waste industry investor." In two areas in particular, innovative ideas are cropping up:

[6]***Newsprint*** Paper, especially newspaper, is the biggest component of landfills—about 40%. Despite being the most widely recycled material, newsprint is not at all easy to process or market. "Often we can't give the stuff away," says James Harvey, owner of E.L. Harvey & Sons, Inc., a Westboro, Massachusetts, hauler. Facilities to remove ink from newsprint—a necessary step before it can be pulped to make new paper—are enormously expensive. To justify the investment, recyclers need the sort of arrangement just announced between the city of Houston and Champion Recycling Corp. In return for building an $85 million de-inking plant, Champion Recycling, a subsidiary of Champion International Corp., a leading paper manufacturer, was assured of getting the city's entire collection of old newspapers and magazines. "Our customers not only want to buy recycled materials; they are insisting on it," says Champion International president Andrew Sigler. "This is a market-driven operation that's great for Houston and gives us the assured supply we need for economic efficiency."

[7]***Plastics*** Though plastics constitute 8.3% of all municipal solid wastes and are proliferating faster than any other material, less than 2% of waste plastic gets recycled. Largely this is because it is cumbersome and expensive to separate the seven basic types and relatively cheap simply to manufacture virgin plastics. Wellman Inc., of Shrewsbury, New Jersey, has emerged as a leader in recycling so-called PET bottles, the most common clear plastic containers for liquid, turning discarded ones into furniture textiles, tennis balls, electrical equipment and yarn for polyester carpet. The Coca-Cola Co. services major markets nationwide with two-liter bottles made of 25% recycled PET plastic.

[8]"It will always cost you money to get rid of garbage," asserts Marcia Bystryn, a recycling official in New York City. The trick is to encourage behavior that minimizes the costs, allocates them as equitably as possible and creates productive economic activity wherever possible. In large measure, the present disequilibrium in recycling is the result of policies that work at cross-purposes with those goals and with one another. Environmentalists argue—correctly—that recycled materials suffer in the marketplace against virgin materials because of government subsidies. Newsprint producers, for instance, are indirectly subsidized through public-area logging and logging access roads. The depletion allowance for petroleum subsi-

dizes producers of oil-based plastics. "If these costs are taken into consideration," contends Allen Hershkowitz, senior scientist at the Natural Resources Defense Council, "recycling looks economically a lot more competitive."

[9]Even with such disadvantages, there are profitable recycling operations. Three years ago, J.J. Hoyt, recycling manager at the U.S. Naval Base in Norfolk, Virginia, took over a solid-waste disposal program that had been costing taxpayers $1 million a year. A shrewd businessman, Hoyt was sensitive to hauling managers' needs and negotiated lucrative deals. Now, says one Navy officer, "not a tin can or newspaper falls to the ground on base." This year Hoyt's program is earning close to $800,000. "The key is knowing the market," he says.

[10]New York City's experience is decidedly more mixed. Its primary landfill, Fresh Kills on Staten Island, already covering 2,200 acres and rising to a height of 155 ft., is rapidly filling up. And the city, which recycles only about 6%, of its waste, must turn increasingly to recycling or incineration. A program launched in 1989 to recycle 25% of the city's daily output of 26,000 tons of solid waste has fallen short. Only 29 of the city's 59 community board districts participate in the program. Although Mayor David Dinkins hopes to expand this to 39 by the end of the year, officials admit that recycling faces heavy slogging. "Recycling began with a real naive sort of optimism," says Bystryn. "I think it is important to come back somewhere near to reality." The Dinkins administration succeeded against intense environmentalist opposition in enacting a waste-disposal plan that includes construction of an incinerator in Brooklyn.

[11]Critics of recycling in the U.S. claim that it weakens the economy, but Germany, one of the world's strongest economies, is showing that isn't necessarily so. Since last December, manufacturers and retail stores in Germany have been required to take back such transport packing materials as cardboard boxes and Styrofoam. This spring the requirement was extended to "secondary packaging" such as cardboard boxes for toothpaste or deodorants. By next year, consumers will be able to return sales packaging—from yogurt cups to meat wrappers—to the point of purchase for disposal. In mid-1995 German manufacturers will be responsible for collecting 80% of their packaging waste. Augmenting the government's program is the Duales System Deutschland, a private-industry-initiative recycling program that has already distributed collection bins to more than half of Germany's 80 million people and expects to reach virtually 100% before the end of the year.

[12]Japan's recycling rate is almost double that of the U.S.—40% of municipal solid waste, vs. 17%. But the Japanese program shares some of the problems familiar to American recyclers. Milk cartons, one of the favorite recycling items, are piling up high in warehouses. Like America, says Hiroshi Takatsuki, a professor at Kyoto University, "Japan emphasized collection before coming up with an appropriate infrastructure for reuse."

[13]Americans dispose of far and away more waste than anybody else on the planet. The EPA estimates the annual cost of this disposal at more than $30 billion, a figure rising 17% a year and predicted to reach $75 billion by the end of the century. On the other hand, despite the dire predictions of some environmentalists, dis-

posal is less of a problem than in many other countries. There are still plenty of landfills available, and they will continue to play an important role. So will new incinerators, despite their many environmental shortcomings. For America to catch up in recycling, experts call for action in four areas:

[14]***Economics*** Recycled materials deserve at least the same tax and subsidy treatment that is provided for virgin materials—especially paper and plastics. Potential investors in recycling equipment and research should be encouraged with tax incentives.

[15]***Packaging*** About 39% of the paper and paperboard going into landfills and incinerators comes from packaging. The German example shows how that number can be dramatically reduced. Lever Bros., for instance, manufactures a superconcentrated powder laundry detergent in small boxes, saving the equivalent of 13 million plastic bottles a year. L & F Products sells its Lysol brand and other liquid cleaners in Smart Packs that take up 65% less landfill space than the jet-spray containers they are designed to refill. Imperial Chemical Industries of London has developed a plastic, soon to be distributed in the U.S., that biodegrades without exposure to air and sunlight.

[16]***Research and Development*** Recycling is a new frontier for technical innovation. New processes, for instance, are needed to remove contaminants. Sorted solid wastes often include contaminants that gum up recycling systems, such as clear plastic tape on envelopes or sticky yellow Post-its on office paper. A single ceramic cap from a bottle of the Dutch-brewed Grolsch beer can contaminate an entire batch of green glass. "We haven't begun to tap the potential for technical innovation in recycling," says Lloyd Leonard, legislative director for the League of Women Voters.

[17]***Legislation*** The New Jersey mandatory recycling law—achieving 34% recycling, or double the national average—demonstrates the virtues of a legal prescript. Minimum-content laws such as those in Oregon and California, mandating the use of recycled materials in new products, have proved effective. So have "pay by bag laws" that increase the price tag for garbage removal according to volume. Last fall the White House issued an executive order requiring federal agencies to give preference to recycled materials when purchasing products. But that's just a start. "Unless the government mandates more use of recycled material in products," warns Dan Weiss of the Sierra Club, "recycling will be discredited."

[18]For all its promises, recycling remains only part of the world's waste-disposal solution. Despite the enormous energy and enthusiasm with which Americans and others collect recyclable products, the real breakthrough can come only when similar effort is expended on reducing waste in the first place and in enticing more markets to absorb recycled materials.

## Content Questions

*True or False*

If the statement is false, rewrite it to make it true.

1. Recycling is the answer to the world's waste-disposal problem.
2. It will always cost money to get rid of garbage.
3. Plastics are the biggest component of landfills.
4. One reason less than two percent of waste plastic gets recycled is because there are so many different kinds of plastic.
5. Americans dispose of more waste than anybody else on the planet.

*Completion*

6. What is the "dirty secret" of recycling?
7. What does Van Voorst mean by "the economics of recycling are out of whack?"
8. Currently, what are the two most profitable recycle items?
9. Name three examples of how companies can reduce packaging.
10. For Americans to catch up in recycling, experts call for action in four areas. What are they?

## Vocabulary

Explain each of these words or phrases:

1. recycling is in vogue (¶3)
2. used-glass market is soft (¶3)
3. laments (¶3)
4. recyclonomics (¶5)
5. interim (¶5)
6. disequilibrium in recycling (¶8)
7. naive sort of optimism (¶10)
8. augmenting (¶11)
9. appropriate infrastructure for reuse (¶12)
10. dire predictions (¶13)
11. demonstrates the virtues of a legal prescript (¶17)

## Content Analysis Questions

1. What is Van Voorst's purpose?
2. State Van Voorst's thesis.
3. Compare and contrast recycling in Germany and the United States. Compare and contrast recycling in Japan and the United States.
4. Why does Van Voorst say that recycling is only part of the world's waste-disposal solution?
5. Review the major ideas proposed by each of the authors in this Theme about "living in a throwaway society." What do you see as a primary, common theme?

**Application Questions**

1. What items do you currently recycle? What do you gain from your recycling? What are the disadvantages of your recycling efforts? What would make you recycle other items? What do you think would make others recycle more often?

2. Do you think that the United States will adopt the German plan of requiring stores and manufacturers to take back their packaging materials? Why or why not? Do you think it's a good idea? Why or why not?

# Theme 3
## "Doing Philosophy" in Everyday Life

You're walking to your car in a shopping center parking lot. You see two people struggling and hear one of them calling for help. What do you do?

You're taking a biology course. A friend who has a later section of the class asks you for the answers to today's test. What do you do?

You're a food server in a restaurant. After closing tonight, you see one of the other food servers take money out of the cash register. What do you do?

What you decide to do in each situation depends partially on your values. Values are your subjective reactions to the world around you. Your value system determines everything you do: how you relate to those around you, what you buy, how you vote, what television shows you watch, how you perform in school, what you do with your leisure time, how you perform your job, and who you believe is an authority.

This theme examines values with a focus on school experiences. "Beyond Materialism: Dark Hearts," a brief report on the "philosophical malaise of modern America" from research by psychologist Susan Krause Whitbourne, opens this theme. Then, "What Is Philosophy?" a textbook chapter by Dr. Thomas White, provides a framework for thinking about the basic issues of philosophy, life, and some less abstract issues.

Next, Pulitzer-Prize-winning author James Michener proposes that the nation's survival depends on our schools' teaching values. His article, "What Is the Secret of Teaching Values?" is followed by social studies teacher Helmut Manzl's "Feeding on Fast Food and False Values." This article describes the pressure on schools to counteract society's "undesirable values." Then, a group of *Newsweek* writers from around the United States review how some schools are handling the teaching of values in the '90s in "Values in the Classroom."

The next two articles focus specifically on the college experience. Albert Yates, president of Colorado State University, proposes that "Universities Must Teach Both Facts and Values to Stave Off Barbarism." However, in "Not to Worry: The Mold Doesn't Hold," Philip Altbach and Lionel Lewis review research that says college students "remain remarkably untouched in terms of attitudes and values by academic experiences."

And finally, Muriel Whetstone shares an example of "doing" philosophy in everyday life in "Beginning Anew."

---

**Strategies for Success**

- Develop a plan for each of the readings.
- Determine who the author is and why he or she is writing.
- Know the vocabulary the author uses.
- Identify what the author is writing about.
- Establish how the author develops the writing.
- Integrate graphic and text information.
- Organize the information you need.
- Recognize the author's stance.
- Decide what you can do with the author's information.

---

# *Beyond Materialism: Dark Hearts*

## PSYCHOLOGY TODAY STAFF

[1]A funny thing happened to psychologist Susan Krause Whitbourne. She thought she was researching how personality changes over the course of adulthood. But when she looked at the results of her longitudinal study, she was staring straight at the philosophical malaise of modern Americans.

[2]What she found was that since the mid-1960s, when she started her study, Americans have lost a sense of personal meaning. They're working more—but far more full of despair.

[3]In all three cohorts of adults she has added, tested, and retested over 22 years, every measure of psychosocial development improved with age. Except one. In her most recent round of testing, she was surprised to see a "precipitous decline" in ego integrity, a personality factor relating to wholeness, honesty, and meaning in life and to having a sense of connection with others.

[4]At first she thought it was restricted to the yuppie generation of her study—people with a "notoriously empty lifestyle focused on wealth and possessions," she reports in the *Journal of Personality and Social Psychology* (Vol. 63, No. 2). But when it turned up in all

three groups at the same time, she could only conclude it reflects "a more general society-wide crisis of morality and purpose affecting adults of all ages."

[5]A professor of psychology at the University of Massachusetts, Whitbourne began testing personality variables at the University of Rochester in 1966. Students scored low on industry; they lacked "a focus on work and material success." Like others of their era, they were disenchanted with the work ethic.

[6]Over time, and with exposure to the real world, their personal industry began to climb. By 1988, when yet another cohort joined the study, the three groups were equally slaving away. But ego integrity had plummeted. All three groups were now questioning life's worth.

[7]What happened between 1977 and 1988? "People got caught up in chasing the materialistic dream. They got recognition for their achievements, yet don't feel that what they are doing matters in the larger scheme of things."

[8]The scores on life satisfaction were so low, Whitbourne says, they couldn't go any lower. She thinks people are now looking for ways to put more meaning in life. There are no data. "My belief:" she confides, "is based on hope."

### Questions

1. What was Whitbourne's primary finding: In 1966? In 1988? Today?
2. In general, what has happened to Americans since the mid-1960s?
3. What does Whitbourne hope is happening now?
4. Are you surprised by Whitbourne's findings? Why or why not?
5. Identify one thing that you think would help people to feel that what they do matters.

### Vocabulary

1. longitudinal study (¶1)
2. philosophical malaise (¶1)
3. cohorts of adults (¶3)
4. precipitous decline (¶3)
5. disenchanted (¶5)
6. ego integrity had plummeted (¶6)

# What Is Philosophy?

## THOMAS WHITE

*Thomas White is a professor at Rider College in New Jersey. This selection is from* Discovering Philosophy.

# What Is Philosophy?

Most of us have either the wrong idea or no idea at all of what studying philosophy is all about. If you're feeling uncomfortable about the prospect of taking a philosophy course, perhaps the following will help ease your mind.

First off, you're probably feeling uncertain because you don't know what to expect from a philosophy course. You've already studied subjects like mathematics, history, English, foreign languages, biology, and chemistry. You've probably also done a little anthropology, sociology, or political science in some of your social studies courses. You have worked with computers. You know what art and music are, whether you studied them or not. Your previous experience, then, gives you some idea of what's coming in college courses on these subjects.

But philosophy? That's different. You haven't encountered anything like philosophy. So it's natural that you would be uneasy about a subject so new and different.

There is also something about philosophy and philosophers that's alien to the way average people see themselves. After you graduate, you probably expect to be a lawyer, computer programmer, sales manager, teacher, or corporate executive. You may even be able to imagine yourself as a rock-and-roll singer, or a movie star, or the president of the United States. But who wants to be a philosopher? You know the image most of us have—someone impractical, unrealistic, and absent-minded, some character with hair flying in every direction, lost in thought while pondering "great ideas."[1]

This image of the philosopher being "out of touch" is even suggested by the very word "philosophy." Literally, the word means "love of wisdom." (It derives from two ancient Greek words: *philia*, "love," and *sophia*, "wisdom.") And who's going to go around saying that they "love wisdom" except somebody who's a little strange? Would anyone want to be like that?

Besides these concerns, you may also be feeling a little afraid. You don't know what to expect, and most people are afraid of the unknown. You don't know if you'll be able to do whatever it is when you've never done anything like it before, especially something so theoretical.

You will find, however, that philosophy is a natural activity. In one way or another most people either already think like philosophers or can do so with just a little help. That's because when it comes down to it, as you're about to see, philosophy is a way of thinking that comes naturally. So you really have nothing to be anxious about.

## What Is Philosophy About?

**philosophy**
Philosophy is an active, intellectual enterprise dedicated to exploring the most fundamental questions of life.

What is **philosophy** about?[2] And how is philosophy such a natural thing to do that you're probably already doing it without knowing it?

More than anything else, philosophy is *thinking*. The main instrument that philosophers use in conducting their investigations is the human mind. They don't try to solve philosophical problems by conducting scientific, empirical research. They think. And so do you. You think just because you're human.

---

[1]One of the first caricatures we have of a philosopher is that of the Greek thinker Socrates. In the comedy entitled *The Clouds*, Aristophanes portrays the philosopher as someone absolutely useless and ridiculous. When we first meet Socrates in the play, he's sitting in a basket suspended midair and staring at the sky.

[2]The first time a word listed in the glossary appears, it will be in boldface.

Of course, philosophers don't just think about whatever crosses their minds. They think about *life's most basic questions*:

—What is the purpose of life?
—Is there a God?
—How do we know the difference between right and wrong?
—Are our actions free or determined?

But who doesn't think about some very basic questions every now and then? You may not make a career out of it, but you have done it. You can't be human without doing it sometimes.

Philosophers also try to come up with answers to these questions, to explain them to other people, and to defend them against criticism and opposing answers. And you have surely also done some of that.

Philosophy even tries to get something positive out of uncertainty, confusion, and argument. If disagreeing philosophers can't prove which answer is right, they believe that discussion can still produce a greater understanding of the issues at stake. And you have probably had that experience as well.

## "Doing" Philosophy in Real Life

Imagine, for example, that your friend Sam asks you to help him cheat on an assignment. You're torn between loyalty to a friend and uneasiness about doing something dishonest. You tell Sam you would rather not help him cheat. Sam tries to get you to change your mind, explaining that he doesn't see anything wrong with what he's asking. But you don't see it that way. The two of you get into a long discussion of cheating—why you think it is wrong, why he doesn't, why he thinks friendship is more important, and why you do not. It may surprise you to hear that this fairly typical event in the life of a college student contains all the basic elements of doing philosophy.

How you determine the difference between right and wrong is certainly a basic issue. We base all our actions on our sense of right and wrong. So the subject of your disagreement with Sam is philosophical. In your discussion with him you're forced to explain your decision, so you have to think seriously about your assumptions. In order to handle his objections, you have to think further about the issues and defend your position against his arguments. Let's say that ultimately neither one of you convinces the other. Has the discussion produced anything? Sure—a better understanding of the issue and of each other.

This is what philosophers do too. They think about basic questions and come up with answers, explain why they think that way, and defend their positions against people who disagree. Philosophers do this in the hope of either settling the matter or at least producing a greater understanding of the issues involved.

Now consider all the times you think about fundamental questions. You wonder whether God exists and if there is any way of proving it. Your best friend discovers she's pregnant and the two of you talk about whether she should have an abortion. You consider taking drugs, even though you know it's illegal. In all these cases, you're thinking about standard philosophical questions, coming to some personal answers, and growing in your understanding. The only difference between you and a professional philosopher is that he or she thinks about the same questions in a more technical, disciplined, and informed way.

So, you see, doing philosophy is one of the most common activities of life, something natural, normal, and, best of all, familiar.

**6** WHAT IS PHILOSOPHY?

### Philosophy—Activity, not Content

Note in particular that philosophy is an activity. Philosophy is active, not passive. It's a way of thinking, something you do, a skill you get better at as you practice, not a body of facts that you memorize. And there is a good and bad side to that.

The good news is that once you get the hang of it, philosophical thinking expands your ability to see things. It also encourages you to think independently. You can entertain all kinds of ideas or theories about an issue, then make up your own mind. No philosophy teacher will ever say to you, "I don't care what you think, just give me the correct answer to my question." How you think about the questions and about other philosophers' answers and how you explain and defend what you think is what it's all about.

Moreover, philosophers are not "authorities." They are only as good as their arguments. If their arguments are not convincing, forget it. The ancient Greek thinker Socrates may have been a great philosopher, but that doesn't mean that what he says is true. He still must convince you.

The bad news, however, is that since you probably haven't studied anything like this before, you're going to have to learn new ways of handling things. In a philosophy course, you can't fall back on memorizing the theories of great philosophers like Plato and Aristotle. You have to know what different thinkers say, but you also have to genuinely understand their ideas. And that's not all. After you think about it, you have to come up with your own reaction.

For example, do you agree or disagree with Plato's description of the ideal society? Totally? Partially? What are the strengths and weaknesses of his ideas? What would you change? Why? How would you convince Plato to change his mind? Suppose the person sitting next to you disagrees with you. How would you try to change her mind?

Philosophy is a dynamic process. That is one of the things that makes it so interesting—and hard to get used to. It isn't just learning the answers that earlier philosophers have come up with. It's also coming up with your own answers. So get used to the idea that you are about to embark on an active enterprise.

## The Basic Issues

Since the subject of philosophy is the "basic issues" of life, it's not surprising that we encounter a very wide range of issues when we study philosophy. Fortunately, philosophers are very logical, so philosophy has been divided into several branches, each devoted to different, but still basic, questions. What are these issues and what are the parts of philosophy?

### The Most Fundamental Issues

Every philosophical question is basic. But some questions are more basic than others, and philosophy starts with those.

#### Reality

What's the most elementary thing you can say about yourself? That you're tall? Short? White? Black? No. That you are male, or female? Simpler than that. That you are human? Still simpler. Just that you *are*. What's the most fundamental characteristic of any object you can describe? Distinguishing characteristics? No. Simply that it is real. It exists. Now we've hit bedrock because the nature of reality, or of existence, is the most basic issue we can talk about. The most fundamental philosophical question, then, is: What is the nature of *reality*?

What do we mean when we say something is "real"? What's the difference between "real" and "not real," or "imaginary"? Does something have to exist physically to be real? Or is it enough that it exists in our minds? Which are more real? Chairs and tables that present themselves to our eyes, but that will eventually wear out, break up, and be thrown out precisely because they're material objects? Or the circles and triangles that we see only with our mind's eye, which are "perfect" and haven't changed or decayed a bit since humans discovered the abstract world of mathematics thousands of years ago?

### Personhood

Think again about yourself and the other things and people in your life. We've already seen that they have existence in common. They're alike in that they're real. But what makes each of these entities different from all the others? One way to account for these differences is through some distinguishing set of properties or characteristics. How are you different from this book in your hand, for example? For openers, you're alive and the book isn't. So now we're talking about the defining characteristics that make something be what it is. We're referring to what we call the "nature" or "essence" of a thing.

To narrow this down, let's focus just on human nature. What is a very basic characteristic of human beings? We're alive, but then so are all nonhuman animals, so we need something more specific. What in our life sets us apart from other living beings? Probably that each of us is a "person." This brings us to a point where we can frame another basic philosophical question: What is the essence of the special property, *personhood*?

Does the ability to communicate by sign language suggest personhood?

8    WHAT IS PHILOSOPHY?

What does it mean to be a "person"? To answer this question, use yourself as an example and contrast your kind of life with that of plants and animals. Notice that you have a particular kind of self-awareness and high intellectual abilities. You can communicate with other people. And you can control your own actions.

But are all humans "persons"? Fetuses don't have any of these characteristics, so some thinkers argue that they are not "persons" in their own right. But, then, infants cannot do most of these things either, and most of us recognize them as "persons." Furthermore, must a "person" be "human"? How about other animals? Some chimpanzees have learned sign language. Some people think that dolphins may be as intelligent as humans. And many individuals claim they've had encounters with intelligent beings from another planet. None of these entities is human, but they seem to have many characteristics and abilities that humans do. Should we think of them as "persons"?

## Free Will

Consider another basic aspect of life. Think again about the most fundamental things you can say about yourself. You exist. You're alive. You're a person. Part of being a person means that you can control your actions, that is, your deeds are not merely automatic products of instinct. You have what philosophers call *free will*.

But now think about it. Sure, we all *feel* free. Yet aren't our choices influenced by our upbringing, the values we're taught, the norms provided by our culture? Perhaps some of our behavior is determined by our genetic makeup. What about the impact of our worst, irrational fears? What about the power of the unconscious mind? Perhaps you believe that God has people's lives all planned out; perhaps you believe in fate. And if the future is somehow already determined, what room is left for choice? These problems lead us to yet another basic philosophical question: How "free" are we?

## Knowledge

Think back for a moment to our discussion of what makes a person. Surely one of the most important characteristics a person has is intelligence. A person can think and know things. Intellectual activity is such a basic part of human life that our species is named for this ability—*Homo sapiens* ("thinking man"). This brings us to another philosophical issue: What is involved in *knowing* something?

At first this might look like a simple question. We say we know something when we have acceptable reasons or proof for what we claim. I can say that I know that my computer is sitting in front of me because I can see it. I also know that the great English humanist Sir Thomas More died in 1535 because I've done research on More for years, and that is what the historical records show. I even know that the sum of the interior angles of every triangle that ever has or ever will exist is 180 degrees. Have I measured them all? Not very likely. How do I know it? Because this is, in fact, the definition of a triangle.

Each of these three examples involves knowledge, but each example is different. I claim to know something in each case, but the reasons I give keep changing. My first claim is based on direct sense experience. The second involves secondhand evidence, or hearsay, ultimately based on someone else's firsthand experience. And the third doesn't rely on sense experience at all. If they're all so different, do all these examples involve knowledge? The same kind of knowledge?

Here's a very different example that involves knowledge. You may have a friend who consults with someone who claims to predict the future. But can such a seer offer any proof that he's right? Certainly not the usual kind of proof, since his predictions are based on direct "insight" or "intuition." Does he know the truth of what he's just foretold? He would probably say so. If the prediction comes true, is this legitimate, physical proof that the psychic knew what was going to happen? That's a good question. Can we say that the psychic actually had "knowledge" of the future, or should we call that something else? As you see, questions about knowledge can be quite complicated.

So far our questions have focused mainly inward, on what it means to be a living person from the inside. When we turn our attention outward, however, we encounter different kinds of philosophical questions.

### God, Life After Death, the Purpose of Life

What do we see when we look outside ourselves? We, and others of our kind, exist, but we're not alone. Plants and other animals also exist. So does the enormous universe that surrounds us. And if we reflect on its complexity and majesty, we've got to ask ourselves, "Where did it all come from?"

We didn't create our universe, so how did it get here? Is it the result of natural processes operating over billions or trillions of years? Or did someone create it? Are we alone in this universe, or is there a *God* as well? Not surprisingly, proofs for the existence of God have been debated by philosophers for thousands of years.

The question of God's existence raises other fundamental questions. For example, if there is a spiritual dimension to reality, does that mean that we have "souls" or "spirits" which continue to exist after our bodies wear out? Is there life after death? For that matter, have we lived other lives before this one? More people on this planet believe in reincarnation than reject the idea. Who is right?

And the idea of an afterlife, or of other lives, leads us to wonder, What is the *purpose of life*? Is it a test of some sort? If so, what counts as "passing"? Making a lot of money and becoming rich and famous? Doing some kind of important work? Devoting our lives to helping people less fortunate than ourselves? Growing personally or spiritually as much as

These classical representations of heaven and hell address the question, What is the point of life? Is it a test in which we are rewarded for the good we do and punished for our wrongdoing?

possible? Questions of the ultimate purpose of life, then, are also common grist for the philosopher's mill.

So far we've identified the most basic questions of philosophy.

—What is the nature of "reality"?

—What is a "person"?

—How free are we?

—What can we "know" and how can we "know" it?

—Is there a God?

—What is the purpose of life?

These, then, are the most fundamental, theoretical questions we ask in philosophy. But we also take up more practical issues.

## Practical Issues

We've been looking at the issues raised by the simple fact that we exist (reality, personhood), that we do things (free will), and that we know (knowledge). What else is characteristic of human beings, but a little less abstract?

### Standards of Conduct: Right and Wrong

When we choose what to do, we use certain standards or values to guide us. We also use these values to evaluate what other people do. Our society, like all societies, suggests some standards for our behavior, the most important of which are laws and customs. Organizations we belong to, schools we go to, churches we belong to, and companies we work for also have their rules, regulations, and policies.

But sometimes those are not enough, or they may conflict with each other. For example, even though it is illegal, many underage students use false IDs to buy liquor. Do you think they're doing something wrong? The traffic laws say you should stop at red lights and stop signs. But what should you do if you are rushing a sick friend to the hospital? Your religion tells you that sex before marriage is wrong, but you are deeply in love with someone and you don't feel that anything you do would be wrong. These ethical dilemmas lead us to yet another philosophical question: How do we separate *right* from *wrong*?

Questions about right and wrong can get as complicated as those about reality or knowledge. We need an ultimate standard of conduct. But where do we find something like that? How do you choose between two actions, both of which seem wrong to you? How would you explain the basis of your standard of right and wrong to someone who disagrees with you? Maybe your standard is influenced by your personal religious beliefs. Yet how could you convince an atheist that you were right? Even if you do have some standard for separating right from wrong, why should you act on it? Why should you do right and not do wrong? What if you can't afford to fix your car and you can steal a few hundred dollars from somebody who's rich? Is there any good reason not to steal, especially if you can get away with it?

So you see, many questions come up when we look at the everyday problem of evaluating human actions against some fundamental standard. And, it will come as no surprise, these are philosophical questions.

### How Do We Organize Our Communities?

Questions of right and wrong come up because we live with other people and we need some standard for judging their conduct, as well as our own. But the fact that we live with other people in communities also creates some issues on a larger scale—and still more

Abortion presents an ethical dilemma to modern society.

philosophical questions. How should decisions be made that affect the common good? Does everybody vote about every little thing? Or do you assign some of these decisions to others—that is, do you create a government? What kind of government do you want? Who gets to make the rules that everybody in the group must live by? What if the group's rules force some people to do things that they find wrong according to their personal standards? Are they entitled to disobey those rules? How do you decide if a law is "just" or not?

These are just a few of the more obvious problems that have to be solved when people live together. When we turn to these issues later in this book, we take up two particular questions: What would an *ideal society* look like? and Is *democracy* a good form of government? The first question has been asked by many philosophers over the last two thousand years. The second question raises more particular issues about the strengths and weaknesses of the type of government we live under in the United States.

## Other Concerns of Philosophy

We exist. We choose our actions. We know things. We evaluate what we do and what others do. We live among other people. Trying to understand and explain these most basic facts of life is what philosophy mainly does.

Yet philosophy also studies the conceptual foundations of some of the more complicated dimensions of human life—art, science, religion, law, education, artificial intelligence, genetic engineering, ethical issues in business and medicine and the other professions. In fact, the most abstract ideas of virtually every human endeavor are the domain of philosophy.

### The Subject Matter of Philosophy

This quick survey of a few basic questions should give you a decent idea of what philosophy is all about. It is not some arcane study that has nothing to do with real life. It is an intellectual activity devoted to understanding the most basic dimensions of what it means to exist as a human being alone and in community with others. As such, it has everything to do with real life.

Capital punishment has been a traditional practice in U.S. society. Would it exist in an ideal society?

## Philosophical Questions

The questions that philosophers ask are obviously varied. One thing they have in common is that all these questions arise from thinking about the fundamental aspects of life. But they also share something else that is distinctive of a philosophical question—their *conceptual* nature.

If I ask you if it's raining, how do find out the answer? You look outside. And if I ask you how many students are in a particular classroom at noon on Monday? You go and count the people. In each case, you get the facts. Many questions are like this. They're answered by doing some empirical investigation. Scientific questions are empirical questions: they can be answered by "getting the facts." Questions that have factual answers are not philosophical questions.

Or what if you want to know if you can leave your car somewhere overnight without getting a ticket? You call the police. Or if you want to know what the Catholic church says about the morality of birth control? Ask a priest. In these cases, you're still getting facts, but they're facts of a different kind. There are specific answers that will settle your questions, but you must find the right person, book, or body of law that tells you what they are. You must seek the judgment of an authority. Questions like these are not philosophical questions either.

Instead, philosophical questions involve conceptual issues. Think about the account of the philosophical topics you just read. All those philosophical questions boil down to basic concepts, or principles. And that is the defining feature of a philosophical question. Reality, personhood, right, wrong, justice, and the like are all concepts. The challenge of a philosophical investigation is exploring the principles and concepts at issue, and applying the results to situations that involve those ideas.

### Philosophical "Answers"

Similarly, the "answers" to these questions share an important property that also characterizes philosophy. Because of the conceptual nature of the fundamental issues philosophy considers, philosophers can never give absolute proof that they are right.

Philosophical questions do not get "solved," as empirical questions do. The empirical question, "How many pages are in this book?", has a single, correct answer; all others are wrong. But a philosophical question like, "Is abortion wrong?" has more than one plausible answer. Depending on the positions taken on such debatable issues as "life," "personhood," and "rights," we can find even completely opposing arguments that are reasonable and believable. Similarly, we can make a plausible case for saying that we have a totally free will, and that we're free to choose anything we want whenever we want to. On the other hand, we can also make an intelligent case for saying that our sense of freedom is an illusion—that we fool ourselves into thinking we're free when our behavior is actually determined. It is simply a characteristic of philosophical issues that we fall short of absolute certainty. And this means that philosophical thinking deals more in probability and plausibility than absolute truth and falsehood.

## The Parts of Philosophy

You now have an understanding of the subjects that philosophy discusses and something of the nature of philosophy. However, without realizing it, you also have acquired a sense of the primary branches of philosophy.

Very fundamental and abstract issues relating to existence in general (like the nature of reality and the existence of God) and human existence in particular (such as personhood

## 14   WHAT IS PHILOSOPHY?

**metaphysics**
Metaphysics is the part of philosophy concerned with the most basic issues, for example, reality, existence, personhood, and freedom versus determinism. Metaphysics was originally referred to by Aristotle as "first philosophy."

**epistemology**
Epistemology, also called "theory of knowledge," is the part of philosophy concerned with "knowledge" and related concepts.

**ethics**
Ethics, also called "moral philosophy," is the part of philosophy concerned with right, wrong, and other issues related to evaluating human conduct.

**logic**
Logic is the part of philosophy devoted to studying reason itself and the structure of arguments.

and free will) are taken up in the part of philosophy called **metaphysics.** The ancient Greek philosopher Aristotle called this branch of philosophy "first philosophy," and that's a good way to think about it. Metaphysics concentrates on the first or most fundamental questions we encounter when we begin studying the most basic issues of life.[3]

Another fundamental part of philosophy is theory of knowledge, or **epistemology,** which takes up the questions we saw above related to the nature of knowledge. "Episte-mology" combines two Greek words, *epistéme* and *logos,* and literally means "the study of knowledge." *Epistéme* means "knowledge." *Logos* has many meanings, but in this context it means "the study of." The suffix "-logy" can be found at the end of many English words: "biology" (the study of life), "geology" (the study of the earth), and so on.

When we encounter the practical issues of philosophy, we move into **ethics,** or *moral philosophy,* and **political philosophy.** "Ethics" is the part of philosophy that discusses right and wrong, and the word is derived from the Greek word for "custom, habit, or character," *ethikos.* ("Moral" comes from the Latin word for "character," *mores.*) "Political philosophy" takes up the wider issues that arise from our living together, such as legitimate authority, justice, and speculation about the ideal society. Its root is *polis,* another Greek word, which means "city."

Metaphysics, epistemology, ethics, and political philosophy are the main divisions of philosophy. But given the wide range of topics that philosophers study, it should come as no surprise that there are also many important, but more narrowly focused branches of philosophy, like philosophy of art, philosophy of science, and philosophy of language. Finally, in a class by itself, there is **logic,** the part of philosophy devoted to studying reason itself and the structure of arguments. Logic is the foundation on which any philosophical investigation is built, and modern philosophy of logic explores some highly technical philosophical questions.

## Why Studying Philosophy Is Valuable

**political philosophy**
Political philosophy is the part of philosophy that addresses the philosophical issues that arise from the fact that we live together in communities. These issues include the nature of political authority, utopias, justice, and the problem of harmonizing freedom and obligation.

So far you have seen that philosophy stems quite naturally from thinking about life's basic questions. And you have been introduced to some of those questions and to the different branches of philosophy. You should now be ready for what we're going to study in the chapters ahead.

Before we move on, however, we should address one more issue—why studying philosophy is worthwhile. Whatever you imagine you will get out of a philosophy course, let me assure you that if you work hard through this course, you will develop skills, abilities, and insights that will help you for the rest of your life.

---

[3]"Metaphysics" comes from two ancient Greek words, *meta* "after," and *physika* "physics." In light of contemporary usage, where "metaphysical" usually means "abstract" or "abstruse," you might think that "metaphysics" takes its name from the fact that it studies highly abstract issues "beyond the physical realm." While such questions are "metaphysical," the word is actually a historical accident. The Greek philosopher Aristotle gave a series of lectures dealing with the most basic questions in philosophy; as I mentioned, he called this, "first philosophy." The treatise containing these lectures was never given a title, but after Aristotle's death his students traditionally filed it after Aristotle's lectures on nature, which the philosopher called "the physics." Thus, *Metaphysics* meant something more like "the scroll filed after *The Physics*" than "lectures on transcendental questions." That is why the best way to understand metaphysics is to remember that Aristotle called it "first philosophy," that is, think of it as the part of philosophy that asks the "first" or most basic questions.

### Analytical Abilities

The skills you will pick up are easy to describe. You will develop better analytical abilities. You will handle abstract problems better. You will learn how to argue more effectively. And you will have a stronger imagination. Philosophy helps to shape in a positive way what we might call the "general cut of your mind." This is invaluable in whatever career you choose to follow. The most successful people use analysis and argument all the time. Successful people make their mark by solving difficult problems and convincing other people they're right.

In preparing this book, I asked several successful executives to tell me what they thought students should study if they wanted to succeed in business. They listed only a few technical subjects—accounting and finance, for example. (The technical end of business, they said, you learn mainly on the job.) Otherwise they suggested courses that help develop your ability to think about problems analytically and to communicate your analysis and recommendations to other people. Time and again, these executives identified philosophy as one of the most important areas you can study for learning how to think in a disciplined, analytical, and imaginative way.

### Vision and Insight

The way that philosophy helps you see the world is no less real than its practical benefits to your career. Studying philosophy exposes you to a wide range of problems that you wouldn't meet otherwise. It simply lets you see more of the world. It stretches your imagination. It challenges you to come up with your own answers to tough issues that do not have ready-made solutions. If you take it seriously, philosophy teaches you different ways of looking at the world.

Studying philosophy helps you to develop insight into some of life's great puzzles and to fashion your own vision of what life is all about. As you go through life, you will be challenged all along the way to make decisions about who you are and what's important to you. What will you do with your life? What career will you pursue? Will you marry? And if so, what kind of person? Will you have children? How will you rear them? What will you tell them is important? What are you willing to do for money and success? How will you cope with the crises you will encounter in your own life or in the lives of those you love— illness, accidents, problems on the job or at home, death? Philosophy helps you develop a sense of what life is all about and where you're going.

In fact, Socrates, one of the first great philosophers, thought that philosophy is the single most important element in making our lives worthwhile. "The unexamined life," he said, "is not worth living." The habit of thinking philosophically lets us scrutinize our values, our goals, and the means we've chosen to achieve them, and it helps us keep our lives on course. In Socrates' mind, at least, philosophy makes it possible for us to control our own destiny. And that's no small matter.

As you now know, philosophy is simply thinking systematically about life's most basic issues. When it comes down to it, there is no way that thinking about these questions cannot make you better prepared for your life.

## Previews of Coming Chapters

Now that you have a sense of what philosophy is, you're ready to plunge in yourself. What's coming up in the rest of this book? We cannot cover every important aspect of such a large

**16**    WHAT IS PHILOSOPHY?

subject in an introductory text. We will, however, talk about all of philosophy's basic topics and a few specialized ones.

We'll start preparing ourselves by "tuning the instrument," that is, the mind. Since we do philosophy by thinking, the best place to begin is by studying some of the "rules of reason" alluded to earlier. Chapter 2, "Philosophical Thinking," will introduce you to the ground rules regarding logic and critical thinking.

In the next section, "Exploring the Basics of Who We Are," we look at some of the most fundamental characteristics of our existence. We start by asking "What Is a Person?" (Chapter 3), then explore whether nonhuman persons might already exist (Chapter 4, "Is a Dolphin a Person?"). The next two chapters consider two approaches to another fundamental condition of our existence—our freedom. In "The Case for Determinism" (Chapter 5), we explore the arguments in favor of determinism, and we look at the case for free will in Chapter 6 ("The Case for Freedom").

In the fourth section, "Dealing with Other Humans," we take up some questions raised by our living with other people. We look at how philosophers talk about "right" and "wrong" in Chapter 7, "Right and Wrong." In Chapter 8, "Why Virtue?", we ask why we should bother doing what's right. We next shift to some philosophical issues related to human communities. Chapter 9, "Ideal Societies," examines a couple of utopias. And Chapter 10, "Democracy," inquires into the underpinnings of the political system we live under.

In the chapters that make up "The World of Theory," we explore both basic and specialized theoretical issues. We start with absolute bedrock—the nature of reality in Chapter 11 ("The Nature of Reality"). Chapter 12, "What Is Knowledge?", looks at the basic ways philosophers have looked at knowledge. Chapter 13, "Scientific Explanations of Reality," looks at philosophical issues raised by the ideas of theoretical physicists about the nature of the world. Then we consider some philosophical questions raised by some fascinating psychological theories that women and men have unique ways of thinking about knowledge and of engaging ethical problems (Chapter 14, "Psychology, Gender, and Thinking").

We conclude with a couple of "big picture" issues in "Ultimate Questions." In Chapter 15, "Does God Exist?", we examine the main "proofs" for the existence of God. In Chapter 16, "The Purpose of Life: Marx and Buddha," we tackle one of life's most perplexing questions as seen through the eyes of two very different philosophers.

This book, then, will give you a basic, but solid understanding of what philosophy is all about. It will serve as a road map for what many of us feel is one of life's most exciting, enriching, and engaging adventures—discovering philosophy. You will see new sights, explore new worlds, expand your horizons, and, most importantly, learn much about yourself. As with any journey, what you get out of it is mainly up to you. But if you give philosophy half a chance, it just might take you to a place you never want to leave.

## Main Points of Chapter 1

1.   Philosophy is a conceptual discipline which focuses on life's most basic questions. It is the activity of thinking about these issues yourself, not simply understanding what philosophers from the past have said about these questions.

2.   The most fundamental issues that philosophy investigates are highly abstract: the nature of reality, personhood, free will, knowledge, the existence of God, and the purpose of life. Philosophy also addresses more practical issues: right and wrong, and the organization of societies.

3.   The main branches of philosophy include: logic, metaphysics, epistemology, ethics, and political philosophy.

4.   Studying philosophy will strengthen your analytical abilities, your capacity for abstract thought, and your ability to argue.

## Discussion Questions

1. Have you already thought about any of the philosophical questions identified in this chapter? What spurred this? Another course? A debate about a controversial issue? An experience in your life? Your own proclivity to think about life?

2. Later chapters of this book will explore in depth the main philosophical issues identified above. But try your hand at taking a position and fashioning an argument on any of the following questions: How free are our actions? What makes an action morally wrong? Does God exist?

3. What do you expect to get out of studying philosophy? What will make it worth all the time and effort you will put in? Will just a good grade do it? If philosophy doesn't help you become more successful in your career, does that mean it has no value?

## Suggested Readings

A superb source for detailed information about almost every philosopher and philosophical issue is *The Encyclopedia of Philosophy*, edited by Paul Edwards, 8 volumes (New York: Macmillan and the Free Press, 1967). For an excellent history of philosophy, see F. C. Copleston, *History of Philosophy*, 8 volumes (Garden City, N.Y.: Doubleday, 1965). For a popular account of the development of philosophy, consult Will Durant, *The Story of Philosophy* (New York: Pocket Books, 1953).

# What Is the Secret of Teaching Values?

## In an increasingly complex society, old ways are no longer guaranteed to work

### JAMES A. MICHENER

*A Pulitzer Prize winner, best-selling author James Michener has also been awarded the U.S. Medal of Freedom. This selection is from* Money.

[1]Values are the emotional rules by which a nation governs itself. Values summarize the accumulated folk wisdom by which a society organizes itself. And values are the precious reminders that individuals obey to bring order and meaning into their personal lives. Without values, nations, societies and individuals can pitch straight to hell.

[2]I was a tough, undisciplined youngster, suspended three times from school, twice from college. I was a vagabond at 14, rode freight trains in my late teens. But because I had accumulated an iron-clad set of values, I was able to hack out a fairly acceptable life. In my day—and I am 84—young people acquired their system of values first in the home. I was raised in a terribly broken home, which never had enough money for normal living. But I had an adoptive mother who took in abandoned children, who worked around the clock, and who read to us at night. By the time I was five, I had the great rhythm of the English language echoing in my mind.

[3]I learned values in church, in school and on the street. I learned them through travel, military service and the movies. I acquired values through athletics, where a high-school coach took me, fatherless and without a rudder, and pointed me in the right direction. I learned values in the library and, in fact, it could be that my intellectual life was saved by the little library opened in our town of Doylestown, Pa. about the time I was seven. Records recently recovered showed that the first two cards taken out were issued to Margaret Mead and me. What a start for us; what a start for the library.

[4]Modern kids, regrettably, face extreme pressures that I simply didn't. This is a more complex world and the youngster of the 1990s absorbs a heavy hammering. There's an assault from all sides by news that's threatening; there's been a break-down of traditional safeguards like the family. Stanford University professor John Gardner, the founder of Common Cause, notes, however, that after many years of exploring "the limits of living without ethics, a lot of people are saying, 'It won't work.' I think there's a movement back toward commitment to shared goals." If so, it's mighty welcome.

[5]What should these goals be? Nationally, there must be a drive for public service, to see society protected and moved ahead. There must be encouragement to blow the whistle when something goes wrong.

⁶Individually, we must develop compassion, a willingness to work, loyalty to family and friends and organizations, the courage to face temporary defeat and not lose forward motion. I think we must learn fairness and honesty in economic matters. And we've got to keep reviewing our value decisions from decade to decade. You're never home free just because you went one way one time.

⁷Adults can keep updating their value systems from the best of what they read and see on television—and from the very fine adult study programs I've observed in places as diverse as Alaska, Maine and Florida. For young people, the home still ought to be the cradle of all values, but unfortunately a staggering proportion of them do not live in stable homes. It is thoughtless beyond imagination for older people to say rigidly, "The child must learn his or her values at home" when there is no home. Some substitute must be found.

⁸Religious training? It would be wonderful if every child had the warm, comforting experience I had in my Sunday school, with its songs, its stories, its bags of candy at the holiday, but many are denied that. And while religion is an admirable teacher for those connected to it, it is a silent voice for those who are not.

⁹The school is the only agency legally established by organized society and supported by taxation whose sole job it is to teach the child the knowledge, the skills and the values required for a successful adult life within the bounds of society. Its task is formidable, its achievement when things work well—that is, when teachers, children and parents unite in a common effort—can be magnificent. I know, for I attended such a school and taught in several. But it is obvious that today most schools fall far short of that ideal. They seem to stultify intelligence, not enhance it. Their deficiencies are deplorable, for the average student can spend twelve years in them and learn little, while gifted students are not challenged or helped to achieve at the maximum.

¹⁰I doubt that I could teach in a modern school, and for good reason. In my day parents and administrators both supported my efforts to be the best teacher possible; today it seems that teachers are not supported by anyone, and I doubt that I could fight undefended. Yet, even those of us who brood about the failure of schools must rely on them to help students build ethical codes and value systems. We must encourage the schools to demonstrate to a child that fair play pays off. That kindliness to peers pays off. That fairness in giving grades is taking place. The child has to see all this going on. We must show, as well as tell, what good values are all about.

¹¹Young people these days are thrown into a hot-house of competition and social exchange that test their decision-making skills rather strenuously. The peer pressure I had to put up with was relatively simple. A boy would gain access to a jalopy and expect the rest of us to tag along on a joy ride. Today, there are drugs and gangs and unprecedented violence. There is the incessant influence of TV, heightening peer pressure to regard fashion and style, for example, as the highest values to which a young person can aspire.

¹²What television offers is so enticing. There was nothing in my youth to compare with its power. Statistics show that the eight or ten hours a week my generation of kids spent reading books are superseded by the 30 hours modern kids spend at the television set. The difference produces a radically different set of values. Beyond the

distorted consumerism, there is an appalling amount of violence. Each week on TV I see endless shootings, stabbings and gruesome deaths. At Halloween I see sadism, abuse of women and slaughter for the fun of it. Young people cannot feed on such a diet without its having a deleterious effect, and studies that purport to prove otherwise are rubbish.

[13]I am disturbed by the demeaning way television depicts the American school. In too many shows, teachers are comic or pathetic and a student who works hard at his lessons is a wimp or a nerd. With so many people needing to rely on schools as the place to learn values, television could be of critical service to the future of our nation by rediscovering respect for the school. And schools, in turn, should direct youngsters to the best of television, to the portion of TV in which the disabled get support, racism is decried, minorities are depicted as heroes and heroines, and patriotism is extolled and rewarded. If young viewers select programs to ensure a mix of good with the violent and vicious, they can find material which illuminates the fight of the American people for justice and a decent society. Pressure can be—must be—mounted to promote the best, not the worst, of TV.

[14]As a young man I was taught to treat all races with justice, and I wrote numerous books testifying to that belief. I was taught that loyalty to one's nation was an obligation, and I have seen men who dabbled in treason come to mournful ends. I was taught the good citizen pays his taxes, supports schools, libraries and museums, and much of my adult life has centered on such activity. It was drummed into me that one looked after his own health and that of others, and I have tried to do so. At all levels of my education and upbringing I was advised to cling to good people and shun the bad, and I have tried. I realize there are considerations and pressures for young people today that did not exist for me—among them, drugs, AIDS and nuclear weapons. Yet, the values I learned must endure—and be taught—as the foundation for the America of tomorrow. They must be taught in the home, in religious training, in the Boy Scouts and Girl Scouts, in Little League, in the media. And most critically, as a guarantee that everyone will be exposed to them, they must be taught in school.

**Content Questions**

*True or False*

If the statement is false, rewrite it to make it true.

1. People and society cannot function without shared values.
2. Today's young people spend approximately the same number of hours watching television as Michener's generation spent reading.
3. Nationally, there appears to be a movement back toward a commitment to shared goals.
4. Value systems should be reviewed and updated.
5. Michener has always been rich and successful.

*Completion*

6. Where did Michener learn his values?

7. What does Michener think two of the nation's shared goals should be?

8. What does Michener think six individual goals should be?

9. What are three sources adults can draw on to help them update their values?

10. What are four of Michener's fundamental values?

## Vocabulary

1. without a rudder (¶3)

2. task is formidable (¶9)

3. stultify intelligence (¶9)

4. deficiencies are deplorable (¶9)

5. incessant influence of TV (¶11)

6. young person can aspire (¶11)

7. distorted consumerism (¶12)

8. deleterious effect (¶12)

9. demeaning way (¶13)

10. patriotism is extolled (¶13)

## Content Analysis Questions

1. What is Michener's purpose?

2. What is Michener's thesis?

3. Explain what Michener means by "We must show, as well as tell, what good values are all about." Do you agree or disagree? Explain your answer.

4. Although Michener says "the home ought to be the cradle of all values," why does he think some substitute must be found? Do you agree or disagree? Explain your answer.

5. Why doesn't Michener think he could teach in a modern school? Do you agree or disagree with him? Do you think you could teach in a modern school? Explain.

## Application Questions

1. Assume that you have been asked by one of your professors to work with a committee to prepare recommendations for parents on "what's good, and not so good, to watch on television." What type of programming would you recommend as "good" and "not so good"? Explain your rationale.

2. Assume that the local elementary school announces it is going to teach an "Ethics and Values in America" unit in all classes in all grades. How would you decide whether to be for or against the unit? Once you decided, what constructive steps would you take to convince school officials of your point of view?

# Feeding on Fast Food and False Values

## Can students overcome instant gratification?

### HELMUT MANZL

*Helmut Manzl is a social science teacher at Oakville-Trafalgar High School, in Oakville, Ontario, Canada. This selection was condensed from* Education Forum, *XV (Spring 1989), pp. 34–37.*

[1]Schools are under great pressure to counteract the hidden curriculum promoted by the social environment. Today, many students have unrealistic attitudes and expectations as a result of such sources of popular culture as the electronic media, advertising, and fast food. This has led to boredom, a degeneration in work habits, and a high dropout rate.

[2]The content of television programs places unrealistic expectations on schools and teachers. Programming is based on fast action, excitement, and glamour. Teachers are unable to compete. Students often have difficulty making the transition from the slick television world to the more routine, matter-of-fact daytime world of education.

[3]But it is also the process of interacting with a medium that shapes us. With the advent of cable systems, videotape, and remote channel changers, television offers a vast selection of programs, and this has considerable impact on how children approach learning. Their expectations for change and manipulation have been heightened by the media experience. Today's learner has a shorter attention span and a lower threshold of boredom than students from previous generations. Student boredom can often be attributed to preconceived notions about what should be going on in real life, based on television experience.

[4]Computers also affect how students learn, giving them a greater sense of control over the pace, content, and direction of learning. Schools do not follow that same regimen. Classrooms housing 30 or more students do not lend themselves to programming demands. Few teachers can give individual students the kind of undivided attention extended by the computer.

[5]The educational system cannot duplicate the electronic world outside. The increasingly obvious learning problems with which many students must cope do not stem from some inborn learning disability but from the incompatibility between the electronic environment and the classroom.

[6]But there are other equally powerful environmental messengers affecting the attitudes of young people. All around them, they receive messages that one's needs will be instantly gratified. From hamburgers to microwaves, from remote channel changers to computers, "fast" or "instant" have become important words in the student vocabulary.

[7]At McDonald's fast-food outlets, hamburgers are ready in 7.5 seconds, served with perpetual smiles. Television ads promise pizza

delivery in 30 minutes or less and quick relief for a headache or other discomfort. Department stores promote total customer satisfaction. Dissatisfied patrons are told they can return products for a complete refund.

8This subordination of trade to the whims of the buyer falters beyond the marketplace. Students are well versed in their consumer rights and freedoms: They drop out of school and quit courses with the same frequency with which they would exchange an unacceptable garment or stereo.

9In schools, the instant gratification mentality translates into lack of application and hard work. Schools just seem to go too slowly. Many students believe they are entitled to fast, painless education. Trying harder to stay in school or working to meet the academic requirements of a course escapes many young minds predisposed to consumerism.

10Other equally powerful forces shape the attitudes of teenagers. Major credit card companies promise that everything is within the cardbearer's reach. No real effort is required to acquire even the most coveted consumer items.

11This message is not lost on young people. What they are often unaware of, however, is a lesson that many adults have learned the hard way: Instant gratification usually has to be paid off later, with interest. The motto of the credit card world is "Fun first, pay later." But the opposite is true in virtually all meaningful endeavors. The debt, in terms of work or energy expended, must be paid up front, and the gratification or payoff comes later, in the form of a job, a promotion, or a profit.

12What thus emerges is the attitude that one is entitled to goods and services whether one has the means to acquire them or not. The doctrine of entitlement runs contrary to the values of hard work, saving, and postponement of gratification. Success comes through struggle and hard work, and, in order to achieve, one must be prepared to compete in the social and economic arena.

13The Xerox machine may yet become an apt symbol for North American youth. Teachers are all too ready to fall into lockstep conformity while originality is sacrificed to the photocopy mentality engineered by the fashion industry and advertising.

14One of the principal reasons for the percentage of high school students who have part-time jobs is the need that young people feel to compete in our consumer-oriented society. They frequently hold down a part-time job because the youth culture places inordinate stress on money, and they want to fit in.

15The end result of this is a generation of followers. In a world where substance is subordinated to image, the designer-label generation equates status not with worthwhile achievement but with material gain.

16Teenagers and young adults may have an entirely unrealistic set of expectations. Inordinate numbers of young people think they will have a high-paying job and will soon be driving a luxury car, living in an expensive home, and spending large chunks of time on leisure activities.

17Our electronic and mechanized society tends to supplant qualitative judgment in favor of quantitative judgment. This is a most unfortunate attitude to take into the highly competitive career market where the doctrine of entitlement breaks down. Never before have so many young people competed for jobs and university and graduate school positions. Many universities have responded by raising their entrance standards. Likewise, job promotions are becoming more difficult to attain as competition intensifies.

[18]One of the most debilitating aspects of the hidden curriculum is that it requires little communication. Instant bank-tellers, fast-food outlets, drive-through services, television, and computers require a very limited amount of speech or no speech at all. But in the world of employment, communication skills will be even more important in the future.

[19]Parents, teachers, and educational administrators will be increasingly called upon to counteract the vocal isolation of the drive-through world in which children live. In the next 20 years, given the shift from an industrial to an information society, the majority of workers will be occupied with the creation, processing, and distribution of information.

[20]In the future, we will be compelled to challenge in some systematic way the pervasive environmentally generated values and attitudes to which children are daily exposed. If we fail to do so, no amount of curriculum shuffling will bring students closer to a sound education.

## Content Questions

*True or False*

If the statement is false, rewrite it to make it true.

1. Today's students have about the same attention span as students in previous generations.
2. The media may be giving teenagers and young adults a very unrealistic set of expectations about their world.
3. Instant gratification means getting what you want when you want it.
4. In the world of employment, communication skills will be even more important in the future.
5. Credit cards often encourage people to play first and pay later.

*Completion*

6. What is the social environment's hidden message?
7. What are three "powerful forces" that shape the attitudes of teenagers?
8. What is the "lesson many adults have learned the hard way"?
9. Why does Manzl think so many high school students have jobs?
10. What is the "photocopy mentality?" Give an example of it.

## Vocabulary

1. degeneration in work habits (¶1)
2. advent (¶3)
3. attributed to preconceived notions (¶3)

4. regimen (¶4)

5. instantly gratified (¶6)

6. perpetual smiles (¶7)

7. subordination of trade (¶8)

8. predisposed to consumerism (¶9)

9. coveted (¶10)

10. supplant (¶17)

### Content Analysis Questions

1. What is Manzl's purpose?

2. What is Manzl's thesis?

3. Does Manzl use primarily facts or opinions to support and develop his thesis? Give two examples to support your answer.

4. Explain what Manzl means by the "doctrine of entitlement." Do you agree or disagree that such a doctrine exists with Americans? Why?

5. Do you agree or disagree with Manzl that today's youth have "fast-food values"? Explain your answer.

### Application Questions

1. Assume that a good friend of yours asks you to talk with her twelve-year-old son. She is concerned because his grades are dropping and he's cutting classes. He tells you that school is boring and doesn't have anything to do with "real" life. What do you say to him?

2. Assume that the professor in one of your required classes spends every minute of every class period lecturing in a monotone voice. You've been spending most of your time complaining to classmates or falling asleep. Now, however, you decide you want to take a positive approach to learn the information. What do you do?

# *Values in the Classroom*

Eloise Salholz
with Tony Clifton, Patricia King, Karen Springen,
Howard Manly, and Debra Rosenberg

*The authors are* Newsweek *correspondents: Eloise Salholz in Washington, Tony Clifton in New York, Patricia King in San Francisco, Karen Springen in Chicago, Howard Manly in Atlanta, and Debra Rosenberg in Boston.*

[1]The spring and summer of '89 were a notably sad time for young people, race relations and civic values. A band of wilding black and Hispanic youths attacked the white Central Park jogger that year, and a group of whites set upon the black 16-year-old Yusuf Hawkins, in Bensonhurst. Norman Siegel, the executive director of the New York ACLU, was on a protest march in Brooklyn when he got the idea for an ethics program for teenagers. Several of the young men convicted in connection with the Hawkins killing had attended New Utrecht High, Siegel's alma mater, so he went there to teach his first class in racial tolerance. Siegel says the values course, which

has spread to 15 other New York schools in the last three years, is "a cross between law school and 'Donahue,' with people clamoring to put [across] their point of view."

[2]The teaching of values in schools is nothing new, but it is as subject to fashion as hemlines and hats. From ancient Greece to cold-war America, educators felt comfortable making absolute distinctions between right and wrong; family, church and school were considered a triangle of moral education, with each corner pulling equal weight. Then came the social revolutions of the '60s. After that, "if you even mentioned teaching values, people immediately saw it as indoctrination," says Charles Quigley, executive director of the California-based Center for Civic Education. Now the pendulum has swung back—educators are openly in the beliefs business again. "Schools cannot be value-neutral," says Prof. George H. Wood, coordinator of the Institute for Democracy in Education at Ohio University, Athens.

[3]Some '60s-era discomfort has remained. "If you [tell] a community that you're going to teach values, some people go nuts," says Peter Benson, head of the Minneapolis-based Search Institute, which surveys student attitudes. "What values? Whose values?" Schools try to avoid hot-button issues like abortion, birth control and capital punishment. Some even shy away from race. "Teachers find it kind of awkward to ask an African-American kid to stand up and talk about racism," says Morris Dees, executive director of the Southern Poverty Law Center. They "would rather just teach the ABCs and go from there."

[4]But many educators say there's a core of basic beliefs—tolerance, honesty, respect, diligence—that belongs in the classroom, especially in the formative years. Experts say the sooner a school starts instilling those values, the better. "After all, a kindergarten child shows some appreciation of values the first time he says, 'It's not fair,' even if that almost always means 'It's not fair to me'," says Thomas Lickona, author of a recent book called "Educating for Character" and an education professor at the State University of New York, Cortland. Around the country, schools have been implementing programs that provide a moral education, 1990s style. A look at some winners:

[5]•*Teaching Tolerance.* After a career spent fighting racism in the courts, Dees of the Southern Poverty Law Center decided to try to nip it in the bud. Last year he launched "Teaching Tolerance," a magazine to teach teachers how to foster racial harmony among school kids. Published twice a year, the magazine provides ideas, resources and tactics. "We can't simply play a video and have kids like each other," says editor Sara Bullard. "We must use a lot of tools and techniques—and be mindful that we can't beat them over the head with it."

[6]•*Learning by Serving.* A number of high schools consider volunteer work a prerequisite for graduation. "A student can go through 12 years of school never having helped anybody else," says Sheldon Berman, president of the Cambridge-based Educators for Social Responsibility. In Atlanta, students must perform 75 non-school hours of service at approved nonprofit organizations like hos-

pitals, libraries, nursing homes or shelters for the homeless. "Citizenship skills, responsibility and respect are all equally important to a democratic society," explains assistant superintendent Barbara Whitaker. One impediment: in their eagerness to keep out unpaid workers of any stripe, unions have on occasion overreacted to such programs.

7•*Learning from the Past.* "We're trying to teach kids the difference between good and evil," says Margot Stern Strom, executive director of a program called Facing History and Ourselves. Based in Brookline, Mass., the outfit gets students to examine racism, prejudice and anti-Semitism through a study of 20th-century genocide. More than 30,000 teachers have participated in Facing History workshops, exposing some 450,000 students each year to the moral complexities of the Holocaust. It has a tremendous impact because the tragedies actually happened. "You don't need to make hypothetical dilemmas for kids," says Stern Strom, who suggests that young people do better when given real ideas to debate.

8•*Creating a Community.* The Child Development Project, a veteran California program, in effect teaches schools to practice what they preach. Specialists go into select schools and help create environments that promote tolerance, respect and grass-roots decision making. For children to really learn the lesson, says director Eric Schaps, "The school has to be a place where these values prevail. . . . This notion of a caring community is the neglected paradigm in American education right now."

9Even educators who welcome the return to values believe there's a limit to what classrooms can accomplish—and no end to what's expected of them. In the face of poverty, family instability and social disorganization, parents want schools to fill what Benson of the Search Institute calls a "values vacuum." That they cannot do. But as microcosms of society at large, schools offer the perfect setting for ethics in action. "In every school there is a hidden curriculum, which is about the way people treat each other, how teachers treat kids, how kids treat kids," says Lickona. The lesson for everyone: do as we do, not as we say.

## Content Questions

*True or False*

If the statement is false, rewrite it to make it true.

1. The teaching of values in schools is a new concept.
2. The social revolutions of the '60s encouraged schools to deal with values issues.
3. Many teachers would prefer to teach the ABCs and avoid values issues.
4. A number of high schools have a volunteer requirement for graduation.
5. There is a limit to what values in the classroom programs can accomplish.

*Completion*

6. What do the authors mean by, "The teaching of values in schools is nothing new, but it is as subject to fashion as hemlines and hats"?

7. What entities made up the "triangle of moral education"?

8. What are the four core beliefs that many educators say belong in the classroom?

9. What are three "hot-button" values issues?

10. What is the "hidden curriculum" of every school? Do you agree that it exists? Explain.

## Vocabulary

1. indoctrination (¶2)
2. instilling (¶4)
3. impediment (¶6)
4. 20th-century genocide (¶7)
5. hypothetical dilemmas (¶7)
6. prevail (¶8)
7. neglected paradigm (¶8)
8. microcosm of society at large (¶9)

## Content Analysis Questions

1. What is the authors' purpose?

2. What is the authors' thesis?

3. What does Professor Wood mean by "schools cannot be values neutral"? Do you agree or disagree? Why?

4. Do you think "educators are openly in the beliefs business again"? Give an example to support your answer. Do you think educators and schools should be in the beliefs business? Why or why not?

5. Of the four "winning" programs described, which one do you think will have the longest-lasting affect on people? Why? Which one of the programs do you think will have the least affect? Why?

## Application Questions

1. Assume that a campus organization you work with has been asked to suggest the components of a "values" program for the college's child development center. What "values" would be the core of your program? Why?

2. Assume that the college administration is conducting a survey on campus to determine "what are our most serious problems" and suggestions for positive action. How do you respond?

# Universities Must Teach Both Facts and Values to Stave off Barbarism

## ALBERT C. YATES

*Dr. Yates is president of Colorado State University, Fort Collins, Colorado, and chancellor of the CSU system. This selection is from* The Denver Post.

[1]Some forty years ago, as a boy of 10 or 11, I strayed some distance from my home. The unfamiliar surroundings seemed like an unknown, safe place where I could do as I pleased—and so I misbehaved. Unknown to me, I was watched. By the time I arrived home, my mother knew of my whereabouts and behavior—and I paid.

[2]During those times, our neighborhood manifested and nurtured the values we learned at home. There were accepted community standards of behavior which children were expected to uphold. We learned that if we crossed the line—if we strayed too far—there was a community of adults who had their eyes on us and were willing to step in and reinforce our parents' values.

[3]The world for most of us is quite a different place now, changed by a redefinition of family, an increasingly mobile society and the contracting boundaries of our neighborhoods. Community standards are more ambiguous, less easy to define.

[4]As a result of these dramatic cultural shifts, expectations of and demands on elementary and secondary schoolteachers have changed over the past two decades as well. A few decades ago, teachers accepted the reinforcement of parents' standards as part of their responsibility. Now, teachers often are expected to introduce children to the values and standards of behavior requisite to membership in a civil society.

[5]At the same time, changes of a different kind have occurred in our system of higher education. Once, under the philosophy of *in loco parentis,* universities acknowledged an obligation to monitor and discipline students as their parents might—a practice correctly abandoned during the social upheaval of the 1960s.

[6]Since that time, higher education has evolved effectively to meet the needs of a changing world in a host of important areas—technology transfer, educational access, research, economic development, extended studies and more—but with one notable exception. We have failed to address as well as we might questions critical to the shaping of our humanity. What, for example, is the academy's role in directing, or reacting to, the changing social fabric of our country? What level of responsibility should be assumed by our colleges and universities in inculcating and refining values? In preparing our graduates for citizenship? As higher education strives to regain the public trust, our institutions must become more certain of their responses to such questions. I don't pretend to have the answers, but some things are clear. We must resurrect the notion that universities play a critical role in developing human beings, and that our

institutions themselves have an active part to play in determining the course of future societal events.

[7]In a 1981 essay, Colorado State Professor Willard Eddy warned of the danger of universities graduating students who are highly skilled in technical fields but lack an essential humanity. "Decency, civility, respect for others, are not stored in libraries or computers," he wrote. "Each generation comes into the world with more potential for becoming barbarians than for becoming saints. Consequently . . . a decent society is not easily sustained."

[8]No institution is better positioned to sustain such a society than a university. These are places which, by their very nature, are expected to model the highest values of civilization.

[9]For the public university, discussion and expression of values seem to occur in two contexts: The first is within the academic program itself; the second is within the example set by the university through the general conduct of its activities. These two settings are not unrelated and often at odds. But this tension between them—brought on by our quest for objectivity and dispassionate discourse on the one hand and our need to stand for something on the other—is a necessary part of the university's search for truth.

[10]Students come to college, in large measure, unshaped and uncertain. But they come with strong beliefs and assumptions, looking to the university for knowledge and guidance. Just as we expect a kindergarten teacher to educate young children in those simple rules that teach discipline and good behavior—say "please" and "thank you," don't cut in line, respect others' belongings—we should expect college professors to help students achieve understanding at a higher level of the finest attributes of a civilized society: the ability to act fairly, reason plainly, express oneself gracefully, behave honestly, define a position worth defending, and accept responsibility for actions taken.

[11]As well, our society expects university graduates to be intelligent people. J. Martin Klotsche, former chancellor of the University of Wisconsin-Milwaukee, once described an intelligent person as "one who has learned 'to choose between'. One who knows that good is better than evil, that confidence should supersede fear, that love is superior to hate, that gentleness is better than cruelty, forbearance (more noble) than intolerance, compassion (greater) than arrogance, and truth more virtuous than ignorance."

[12]A university's job is to help its students acquire the knowledge to choose wisely and to understand the consequences of their choices. In our classrooms and on our plazas, we must permit all manner of thought and debate, no matter how controversial or offensive. And within such forums we must be especially guarded in our advocacy of one position over another.

[13]But we still can do our very best to say, "Here are the results of choosing one set of actions over another. Here is what happened when someone embraced this course, and here is what happened to someone who chose a different path."

[14]In educating people to choose wisely, the true mettle of a college or university is gleaned through the aspirations of its general education program. Father Theodore Hesburgh, former president of Notre Dame University, captured the ideal in characteristic eloquence as he reviewed the possibilities of the curriculum:

[15]*"Language and mathematics stress clarity, precision, and style*

*if well-taught; literature gives an insight into that vast human arena of good and evil, love and hate, peace and violence as real living human options. History gives a vital record of mankind's success and failure, hopes and fears, the heights and the depths of human endeavors pursued with either heroism or depravity but always depicting real virtue or the lack of it. Music and art purvey a sense of beauty seen or heard, a value to be preferred to ugliness or cacophony. The physical sciences are a symphony of world order, so often unsuccessfully sought by law, but already achieved by creation, a model challenging man's freedom and creativity. The social sciences show man at work, theoretically and practically, creating his world."*

[16]Such values, expressed and debated throughout the academic program, offer the substance to permit an assessment of how the university itself chooses to conduct its business. Any university has a set of values it embraces and displays in decision-making, aesthetics, concerns about safety, about people and about funding—even in the programs and courses of study it offers.

[17]The emphasis universities place upon qualities such as service, community, integrity and decorum are manifestations of the things we treasure.

[18]Interpreted in this way, our universities model (or should) for their students—and others—principles and standards deserving of preservation and emulation. In the ideal, faculty and staff elaborate the culture broadly articulated by the institution. Through their behavior in the classroom and laboratory, as well as through personal contact with students, faculty can encourage students to embrace simple truths, like those which Klotsche named, which we know to be right and good.

[19]It is most important that the university be preserved as a forum for speech and debate that is unconstrained and unabashed. During their time on campus, students need to feel safe to venture into unknown territory, to push against the boundaries of what they know and draw conclusions based on their judgment and experience.

[20]But they should do so within the context of an environment which is itself secure and well-founded.

[21]The world is a different place from that in which many of us grew up. Those neighbors who watched me wander from home and get into mischief were part of a system of needed oversight and reinforcement of important things learned, but not yet owned.

[22]Much has now changed and new systems must be invented: Our colleges and universities surely must play a crucial role.

## Content Questions

*True or False*

If the statement is false, rewrite it to make it true.

1. When Yates was growing up, neighbors felt a responsibility for neighbors.

2. Yates would like to see the university return to the philosophy of *in loco parentis*.

3. All colleges and universities have a set of values that they believe and use.

4. Yates thinks some controversial topics should be off-limits on college and university campuses.

5. Yates thinks it is important that higher education be a forum for free speech and debate.

*Completion*

6. What four changes does Yates say have made the world a different place today than when he grew up?

7. What does *in loco parentis* mean?

8. What six "attributes of a civilized society" does Yates think professors should help students achieve?

9. How does Yates think professors can help students achieve these "attributes of a civilized society"?

10. What is the importance of a college or university's general education program?

**Vocabulary**

1. manifested and nurtured (¶2)

2. requisite to membership (¶4)

3. inculcating and refining values (¶6)

4. true mettle (¶14)

5. gleaned through (¶14)

6. aspirations of its general education (¶14)

7. characteristic eloquence (¶14)

8. manifestations of (¶17)

9. preservation and emulation (¶18)

10. faculty and staff elaborate the culture broadly articulated by the institution (¶18)

**Content Analysis Questions**

1. What is Yates' purpose?

2. What is Yates' thesis?

3. Explain what Eddy means by "Decency, civility, respect for others, are not stored in libraries or computers." What kind of advice do you think he would give professors?

4. In what ways do you agree or disagree with Klotsche's description of an intelligent person? Explain.

5. Yates writes, "A university's job is to help its students acquire the knowledge to choose wisely and to understand the consequences of their choices." In what ways do you agree or disagree? Explain.

**Application Questions**

1. Assume that your campus has an unofficial "soapbox corner" where students gather between classes to talk about events and issues. Recently there have been student complaints that the topics and lan-

guage are offensive. You're now on a committee to decide what, if any, rules and regulations should be established. What is your personal point of view? How would you proceed?

2. Assume that as part of your English course you are going to be required to participate in a computer-networked electronic forum each week. Your professor asks your class what, if any, rules and regulations it wants to govern the topics and responses. How do you respond? Would your stance change if some student responses consistently contained views or language you found objectionable?

# *Not to Worry: The College Mold Doesn't Hold*

## PHILIP ALTBACH AND LIONEL LEWIS

*Philip Altbach is professor of education and director of the Comparative Education Center at the State University of New York at Buffalo. Lionel Lewis is professor of sociology at the State University of New York at Buffalo. This selection is from* Commonweal.

[1]On one side of the often acrimonious debate about "political correctness" and the sanctity of the traditional curricular "canon" are faculty who would like their teaching to have a liberalizing influence on the attitudes and values of American college students. The other side is concerned that these humanists will be successful, that those who take a certain ideological line in the classroom will impose a dubious worldview on students. The latter, conservatives like Dinesh D'Souza and Charles J. Sykes, are, at present, the most vocal. They are convinced that the Left has captured the curriculum and that students are being subjected to the politically correct radical ideology of the campus Left. Sykes, for example, reminds us about the "distinction between teaching and indoctrination; the abyss that separates the Socratic method from propaganda." The traditionalists have pitted themselves against those whom they describe as radicals who worry about the rise of racism on campus and a general intolerance and separatism among students. These "radicals" have become intensely involved in rethinking the curriculum and adding various courses dealing with multiculturalism, minority perspectives, and human relations in an effort to influence the attitudes and values of students.

[2]Everyone should relax. The wangling is unnecessary if the concern is about changing or safeguarding the social attitudes or civility or character or ethics of students. For the most part, students are pretty well inoculated against ideological and intellectual currents. The fact is that students are only marginally influenced in terms of attitude change, politics, or broader societal perspectives by their experiences in higher education. There is little doubt that students do learn as a result of going to college, but they remain remarkably untouched in terms of attitudes and values by academic experiences.

[3]A new book reminds us of the illusory nature of attitude change on campus. Ernest T. Pascarella and Patrick T. Terenzini,

following in the tradition of earlier studies, have summarized the massive but not very conclusive research on students in *How College Affects Students* (Jossey-Bass, 1991). Their survey of 2,600 studies carried out over the last two decades on American students tells us that college has only a modest and mostly ill-defined impact on students. And these two authors are not the first to look at student change and not find much. Back in 1957, Philip Jacob found that students were hardly changed by their collegiate experience. In 1969, Kenneth Feldman and Theodore Newcomb were more optimistic about college impact, but their massive synthesis did not come up with convincing or unambiguous evidence. One could add the annual surveys of American college freshmen done by UCLA and the American Council on Education. Although 1991 freshmen may not see the world precisely as freshmen did in 1971, throughout individual college careers there is remarkable stability in attitudes toward politics, life-styles, and ideology. To be sure, there was some radicalization in the 1960s, a modest although noticeable conservative trend in the Reagan years, and most recently there is evidence of some resurgent liberalism among students. But students come to campus with these predispositions. As entering freshmen during the Reagan years, students had their sights on professional degrees and careers.

⁴Just what does college do for students? The academic experience imparts knowledge—students seem to learn something in college. If they use what they learn, they retain it. College graduates also benefit economically from having obtained a university degree. Studies indicate that those with a degree earn more than their counterparts without one. The skills and knowledge, and most particularly the discipline, that are learned in college are valued by employers—we know this because employers pay more for college graduates.

⁵But when it comes to attitudes and values, the evidence is less persuasive. For example, the new Pascarella and Terenzini study notes that, on the following items: social liberalism, political liberalism, civil rights and liberties, secularism, and modern gender roles, the net effects of college on attitudes and values are either unclear or small. But these are precisely the areas which are so bitterly contested today. If a wealth of evidence shows that over the past two decades a college education has not greatly affected the attitudes and values of students, perhaps educators are spending too much time on attempting to manipulate the curriculum with the idea of changing attitudes. We should remember that the much-studied women from Bennington College, who were saturated with New Deal ideas in the 1930s, were not discernibly different when compared with their sisters and other close relatives a decade later. Spouses and children, community activities, and social class were clearly more salient than vaguely remembered Keynesian theory and liberal ideas imbibed on campus.

⁶All this leaves us with several important questions. Why do the attitudes and values of students change over time? Why has there been a deterioration in racial and ethnic relations? And what should the academic community do to improve the present problematical situation? Clearly, there are differences in college students

over time. During the 1960s, students became more liberal and their choice of majors reflected a concern with social activism and service. For example, classes in sociology were full and faculties doubled or tripled in size. Later, in the 1970s and 1980s, students of the "me-generation" flocked to fields such as law and business, fields that would yield high incomes. Service-related majors or those majors which did not promise instant economic gratification languished. Student generations change because young people are affected by the same societal trends and conditions as the rest of the population. After the 1960s, students were buffeted by the economic uncertainties and declining job market of the 1970s; in the 1980s they were affected by the conservative ethos and instant gratification of the Reagan years. It is not surprising that the campus felt the influence of these basic economic and social factors. In the past few years, cutbacks in higher education and a tough job market have led to worries on campus. Further, "Willie Hortonism" has combined with real fears and tensions to produce a deterioration in campus race relations. Moreover, opposition in high places to affirmative action, quotas, and other efforts to ensure racial equality, as well as recent decisions by the Supreme Court have all signaled significant change. It is becoming more respectable in American society to blame minority groups not only for society's ills but also for one's own individual problems. In colleges and universities across the country, many white students see affirmative action and other programs favoring minorities as hurting themselves—a zero-sum game. They feel threatened by admissions programs that seem to favor someone else; they believe that the bulk of student aid is going to others more favorably placed. Not surprisingly, many college students buy into these new attitudes and values. They hear them at home and believe them before attending their first college lecture.

[7]What, then, should colleges and universities do? The effort to marry the curriculum to social and attitudinal change would seem to be fruitless. The debate about the curriculum should be based on questions about what knowledge is intrinsically important and what is useful in an increasingly complex and technologically oriented society. What is worth knowing? What do we need to know? Perhaps the "core curriculum" proponents who devised the Chicago "Great Books" program or the Columbia general education core were right. They focused on what they felt was important to learn. It should be kept in mind that these core programs were not static—they changed as ideas about knowledge expanded and society presented new challenges. Thus, a broadened concept of the role of minorities in American life and a multicultural approach to history and society would not be inimical to a coherent curriculum.

[8]Our point is that American higher education has been led astray by the idea that the curriculum, the impact of professors, and the "collegiate experience" change attitudes. The evidence shows that these do not significantly alter student ideologies; it is a conceit to believe otherwise. Once this is recognized, the heat can be lowered on the curriculum debate. Political correctness will lose much of its salience and the Right will be able to stop worrying about students being brainwashed. We can focus on what is important.

⁹Improved race relations and a greater degree of tolerance on campus will not come from restricting freedom of expression or mandatory human relations courses. American colleges and universities are an integral part of American society: so far as there are social, racial, and economic tensions in society, these will be reflected on campus. How could it be otherwise? The best that higher education can do is to ensure a stimulating environment for learning, study, and research.

### Content Questions

*True or False*

If the statement is false, rewrite it to make it true.

1. Most students' attitudes, values, and politics are highly influenced by their college experience.
2. College freshmen in 1991 viewed the world basically the same as college freshmen in 1971 did.
3. Students come to campus with most of their attitudes, values, and politics already formed.
4. There are differences in college students over time.
5. Requiring all students to take a human relations course would assure more tolerance on campus.

*Completion*

6. What are the two sides of the curriculum debate?
7. What are two things college does for students?
8. Why do employers pay more for college graduates?
9. Why do the attitudes and values of college students change over time?
10. What do Altbach and Lewis think the curriculum debate should be centered around?

### Vocabulary

1. acrimonious debate (¶1)
2. sanctity of the traditional (¶1)
3. ideological line (¶1) and student ideologies (¶8)
4. illusory nature (¶3)
5. unambiguous evidence (¶3)
6. resurgent liberalism (¶3)
7. salient (¶5) and salience (¶8)
8. imbibed (¶5)
9. languished (¶6)
10. buffeted by (¶6)

11. conservative ethos (¶6)

12. intrinsically important (¶7)

13. inimical (¶7)

**Content Analysis Questions**

1. What is Altbach and Lewis's purpose?

2. What is Altbach and Lewis's thesis?

3. Why do Altbach and Lewis think educators may be "spending too much time on attempting to manipulate the curriculum with the idea of changing attitudes"? Do you agree or disagree? Why?

4. During the '60s, students selected majors for social activism and service; during the '70s and '80s for high incomes. How would you characterize the primary motives for selecting majors now? What makes you think so?

5. Do you agree or disagree that "The best that higher education can do is to ensure a stimulating environment for learning"? Why?

**Application Questions**

1. Assume that you are serving on your campus curriculum committee that is charged with developing or revising a "core curriculum." Who would you ask for help? Why? What are two concepts or courses you would want included in a core curriculum? Why?

2. What are two things you think the academic community should do to strengthen the attitudes, values, and human relations of students?

# *Beginning Anew*

### MURIEL L. WHETSTONE

*Muriel Whetstone was a journalism student at Columbia College in Chicago when she wrote this article for* Essence. *She graduated and is a full-time professional journalist in Chicago.*

¹I dreaded Sundays. I began living for the weekend at 8:30 Monday mornings. I resented my boss. The mere thought of answering other people's telephones, typing other people's work and watching other people take credit for my ideas and opinions would throw me into week-long bouts of depression. I hated my job. I hated my life. I hated myself for not having the guts to change either one.

²When most of my friends were planning college schedules and partying into the night, I was changing dirty diapers and walking the floor with a colicky baby. At 19 years old I was the mother of two, and a pitifully young wife. Everything I did for years, every decision I made, was done with my family in mind.

³And then I turned 29, and 30 was only a breath away. How long could I live like this? Certainly not until I retired. I began to feel that if I didn't do something soon, something quickly, I would die of

unhappiness. I decided to follow my childhood dream: I was going to get my undergraduate degree and become a full-time journalist.

[4]I quit my job on one of my good days, a Friday. Almost at once I was filled with trepidation. What would I tell my husband and what would be his reaction? How would we pay our bills? *I must be crazy,* I thought. I was too old to begin again. I prayed, *Lord, what have I done?* I wondered if I was experiencing some sort of early mid-life crisis. Perhaps if I crawled back to my boss on my hands and knees and pleaded temporary insanity, he'd give me my job back. I spent that entire weekend in the eye of an emotional cyclone.

[5]But while I was feeling uneasy about the bridge I'd just crossed, I also began to feel a renewed sense of hopefulness about the possibilities on the other side. I had had a long love affair with the written word that was separate and apart from any of my roles. What we shared was personal: It belonged to me and would always be mine despite anything going on outside of me. I wasn't quite sure what my journey would entail, but I was positive who would be at the other end. I steeled myself to travel the road that would lead me to a better understanding of who I was and of what I wanted out of life. I shared my mixed feelings with my husband. He was as apprehensive as I was, but he was also warmly supportive. And so I stepped off the bridge and onto the path, nervous but determined. I soon discovered that I loved to learn and that my mind soaked up knowledge at every opportunity. My decision at those times felt right. But sometimes, after realizing what was expected of me, I would be engulfed in self-doubt and uncertainty.

[6]I was older than a few of my instructors and nearly all of my classmates. I was a social outcast practically that entire first semester. Finally I met a group of older female students who were, like me, beginning anew. We began to share our experiences of returning to school, dealing with husbands, lovers, children and bills that had to be paid. Over time we have become sisters, supporting ourselves by encouraging and supporting one another.

[7]I eventually had to seek employment to help with expenses. In fact, I've had more jobs in the last couple of years than I care to count. Many times I've had to stir a pot with one hand while holding a book with the other. More than a few times I've nearly broken under the pressure. I've shed tears on the bad days, but smiles abound on the good ones.

[8]However, I would not take back one tear or change one thing about the last couple of years. It hasn't been a snap: From the beginning I knew it would not be. And it's not so much the results of the action that have reshaped me (although that's important, too) as it is the realization that I have within myself what it takes to do what I set out to do. I feel more in control these days and less like a flag on a breezy day, blowing this way or that depending on the wind.

[9]I no longer dread Sundays, and Wednesdays are just as pleasant as Fridays. Now I get credit for my ideas, and my opinions are sought after. I love my new career. I love my life again. And I can clearly see a new woman waiting patiently just a little way down the road, waiting for me to reach her.

**Vocabulary**

1. filled with trepidation (¶4)
2. what my journey would entail (¶5)
3. I steeled myself (¶5)
4. engulfed in self-doubt (¶5)

**Content Analysis Questions**

1. What is Whetstone's purpose?
2. What is Whetstone's thesis?
3. When Whetstone writes, "I wasn't quite sure what my journey would entail, but I was positive who would be at the other end," who does she know will be at the other end?
4. Explain what Whetstone means by "it's not so much the results of the action that have reshaped me . . . as it is the realization that I have within myself what it takes to do what I set out to do."
5. Describe the "new woman" Whetstone sees waiting patiently down the road. When do you think she'll meet her?

**Application Question**

1. Describe the "new person" waiting patiently down the road to meet you.

# Theme 4
# Working in a
# Global Economy

"Today's students and workers need to prepare themselves for a radically different job market by the year 2000," warns Selwyn Enzer, director of the University of Southern California's Project Overlook.

The readings in this theme consider information about predictions like this and encourage you to think about how changes in society and business will affect you and your future work.

The textbook chapter, "Recognizing Business Trends and Challenges" by Professors Griffin and Ebert, provides the big picture—why the world you work in is so different from past decades. Among the trends and issues they examine are the impact of high technology, the transition from manufacturing to information services, the changing demographics of the workforce, and the international trade dilemma.

The articles that make up the rest of the theme focus on specific workforce changes or job issues. First, newspaper feature writer Laura Anderson gives a glimpse of the workforce in the year 2000. Next, J. F. Coates, Inc., a firm specializing in futures research, supplies an in-depth look at how changing demographics, modern technology, and new demands on workers will bring sweeping changes to your workplace in the next fifteen years.

"Solving The Job Puzzle," by Clymer and McGregor offers some insight into the complex task of choosing a career. Then, in "Where the Jobs Are," five *Business Week* correspondents combine their resources to tell you where to look for new jobs in the 90s.

The last two articles deal with a specific workplace issue: contingent, or part-time, work. "Current Situation: Contingent Work Force," by the staff of *CQ Researcher,* serves as an overview of the issue. Then, in "Disposable Workers," the last article in this unit, Robert Lewis asks you to look at contingent work as it affects a particular segment of American workers.

Each of the readings is by a different author(s), of a different length, and requires different tasks.

---

**Strategies for Success**

- Develop a plan for each of the readings.
- Determine who the author is and why he or she is writing.
- Know the vocabulary the author uses.
- Identify what the author is writing about.
- Establish how the author develops the writing.
- Integrate graphic and text information.
- Organize the information you need.
- Recognize the author's stance.
- Decide what you can do with the author's information.

---

# *Recognizing Business Trends and Challenges*

## RICKY W. GRIFFIN AND RONALD J. EBERT

*Ricky W. Griffin teaches at Texas A & M University. Ronald J. Ebert teaches at the University of Missouri-Columbia. This selection is from* Business, *3rd ed.*

CHAPTER

3

▼

# RECOGNIZING BUSINESS TRENDS AND CHALLENGES

## *L*EARNING OBJECTIVES

After studying this chapter, you should be able to:

1. Describe five major trends that affect U.S. business today.
2. Explain why the U.S. government sometimes regulates businesses and how business seeks to influence the government.
3. Discuss changes in the U.S. labor pool and their effects on business.
4. Describe changes in demographics and consumer rights and their impact on U.S. business.
5. Identify and discuss four major challenges for U.S. business in the 1990s.

## *C*HAPTER OUTLINE

Opening Case: Buttoning Up Profits

Business Trends in the 1990s
  The Impact of High Technology • The Shift to Services • The Shift South and West • Mergers, Acquisitions, and Alliances

Business and Government
  Government Regulation of Business • The Move Toward Deregulation • How Business Influences Government

Business and Labor
  The Changing Demographics of the U.S. Labor Force • The Declining Unionization of the Labor Force • Worker Participation

Business and Consumers
  Consumer Rights • The Changing Demographics of U.S. Consumers

Business Challenges of the 1990s
  In Search of Higher Productivity • The International Trade Deficit • The Continuing Challenge of Pollution • Technology: Friend or Foe?

Opening Case Wrap-up

Concluding Case: Rolling in Dough

*O*PENING CASE

## BUTTONING UP PROFITS

O nce upon a time, in the year 1853, a German immigrant arrived in San Francisco and thought he saw an opportunity to sell tents to miners. As it turned out, miners weren't much interested in the tents he had to sell, but they were interested in buying rugged clothes. To salvage his investment, the merchant took his tent canvas and cut it into pants that proved sturdier than most. Encouraged by brisk sales, he took advantage of a good price on denim from a French firm (the word *denim* is from the French *serge de Nîmes,* Nîmes being the town that manufactured the cloth) and dyed the fabric a dirt-concealing dark indigo. In doing so, Levi Strauss built the foundations of an empire.

Not until the 1960s, though, did blue jeans truly take off. Adopted by the baby boomers—that fickle but huge generation beloved by businesses large and small—as a statement against "materialistic" culture, jeans became the uniform of the day and a symbol of the United States itself. Throughout the 1970s, sales of jeans continued to skyrocket. By the end of the decade, some companies had begun to market "designer" and "dress" jeans at prices that pronounced them a fashion item.

Unfortunately for jeans makers, however, jeans are most appealing to the young. As the baby boom generation grew older, its members—like generations before them—put on the weight that made jeans uncomfortable and unflattering. And like most other fashion statements, jeans eventually lost their cachet. At the same time, the new generation of teenagers—the so-called "baby bust"—was much smaller. In 1990, there were 16 percent fewer 14–24-year-olds—the age group that wears the most jeans—than there were in 1980. As a result, sales of jeans began to fall, sending Levi's profits downward.

Like many companies in the early 1980s, Levi's attempted to recoup its losses by diversifying. Selling suits and hats proved to be very different from selling jeans, however, and soon the company was in even deeper financial trouble. Convinced that drastic changes were needed if the company

was to survive, Robert D. Haas (great-great-grand-nephew of Levi Strauss) turned to that other business boom of the 1980s—the leveraged buyout. Buying out all the Levi's stock then held by members of the public wasn't cheap: the company took on $1.65 billion in debt in 1984 to finance the buyback.

Unlike many other leveraged buyouts of the 1980s, however, Haas's results at Levi Strauss have more than justified the buyout's cost. By the end of 1988, the firm had paid off more of its debt than anticipated—$950 million, to be exact. This success has continued into the 1990s. In 1990, Levi's sales rose to $3.6 billion and its profits increased to $272 million. In the first quarter of 1991, the company posted an 89 percent surge in net income over the previous year.

Levi's managers credit the company's improved financial picture to the leveraged buyout. They argue that the kinds of sweeping and often expensive changes they had to make to become highly profitable again could never have been made under public ownership. Publicly traded companies are often at the mercy of Wall Street brokers' projections of their short-term results. Levi Strauss's management has only to answer to the Haas family, which now owns 90 percent of the firm's stock. (The rest of the stock is held by Levi's employees.)

Moreover, Haas argues that being free from the pressure of outside investors has enabled the firm to commit itself not only to temporarily unprofitable activities but also to six long-term goals: communications, diversity, empowerment, ethical management, new behavior, and recognition. These items, Haas maintains, cannot be summarized in a line in an income statement, but they are vital to the continued prosperity of the firm. If such "aspirations," as Haas terms them, are unusual goals for a businessman, they are certainly understandable coming from a man who was once a part of another symbol of the 1960s—the Peace Corps.

Changing its product line to meet the needs of a new generation was just one of the challenges Levi Strauss met in the 1980s. But Levi's is not unique: today nearly every company must contend with shifts in its relationships with its competitors, the government, its workforce, and its customers.

In this chapter, we explore the nature of today's business world. We begin by discussing interactions among businesses within the United States. We then consider how businesses interact with other segments of the economy. For example, in discussing the production era in Chapter 2, we noted that business, government, and labor traditionally have acted as countervailing powers in the U.S. economy. In recent years, this balance has begun to change in subtle ways. Government and business remain strong, but labor's influence has eroded. At the same time, consumers have gained more power in their interactions with business. Thus business must contend not only with government and labor, but also with consumers. Only when you understand the complexities of these interactions can you appreciate the challenges facing business in the 1990s.

## ▼ BUSINESS TRENDS IN THE 1990S

Some of the changes and challenges confronting modern businesses involve the organizations themselves. Among the most important of these changes and challenges for U.S. businesses are the development of high technology, the shift toward a service-based economy, geographical shifts, and an increase in mergers and acquisitions.

### THE IMPACT OF HIGH TECHNOLOGY

One trend that has affected virtually every aspect of the contemporary business world is the development and spread of high technology. The Bureau of Labor Standards defines a **high-technology (high-tech) firm** as one that spends twice as much on research and development and employs twice as many technical employees as the average U.S. manufacturing firm. The term *high-tech* often conjures up images of computers and robots. Firms that make these products are definitely high-tech, but so are firms in the aircraft, pharmaceuticals, biotechnology, and communications industries.

> **high-technology (high-tech) firm**
> A firm that spends twice as much on research and development and employs twice as many technical employees as the average U.S. manufacturing firm.

Several parts of the United States, including the Boston area, California's Silicon Valley, and Austin, Texas, have become centers for high-tech firms. The products offered by these high-tech ventures are affecting many other businesses. For example, high-tech robots produced by Fanuc Corporation, a Japanese firm, are used in virtually all automobile plants today.

High-tech has not delivered all that it originally promised. For example, it has not created the number of new jobs that many economists predicted. Some of the production jobs it has created have been in foreign factories. Many workers trained for industrial jobs have been unable or unwilling to make the transition to high-tech jobs. Finally, many entrepreneurs who rushed into the high-tech area did so with poorly conceived plans and were unsuccessful. While some high-tech companies like Sun Microsystems, Cypress Semiconductors, and Conner Peripherals have succeeded, many others have fallen by the wayside.[1] Still, high-tech is clearly here to stay and will play an increasingly important role in the U.S. economy.

> **M**any workers trained for industrial jobs have been unable or unwilling to make the transition to high-tech jobs.

### THE SHIFT TO SERVICES

Developments in high technology have also contributed to another change in the business world. In recent years, the manufacturing sector—long the backbone of the U.S. economy—has declined in importance as an employer of workers, while the service sector has grown steadily. The **service sector** consists of jobs that involve providing a service rather than creating a tangible product. Banks, restaurants, retailers, transportation, and entertainment businesses are examples of service firms.

> **service sector**
> The sector of the economy consisting of jobs that involve providing a service rather than creating a tangible product.

The growth of the service sector since 1960 is illustrated in Figure 3.1. In 1900, only about 28 percent of U.S. jobs were service jobs. By 1950, the figure was 40 percent, and by 1991, it was almost 78 percent. No wonder, then, that many have begun referring to the U.S. economy as a "service economy."

Some service industries have grown less than others. While employment in traditional service industries has risen as a percentage of total employment, the growth of **informational services** in recent years is most notable. Informational services include those provided by lawyers, accountants, data processors, computer operators, financial analysts, office personnel, and insurance agents —all those who work on or with information.

> **informational services**
> Service industries that provide information for a fee. Examples are law, accounting, and data processing.

The demand for informational services has grown for many reasons. The increasing need to acquire and manage vast amounts of information in a highly competitive marketplace is one major reason. Another is the increasing govern-

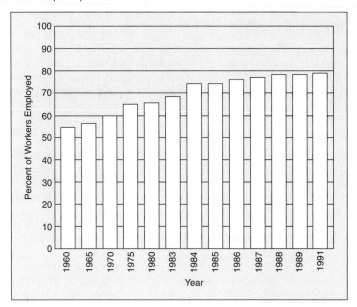

**FIGURE 3.1** Service Sector Employment in the United States

*The service sector of the U.S. economy has grown steadily over several decades. Today, it provides more than three-quarters of all jobs in the United States.*

ment regulation of business. With more government regulations, companies have had to hire more people to study the regulations and to construct and implement appropriate policies to comply with them. Filling out government forms is another major task.

### THE SHIFT SOUTH AND WEST

Another trend affecting business has been a gradual population shift to the so-called Sunbelt. The shift south and west picked up momentum at the start of the 1970s, when rapidly rising energy prices drove up the costs—and prices—of virtually everything. Consumers responded by buying less, causing many industries to lay off workers. But businesses in southern states like Florida and Texas and western states like Colorado and Arizona continued to hire. As people rushed to these areas, houses, retail stores, and restaurants could not be built fast enough to serve the growing population.

A favorable climate, a nonunionized workforce, and low taxes in the South and West have since resulted in a substantial relocation of the U.S. population. Some businesses have moved their headquarters from northern cities like New York to southern cities like Dallas and Houston. Other businesses have expanded to serve new population centers like Phoenix and the entire state of Florida. Such expansion, of course, carries with it more sophisticated communication networks, higher transportation expenses, and sometimes a loss of valuable employees who decide not to relocate.

The shift south and west continued through most of the 1980s. In the latter part of that decade, however, a glut in the world supply of petroleum hurt the economies of states like Texas and Louisiana. Major southern cities like Houston experienced dramatic economic downturns, and growth elsewhere in the Sunbelt stabilized a bit. But as the 1990s began, things started to pick up again and the shift continues. For example, J. C. Penney and Exxon both recently moved their corporate headquarters from New York to Dallas.[2]

### MERGERS, ACQUISITIONS, AND STRATEGIC ALLIANCES

Another trend in modern business has been an increased emphasis on mergers, acquisitions, and alliances. In Chapter 2, we saw that businesses today buy and sell other companies like farmers used to buy and sell produce. An **acquisition**

**acquisition**
The purchase of one company by another.

occurs when one firm buys another. A **merger** is a consolidation of two firms. Under the terms of **a strategic alliance,** individual firms retain their independence but agree to work together in one or more areas.

In acquisitions, one firm (usually the larger) buys the other (the smaller). The transaction is similar to buying a car that becomes your property after the sale. In a merger, however, the firms are usually similar in size and the arrangement is more collaborative. A strategic alliance may involve the creation of a new enterprise jointly owned by the partners or may simply involve collaboration on new technology or marketing.

After a merger or acquisition, three things can happen. One possibility is that the acquired company will continue to operate as a separate entity. Even though K Mart bought Waldenbooks several years ago, the bookstore chain has continued to operate autonomously. Another possibility is that the acquired business will be absorbed by the other and simply disappear. For example, when Chevron bought Gulf, the latter company essentially ceased to exist—its service stations were either closed or converted to Chevron stations. Finally, the two companies may form a new company. For example, when Warner and Time merged, they formed a new company called Time Warner.

***Types of Mergers.*** As Figure 3.2 shows, mergers can take several forms. A **horizontal merger** is a merger between two companies in the same industry.

**merger**
The union of two companies to form a single new business.

**strategic alliance**
A collaboration between two or more organizations.

**horizontal merger**
A merger between two companies in the same industry.

**FIGURE 3.2**   Types of Mergers
*The three most common types of mergers are horizontal, vertical, and conglomerate.*

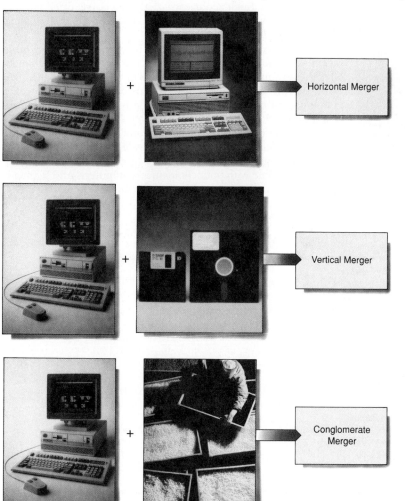

**vertical merger**
A merger in which one of the companies is a supplier to or customer of the other.

**conglomerate merger**
A merger of two firms in completely unrelated businesses.

**friendly takeover**
An acquisition in which the acquired company welcomes the merger.

**hostile takeover**
An acquisition in which the acquiring company buys enough of the other company's stock to take control, even though the other company opposes the takeover.

**greenmail**
A buyback of a company's stock at a large profit to one or more investors who are threatening a hostile takeover of the firm.

**raiders**
Investors who acquire a large block of a company's stock and initiate a hostile takeover.

**A**lliances offer the advantage of allowing each firm to remain independent while sharing the risk of a new venture with another firm.

Ford's purchase of Jaguar was a horizontal merger. A **vertical merger** takes place when one of the companies in the merger is a supplier or customer of the other. For example, Du Pont bought Conoco in part because it wanted a reliable source of petroleum for its chemical business. A **conglomerate merger** occurs when the companies are unrelated. Kodak's acquisition of Sterling Drugs falls into this category.

*Takeovers and Greenmail.*   Mergers and acquisitions can take place in several different ways. Indeed, as summarized in Table 3.1, merger and acquisition activity has its own unique vocabulary. In a **friendly takeover,** the acquired company welcomes the merger, perhaps because it needs cash or sees other benefits from joining the acquiring firm. Chevron's purchase of Gulf was friendly. But in a **hostile takeover,** the acquiring company buys enough of the other company's stock to take control, even though the other company opposes the takeover. NCR initially fought AT&T's takeover bid and dropped its fight only after AT&T raised its offer price.

Closely related to the hostile takeover is the practice of paying **greenmail.** In this situation, investors (called **raiders**) acquire large blocks of a company's stock, threaten a hostile takeover, then let the target company buy back its stock at a price that gives the raiders a substantial profit. For example, Kroger recently had to pay a special dividend to all of its stockholders to fend off a takeover bid by a small group of investors. Such actions are costly, of course; often the firm has to borrow money to finance the stock purchase. Paying greenmail to some stockholders may also anger other stockholders.

While merger and acquisition activity has leveled off a bit in recent years, the number of alliances has skyrocketed. Alliances offer the advantage of allowing each firm to remain independent while sharing the risk of a new venture with another firm. For example, Nestlé and General Mills recently formed a new venture called Cereal Partners Worldwide (CPW). CPW will produce General Mills's cereals (such as Cheerios and Golden Grahams) and market them under the well-known Nestlé name in Europe. IBM and Apple have recently agreed to work together to create a new operating system that will be compatible with both companies' computers. And Boeing is working with three different Japanese companies to build a new long-range, wide-body jet.[3]

### Table 3.1   The Language of Mergers and Acquisitions

**Friendly Takeover**
A merger or acquisition in which the acquired firm welcomes the takeover.

**Hostile Takeover**
A merger or acquisition in which the company being acquired does not want to be taken over.

**Raiders (also called *Sharks*)**
Investors who buy a large block of a business's stock and threaten a hostile takeover.

**Greenmail**
The buying back of stock from a raider for more than its market value.

**Poison Pills**
Actions taken by a business to make it less attractive to potential raiders (such as taking on additional debt or selling off valuable assets).

**Golden Parachutes**
Contracts with senior managers that guarantee them a large payment if the business is acquired and they lose their jobs.

**White Knight**
A company that takes over another company but allows the acquired firm to remain independent and to keep its existing management.

Because of the enormous complexities of large mergers, acquisitions, and alliances, and because of the potential for virtual monopolies to arise as a result of them, the government has become increasingly watchful of these activities. As you will see in the next section, this is just one of the areas in which business is affected by the government.

## ▼ BUSINESS AND GOVERNMENT

A few years ago, within the space of a few days, PepsiCo announced plans to acquire Seven-Up and the Coca-Cola Company declared that it would buy Dr. Pepper. The government intervened, however, and blocked both mergers, arguing that the mergers would place 81 percent of the soft-drink market in the hands of two companies.

At first glance, this type of governmental intervention might seem contrary to the nature of private enterprise and capitalism as we explained them in Chapter 1. Nonetheless, mergers are just one area of business that the U.S. government regulates and controls.

### *GOVERNMENT REGULATION OF BUSINESS*

**Regulation** is the establishment of governmental rules that restrict business activity. Government regulates business for a variety of reasons, the two most important of which are to protect competition and to meet the nation's social goals.

**regulation**
The establishment of governmental rules that restrict business activity.

*Protecting Competition.* One of the reasons that government regulates business is to ensure competition. Regulation in this area protects both consumers and other businesses. As we saw in Chapter 1, competition is crucial to a market economy. If competition did not exist, monopolists would be able to charge high prices for low-quality goods. Laws prohibiting monopolies thus preserve competition and allow companies to offer goods that meet consumers' expectations at a reasonable price.

Similarly, without government restrictions, a large business with vast resources could cut its prices so low and advertise so much that smaller firms lacking equal resources would be forced to shut down. It was exactly this threat that prompted the Department of Justice (DOJ) to block the acquisition plans of PepsiCo and Coca-Cola. The DOJ feared that small companies like Royal Crown Cola (4.5 percent market share) and Cadbury Schwepps (3.7 percent market share) would go bankrupt if the larger companies were allowed to proceed. The DOJ's antitrust division and the Federal Trade Commission (FTC) are also empowered to enforce the laws relating to illegal competitive practices and deceptive advertising.

In some cases, monopoly may be desirable from society's point of view. In these instances, government regulation prevents companies from price gouging. For example, telephone, utility, and cable television rates are controlled by state agencies, city councils, or other governing agencies. Government regulation is also common in industries in which only limited competition exists. Fears that oligopolies such as the trucking, airline, and railroad industries will collude on prices have led the federal government to set rates in these industries at various times. Fears of the power of television and radio stations have been used to justify government rules and pressure on these organizations to run public service ads and to give equal time to opposing views.

*Meeting Social Goals.* Another reason that the government regulates business is to help meet social goals. Social goals promote the general well-being of society. In the United States, as in any market economy, consumers must have money to purchase goods and services. But our sense of fairness dictates that the ill should be treated, regardless of their ability to pay. Medicare (a federal insurance program for the elderly established during President Lyndon Johnson's administration) has not only made medical care available to many elderly citizens, but has also had a major impact on medical fees. For example, regulations now limit how much hospitals and doctors can charge Medicare patients for certain services. These limits have effectively created fixed rates.

Another social goal—a safe workplace—has also generated extensive government regulation of businesses. OSHA (the Occupational Safety and Health Administration) is the primary government agency charged with ensuring worker safety. In addition, state-mandated worker compensation programs require businesses to contribute to a fund that pays workers who have been injured on the job.

Through the EPA (the Environmental Protection Agency), the federal government has become the chief regulator of industrial pollution. But many states, counties, and cities have imposed additional restrictions on business activities that generate pollution. For example, New York and Florida forbid the sale of detergents that contain phosphates, which have been shown to affect water purity. In an effort to promote recycling, some states require bottle deposits. And California has placed strict limits on the level of emissions that cars sold and operated in that state may give off. OSHA and the EPA can affect a firm's profits by levying fines or even shutting down plants that violate government regulations.

Other federal, state, and local laws regulate countless aspects of business in order to "protect" the public. Federal laws regulate banks and stock sales. States license physicians, insurance agents, and barbers. Local ordinances establish where garbage can be dumped and who can serve liquor. Indeed, millions of laws, licensing rules, and legal actions regulate every aspect of business in the United States today, a pattern some small businesses find threatening, as the Small Business Report "David and Goliath: Small Business versus Federal Regulation" explains.

### THE MOVE TOWARD DEREGULATION

Although government regulation has benefited the United States in some ways, it is not without drawbacks. Businesspeople complain—with some justification—that government regulations require too much paperwork. For example, to comply with just one OSHA regulation, Goodyear once generated 345,000 pages of computer reports weighing 3,200 pounds. It costs that company $35.5 million each year to comply with the regulations of six government agencies, and it takes 36 employee-years (the equivalent of one employee working full-time for 36 years) to fill out each year's required reports. In some cases, rate regulation has resulted in prices higher than those the market would have set without regulation. For these and other reasons, the federal government began deregulating certain industries in the 1970s, with mixed results. **Deregulation** is the elimination of governmental rules that restrict business activity.

> **T**o comply with just one OSHA regulation, Goodyear once generated 345,000 pages of computer reports weighing 3,200 pounds.

**deregulation**
The elimination of governmental rules that restrict business activity.

***The Airline Industry.*** For many years, the Civil Aeronautics Board set fares and assigned routes in the airline industry. Fares were so high that many airlines could cover the costs of a flight by selling only 15 seats on that flight! Because everything was regulated, the airlines had little incentive to control operating costs.

Since deregulation, however, the airlines have had to compete for customers by lowering their fares and costs. In recent years, many airlines that could not compete effectively have gone bankrupt, sold their assets to other airlines, or

*Small Business Report*

## DAVID AND GOLIATH: SMALL BUSINESS VERSUS FEDERAL REGULATION

The statistics are frightening. Owners of small businesses spend as much as one-third of their time filling out forms to comply with government reporting requirements. These and other federal rules cost each of the United States's small businesses about $2,000 every year. Horror stories are common:

► A Virginia store owner ran afoul of Labor Department overtime rules when he let two of his employees have time off during the week in return for working for free on Saturdays and during lunch breaks. Getting the charge dismissed cost the Virginian $3,000.
► A Michigan gravel pit owner had to buy a first-aid stretcher for his facility—even though it's a one-man operation.
► A Wisconsin meatpacker with only eight employees had to spend $6,000 to sandblast a wall when a federal meat inspector was able to pry off a piece of paint—even though the wall was nowhere near the meatpacking area.

Worse yet, federal regulation of small businesses seems likely to increase. Under COBRA, the Consolidated Omnibus Budget Reconciliation Act, employers must continue benefits for ex-employees and their families at the employees' expense for 18 months. Adding to the paperwork burden, firms must give written notice of the benefits available to employees and to each of their family members.

Under amendments to the Resource Conservation Recovery Act, firms producing as little as 220 pounds of hazardous waste per month must obey complex disposal regulations and may be liable for damages if a disposal plan that is legal today is outlawed tomorrow.

Feeling buried under so much paperwork and regulation, small business has begun to fight back. Pressure on Congress and the White House has won some regulatory exemptions. For example, firms with fewer than 250 employees no longer have to have a written affirmative action plan. The Occupational Safety and Health Administration now performs routine safety checks only if a small firm has a higher-than-normal injury rate. Under the Equal Access to Justice Act, small businesses that can show arbitrariness on the part of regulators will be entitled to government payment of legal fees to defend themselves.

Then there are the small, private victories of small businessmen like George Poppas. Poppas owns a modest taxi operation. When the Federal Trade Commission threatened to send U.S. marshals to close down his business because he had failed to send in one form, Poppas let the FTC know that he would welcome the marshals. In fact, he promised to have a local television crew on hand to film their arrival. The FTC promptly lost interest in sending marshals and even in receiving Poppas's form.

reduced their operations substantially. For example, Continental declared bankruptcy twice, and Eastern and PanAm have shut down altogether.[4]

Ironically, the competition that has resulted since deregulation has not brought about any structural change in the airline industry. Some major firms did not survive the competition or grow as quickly as other airlines. But the overall structure of the industry—with international carriers, regional carriers, and local carriers—has not changed. What has changed is the cost of flying. It is now cheaper to fly than it was before deregulation. In addition, only those companies whose management was able to operate successfully in the new, deregulated environment have survived. For example, American, Delta, and United Airlines have thrived under deregulation.

***The Banking Industry.*** Deregulation has also affected the banking industry. For years, savings and loan companies and banks were regulated by several different agencies. Since deregulation, some banks, like Nations Bank in North Carolina, have expanded rapidly and prospered. Many banks have also increased the range of services they offer. For example, some now offer a wide array of savings plans, discount brokerage services, and so forth.

*Deregulation has forced the airline industry to cut costs and improve service to remain competitive. The result has been a wave of airline bankruptcies in the past five years. Northwest Airlines, for example, bought the planes of the now defunct Republic Airlines.*

Deregulation of the banking industry has created some serious problems, however. To compete, some banks took greater risks in their loan making—a policy change that contributed to the large number of bank failures in recent years. Decreased regulation has contributed to hard times in the savings and loan (S&L) industry, too. A number of Sunbelt S&Ls, plagued by mismanagement of funds, bad debts, and outright fraud, have collapsed. Indeed, the federal government has had to pledge billions of dollars to avert a financial crisis in the industry. Several S&Ls have been taken over by other banks and many others have closed.

### HOW BUSINESS INFLUENCES GOVERNMENT

As we have noted, not everyone agrees on the benefits of government regulation —or deregulation. Naturally, businesses want laws regarding regulation and taxation to do them the least harm and the most good. Toward this end, businesses attempt to influence the government through lobbyists, trade associations, advertising, and political action committees.

A **lobbyist** is a person hired by a company or an industry to represent its interests with government officials. Some business lobbyists have training in a particular industry, public relations experience, or a legal background. A few have served as legislators or government regulators. But all are required to register with the government as paid representatives of interest groups or particular businesses.

Employees and owners of small businesses that cannot afford lobbyists often join **trade associations,** which assist and promote the interests of their members. A trade association may act as an industry lobby to influence legislation. It may also conduct training programs relevant to its particular industry and arrange trade shows at which members display their products or services to potential customers. Most trade associations publish newsletters featuring articles on new products, new companies, changes in ownership, and modifications in laws affecting the industry.

Businesses can also influence legislation indirectly by influencing voters. For example, a company or an industry can launch an advertising campaign

**lobbyist**
A person hired by a company or industry to represent its interests with government officials.

**trade association**
An organization dedicated to assisting and promoting the interests of its members.

designed to get people to write their representatives demanding passage—or rejection—of a particular bill. (Figure 3.3 shows an ad used by Mobil to make a point about governmental actions.)

Finally, businesses may attempt to influence legislation by contributing to **political action committees (PACs),** which are special political fund-raising groups. The Federal Election Campaign Law limits corporate political contributions to individual candidates. But PACs can accept voluntary contributions from individual employees and distribute them to specific candidates. The enormous sums of money—millions of dollars each year—raised by PACs give them great power and influence in government.

Critics have argued that the growth of lobbying and the increased number of PACs in recent years have distorted the legislative process. They charge that legislators have become most sensitive to the best-funded arguments. For

**political action committee (PAC)**
A political fund-raising group that accepts contributions and distributes them to candidates for political office.

# The wrong prescription

In an apparent response to the recent string of oils spills, the House of Representatives has expanded, by a wide margin, the existing moratoriums on the leasing of offshore tracts for oil and gas exploration. In addition, it voted for the first time to prohibit such leasing off the coast of Alaska. The measure makes as much sense as slapping a cast on the leg of a man with a broken arm.

The measure, attached to a bill for the fiscal 1990 funding of the Interior Department and other agencies, would prohibit, at least until October of 1990, all leasing and pre-leasing activities off California and a large area of the Atlantic stretching from Massachusetts to Maryland, including the Georges Bank, and including also the eastern Gulf of Mexico. Another affected area is Bristol Bay in Alaska, where some companies already have paid almost $100 million for leases, and where the government may have to buy them back.

Why is the House action the wrong prescription? For one thing, because if affects the wrong part of the oil business. The recent spills occurred as oil was being transported by large tanker. The industry has already recommended a detailed program to increase tanker safety, including the creation of a new spill-response organization, deeper involvement of the Coast Guard, improved maneuvering devices on vessels, and an ongoing research effort on how to clean up spills more effectively. To equate oil exploration and production with oil transportation is the archetypical—and erroneous—admixture of apples and oranges.

While a major oil spill at an exploration or production site offshore remains a possibility, that possibility is quite remote. The Minerals Management Service of the Interior Department recently reported that over the last 17 years, there has not been an oil spill resulting from a blowout at an exploratory well. Over the same period of time, only 840 barrels of oil were spilled during blowouts at production wells. Production in U.S. waters

during those years totaled five billion barrels.

Furthermore, the House action is wrong because it would be counterproductive. Most of the oil from wells in U.S. waters comes ashore by pipeline, not by tanker. At a time of dwindling U.S. production, any damper on the effort to find more domestic oil means an increase in imports to meet demand. Imported oil—currently 45 percent of consumption—does arrive by tanker, so more imports mean more tanker traffic in and around American ports.

There are also sound budgetary arguments against the banning of offshore exploration. The federal Treasury receives some $2.3 billion a year in royalties from offshore production. Cut the exploration rate and the production rate will eventually follow, and so will royalty income.

Other financial considerations are involved. We've already mentioned the $100 million or so that may have to be refunded because of the Bristol Bay moratorium. And another $184 million may have to be refunded for leases off the Florida coast. It hardly makes sense for Congress to frantically scramble for more revenues as it writes a tax bill with one hand, while the other hand busily adds to the budget deficit. Besides, as we have already noted, a slowdown in the domestic search for petroleum means an increase in imports—which translates into additional pressure on America's balance of payments.

In the decade of the 1970s, with its recurrent oil crises, the industry was often made the scapegoat during a frenzied search for easy answers and identifiable villains. The '90s is no time to replay past errors. Oil spills are tragic, but to compound the tragedy through hasty, ill-considered legislation benefits neither the nation nor its people.

We respectfully urge that common sense prevail when the Senate considers the House measure. Immobilizing a healthy leg won't heal a broken arm.

**Mobil**

© 1989 Mobil Corporation

This ad appeared in *The New York Times* on Thursday, August 3, 1989.

**FIGURE 3.3**   Advertising for Influence
*Mobil attempts to influence legislators by advertising its position in the media. For example, this recent ad in* The New York Times *criticizes governmental action regarding oil spills.*

*Business Ethics*

## WHERE THERE'S SMOKE, THERE'S MONEY

"[P]olitical] power is an illusion . . . beautiful blue smoke rolling over the surface of highly polished mirrors," wrote Jimmy Breslin in *How the Good Guys Finally Won*. Thus it is perhaps fitting that until recently few in Washington have wielded more power over the Congress than the tobacco industry.

The industry's long-time influence depended on two factors: money and organization. Tobacco is a $35-billion-a-year industry in the United States, accounting for $4 billion in U.S. exports. Few members of Congress are prepared to write off the income the industry generates and the jobs it provides. Moreover, the tobacco industry is accustomed to "sharing" its profits with Congress. Long before political action committees became the fashion, the Tobacco Institute was funding political campaigns. In the 1988 election year alone, tobacco companies supplied $1 million just to congressional candidates.

But money and organization have not been able to protect the tobacco industry from increased governmental restrictions in recent years. As report after report from the U.S. Surgeon General has linked cigarette smoking and tobacco chewing to various forms of cancer and heart disease, the public has become more and more opposed to tobacco products. And reports that "second-hand smoke" (being in the presence of someone smoking) may also be a health threat have led to increased cries for limits on public smoking.

Today, antismoking forces are as well organized as the tobacco industry (if less affluent) and are successfully challenging the use of tobacco in many settings. Many of the restrictions on tobacco use thus far have been at the local level, but a few years ago Congress passed laws prohibiting smok-

*The tobacco fields of Tennessee are just one small part of an industry that generates more than $35 billion a year.*

ing on all domestic flights. In addition, many on the antismoking side are now calling for an end to cigarette vending machines. They point out that such machines make it impossible to prevent minors from buying cigarettes and that, of the 1 million new U.S. smokers each year, 80 percent are teenagers and 100,000 are aged 12 or under. (Indeed, the current U.S. smoker is most likely to be young, poor, and relatively uneducated.)

The tobacco industry is not giving up, though, and still wields considerable power in Washington. When the Environmental Protection Agency assembled a panel in 1990 to assess EPA studies on the effects of second-hand smoke, six of the eight panel members had ties to tobacco industry research groups. Only after word of the makeup of the panel was leaked to the press was one scientist who had previously expressed opposition to smoking named to the panel (over the objections of the tobacco industry, of course). It would appear that where there's smoke . . . there's still money.

example, they note that while public opinion polls show that most U.S. residents favor some form of gun control, the National Rifle Association's lobbying has kept such laws off the federal books. Similarly, farmers and ranchers have been given government subsidies not to grow or produce certain foodstuffs. And the same government that warns of tobacco's dangers allows the tobacco industry to make large contributions to political campaign funds, as the Business Ethics box "Where There's Smoke, There's Money" discusses.

For many lobbying efforts, however, there are opposing efforts. The American Cancer Society and the American Tobacco Institute have very different points of view on cigarette smoking and cigarette advertising, for example. So, in looking at business and its influence on government, it is important to keep in mind that competing interests can have vastly different effects on political processes. (We will discuss the legal and regulatory environment of business in more detail in Chapter 24.)

## ▼ BUSINESS AND LABOR

Because workers are an important resource to every company, relations with the labor force are another important dimension of the contemporary business world. As we noted earlier in this chapter, however, the influence of organized labor has been declining in recent years. This trend stems from several factors, including the changing demographics of the labor force and declining membership in many unions. At the same time, though, some organizations are giving their employees more power through increased participation.

### *THE CHANGING DEMOGRAPHICS OF THE U.S. LABOR FORCE*

The statistical makeup—the *demographics*—of the U.S. labor force has changed gradually over the past several years. As Figure 3.4 shows, these changes have been in terms of age, the role of women, and the impact of immigrants.

*The Graying Workforce.* The age of the average U.S. worker has gradually increased over the past few decades. As you might expect, this increase is the result of more older workers and fewer younger workers. Americans are living longer than ever before, and some older individuals are taking advantage of changes in retirement laws and continuing to work beyond age 65. More important, however, is the so-called baby bust generation, those individuals born after the baby boom of the immediate post–World War II period. It was the baby boomers who embraced the jeans offered by Levi Strauss in the 1960s. The baby bust generation is relatively small, not only in comparison to the giant baby boom generation, but also in comparison to the individuals now in their 50s and 60s.

This trend has affected business in two ways. First, older workers tend to put greater demands on a company's health insurance, life insurance, and retirement benefit programs. Second, younger workers taking the places of retirees tend to want different things from employers—things like more opportunities for self-expression or more leisure time.

On another front, many businesses are now hiring retirees as part-time employees. Many retirees have a great deal of experience, are dependable, and require fewer benefits than do full-time employees.

*Women in the Workforce.* Another employment trend in the United States is the growing number of women in the workforce. In 1950, only 34 percent of the female population worked outside the home. By 1990, the figure exceeded 57 percent.[5]

There are many reasons for the increase in the number of women who work outside the home. Faced with rapid increases in the prices of goods and services during the 1970s, many couples found that they needed two incomes to maintain their standard of living. In addition, the women's movement and the greater number of women graduating from college have resulted in more career opportunities for women.

The large percentage of women in all types of careers has had and will continue to have a major impact on U.S. business. Millions of young children have mothers who work outside the home. Government leaders have described

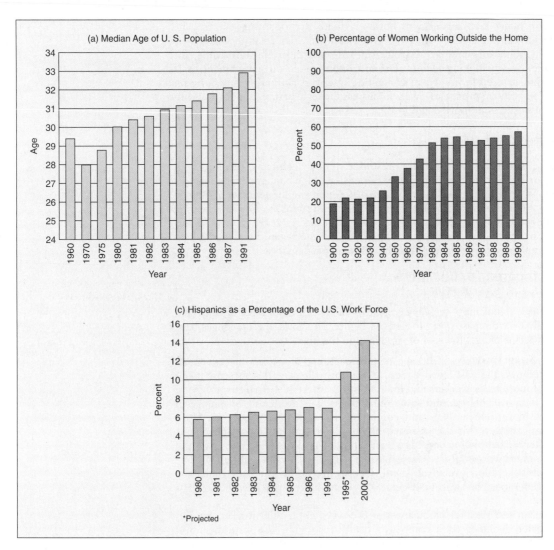

**FIGURE 3.4**   Demographics of the U.S. Labor Force

*The demographics of the U.S. workforce are changing. The median age of the average U.S. worker is increasing, and women and Hispanic-Americans are a growing percentage of the workforce.*

the problem of child care as one of today's most important business challenges. While everyone agrees that there is a problem, there is little agreement over how to solve it. Some people believe that the government should own and operate child-care centers. Others argue that companies should sponsor child-care centers for their employees. Indeed, many major companies have started offering such services in recent years.

> Immigrants have not merely melted into U.S. society; they have also changed it.

**Immigrants in the Workforce.** Immigrants have long been said to make the United States a "melting pot." But immigrants have not merely melted into U.S. society; they have also changed it. For example, workers from some countries have religious holidays different from those celebrated in the United States. Some want more participation in decision making than is customary in the

*Partially as a result of changes in retirement laws, older workers are staying in the workforce longer. Recent years have also seen an increase in the number of older Americans serving as volunteers for worthy causes after retirement. Volunteers are essential to many organizations, including this school in Donna, Texas, where Hispanic-American children receive special tutoring to learn reading skills.*

United States; others want less. Some workers from hot climates are used to long lunch breaks, while others are accustomed to work weeks much longer than 40 hours. As a result of these various influences, some businesses have altered their policies regarding religious holidays, employer-employee relationships, and work-ethic expectations.

Tougher immigration laws have also increased labor costs for many companies in border towns. Accustomed to using the cheap labor of illegal aliens for temporary jobs like construction and agriculture, these firms now face stiff fines for such hiring practices. In addition, many companies have had to process additional paperwork (at additional costs) in order to document the citizenship of their workers.

## THE DECLINING UNIONIZATION OF THE LABOR FORCE

Another important element affecting business's dealings with labor is the steady decline in union membership over the past several years. Several factors account for this trend. For one thing, the number of jobs in manufacturing, long a union stronghold, has declined. For another, younger workers entering the labor force in recent years have not been as interested in joining unions as their predecessors were. Furthermore, unions have been slow to enroll women and minorities.

Business, of course, reaps certain benefits from this trend. Labor costs don't increase as rapidly, strikes are not as likely, and there are fewer union-demanded "work rules" to worry about. (We will cover these and many related issues in more depth in Chapter 11.)

## WORKER PARTICIPATION

Yet another trend in business-labor relations is the increase in worker participation. Traditionally, at least in the United States, managers made decisions and decided how things were going to be done. Workers carried out management's orders and had little voice in how they performed their jobs. In recent years, however, U.S. firms have learned that most successful Japanese firms give their

*You might think this photo was snapped by an American on a visit to the Far East, but it was really taken in Los Angeles' Koreatown. Experts have projected that ethnic minorities will account for half of California's population by the year 2000. In Los Angeles, where they already do, shopping malls like Seoul (Na Sung) Plaza have sprung up to cater to the needs of various ethnic groups.*

workers considerable responsibility. Impressed by the success of these firms, U.S. businesses have tried to become more participative as well. At Xerox, Federal Express, Westinghouse, and Apple (to name just a few), many managerial functions are being turned over to teams of workers. And those workers are not only accepting the responsibility for getting their own work done but are also doing a far better job than before.[6] (We will cover this trend in more detail in Chapter 8.)

## ▼ BUSINESS AND CONSUMERS

In addition to adjusting to the demands of government and labor, businesses have also had to adjust to a steady increase in the power of the consumer. Gone are the days of *caveat emptor,* "let the buyer beware." A business following that dictum today is apt to face boycotts, lawsuits, and government intervention. Consumer tastes and preferences are also more complex than in the past. There are several reasons for this trend, including demographic changes and the rise of the consumer rights movement.[7]

### *CONSUMER RIGHTS*

**consumer movement**
Activism on the part of consumers seeking better value from businesses.

Activism on the part of consumers seeking better value from businesses—the **consumer movement**—has altered the conduct of many businesses. Although the consumer movement traces its roots back to the turn of the century, Ralph Nader's much-publicized attack on the unsafe cars being produced by General Motors in the 1960s (*Unsafe at Any Speed,* 1965) really gave consumerism its momentum.

**consumer rights**
The legally protected rights of consumers to purchase the products they desire, to safety from the products they purchase, to be informed about what they are buying, and to be heard in the event of problems.

Over the last decade, legislation has broadened **consumer rights** considerably. In particular, laws now guarantee consumers the right to purchase the products they desire, the right to safety from the products they purchase, the right to be informed about what they are buying, and the right to be heard in the event of problems. As a result, most products today come with extensive instructions regarding their use and, in the case of food products, a detailed list of their ingredients. Most products also have a guarantee or warranty, and many list telephone numbers or addresses to contact in the event of problems. We will consider consumer rights and related issues more fully in Chapter 16.

### THE CHANGING DEMOGRAPHICS OF U.S. CONSUMERS

The same pattern of demographic changes that are affecting the U.S. labor force also reflect changes in consumer demands.

*A Graying Population.* Just as the average age of U.S. workers is increasing, so is the average age of the entire U.S. population. Because of this trend, companies are finding new market opportunities and challenges. Older adults are demanding recreational facilities, health care, housing, leisure-time products, and personal-care items designed specifically for them.

*Working Women.* Working women are also providing many new opportunities for business. For example, in recent years, there has been increased demand for convenience foods that require little preparation, such as microwaveable dinners and frozen pizzas. Products like telephone answering machines and home computers have increased in popularity, partly because of the increase in two-career families. Restaurants and home-cleaning services have benefited too. In addition, there has been more demand for professional "gear" for working women: business attire, briefcases, and the like. The fact that women are not staying at home to care for children has even created a whole new industry—the day-care industry.

*Increased Cultural Diversity.* The increased buying power of various ethnic and cultural groups has led businesses to respond with products requested or demanded by these consumers. Radio stations and even some television stations offer programming in several languages, along with special programs oriented to specific ethnic groups. Large grocery stores routinely offer Mexican and Chinese food products. Fiesta Markets in Houston has prospered by catering to Hispanic-American consumers. And the cosmetic industry now manufactures products designed for people with a wide range of skin tones.

> The increased buying power of various ethnic and cultural groups has led businesses to respond with products requested or demanded by these consumers.

### ▼ BUSINESS CHALLENGES OF THE 1990S

Given the nature and complexities of today's business environment, it is not surprising that U.S. business faces a number of challenges in the 1990s. As Figure 3.5 shows, the four most important challenges relate to productivity, international trade, pollution, and technology.

### IN SEARCH OF HIGHER PRODUCTIVITY

As we saw in Chapter 1, productivity is a measure of an economy's success. It is also a measure of a business's success, because it reflects the efficiency with

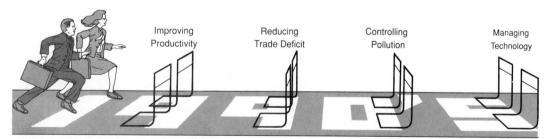

Improving Productivity    Reducing Trade Deficit    Controlling Pollution    Managing Technology

**FIGURE 3.5**    The Four Basic Challenges of the 1990s
*U.S. business must confront four basic challenges in the 1990s: improving productivity, reducing the trade deficit, controlling pollution, and managing technology.*

*Carolyn Blakeslee, who singlehandedly produces every issue of* ArtCalendar *(a monthly publication for visual artists that lists grants, juried shows accepting applications, and other forums to which artists can submit their work), is just one of many working mothers in the United States today.*

which a company uses resources. A company that uses fewer resources (whether materials, management, or labor) to make the same number of products as another firm is more efficient. While U.S. workers are the most productive in the world, for the last several years the growth of productivity in the United States has been slower than that in many other nations such as Japan and Germany. This has prompted U.S. managers to look actively for ways to improve productivity. The complex nature of the productivity problem and some proposed solutions are discussed in Chapter 26.

### THE INTERNATIONAL TRADE DEFICIT

**trade deficit**
The situation in which a country imports more than it exports; sometimes called a *negative trade balance.*

**trade surplus**
The situation in which a country exports more than it imports.

Another significant challenge facing managers in the 1990s is the U.S. **trade deficit.** A trade deficit occurs when a nation is importing more products than it is exporting. For decades, the United States had a **trade surplus**—that is, it exported more than it imported. But the surplus turned to a deficit in the 1980s. The mid-1991 surplus was the first surplus in the United States in over 15 years, and it didn't last very long.

Why have so many foreign companies been more successful in the international market of late than their U.S. competitors? Some economists blame conflict among business, the government, and labor in the United States. Certainly, cooperation among these elements has helped Japan gain an advantage in the contemporary business world. If the United States is to compete more effectively in the international business arena, these economists argue, it must operate with more coordination and less antagonism. Perhaps the system that served us well domestically for so long must change to meet the challenges of today's global environment.

Some reasons for U.S. trade imbalances relate to the characteristics of other countries. For example, some countries pay their employees lower wages. This is one of the reasons that Levi Strauss recently made the decision to transfer some of its operations overseas. Lower safety standards and fewer pollution controls in many foreign countries translate into lower costs of producing goods. Fewer "paperwork" requirements mean that foreign companies do not have to employ as many accountants and lawyers—a substantial cost savings that is passed on to consumers in the form of lower prices. In addition, many countries have complex rules that restrict the import of U.S.-made goods. Some impose tariffs (taxes) on imports. Others have complicated inspection procedures that cost U.S. companies much time and money.

Finally, if unemployment threatens a particular industry, some foreign governments will subsidize that industry through grants, low-interest loans, or government purchases at inflated prices. Subsidies enable foreign companies to sell their products in the United States at prices lower than their actual production costs.

Because so many factors are involved in the international trade problem, any solution will have to be equally complex. We discuss the international business world throughout this book and devote a special chapter to the topic later on (Chapter 25).

## THE CONTINUING CHALLENGE OF POLLUTION

By the end of the twentieth century, there will be no unused landfills in the United States. How will we dispose of solid waste then? Will we burn it? Will we recycle it? How will we meet the energy needs of the future? Will we use conventional power plants that damage the air and land? Or will we turn to nuclear-powered plants that raise the issue of safe nuclear waste disposal?

Unfortunately, this problem is not unique to the United States. Indeed, many areas of Eastern Europe are among the most polluted in the world. As the Executive Report "Turning Garbage into Gold" describes, pollution cleanup may be a new source of business profits. We explore environmental issues in more detail in the next chapter.

## TECHNOLOGY: FRIEND OR FOE?

We have already introduced some of the opportunities and issues posed by technological innovation and advancement. Dealing with such technology and its role in modern society will continue to be a major business challenge of the 1990s. Is high technology friend or foe to U.S. workers and businesses? Critics fear the replacement of traditional middle-class jobs with automated machinery, predicting a depersonalized society in which people become nothing but numbers to a computer that receives telephone calls, handles banking transactions, maintains the temperatures in our homes, and even answers our doorbells. This fear of technology is not new. Charlie Chaplin movies in the 1920s satirized the industrial production line and George Orwell's *1984* (first published in 1949) painted a grim vision of a future government using technology to control society.

> Is high technology friend or foe to U.S. workers and businesses?

## DAVID L. SOKOL: TURNING GARBAGE INTO GOLD

It may be today's ideal industry. With so many disposable goods—disposable diapers, disposable lighters, and disposable razors, to name just a few—the United States is confronted with an ever-increasing garbage pile and an ever-decreasing number of places to dump that garbage. At the same time, everyone is worried about finding energy substitutes for expensive foreign oil. What could be more perfect than a company that burns garbage at high temperatures that generate steam, which, in turn, can be used to produce electricity? In the opinion of Ogden Projects' youthful president and CEO, David L. Sokol, nothing.

Sokol certainly seems justified in his optimism. Ogden Projects' first facility didn't open until 1986, yet by 1989, it had become the industry leader, beating out older firms such as Wheelabrator and Westinghouse. Of the 42 projects on which Sokol bid between 1984 and 1989, Ogden Projects won 22 contracts.

Much of the credit for Ogden Projects' success goes to Sokol's choice of market. Because Ogden Projects has confined itself to the municipal market, working with cities to build the necessary plants, it has faced less public opposition than its rivals.

Sokol's choice of technology has also helped Ogden's sales and profits. Because all of Ogden's facilities are exactly the same, the company has been able to construct them on time and at a relatively low cost. Because Ogden Projects has exclusive rights to the Martin incineration technology—which many say is the best available—Ogden has earned an attractive reputation for reliability.

Finally, under Sokol, Ogden's pricing policy has appealed to the cities with which it seeks to do business. Typically, Ogden Projects builds its plants for cost. It earns its money on 20- to 25-year guaranteed contracts with municipalities. Thus cities get low initial costs, while Ogden gets solid future profits that include a percentage of the energy revenues.

*Occasionally, a hardworking entrepreneur finds himself riding the crest of a wave. The "Green Movement" of the 1990s, with its emphasis on environmentally sound trash disposal and recycling, has opened up a world of opportunity for David Sokol and Ogden Projects.*

Ogden Projects' parent company, Ogden Corporation, couldn't be more delighted. Having pared its once far-flung holdings to focus on cleanup (everything from building maintenance to toxic waste disposal), Ogden Corporation is now reaping the benefits. And chief among these benefits is Sokol's Ogden Projects. In 1988, waste-to-energy provided Ogden Corporation with over $18 million, a third of the company's entire income.

And it seems that the best is yet to come. The firm's earnings have continued to increase substantially each year. Seven new plants were built in 1990 and 1991, and seven more are planned for 1995. With a recent ruling by the Environmental Protection Agency that incinerator projects must recycle 25 percent of their output by 1994, Ogden appears to have found a treasure trove in trash.

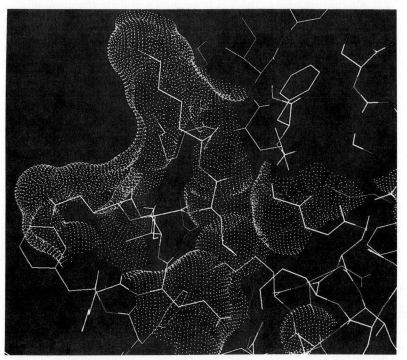

*This is a small portion of the crystal structure of Actimmune gamma interferon, a virus-fighting agent produced by Genentech and pending approval by the U.S. Food and Drug Administration. Rapidly advancing genetic technology promises a safer world and a healthier population, but is not without its ethical problems. Should animals be used for experimental purposes? How extensively should a new drug or technology be tested before it is approved for use?*

Defenders of technology point to its many benefits. New genetically engineered seeds that will increase agricultural production for a hungry world are now coming on the market. New vaccines that may help win the battle against cancer are in development. And new employment opportunities in safer work environments than the blistering hot and dangerous steel mills of the past are a reality for many workers today.

Some people argue that technology will provide solutions to the pollution problem and ways to increase productivity. Others raise complex questions about whether we will be able to control the technology we create. As future business and government leaders, you will be confronted with these and many other challenges in the decades ahead.

## SUMMARY OF LEARNING OBJECTIVES

**1** **Describe four major trends that affect U.S. business today.**   Business, the government, labor, and consumers are four countervailing powers that influence and are influenced by one another. Over the last two decades, the influence of labor has declined, while that of consumers has been on the rise. The U.S. business world has also experienced a shift from manufacturing to services, a geographic shift toward the Sunbelt, the advent of high technology, and increased merger activity.

**2** **Explain why the U.S. government sometimes regulates businesses and how business seeks to influence the government.**   Government regulates business in order to promote competition and to help achieve social goals. Recent years have seen a trend toward deregulation, but businesses continue to use lobbying, trade associations, advertising, and political action committees (PACs) to influence government.

**3** **Discuss changes in the U.S. labor pool and their effects on business.** Changing demographics in the labor force have influenced how business managers deal with labor. The most notable of these changes are an aging population, more working women, and increased ethnic and cultural diversity. In addition, the decline of labor unions has meant lower labor costs, fewer strikes, and fewer union-demanded "work rules." More organizations are giving their workers increased responsibility and allowing them greater participation.

**4** **Describe changes in demographics and consumer rights and their impact on U.S. business.** The same pattern of demographic changes that has affected management-labor relations (see number 3 above) has also influenced business-customer relations, particularly in terms of the goods and services that customers are demanding. Consumer rights activism has forced businesses to become more sensitive to consumer desires and complaints.

**5** **Identify and discuss four major challenges for U.S. business in the 1990s.** Businesses face a variety of challenges in the 1990s. Foremost among these are the need to increase productivity, the need to regain a competitive edge in international trade and reduce the U.S. trade deficit, the need to control pollution, and the need to harness technology.

---

*O*PENING CASE WRAP-UP

## BUTTONING UP PROFITS

**W**hile Haas's commitment to creating a positive corporate culture has been a major factor in the success of Levi Strauss since 1985, of at least equal importance has been a host of internal changes to meet external challenges.

*New Products.* Much of Levi's increased sales come from several "new" products. The first of these new products is actually an old one—the revival of the company's trademark button-fly jeans, now hawked as "501 jeans." A switch to more stonewashed, acid-washed, and other "treated" denim has also helped to revitalize the firm's line of jeans.

More radical and possibly even more important is the introduction of the Dockers line. These casual nondenim pants, cut wide at the top and tapered toward the ankle, meet two baby boomer needs: comfortable fit and a more polished appearance than jeans. How successful is the Dockers' line? In just four years, it has become a $500-million-a-year line. Industry analysts describe Dockers as the fastest-growing product line in the history of the apparel industry. Little wonder that it has been expanded beyond Dockers pants for men to include coordinated tops and women's and children's wear.

*New Promotion.* Free of the short-term constraints of public ownership, the management of Levi Strauss has pumped millions of dollars into advertising. In 1991, the firm spent $15 million for the 1991 edition of its "Button Your Fly" campaign, directed by popular filmmaker Spike Lee, for its 501 jeans.

*New Distribution.* Levi's jeans have long been popular in Western Europe. By expanding sales and manufacturing operations into Eastern Europe and Asia, Levi's has been able to take advantage of relatively low production costs in these nations. Today over half of Levi's profits come from its overseas operations.

*New Organization.* Streamlining the firm's organization to eliminate layers of management has translated into substantial cost savings—and increased the speed with which other changes can be made. After maintaining a paternalistic attitude toward job security for employees for many years, Haas and other upper-level managers recently decided to shut 26 Levi's manufacturing plants in the United States. (Union officials admit that the severance plan for those let go was generous, however.)

*New Technology.* Thanks to the firm's LeviLink computer system, vendors can place orders and make payments electronically. The system also allows Levi's to order supplies and produce goods on a just-in-time basis to meet customers' needs (thus saving both Levi's and its suppliers the costs of high inventories). A sophisticated computer-aided design system takes initial designs, turns them into pattern pieces for a range of sizes, and designs a layout of the pieces to get the most out of the fabric.

What will the future hold? Will baby boomers abandon Dockers, as they have so many other products? Perhaps. But if so, count on Levi Strauss to find a way to get business "booming" again.

## CASE QUESTIONS

1. Why do you think Levi Strauss's attempt to sell other forms of clothing in the 1980s failed?
2. What other savings might Levi Strauss realize by utilizing more high-technology equipment?
3. What changes in the labor force would you expect to see at Levi Strauss in the next decade? Why?

4. How do you think continued changes in U.S. demographics will affect Levi Strauss's products and sales in the next 10 years? The next 20 years?
5. In 1990, Levi Strauss agreed to sell stock in its Japanese operation to Japanese investors. The firm's management argues that such a sale is no threat to its management plans because Japanese investors are "in it for the long run." Do you agree or disagree with this decision? Why?

# *C*ONCLUDING CASE

## *ROLLING IN DOUGH*

**T**hough sometimes nicknamed "sinkers," doughnuts can float you to the top . . . just ask the folks at Dunkin' Donuts. While many firms in the United States spent much of the 1980s buying up unrelated firms and building conglomerates, only to dismantle them later (or see them fall apart), Dunkin' Donuts has stayed with what it knows.

Since its founding in 1950, Dunkin' Donuts has had a clear mission: "to make and sell the freshest, most delicious coffee and donuts." And quarter after quarter, year after year, that mission has translated into growth and profits. Today over 2,000 Dunkin' Donuts range from Massachusetts (the original store) to Europe and Asia, with more opening every year.

In the late 1980s, this very success made the firm a takeover target of Canadian oil and real estate magnate George Mann. But Bob Rosenberg, chairman of Dunkin' Donuts and son of the founder, fought back, deliberately taking on debt (a "poison pill" against a takeover). The firm also sold a large block of stock to its employees and additional stock to friendly General Electric Corporation. Left with only 15 percent of the firm's stock and the chance to buy only 20 percent more, Mann was stymied.

Unlike many firms that took on debt in the 1980s to prevent a takeover, however, Dunkin' Donuts may be in better shape than ever. For even as he took on debt, Rosenberg cut $7 million from operating expenses

*Dunkin' Donuts' latest brainstorm is the "mini donut," a miniaturized version of its traditional donut. The minis were introduced in early 1992 at a price of five for 99 cents and were an immediate success.*

by paring 14 percent of the staff—more than enough to service the debt. Remaining employees' morale remained reasonably high, thanks to the new stock ownership plan implemented by Rosenberg.

Rosenberg is also looking for new ideas to enable the company to continue to grow in ever more profitable ways. In the decade before Mann's takeover attempt, Dunkin' Donuts had expanded its kitchens to include ovens, its menu to include muffins, cookies, brownies, croissants, and soup, and its offerings to include lunch as well as breakfast. But such operations are expensive and space-consuming. Thus the company is now experimenting with kitchenless "satellite" shops in airports, train stations, shopping malls, and convenience stores. These shops sell products made and supplied by nearby full-service franchises. Not only are these satellite shops less expensive to build and operate, but they also provide an outlet for any excess production capacity at the supplying store.

All of which may make it a "hole" new ball game for Dunkin' Donuts.

### CASE QUESTIONS

1. Do you think Rosenberg was wise to fend off Mann's attempted takeover? Why or why not?
2. What shifts in the marketplace do you think Dunkin' Donuts was trying to address with its addition of muffins? Of lunch?
3. What do you believe will be Dunkin' Donuts' greatest challenge in the next decade?
4. What demographic changes may force alterations at Dunkin' Donuts in the future?

### KEY TERMS

high technology (high-tech) firm  51
service sector  51
informational services  51
acquisition  52
merger  53
strategic alliance  53
horizontal merger  53
vertical merger  54
conglomerate  merger  54
friendly takeover  54
hostile takeover  54

greenmail  54
raiders  54
regulation  55
deregulation  56
lobbyist  58
trade association  58
political action committee (PAC)  59
consumer  movement  64
consumer rights  64
trade deficit  66
trade surplus  66

### STUDY QUESTIONS AND EXERCISES

*Review Questions*

1. Identify four significant forces of change that businesses must contend with.
2. In what ways do businesses attempt to influence government? What ethical implications can be drawn regarding these actions?
3. Why is union membership in the United States declining?
4. Why is productivity such an important issue today?
5. What four major hurdles face business in the 1990s?

*Analysis Questions*

6. Using periodicals such as *Fortune* and *Business Week*, identify six recent alliances. What do you think each organization expects to gain from its partnership in the alliance?
7. Locate three instances in which you believe business has been more responsive to consumer expectations recently than it was in the past.

8. Do you think that the continuing challenge of pollution will ever be solved? Why or why not?

*Application Exercises*

9. Interview a local bank manager. Identify ways in which deregulation of the banking industry has made banking more risky and more profitable.

10. Visit a local manufacturing company. Identify ways in which it has been affected by high technology.

# *Employment Challenges of the 1990s*

### LAURA ANDERSON

*Laura Anderson is a marketing features writer for* The Denver Post.

[1]Just 40 years ago, a man could expect to find a job relatively easily, work hard and stay with it, and retire at age 65 with a gold watch and a comfortable pension. His wife, in the meantime, stayed at home to give full attention to support of the family and management of the household. Needless to say, those days are gone.

[2]According to projections by the U.S. Department of Labor, by the year 2000, 80% of the United States work force will be made up of women, minorities and immigrants. Women will account for 47% of all workers and will be hired for 64% of all new jobs. By 2000, the largest age group of workers will be those 35 to 54 years old as the baby boomers reach their 50's. The disabled workers will find doors opened that have been otherwise closed, albeit illegally, as the shift in American industry puts more emphasis on intellect than muscle.

[3]Fifty percent of the new jobs created in the 1990s will require some education beyond the high school level and almost 33% will be open to college graduates only. According to recent surveys, 61% of the companies questioned are currently having difficulties finding qualified people to fill professional and technical positions; 66% surveyed indicate that applicants for entry-level positions now "lack basic skills such as reading, writing, mathematics, problem solving and communications."

[4]During the 1980s, the U.S. economy affecting the job market was replaced by the global economy. As imports and exports have broken down the geographic boundaries of business transactions and interests, the job market is being affected just as surely. As exports from the U.S. increase, jobs will increase. This presents a new challenge and great opportunity for businesses and the work force. Only the courageous will survive. Just as competition is stiff in today's American job market, tomorrow the competition will be just as stiff but will encompass the world. . . .

## Content Questions

*True or False*

If the statement is false, rewrite it to make it true.

1. The makeup of the U. S. work force is expected to remain the same into the year 2000.
2. By 2000, the largest age group of workers will be those 35–54.
3. Thirty-three percent of the jobs created in the '90s will require education beyond high school.

4. The global economy is affecting the U.S. job market more than ever before.

5. With a global economy, the job market will be easier.

*Completion*

6. Identify the three major components of the U.S. work force in the year 2000.

7. What are the five "basic skills" many entry-level workers lack?

## Content Analysis Questions

1. What is Anderson's thesis?

2. How do these figures compare with Griffin and Ebert's data on the changing demographics of the labor force?

3. Why do you think a change in the amount of imports and exports has such an affect on the U.S. job market?

4. Explain what Anderson means by, "as the shift in American industry puts more emphasis on intellect than muscle."

5. Explain what Anderson means by, "During the 1980s, the U.S. economy affecting the job market was replaced by the global economy."

## Application Question

1. Would you rather have lived 40 years ago when a man could expect to find a job relatively easily, work hard at the same job all his life, and retire at age 65 with a gold watch and comfortable pension while his wife stayed home with the family, or today? Discuss your reasons.

# Future Work

JOSEPH F. COATES, JENNIFER JARRATT,
AND JOHN B. MAHAFFIE

*Joseph Coates, Jennifer Jarratt, and John Mahaffie are the president, vice president and research associate, respectively, of J.F. Coates, Inc., a firm specializing in futures research and policy analysis. This article is excerpted from the book* Future Work: Seven Critical Forces Reshaping Work and the Work Force in North America.

[1]The North American work force faces wrenching changes in its structure and composition that will radically alter how employers recruit, hire, manage, and hold on to good people.

[2]Some of these changes are demographic. More women, minorities, and immigrants are entering the work force; the work force is aging, as is society in North America; and the number of younger, entry-level workers available is shrinking. Other changes are economic: for example, North American corporations confront growing competition at home and abroad from companies with lower labor costs and faster product-to-market rates. This means employers must contain labor costs and produce higher-quality goods and services with a smaller work force.

³What an individual worker can bring to the workplace—in terms of education, skills, self-reliance, and attitude—is becoming ever more important in reaching an organization's business goals. Businesses are recognizing that a worker is a resource and an asset, rather than merely a fixed cost.

⁴The North American work force has earned its reputation as one of the most vital and hard-working labor forces in the world. Other countries envy its education, mobility, and creativity, as they also admire the U.S. economy's capacity for generating new jobs. Maintaining this reputation and competing effectively in turbulent times will require flexibility and the ability to embrace and incorporate change. The ability of business planners and managers to anticipate changes and their effects on people in an organization thus becomes more critical, and competitive survival may depend on how well planners and managers can think about the future.

⁵More than ever before, people are the dominant factor in both service and production. People plan, invent, design, operate, manage, and service the large corporation. People are its suppliers and its customers.

⁶This increased attention being given to the demand for more-productive and more-effective workers is stimulating new ideas. When one thinks of innovation, one tends to think of science and high technology, such as robots and new ceramics. But now one also thinks of quality circles, innovative rewards, and new work arrangements.

⁷One of the most positive developments is the growing interest on the part of business organizations in identifying and analyzing trends shaping the future work force. This interest in the future is a first step toward planning for work-force needs over the next 10 to 15 years. Actions taken now that are based on an informed look toward the future can prepare a company for changes and shifts in its available work force over time.

⁸We have identified a number of trends that are likely to influence the North American work force in the next 15 years. The potential effect of these trends signals the need for action and response. Actions can range from merely continuing to monitor the trend to reviewing policies and creating major shifts in business strategy.

## INCREASING DIVERSITY IN THE WORK FORCE

⁹•*The Continuing Aging of the Work Force Will Create Problems and Opportunities.* The aging of the baby-boom generation is raising the median age of the U.S. population. The median age, about 33 in 1990, will be 36 by the year 2000. By 2010, one quarter of the U.S. population will be at least 55, and one in seven Americans will be at least 65. The rapid growth of the U.S. labor force has been pushed by the baby boomers who have now matured into working-age adults. Between 1990 and 2000, the number of people between 35 and 44 will jump by 16%, and those between the ages of 45 and 54 will increase by 46%, compared with an overall expected population growth of 7.1%.

**The Middle-Aging of the Work Force**

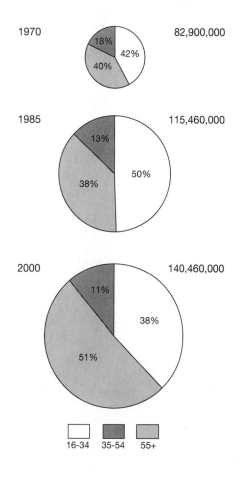

1970    82,900,000

18%   42%   40%

1985    115,460,000

13%   50%   38%

2000    140,460,000

11%   38%   51%

16-34   35-54   55+

[10]In addition to the baby boomers (people born between 1946 and 1964), three age groups are influencing the shifting structure and composition of the work force: 1930s Depression babies (1929–1940); the baby-bust cohort (1965–1978); and the baby-boom echo (1979+).

[11]•*Older Americans Will Increase in Number and Grow in Influence.* Older people are becoming a larger segment of the population, enjoying better health and longer life, and wielding economic and political power. More than 31 million Americans—12.4% of the nation's population—are estimated to be 65 or older. By 2020, when baby boomers reach 65, old people will be 20% of the U.S. population. At that time, there will be at least 7 million Americans over age 85.

[12]This aging of the U.S. society will have several significant effects. First, there will be changes in buying habits and consumer preferences. Second, there will be effects of the work force, such as aging workers and their productivity, health-care needs, retirement plans, rehired retirees as a part of the work force, and so on. Third, society will change with the rise of the four-generation family in which the older generation is active and economically independent.

## PROJECTIONS OF THE U.S. LABOR FORCE—1988–2000
(All population numbers in thousands)

| | U.S. Labor Force | | | Net Change | | % Change/Yr. | |
|---|---|---|---|---|---|---|---|
| | 1976 | 1988 | 2000 | '76–'88 | '88–2000 | '76–88 | '88–2000 |
| **Total, age** | | | | | | | |
| 16 & over | 96,158 | 121,669 | 141,134 | 25,511 | 19,465 | 2.0% | 1.2% |
| **Men, age** | | | | | | | |
| 16 & over | 57,174 | 66,927 | 74,324 | 9,753 | 7,397 | 1.3% | 0.9% |
| 16–24 | 12,572 | 11,753 | 11,352 | −999 | −401 | −0.7% | −0.3% |
| 25 | 35,576 | 46,383 | 53,155 | 10,807 | 6,772 | 2.2% | 1.1% |
| 55+ | 8,846 | 8,791 | 9,817 | −55 | 1,026 | −0.1% | 0.9% |
| **Women, age** | | | | | | | |
| 16 & over | 38,984 | 54,742 | 66,810 | 15,758 | 12,068 | 2.9% | 1.7% |
| 16–24 | 10,588 | 10,782 | 11,104 | 194 | 322 | 0.2% | 0.2% |
| 24–54 | 22,925 | 37,659 | 48,112 | 14,734 | 10,453 | 4.2% | 2.1% |
| 55+ | 5,471 | 6,301 | 7,594 | 830 | 1,293 | 1.2% | 1.6% |
| **White** | 84,767 | 104,755 | 118,981 | 19,988 | 14,226 | 1.8% | 1.1% |
| **Black** | 9,565 | 13,205 | 16,465 | 3,640 | 3,260 | 2.7% | 1.9% |
| **Asian/other** | 1,826 | 3,709 | 5,688 | 1,883 | 1,979 | 6.1% | 3.6% |
| **Hispanics*** | 4,289 | 8,982 | 14,321 | 2,693 | 5,339 | 6.4% | 4.0% |

*Persons of Hispanic origin may be of any race

*Source:* U.S. Department of Labor

[13]•*Hispanics Will Be the Largest Fast-Growing Minority Population in the United States.* Hispanics are changing the face of America. The bureau of the Census estimates that the Hispanic population grew from 14.6 million in 1980 to 21.9 million in 1990, about 50% in 10 years. Hispanic growth is five times that of non-Hispanics. By 2010, there will be 39.5 million U.S. Hispanics. Most U.S. Hispanics live in nine states. Mexican Americans are mostly in California, Arizona, New Mexico, Colorado, and Texas. Puerto Ricans are largely in New York, New Jersey, and Illinois. Cubans are mostly in Florida.

[14]Despite similarity of language, Hispanics are not a homogeneous group. Several different cultures, drawing on different national bases, make up the so-called Hispanic culture. But although there may be cultural differences, most Hispanics in the United States share North American values, including a desire for upward mobility.

[15]•*Most Black Americans Will Advance—But Not All.* In 1987, blacks accounted for 10.8% of the U.S. work force and about 12.2% of the population. They will grow to a projected 11.7% of the labor force by the year 2000. About 70% of black Americans are advancing in nearly every aspect of American life. In their transition to the mainstream, they have already moved from the rural South to cities throughout the country and advanced in large numbers from

unskilled and blue-collar work to white-collar work. They are moving up in corporations and government, making great educational advances, moving toward closer income parity with whites, and gaining political and economic power. In a generation or two, they have risen into the middle class and are moving to the suburbs. They are part of the mainstream.

[16]Nevertheless, 30% of blacks did not make these transitions after the great northward migration, which began in the 1920s and accelerated during and after World War II. They are stuck in a new American social situation—in urban ghettos, in multi-generational poverty, off the upward-mobility ladder—and locked into a goalless culture.

[17]•*Women Will Move Gradually into the Executive Suite.* By sheer force of their growing numbers in management ranks, women will force open the door to the executive suite over the next two decades. They will be counted among the 15 to 25 people in each of the largest corporations who run the show.

[18]•*High-Achieving Asians Are Out-Performing North American Whites in the Classroom and the Workplace.* For the most part, Asian Americans are affluent and well educated, but they are a diverse group differentiated by language, culture, and geography. Seven of the largest Asian groups in the United States are the Chinese, Filipinos, Japanese, Asian Indians, Koreans, Vietnamese, and Laotians. By the turn of the century, the number of Asian Americans will rise to more than 8 million.

[19]Asian Americans are outstandingly successful in education. Japanese males between 25 and 39 have a 96% high-school-completion rate. For Koreans and Indians, the completion rate is 94%; for Chinese, 90%; and for Filipinos, 89%. These rates compare with a white rate of 87%. Young Asian Americans graduating at the top of their class will be well acculturated and will have high expectations of the workplace and their prospects in it.

[20]•*A Shrinking Labor Pool Will Create Opportunities for Traditionally Underemployed Workers.* A shortage of workers in the United States—especially entry-level workers and those with specialized talent—is making many underutilized workers more attractive. These workers fall into two categories: those of limited skill or ability and those who are only partially available for work. The first are underutilized because they lack particular abilities or skills; the second either are not available to work at preferred times and places or do not have the desired commitment. Both categories are a substantial part of the human resource pool. Labor shortages may make workers who are often considered unemployable or problematic—such as the disabled, emotionally impaired, or illiterate— more attractive.

[21]•*The Scientific and Engineering Work Force Is Growing and Becoming More Diverse in National Origin, Gender, and Race.* Nearly 5 million scientists and engineers were employed in the United States in 1986, double the number employed in 1976, demonstrating the increasing importance of science and technology

**SELECTED MARKET CHARACTERISTICS (WITH PERCENTAGES OF PARTICIPATION) OF SCIENTISTS AND ENGINEERS, 1986**

| | All Scientists & Engineers | Scientists | Engineers |
|---|---|---|---|
| Labor-force participation rate | 94.5 | 95.3 | 93.8 |
| Unemployment rate | 1.5 | 1.9 | 1.2 |
| Employment rate | 84.7 | 76.7 | 91.9 |
| Underemployment rate | 2.6 | 4.3 | 1.0 |
| Average annual salary | $38,400 | $35,700 | $40,800 |

*Source:* National Science Foundation, *Science Resources Studies Highlights, 1987*

to U.S. society. At the same time, the scientific and engineering work force is becoming more diverse by gaining more foreign-born workers, women, and minorities. Women and black scientists and engineers are still a relatively small part of this work force, although their numbers are increasing. Universities and employers who need Ph.D. qualifications find themselves increasingly dependent on foreign-born workers.

## HOME LIFE AND WORK LIFE

[22]•*Corporations Will Adopt New Programs to Support Employees' Family Responsibilities.* Although it is currently focused on day care, the issue of workplace support for employees' family obligations is indicative of a larger concern for greater integration of home and work life. Employers, once able to assume that the demands of male workers' home lives were taken care of by wives and families, are now being pushed to pay attention to family issues such as day care, sick children, eldercare, and schooling. One reason why corporations may lag behind in this trend could be that their older senior managers have not experienced these pressures in their own lives.

[23]Drivers of this trend include more families in which both husband and wife work, the dramatic increase in the number of women in the work force who are mothers, and the growing need for long-term care of the aging.

[24]•*Work and Education Will Influence Women's Childbearing Choices and Will Shape National Fertility Patterns.* Of the 50.3 million employed women in 1987, 59.2% were married and most were in their prime childbearing and working years. Women are returning to work after childbearing sooner than ever.

[25]For many women, especially those with more than average education and with career prospects, there is an economic and opportunity cost for bearing children that may be limiting their lifetime fertility, as well as encouraging them to postpone childbearing.

Demographers now expect the average U.S. woman to bear fewer than two children, although she herself may anticipate having at least two. Many more women will be childless than had planned to be. While the consequences of these trends have yet to be fully estimated, one likely outcome is childbearing that is explicitly planned to coincide with career choices.

[26]•*Work Will Move to Unconventional Sites and Arrangements.* Employers are becoming willing to consider almost any work arrangement that will get work done at less cost. Businesses are seeking to contain costs, are responding to the need for flexibility to meet sudden demands or slowdown in work, and are finding workers with critical skills either too scarce or too expensive to hire full time. Workers, on the other hand, find flexible schedules appealing, particularly in terms of childcare, and are more concerned about such factors as long commutes. Temporary workers, part-time contractors, and independent workers constitute the fastest-growing employment category. These workers accounted for half of the growth in the U.S. work force between 1980 and 1987.

[27]Companies are exploring options such as contingent workers and flexible scheduling. Contingent workers are paid only for working, may not qualify for benefits, and are less likely to join labor unions. At the same time, emerging computer and networking technologies are enabling work to be done anywhere, at any time, and at any distance from the office or factory.

[28]•*The New Focus on Workers as an Asset Will Make Attitudes and Values More Central.* Pressed by demands for an adequate return on investment in the work force, managers are becoming increasingly concerned about factors shaping their employees' behavior. More is being invested in training. Expectations of the individual's productivity, skills, and capacity for responsibility are greater. Yet at the same time, the work force is increasingly diverse in its attitudes and lifestyles. It is better educated than ever before and more acquainted with psychology and sociology.

[29]As a result, researchers are prodding workers and their families about their values and attitudes toward work, their bosses, and the workplace. Surveying is becoming a tool for assessing employees' loyalty and productivity.

[30]•*Mobility Continues to Be a Strength of the North American Work Force.* North Americans, more than others, are ready to pack up and go. The average American moves every six years—11 times in a lifetime. During 1986–1987, 18% of people living in the United States moved to a different home. Many of these movers moved more than once in a year. A steady stream of immigrants to North America adds mobility to the work force. Such mobility is a strength for the future work force. Workers can move to where the jobs are, acquiring experience and skills in the process. And a mobile work force means that employers can attract skilled workers to new sites, making it easier for business to relocate closer to markets and resources.

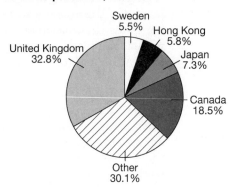

**Countries Most Active in U.S. Mergers
and Acquisitions, 1986**

Sweden 5.5%
Hong Kong 5.8%
Japan 7.3%
Canada 18.5%
United Kingdom 32.8%
Other 30.1%

*Source:* U.S. General Accounting Office, *Foreign Investment,* 1987

## GLOBALIZATION: COMPETING IN A WORLD ECONOMY

[31]•*Mergers and Acquisitions Will Continue—With More International Actors Involved.* Globalization encourages the flow of capital as barriers to the movement of capital fall. The increase in capital movement among countries results in mergers and acquisitions, with more foreign actors involved as nations look for more-productive investments. Over the long term, as a global economy emerges and structural and economic differences fade, there is the potential for large international shifts in corporate ownership and the development of new organizational structures for doing business internationally.

[32]•*Work-Force and Market Demographics in Europe and Asia Will Present New Opportunities.* Birthrates are falling almost everywhere in the industrialized world. Between 2020 and 2025, the birthrates of Europe, Asia (including Japan, South Korea, Taiwan, Hong Kong, and Singapore), and North America are projected to have declined to about 12–14 births per 1,000 population. As the work forces of the industrially advanced nations of Europe and Asia grow in sophistication, those countries will grow economically and reap the benefits of world trade.

[33]•*Sweeping Changes Will Alter Market Basics.* New stresses on time, the increasing diversity of lifestyles, the opening up of overseas markets, and the restructuring of many corporations will shift the basics of marketing. At the same time, workers at all levels will become integral to marketing, sales, and customer relations. Broad change will affect when products and services are marketed (time), what is sold (quality, experience), how marketing and selling are done (technologies and new strategies), to whom products and services are marketed and sold (demographic change and segmentation) and by whom products are marketed and sold (worker as representative, customer as salesperson).

[34]Several factors are also pushing new approaches to marketing and sales. These include overseas competition and competition

for foreign markets; changing social values in the United States and other advanced nations, including new demands for quality and service; and the opening up of new avenues and new markets through electronic technology, such as television, fax copying, videotex, home computers, and satellite transmission. One of the most important of these factors, especially in the United States, is greater demands on time.

[35]•*Worldwide Technical and Scientific Competence Will Sharpen Competition.* Although the United States is the center of scientific and technical education, has the world's largest technically educated work force, and holds a sizable share of world trade in high technology, other countries are catching up. Their efforts are being driven by several factors: the greater significance of technical education as a route to economic success; transborder data flows and technical and scientific exchanges between nations; and new scientific and technical developments occurring world-wide, including the growth in research and development. Scientists and the technically educated are becoming the first truly international, mobile work force.

## THE CHANGING NATURE OF WORK

[36]•*New Critical Skills Are Emerging.* Skills critical to the future of the workplace are emerging, but some are or will be in short supply. Several factors are driving the shift toward new skills for work: greater use of information technologies, the move away from craft and assembly manufacture and toward computer-mediated processes, the larger amount of knowledge work in almost every occupation, new requirements for education and the ability to manage complexity, and the redesign of many jobs to include computer-based work. Frequently, several skills will be folded into one job, often with a new title and greater individual responsibility.

[37]•*Training and Education Budgets Will Stay High as Corporations Stretch for New Results.* To boost competitiveness, many corporations are energetically training and retraining their work forces. At the same time, more managers and executives are exposed to new and sometimes eccentric methods and styles of training, aimed at shaping their behavior toward more effective leadership and greater productivity. In the name of leaner, meaner, and more efficient management, corporate educators are forging ahead, with no evidence beyond the promise that these emerging techniques produce long-term results.

[38]There is, however, a solid base for all the technical training and retraining that needs to be done in factories and offices. In the next five years, four out of five people in the industrial world will be doing jobs differently from the way they have been done in the last 50 years. Most people will have to learn new skills. By the year 2000, 75% of all employees will need to be retrained in new jobs or taught fresh skills for their old ones. Corporate trainers, in the interest of saving time, will explore alternative and faster methods of delivering new skills and learning, including interactive video, audiotapes,

take-home videodiscs, computer-based instruction, and expert systems.

### 39•*The Corporation Will Reach Deeper into the Educational System to Influence the Quality of Its Supply of Workers.*

At a time when the U.S. work force as a whole is becoming better educated than ever—one in four U.S. workers is a college graduate—corporations are troubled by deficiencies in basic skills among entry-level workers. As a result, more corporations are teaching reading, writing, and computing to new hires. More significant, perhaps, are corporations' efforts to influence the U.S. educational system and thus improve the skills of their future supply of new workers.

40To influence the future supply of workers, corporations are reaching into the educational system with a variety of incentives, new ideas, and cooperative agreements. In Minneapolis, for example, corporate contributions underwrote extensive participatory planning, which was used in the successful restructure of the city's school system, particularly its inner-city high schools. In Pekin, Illinois, IBM's "Writing to Read" program helped first graders, cutting the number who needed remedial teaching from 11% to 2%.

### 41•*The Requirements of the Emerging Global Society Are Diverging from the Knowledge Base of the U.S. Population.*

An emerging globally integrated society is demanding more knowledge and education. Sweeping technological change, the rise of worldwide communications, and competition in the global marketplace require specialized knowledge. The United States is failing to meet these requirements and struggles to sustain the literacy, math, and other abilities of previous decades.

### 42•*Office Automation Will Thrive Despite Questionable Productivity Gains.*

Spending on information-processing equipment is rising. Total fixed-capital investment rose an estimated 8.9% in 1988, to $490 billion; about 70% of this investment was on computers and telecommunications equipment. However, productivity in some industries is stagnant or slow to rise, despite increasing capital outlays.

43Office automation is driven by the promises of increased productivity, efficiency, and effectiveness implicit in the technology. No one doubted that automation would streamline operations and increase worker's output. The promise, however, has not been fully realized. The service sector has posted virtually no productive gains despite huge spending on information-processing equipment. Several factors may be responsible: growth in productivity has not been high enough to offset large capital outlays for computers and related equipment, too little training is being put behind the hardware, and productivity in information industries is hard to measure.

### 44•*Artificial Intelligence Is Jerkily Moving from the Laboratory to Practical Application.*

Artificial intelligence (AI) promises a new industrial revolution by the turn of the century. That revolution may be bigger than the one created by microprocessing technology. Artificial intelligence mimics the human mind, and

**Artificial Intelligence Replicating the Functions of the Human Brain**

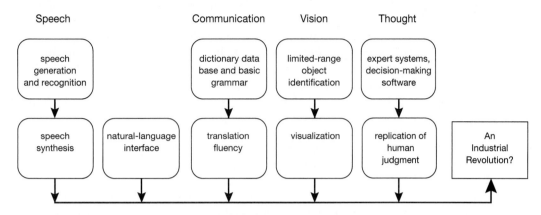

Artificial intelligence will allow computers to utilize many of the thought and decision-making processes of the human brain.

intelligent machines may eventually match humans in speech, vision, language, communication, and thought.

[45]Expert systems are available today that are the forerunners of AI applications. By the year 2000, AI will affect 60%–90% of all jobs in large organizations; it will augment, displace, downgrade, or even eliminate workers. AI's potential for teaching, training, and monitoring will also give us sophisticated new capabilities. The technology will make autonomous machines, free of a central control mechanism or wired networks, practical.

## EMPLOYEES AND HEALTH

[46]•*The United States Is an Increasingly Sedentary Society.* As the United States changes into a post-industrial society, the characteristics of work will change. A feature of this shift is more indoor working and living. About 60% of American adults live sedentary lives. Americans are spending 90% of their time indoors, whether at home, in the office or factory, or in closed spaces during travel. Work is far more sedentary than in the past. Aside from sleeping, eating, and dressing, the big consumer of indoor time is watching television—six hours and 59 minutes daily in U.S. households in 1988–1989.

[47]The trend toward a sedentary society will lead to more exposure to the risks of an indoor environment, such as indoor air pollution; a sharp decline in muscular activity; new bad habits associated with a sedentary life, such as smoking, coffee and soda drinking, and candy nibbling; and even more social friction and interpersonal annoyances. Healthy workers lose less time and have fewer accidents. People in good physical shape live longer and healthier lives. Attention to health at the workplace also may be seen as an amenity and a factor in morale.

[48]•*Strong Long-Term Forces Will Work Against Cutting Health Costs.* The United States spends at least $500 billion a year on health care, more than 11% of its gross national product. As a percent of GNP, national health-care expenditures have almost tripled

since 1940. Cost-containment attempts so far have only slightly slowed an inexorable rise. At the same time, there is no evidence that the quality of health care, of health maintenance, or of disease prevention is improving to match the increase in spending.

[49]At least four strong long-term forces are boosting the soaring cost of health care in the United States—and are likely to keep those costs high. The United States has huge institutionalized health-care obligations, created by factors such as the aging U.S. population. Insurance and liability costs in an increasingly litigious society are enormous. New medical technologies, such as those used for heart and other organ transplants, have been tremendously expensive. And the public's expectation of universal entitlement to health care and health protection continues to grow.

[50]•*The Significance of the Worker's Contribution to Occupational Health and Safety Will Increase.* In the changing workplace, the worker increasingly is responsible for his or her personal health and safety, as well as that of fellow workers. The worker can contribute through awareness of and concern for health and safety or may aggravate workplace risks by inappropriate behavior or attitudes.

[51]New technologies and new workstyles have shifted occupa-

### Workplace Regulation by State
(Selected recent activity)

| | | | |
|---|---|---|---|
| **A** | Parental leave legislation, 1987-1988 | **F** | Ban on lie detectors in the private sector |
| **B** | Family and medical leave | **G** | "Whistleblower" protection for private-sector employees |
| **C** | Raised minimum wage | | |
| **D** | Regulation of smoking in the workplace | **H** | VDT use/computer monitoring regulations considered and/or enacted |
| **E** | Drug-testing bills or legislation | **I** | Health-benefits legislation |

tional health and safety issues from the acute to the chronic and long term. There are also new issues (such as mental stress, eyestrain from computer use, and back fatigue) associated with the white-collar work force. In the blue-collar work force, averting injury is no longer strictly a matter of enforcing safety regulations. Greater use of automation requires more responsibility and cooperation from workers to ensure safety.

[52]•***The AIDS Epidemic Is Killing People in the Prime of Their Working Lives.*** What makes AIDS uniquely important to business is that those who are infected and die at present are mostly young men in the prime of their working years. At the same time, the long incubation period of AIDS will cause greater distress for individuals and higher medical costs for employers than any other acute epidemic.

[53]AIDS-related deaths are expected to rise to 68.63 per 100,000 U.S. population by the end of 1991. Evidence aside, most employers do not view AIDS as a problem. A Harris executive poll for *Business Week* showed little concern among the 1,000 companies surveyed; 89% of the executives reported that their companies did not have an AIDS policy.

## CHANGING AND RESTRUCTURING THE WAY BUSINESS DOES BUSINESS

[54]•***Businesses Will Be Increasingly Committed to Improving Performance through Innovation in Rewards.*** Small, medium, and large firms are exploring innovations in monetary, dollar-equivalent, and symbolic rewards—such as sabbaticals, mental-health benefits, and goodwill gestures such as special concert or other entertaining events for their workers. These innovations have high potential to stimulate and motivate workers without raising fixed costs. Both managers and employers, however, may need some help in thinking of and implementing any nontraditional rewards. Trade-offs between rewards and compensation, benefits, amenities, and perks will be common.

[55]•***Organizational and Work-force Restructuring Will Lead to Changes in Compensation.*** New organizational goals for productivity, cost control, quality, and work-force restructuring are reshaping compensation patterns. Corporations are cutting the layers of managers that separate top executives from other workers. Between 1980 and 1987, 89 of the top 100 U.S. companies reduced their management layers; analysis of performance appears to show that companies with only seven layers perform better than those with 11. Compensation for those at the top, based on the old hierarchy, is rising to new heights, leading many to doubt that a system that is changing underneath can continue to support this pattern for long.

[56]Major new directions in compensation include the increasing popularity of incentive-pay plans in general (long-term plans in particular) and the use of other cash and non-cash methods of compen-

sation—such as employee stock-ownership plans or savings plans—to substitute for wage increases.

⁵⁷•*Competition Will Promote Entrapreneurship and Worker Empowerment.* Encouraging innovation and entrapreneurship is the new goal of corporate management. Following the examples of many smaller companies, large organizations are also experimenting in empowering their workers. "Empowerment" is a voguish term for giving workers discretion, authority, and the power of self-management. To some, this is an old idea—a good business practice—with a new name. Driving the recycling of this idea are the greater use of worker participation as a tool for generating productivity, information technology that makes information available at all levels of an organization, and a better-educated work force, among other factors.

⁵⁸•Downsizing will reshuffle the work-force deck. Begun in the restructuring of heavy industry, downsizing has continued into the white-collar work force and now affects the composition of all industries and companies, in all regions and of all sizes, and affects employees at all levels of skills and education. The resulting reshuffling of jobs will create a new business culture in which most people, as well as having more than one career, will have been laid off at least once, can expect to be laid off again, and are likely to behave as if their current jobs are fleeting.

⁵⁹Some believe that most U.S. corporations had hired too many employees and were suffering from payroll bloat. In any event, by some estimates at least 600,000 middle managers were laid off between 1984 and 1987. Factors driving downsizing include automation, mergers and acquisitions, the use of information technology that makes middle management and some clerical work obsolete, and new management concepts that call for fewer, cross-skilled workers.

⁶⁰•*Pent-up Demand for Solutions to Workplace Issues Will Increase Regulation.* Societal problems that are important to the work force—family support, pay equity, drug abuse, job security, health care, and labor relations, among others—are not being fully addressed by U.S. employers or by the federal government. The relative neglect of these issues in the past decade has created a pent-up demand for new solutions. In response, state governments and the courts are reversing the United States' long-term tendency toward managing labor issues by federal regulation. In the process they are creating a crazy quilt of their own regulatory actions and decisions.

⁶¹•*Corporations Will Be Under Pressure to Explore and Redefine Their Ethics.* Business ethics is a growth enterprise. Frequently cited factors behind this uprush of interest in ethics include an increase in social concerns that began with Watergate; stock-market scandals; sexual-harassment issues; issues of privacy and testing; safety in products (as, for example, in cigarettes); the quality and integrity of advertising; and corporate fervor for belt-tightening mergers, acquisitions, divestitures, and downsizing.

## Content Questions

*True or False*

If the statement is false, rewrite it to make it true.

1. Managers planning for the future are giving most of their attention to the role of technology.
2. The median age of the U.S. population is decreasing.
3. The average American moves every six years.
4. Office automation has reached its peak and there will not be much change in the future.
5. In the next five years, four out of five people in the industrial world will be doing jobs differently from the way they have been done in the last 50 years.

*Completion*

6. Identify three demographic changes in the work force of the future.
7. What is the largest fast-growing minority population in the United States?
8. In the future, why will employers consider more unconventional work arrangements like contingent workers?
9. Name four societal changes that will cause changes in marketing products and services.
10. List three major health issues affecting business in the future.

## Vocabulary

1. Hispanics are not a *homogeneous group* (¶14)
2. moving toward closer income *parity* (¶15)
3. will be *acculturated* (¶19)
4. many *underutilized* workers (¶20)
5. is *indicative* of a larger concern (¶22)
6. better *integration of home and work life* (¶22)
7. List and explain five additional phrases important to the understanding of the article.

## Content Analysis Questions

1. State the authors' thesis. Do you think they presented sufficient evidence to support their thesis? Why or why not?
2. Develop an informal outline of the article.
3. Why are businesses beginning to recognize employees as a resource or asset rather than just a fixed cost?
4. Compare and contrast the trends discussed by Coates, Jarratt, and Mahaffie with the trends and challenges discussed by Griffin and Ebert in their textbook chapter *Recognizing Business Trends and Challenges*.
5. What do "The Middle-Aging of the Work Force" pie charts indicate? What does the text say about this concept?

**Application Questions**

1. According to the authors, the United States is failing the requirements of the emerging global society and is struggling to sustain the literacy, math, and other abilities of previous decades. What does this mean? Do you think this is true? If it is true, how might it affect you?

2. What is artificial intelligence (AI)? What kind of AI applications do you think we'll see in this century? What application do you think will have the most affect on you?

# Solving the Job Puzzle

## ANNE W. CLYMER AND ELIZABETH MCGREGOR

*Anne Clymer and Elizabeth McGregor are economists in the Office of Employment Projections, Bureau of Labor Statistics. This selection is from* Occupational Outlook Quarterly.

[1]"I am myself reminded that we are not alike; there are diversities of natures among us which are adapted to different occupations." These words, which Plato attributed to Socrates, are still true today.

[2]Choosing a career is one of the hardest jobs you will ever have. You should devote extensive time, energy, and thought to make a decision with which you will be happy. Even though undertaking this task means hard work, view a career as an opportunity to do something you enjoy, not simply as a necessity or as a means of earning a living. Taking the time to thoroughly explore career options can mean the difference between finding a stimulating and fulfilling career or hopping from one job to the next in search of the right job. Finding the best occupation for you also is important because work influences many aspects of your life—from your choice of friends and recreational activities to where you live.

[3]Choosing a career is work that should be done carefully. As you gain experience and mature, however, you may develop new interests and skills which open doors to new opportunities. Work is an educational experience and can further focus your interests or perhaps change your career preferences. The choice you make today may not be your last. In fact, most people change occupations several times during their careers. With careful consideration of the wide range of occupations available, you should be able to find the right career.

[4]There are many factors to consider when exploring career options and many ways to begin solving your job puzzle. Everyone has certain expectations of his or her job—these may include career advancement, self-expression or creativity, a sense of accomplishment, or a high salary. Deciding what you want most from your job will make choosing a career easier.

[5]This article can assist you in your search for a suitable career. It discusses things to consider—personal interests, educational and skill requirements, and job outlook—and lists sources of additional information. . . .

## INTERESTS

[6]Identifying your interests will help in your search for a stimulating career. You might start by assessing your likes and dislikes, strengths and weaknesses. If you have trouble identifying them, consider the school subjects, activities, and surroundings that appeal to you. Would you prefer a job that involves travel? Do you want to work with children? Do you like science and mathematics? Do you need flexible working hours? Does a particular industry, such as health services, appeal to you? These are just a few questions to ask yourself. There are no right or wrong answers, and only you know what's important. Decide what job characteristics you require, which ones you prefer, and which ones you would not accept. Then rank these characteristics in order of importance to you.

[7]Perhaps job setting ranks high on your list of important job characteristics. You may not want to work behind a desk all day. Or maybe you always dreamed of a job that involves instructing and helping others; in this case, child care workers, teachers, and physicians are among the occupations that might interest you.

[8]Geographic location may also concern you. If so, it could influence your career decision because employment in some occupations and industries is concentrated in certain regions or localities. For example, aerospace jobs are concentrated in three States—California, Texas, and Washington—while advertising jobs are concentrated in large cities. If you choose to work in one of these fields, you probably will have to live in one of these states or in a large city. Or, if you live in Denver or the Southeast, for instance, you should learn which industries and occupations are found in those locations. On the other hand, many industries such as hotels and motels, legal services, and retail trade, as well as occupations such as teachers, secretaries, and computer analysts, are found in all areas of the country.

[9]Earnings potential varies from occupation to occupation, and each person must determine his or her needs and goals. If high earnings are important to you, look beyond the starting wages. Some occupations offer relatively low starting salaries, but earnings substantially increase with experience, additional training, and promotions. In the end, your earnings may be higher in one of these occupations. For example, insurance sales workers may have relatively low earnings at first; after years of building a clientele, however, their earnings may increase substantially.

[10]Job setting, working with a specific group of people, geographic location, and earnings are just a few occupational characteristics that you may consider. Be open minded. Consider occupations related to your initial interests. For example, you may be interested in health care, and certain qualities of nursing may appeal to you, such as patient care and frequent public contact. Exploring other health occupations that share these characteristics—including doctors, respiratory therapists, and emergency medical technicians—may stimulate your interest in a health field other than nursing.

[11]Don't eliminate any occupation or industry before you learn more about it. Some occupations and industries invoke certain positive or negative images. For some people, fashion designers produce a glamorous image, while production occupations in manufacturing

industries bring to mind a less attractive image. However, jobs often are not what they first appear to be, and misconceptions are common. Exciting jobs may have dull aspects, while less glamorous occupations may interest you once you learn about them. For example, the opportunity to travel makes a flight attendant's job seem exciting, but the work is strenuous and tiring; flight attendants stand for long periods and must remain friendly when they are tired and passengers are unpleasant. On the other hand, many people consider automotive assembly work dirty and dull; however, production workers in the motor vehicle manufacturing industry are among the highest paid in the Nation.

## SKILLS

¹²One way to choose an occupation is to examine the skills required to perform the job well. Consider the skills you already have, or your ability and interest in obtaining the skills or training required for specific occupations. Some occupations that require mechanical ability, for instance, include elevator installers and repairers and automotive mechanics. If you do not plan to attend college, consider occupations that require less formal education. If you are interested in engineering, for example, but do not want to pursue a college degree, drafters and engineering technicians are two occupations you can enter with 1 or 2 years of postsecondary training.

¹³Some skills—analysis, persuading, and mechanical ability, for example—are specific to certain occupations. . . . However, certain skills are needed, in varying degrees, in virtually all occupations, from factory workers to top executives. Because these skills apply to so many occupations, they are discussed here.

## SKILLS COMMON TO ALL JOBS

¹⁴As the marketplace becomes increasingly competitive, a company's ability to succeed depends upon its workers' skills—in particular, basic skills in reading, writing, and mathematics. These skills allow workers to learn and adapt to rapid technological advances and changing business practices in their jobs. This adaptability is crucial to one's survival in the job market.

¹⁵Reading skills are essential to perform most jobs. Workers must often read and understand text, graphs, charts, manuals, and instructional materials. Writing skills are necessary to communicate thoughts, ideas, and information in written forms such as memorandums, invoices, schedules, letters, or information requests. Many jobs require basic mathematical skills to take measurements and perform simple calculations. Lack of these skills can lead to many problems, including poor quality products and missed deadlines. These problems can then result in a decline in sales and increased customer complaints.

¹⁶Reading, writing, and mathematical skills are as important for a research scientist as they are for occupations that require little formal education, such as a stockroom clerk at a manufacturing plant. Although a computer system may be designed to track inventory by electronically recording all transactions, the clerk is respon-

sible for verifying the information. The clerk must be able to read and do simple calculations to confirm that stockroom inventory matches what the computer registers. Any inaccuracies in counting, computing, or recording of this inventory could result in a slowdown in production.

[17]Workers also need good listening and speaking skills to interact with others. Greater interaction among workers is evident in factories, offices, and laboratories. Problems often are solved through communication, cooperation, and discussion, and workers must be able to listen, speak, and think on their feet. When dealing with customers, workers must listen and understand customers' needs and communicate solutions and ideas. It is not good enough to merely take a customer's order; workers must provide customers with useful information.

[18]The banking industry illustrates the importance of listening and speaking skills. Banks face competition from other industries— including insurance companies, credit unions, and investment houses—that offer a growing array of financial products. Tellers, customer service representatives, and bank managers need strong communication skills to explain, promote, and sell the bank's services to potential customers. Customer satisfaction can only be achieved by understanding what the customer wants and by providing that service as quickly as possible.

[19]Good interpersonal skills are critical as the workplace becomes more team-oriented. Apparel plants, for instance, are replacing the traditional assembly line with modular manufacturing. On the traditional assembly line, workers performed a specific task independent of other workers and were compensated accordingly. Today, groups of workers, called modules, work as a team to produce garments, solve problems as they occur, and make suggestions to improve production or working conditions. Group interaction is important because an individual's earnings are based upon the group's performance.

[20]Workers at all levels must be willing to learn new techniques. Computers, for instance, were once found primarily in office settings; today, computers are found in every work setting from factories to classrooms. The introduction of computers into the manufacturing process is transforming many craft and factory occupations; many of these jobs now require the use of computer-controlled equipment. For example, most elevators are computerized and electronically controlled. In order to install, repair, and maintain modern elevators, elevator repairers need a thorough knowledge of electronics, electricity, and computer applications. Even though a high school education generally is the minimum requirement for entering this field, workers with postsecondary training in electronics usually have better advancement opportunities than those with less training. As technological changes continue, retraining will be essential for workers in many fields.

## OUTLOOK

[21]When matching your interests and skills to an occupation, you should also consider the employment outlook for that occupation or related industry. For instance, stiff competition is expected

for jobs as advertising managers because the number of applicants greatly exceeds the number of job openings. On the other hand, job openings for preschool workers should be plentiful due to rapidly growing demand for this occupation and relatively high turnover among preschool workers. Outlook is not addressed in this article but is discussed in detail in the *Occupational Outlook Handbook* and *Career Guide to Industries,* which are revised every two years.

[22]Information about job openings, supply-demand conditions, and susceptibility to layoffs indicate, in part, the ease or difficulty of landing a job. Many factors affect the demand for an occupation, including changes in consumer spending, demographics, and technology. Researching an occupation or industry will help you identify key factors and their impact on employment. For example, increased use of computers has contributed to the rapid growth of computer service technician jobs. On the other hand, the growing use of computers in offices has greatly reduced the demand for typists. This illustrates the diverse effects that technological advances can have on different occupations and emphasizes the importance of learning about specific occupations.

[23]Job growth is a good indicator of favorable opportunities, but the fastest growing occupations do not always equate with the largest numbers of job opportunities. Most job openings result from the need to replace workers who leave their jobs. Consequently, larger occupations—which usually have the highest replacement needs—generally provide the most job openings. As a result of replacement needs, even occupations that are declining can provide employment opportunities.

[24]Knowledge of the industries in which occupations are found also is important in looking for a job. Job opportunities generally are favorable in an occupation found in a wide range of industries, such as receptionists. On the other hand, employment prospects are likely to be unfavorable, and workers more subject to layoffs, in an occupation that is concentrated in a declining industry, such as machine operators in the textile industry. Some workers also may be subject to layoffs because of the nature of the industry. For example, the demand for construction workers is cyclical—employment rises and falls with changes in construction activity—and motor vehicle manufacturing workers may be laid off during periods of slack sales.

## ADDITIONAL INFORMATION

[25]. . . Once you identify an interest in one or more occupations or industries, many sources of additional information are available. The specific sources may vary, depending on the fields which interest you. . . . The following sources may serve as starting points in your career search.

[26]***Libraries.*** A library is a great place to find information about jobs. Libraries have career guidance publications that present occupational information covering job duties, training requirements,

working conditions, employment outlook, and earnings. Librarians can direct you to the information you need.

[27]*Career Centers.* Many career centers have computerized job information systems that match jobs to your skills and interests. These systems usually are easy to use and generate a list of suggested occupations. Also, career counselors at these centers can help you develop jobseeking skills, such as resumé writing or interviewing.

[28]*State Employment Service Offices.* State employment service offices can provide you with information concerning the industrial and occupational composition of specific areas. This is a good place to start if you need to find out what job opportunities a particular area offers.

[29]*Guidance Counselors.* Counselors interview, test, and counsel students to help them discover their skills and interests and how these relate to career opportunities. If you have a particular aptitude for certain subjects, a counselor can direct you toward occupations that require these talents. . . .

[30]*Informational Interviews.* Interviewing individuals to gather information about their occupation or industry is a very effective way to find out about jobs that may interest you. An informational interview is not a job interview. Rather, it's your opportunity to learn from a person who knows the pros and cons of an occupation or industry.

[31]If you don't know someone in the occupation that interests you, network! Ask your parents, neighbors, teachers, or friends if they know someone in the occupation. Most people enjoy talking about their jobs and are pleased to have an audience. . . .

[33]*Internships/Volunteer Work.* There is no substitute for practical experience. Internship programs and volunteer work help students explore a field and develop career skills at the same time. For example, someone interested in politics may volunteer to help a local, state, or national campaign elect a candidate to office. Many local government planning offices offer internships to college and graduate students specializing in urban and regional planning. Through these programs, students gain planning experience that not only improves their chances of finding a full-time job after graduation but also helps them decide whether or not the field interests them.

[34]*Cooperative Education.* This program is similar to internships; students gain practical experience by working in their chosen fields. Students enrolled in cooperative education programs divide their time between school and work, applying the knowledge and theory gained in class to practical situations on the job. Credit and grades are given for both the worksite learning and the related school instruction. . . .

[35]***Trade Unions and Associations.*** These organizations specialize in a particular field and are well informed on the issues affecting the employment of workers in occupations or industries that they represent. They can provide information about training and skill requirements. Local unions sponsor apprenticeships and formal training programs for many occupations.

## Content Questions

*True or False*

If the statement is false, rewrite it to make it true.

1. Most people stay with the same career all their lives.
2. Deciding what you want most from a job will make a career choice easier.
3. Starting wage is a critical factor in selecting a career.
4. Adaptability is crucial to one's survival in the job market.
5. The fastest growing occupations always have the largest number of job opportunities.

*Completion*

6. Identify four job expectations that many people have.
7. List three basic skills common to almost all occupations.
8. Why do workers need good listening and speaking skills?
9. Name three factors that affect the demand for an occupation.
10. Identify five sources that you could consult for additional information on occupations.

## Vocabulary

1. devote extensive time (¶2)
2. invoke certain positive or negative images (¶11)
3. as the marketplace becomes increasingly competitive (¶14)
4. compensated accordingly (¶19)

## Content Analysis Questions

1. What is Clymer and McGregor's purpose?
2. What is Clymer and McGregor's thesis?
3. How do Clymer and McGregor develop and support their thesis?
4. Explain what Socrates meant when he said, "I am myself reminded that we are not alike; there are diversities of natures among us which are adapted to different occupations." Do you agree or disagree? Explain.
5. What do you think Clymer and McGregor see as "the difference between a stimulating and fulfilling career and a job"? Do you agree or disagree? Explain.

**Application Questions**

1. Assume that you have the opportunity to change jobs—to make a new start in a new career. Would you want to change? What is one thing you would look for in a new job that you don't have now? What other factors would you consider?

2. Assume that you are working with a group of students and faculty to set up a job fair on campus. What employers would you definitely want to have represented? Why? What employers, if any, would you not want to be represented? Why? What resource people would you invite? How would you encourage students to attend?

# *Where the Jobs Are*

MICHAEL J. MANDEL, DAVID GREISING, JOAN O'C. HAMILTON, GAIL DeGEORGE, AND SANDRA ATCHISON

*Michael Mandel, David Greising, Joan Hamilton, Gail DeGeorge, and Sandra Atchison are* Business Week *correspondents.*

[1]Let there be no mistake: The current job outlook is bleak. Titans such as IBM, General Motors, and General Dynamics continue to slash jobs. And college seniors are heading for big disappointments. "Last year's graduating class was not facing great prospects," says Kenneth Goldstein, an economist at the Conference Board. "But this class is coming out into a worse labor market."

[2]But cheer up, harried job-hunter, all is not lost. The forces that will produce the new jobs of the 1990s are already in place. Information services will generate new hiring as the computer revolution rolls on. The graying of America will mean strong job growth in health care and leisure activities. And a raft of private companies are springing up to take on tasks that government once did itself.

[3]So powerful are those engines of job creation that not even the recession could check their progress. Over the last year, companies in sectors as diverse as software, skiing, hospitals, and private bus services have added a total of 600,000 jobs, even while overall employment was sinking.

[4]*New Collars.* If history is any guide, that's a sign of many more job openings to come. Industries with enough vigor to grow during hard times typically explode once the economy improves. Look back at the recession of 1981–'82: Financial, legal, and business services all began hiring months before that downturn ended. In the end, they became some of the biggest job producers of the 1980s.

[5]The expansion of the 1980s was the sort of boom that comes along once a generation. The coming recovery almost certainly won't be nearly as strong. Moreover, few new jobs will be of the skilled, well-paid, blue-collar variety that is fast vanishing from the U.S. Nor will some white-collar workers, laid off from a bank or defense company, easily make the shift to the new growth sectors. But the economy of the 1990s will produce its share of good jobs. Here's where you're likely to find many of them:

**FINDING THE HIRING KIND**

CHANGE IN PAYROLL EMPLOYMENT (FEBRUARY,1991-FEBRUARY, 1992)

**INFORMATION SERVICES**

SOFTWARE AND DATA PROCESSING, DIRECT MAIL, AND GRAPHICS SERVICES

| 7.1 % |

With more than 50 million personal computers in U.S. homes and offices, companies providing the software, networks, and services will need more people

**HEALTH CARE**

PRIVATE HEALTH SERVICES, PUBLIC HOSPITALS AND CLINICS, RELATED INDUSTRIES (BIOTECH, PHARMACEUTICALS, ETC.)

| 4.6 % |

More elderly people mean rising demand for health care and the workers who provide it. Advances in biotech and other high-tech health sectors will stimulate whole new industries

**PRIVATIZATION**

PRIVATE LOCAL AND SUBURBAN TRANSIT, PRIVATE SANITARY SERVICES

| 4.7% |

Despite enormous state and local deficits, taxpayers want more government services. The solution: Let the private sector do it

**LEISURE**

AMUSEMENT AND RECREATION SERVICES, TOY AND SPORTING GOODS MAKERS

| 2.4% |

Aging baby boomers will have more time and money to spend on leisure. Rising real income will boost spending on vacations and recreational sports

– 0.3% **TOTAL NONFARM EMPLOYMENT**

DATA: BUREAU OF LABOR STATISTICS, BW

⁶•*Information Services.* Software, data processing, and computer-services companies employ over 800,000 people, more than the auto makers—and they're growing. Personal computer software sales will rise 24% this year, estimates market researcher International Data Corp. Microsoft Corp. added more than 3,000 workers in 1991. Cincinnati-based Structural Dynamics Research Corp., a supplier of software used to design everything from auto parts to satellites, last year hired 100 new programmers, marketers, and customer service personnel. And CEO Ronald J. Friedsam expects to add another 150 employees to the payroll in 1992.

⁷As people start trading vast quantities of text and video across networks, companies will spring up to help transmit, coordinate, and sift through all that information, predicts Jacqueline C. Morby, a senior partner with TA Associates, a venture capital firm in Boston. Information providers will grow as well. One example: Ohio-based Mead Data Central Inc., which publishes on-line data bases, added about 100 workers in 1991.

⁸•*Privatization.* Want to work for the commonweal? Try the private sector. "States will continue to have fiscal stress for most of the 1990s," says Steven Gold, director of the Center for the Study of the States. At the same time, taxpayers want better service. In response, more and more governments will turn to private companies to run prisons, collect garbage, and drive buses.

⁹That's how San Diego expanded bus service to outlying suburbs without draining scarce tax revenues. Today, half of all bus routes in sprawling San Diego County are run by private contractors. Nationwide, while public transit jobs declined by 2,000 over the last year, private local transit employment rose by 5,000, the Labor Dept. reports.

¹⁰Privatization is also creating new jobs at Wackenhut Corp., the giant Florida security company. Wackenhut manages nine prisons in the U.S., employs parking-meter attendants in Anchorage,

and runs two of the nation's largest job training programs. Robert C. Kneip, senior vice-president for planning and development, expects Wackenhut's government service jobs to grow at an annual rate of more than 10% over the next decade, producing openings for security guards, managers, and vocational-education teachers, among others.

[11]•***Leisure.*** If the quintessential 1980s worker was a bank manager or a retail clerk, the 1990s counterpart may be an amusement park owner or an aerobics instructor. As baby boomers and their children grow older, they will spend more on travel and leisure activities. Hints of the trend already show up in consumer-spending patterns. Since the recession started in July, 1990, total consumer spending, adjusted for inflation, has risen only 1.2%. But outlays on toys, sporting goods, and participant sports have risen by 8.1%.

[12]The ski industry, for example, is benefiting from "a boomlet of baby-boomer children, who are going skiing and bringing their parents back to the sport," says John I. Lay, president of Colorado Ski Country USA, which represents 25 areas in the state. Jobs in the skiing industry are expected to grow 3% to 5% a year, and some ski resorts could even have trouble hiring all the maids and ticket takers they need, Lay reports.

[13]The same demographic changes are also fueling growth at Discovery Zone, a Kansas City-based company that franchises indoor playgrounds. For a small fee, children can crawl through plastic piping and slide into wading pools filled with colorful balls. This year, Discovery Zone went from 121 sites to nearly 200. "We didn't just create a new business here, we created a new industry," boasts Jack V. Gunion, president and chief executive of Discovery Zone.

[14]And there has been no downturn in toyland. Ohio-based Little Tikes Co., which makes toys for preschoolers, added 500 people to its payroll last year, a 25% increase. It expects a similar gain this year. With sales booming here and abroad, "we never really felt the recession at all," says Gary S. Baughman, head of Little Tikes, a division of Rubbermaid Inc.

[15]•***Health.*** Job-seekers long have looked to health care as one of their most dependable sources of openings. That's not going to change any time soon, especially as the number of people age 75 and over climbs sharply in the 1990s. Even attempts at cost-cutting can't stop the big health care job machine. "Now, patients are coming out of the hospital quicker and sicker," says Charles H. Blanchard, CEO of Caremark Inc., Baxter International Inc.'s fast-growing home health care subsidiary. That means more work for Caremark, which sends nurses and other health care workers to patient's homes. The company had to boost its nursing staff by 40% last year, and it expects to keep hiring in 1992.

[16]The stock market can take some credit for furious hiring by biotech companies. Since early 1991, more than 100 companies have raised about $5 billion in new equity. That means many hundreds of job openings, predicts Cynthia Robbins-Roth, editor of *BioVenture View,* an industry newsletter. Take CellPro Inc., of Bothell, Wash., a company in the red-hot field of cellular and gene therapy. Having

raised $35 million in an initial public offering last September, the company expects to add 60 workers by yearend, more than doubling its payroll.

[17]The new workers aren't just high-paid, Ph.D.-toting molecular biologists. Newspapers in such hotbeds of biotech as San Francisco and Boston run columns of want ads seeking high school or college graduates who can wash test tubes and assist the scientists. says Robbins-Roth: "It's beginning to get difficult to find people at the technician level."

[18]Those kinds of worries are good news for job-hunters with the right stuff. The long dry period for American workers is not over yet. But if you know where to look, you can see the job opportunities of the 1990s already starting to beckon.

### Content Questions

*True or False*

If the statement is false, rewrite it to make it true.

1. The job outlook in all sectors is poor into the year 2000.
2. Americans are expected to spend more money on travel and leisure activities in the future.
3. The health care industry will continue to be a good source of jobs.
4. In the future you will have to have a Ph.D. to work in the biotechnology field.
5. Toy sales have been hard-hit by the recession.

*Completion*

6. In the '90s, what four major sectors are jobs likely to be found in?
7. In what two areas will the aging of America mean job growth?
8. Because of rising costs, local governments may begin hiring private companies to provide services. List three examples of such services.
9. List four areas of information services.
10. Why is the home health care industry growing?

### Vocabulary

1. titans (¶1)
2. harried job-hunter (¶2)
3. engines of job creation (¶3)
4. vigor to grow (¶4)
5. want to work for the commonweal (¶8)
6. fiscal stress (¶8)

### Content Analysis Questions

1. Write a one paragraph summary of *Where the Jobs Are*.
2. What does "the graying of America" mean? What implications does it have for the job market? How does the authors' view of the graying of

America fit with Griffin and Ebert's view in their textbook chapter *Recognizing Business Trends and Challenges?*

3. What does "privatization" mean in this context? What is the impact of privatization on workers?

4. Who do the authors predict will be the quintessential workers of the 1990s? What does that mean? Why the change from the '80s?

5. What information does the chart "Finding the Hiring Kind" add to the article?

6. What was the most surprising employment prediction for you? Why?

**Application Questions**

1. If you were going to start a new business this year, what effect would this information have on you? What effect do you think this information should have on your current career plans? On the career plans of your classmates?

2. What career planning advice would you give an eighth-grader? What career planning advice would you give a high school senior?

# Current Situation: Contingent Work Force

## CQ RESEARCHER STAFF

[1]Despite the many jobs disappearing across the spectrum of American industry, the unemployment rate measures a surprisingly low 7.1 percent of the labor force. That's high compared with normal economic conditions but by no means as dramatic as the reports of permanent job losses would suggest. During the 1981–82 recession, for example, unemployment peaked at more than 11 percent.

[2]One reason for the relatively low jobless figure is that many unemployed people have simply stopped looking for work. The Labor Department estimates that these "discouraged workers," who are not included in the unemployment figures, number 1.1 million.

[3]Also left out of the statistics are 6.7 million people doing part-time work because they couldn't find acceptable full-time positions. "What we've got is large numbers of people cobbling together an income by doing less than a full week of work," says Audrey Freedman a labor economist at The Conference Board, a business research organization in New York. She calls this approach to the job market "the contingent way of piecing together a living."

[4]The actual number of people who have joined the contingent work force is unknown. That's because the Labor Department has no measure for this group of workers. Some analysts, including Dan Lacey, editor of the newsletter *Workplace Trends,* and economist Richard Belous, who have studied the matter in some detail, estimate that contingent workers make up as much as a third of the total U.S. work force.

[5]But BLS economist Tom Nardone is skeptical, especially since the total may include not only poorly paid temporary and fastfood workers but also well-heeled consultants as well as doctors and lawyers who are self-employed. "It all comes down to a question of

job security, and that is very hard to measure," he says. "The point is, how many lousy jobs are there? We don't have a measure for that."

⁶Whatever the number of workers involved, everyone agrees that there is a marked shift toward contingent workers, and that the change makes sense for business. For one thing, the shift can save employers a lot on fringe benefits, especially health insurance, whose costs are rising faster than any other employer-provided benefit. "If you look at who gets health insurance from their employers, it's much less frequent among part-time workers than among full-time workers," says Nardone, who adds that only 67 percent of full-timers have health coverage.

⁷Reducing the in-house payroll may also help companies become more competitive, says Freedman, enabling them to quickly change their products, their marketing techniques, even their factory or retail locations in response to new business conditions. "The rapidity with which they can adapt is very much affected by whether they have a long-term, stable kind of work force or whether they can pick and choose, in effect, by going to the supermarket and picking up a new crop of people to handle something that may not last more than three months," she says.

⁸According to Freedman, many companies turned to the contingent labor market in the 1980s. IBM is typical. As the company pared its permanent, full-time work force, it brought in outside firms to handle certain operations; it currently has contracts with 1,400 vendors and suppliers and employs about 33,000 contingent workers. "The trend is definitely to contract out to vendors the support-type services we need," says company spokeswoman Ryan. For example, Marriott Corp., the hotel and food service chain, operates some of IBM's cafeterias, while Manpower Inc., a temporary-help agency, provides clerical and secretarial services as well as more highly skilled workers.

⁹Sears also contracts out for many former in-house functions, including maintenance, typesetting, advertising and transportation. "To be competitive today," says spokesman Gordon Jones, "we have to have the cost structure that our competitors do, and one of the ways our competitors keep their costs down is by having outside companies do the work." While Sears offers health and other benefits to some of its permanent part-time workers, so-called "part-time regulars" who put in 30 hours a week, Jones acknowledges that many of the contingent workers do not receive benefits from the subcontractors.

¹⁰"If those outside companies provide minimal benefits, it's probably going to be one of the ways they hold their costs down when we go to them," he says. "In terms of the social impact on the country, I'm sure our senior executives are concerned, but at the same time there's the need to be competitive."

## CORE VS. CONTINGENT WORKERS

¹¹As more and more companies hire contingent workers, some experts say serious morale problems could arise between these lower-paid employees and the better-paid permanent, or "core," workers they often work with. Former United Auto Workers President Douglas Fraser cites the problems that arose in the early 1980s, when airlines and other troubled industries tried to cut personnel

costs by introducing the "two-tier" wage scale, which gave much lower pay to new hires—even when they had better skills than the older workers.

[12]"People lived with it for awhile," Fraser says, "but [the system caused] such friction that the companies that had two-tier just threw up their hands in despair. You rarely see it anymore."

[13]Two-tier wage scales may be on the wane, but some of the same problems afflict contingent work. "There's a big question about who's taking whose job away, and why somebody working side by side on the same job is earning half as much, with no security, no benefits and in most cases no union," says Thomas Kochan, a professor of management and human resources at MIT.

[14]For their part, Kochan adds, the permanent workers "feel that the company has an incentive to give all the work to these cheap folks and take their jobs away." He cites studies showing how resentment between core and contingent workers may even pose physical threats in certain industries, such as oil and chemical manufacturing, where safety risks already abound.

[15]Safety aside, Kochan says contingent work may do more long-term harm than good, even to the companies that promote it to improve productivity. "I don't think this employment relationship is good for the economy," he says. "You've got to have solid personal relationships to get along and solve problems in groups. You have to understand the culture and the setting because that's all part of what an organization is about."

[16]If contingent work becomes entrenched in the labor market, Kochan predicts, "quality and productivity will go down."

## CONTINGENT WORK SPREADS

[17]Once typified by the "Kelly Girl" and other low-level white-collar temporaries, contingent workers are no longer confined to low-wage occupations. "Contingent work is creeping up and becoming much more high-level white collar," Belous says, as corporations begin to subcontract for accountants and providers of other financial services.

[18]But contingent work has also moved much more into blue-collar occupations, particularly through "leasing" of employees for specific tasks. Leasing allows corporations to delegate a task to an agency that assumes all responsibility for the personnel who do the work. Although some leasing agencies provide benefits to their workers, Belous says they are usually less generous than benefits the corporation would normally provide full-time workers. He adds, "It's not unusual to read about some unscrupulous leasing operation that told its employees they had benefits but just pocketed the money."

[19]Contingent workers have fewer defenses against such abuses than full-time workers. "Unions have their collective backs to the wall," says well-known economist Robert Reich, citing the fall in union membership to a mere 13 percent of the work force today. "In most industries, the unions are only a pale reflection of their former selves," he says. "It's very difficult for the unions to put contingent workers at the top of an agenda that's already crowded with the demands by unionized workers for protection from other corporate incursions."

[20]The move to contingent work is not bad for everyone, of course, especially among professional, managerial and technical workers. They can sell their special skills more easily to a number of clients than, say, a laborer or an assembler. "Contingent workers don't necessarily make less," says Dan Lacey. "Some who are consultants make a lot of money. So contingent working is not necessarily downward mobility, but it is certainly less predictable than the paycheck."

[21]Belous agrees that contingent work can prove beneficial for some workers. "Many workers view it as a way to gain increased freedom, and that's what they want. And let's face it, a lot of corporations would be out of business without contingent workers. It's not an unmitigated evil."

## Content Questions

*True or False*

If the statement is false, rewrite it to make it true.

1. Today's unemployment rate is higher than ever before.
2. It is estimated that as many as $\frac{1}{3}$ of the U.S. work force is made up of contingent workers.
3. The shift to more contingent workers makes good economic sense for most businesses.
4. Contingent workers are only found in low-level, blue-collar jobs.
5. Morale problems are likely to increase as more contingent workers are hired.

*Completion*

6. Cite one reason for the relatively low unemployment figure.
7. Name three examples of contingent workers.
8. Identify three reasons companies are hiring more contingent workers.
9. List two reasons some workers like contingent work.
10. Name three reasons for potential friction between core and contingent workers.

## Vocabulary

1. pared (¶8)
2. wane (¶13)
3. entrenched (¶16)
4. incursions (¶19)
5. not an unmitigated evil (¶21)

## Content Analysis Questions

1. What is a "contingent" worker? What is a "core" worker?
2. What is the major reason that companies are hiring more contingent workers and less core workers? Do you think this benefit outweighs the potential disadvantages?

3. What is Thomas Kochan's point of view on the increasing use of contingent workers and its effects? Give examples to support your answer.

4. In what ways do you think the increased hiring of contingent workers can help the quality agenda? In what ways could it be detrimental?

5. What does Belous mean by "It's not an unmitigated evil?" Do you agree/disagree? Explain.

### Application Questions

1. What companies in your local area make use of contingent workers, outside vendors, and/or leased employees? Does your college? What do you think their reasons are? Do you agree/disagree with their rationale?

2. What are two reasons a person might choose contingent work? Under what circumstances would you choose contingent work?

# *Disposable Workers: New Corporate Policies Put Many Older Employees at Risk*

### ROBERT LEWIS

*Robert Lewis is the editor of the* NRTA Bulletin, *a publication of the National Retired Teachers Association division of AARP, from which this selection is taken.*

¹For many older Americans a part-time or temporary job is the ticket to retirement comfort. It generates extra income and provides an outside interest, yet still allows time for leisurely pursuits.

²But for sizable numbers of Americans still a few years shy of retirement, it is quite another story.

³For Barbara McCarthy, for instance, a temporary job became a ticket to the poor house. A marketing and public relations professional, McCarthy, who is in her 50s and lives in Chicago, became an office "temp" in 1990 after her $40,000-a-year full-time job was abolished.

⁴Her income plunged by more than half and she lost her employer-financed health insurance.

⁵"It's the most frightening thing I ever lived through," says McCarthy. "I look at homeless people a lot differently now; it could happen to me."

⁶McCarthy isn't alone in these fears. She is among a burgeoning group of workers age 50 and older who now find themselves clinging to jobs in one of the most risky and unpredictable sectors of the American workplace—the so called contingent work force.

⁷Like McCarthy, most people holding "contingent" jobs get low pay, receive few benefits and, perhaps most troubling of all, enjoy little or no job security. All too often, such jobs end abruptly, with little or no warning.

⁸Yet, contingent work is on the rise. Consisting of part-time, temporary, contract and various types of free-lance jobs, the contingent labor force grew faster than full-time employment during the 1980s.

[9]As a result, contingent workers now hold one in four jobs in America—a total of about 30 million. Not all are happy about this. According to one estimate, more than one million persons age 50 and older are working involuntarily at a part-time, temporary or some other kind of contingent job.

[10]Nominally full-timers, they work at contingent jobs because they're the only kind they can get.

[11]Of course, part-time and temporary jobs aren't new, and they make sense for a lot of people despite their drawbacks. Retirees under age 70, for example, often find full-time work impractical because they lose Social Security benefits if their incomes exceed a certain ceiling.

[12]Many women with care-giving duties also seek part-time jobs. Not surprisingly, women hold three out of five part-time jobs for the 55- and older population.

[13]What is new about part-time, temporary and other contingent workers is the way they're being used by employers these days: as commodities to be plugged into the workplace on an "as-needed" basis, and then to be dispensed with very much like water cooler refills or Dixie cups.

[14]Increasingly, says Martin Sicker, director of the AARP Work Force Programs Department, corporations are moving toward a new "core-ring" job strategy that, in effect, cuts labor costs by converting full-time jobs to contingent jobs.

[15]Under this approach, relatively small numbers of full-time employees (the core) are augmented by contingent workers (the ring) who are hired—and released—to meet cyclical or temporary work demands.

[16]By using contingent workers, labor economists say, employers gain flexibility that allows them to fine-tune payrolls to match business cycles. Labor costs dip because part-time workers typically do not receive health insurance, pensions or paid vacations.

[17]They also are paid less, on average, than those on full-time schedules. In 1990, part-time employees earned 63 cents for every dollar paid to full-time employees, reports the Bureau of Labor Statistics. The disparity for temporary workers was 77 cents.

[18]Despite these shortcomings, most people age 50 and older who work part-time do so by choice, says BLS economist Thomas Nardone.

[19]But the current economic slump, coupled with recent dislocations in the economy, is pushing up the proportion of contingent workers who occupy such jobs involuntarily—because no others are available.

[20]Brandeis University economist James H. Schulz says large numbers of older workers whose careers are being cut short by corporate downsizing are using contingent jobs as a "bridge" to provide income until they reach retirement age.

[21]The transition isn't easy, however. Harold Titus, 51, of Brooklyn, N.Y., thought he would have no trouble finding a new job when he was laid off a year ago as accounting manager for an asset management group. When nothing materialized he took a temporary job—at four-tenths his old salary.

[22]For the wage-earner who needs the income from full-time employment, settling for half a job can be a financial calamity, as Marlene Thornell of Duluth, Minn., discovered six years ago. After earning $7.95 an hour as a counselor in a mental health facility, she now gets $4.25 as a part-time receptionist, surviving with the help of subsidized rent and state medical assistance.

[23]Quite frequently people forced to take contingent work find themselves shunted into low-paying service jobs.

[24]Consider Jeanne Rellahan, a professor of American history at Hawaii Pacific University, who moved to Washington, D.C., last summer. She figured her doctorate degree would lead to a job in the humanities.

[25]When nothing came up, Rellahan, 50, had no choice but to accept a temporary job at the Kennedy Center selling ballet tickets by phone for $4.25 an hour plus commissions. "It was numbing work," she says.

[26]Boredom, however, often coexists with fear. "The real problem with contingent work is that it's just so insecure," says Sara E. Rix, senior analyst with the AARP Public Policy Institute. "You always have to be thinking about the next job."

[27]With the contingent work force continuing to swell, some lawmakers are moving to close the wage and benefit gap between full- and part-time workers.

[28]Rep. Pat Schroeder, D-Colo., last year introduced a bill that would require employers to provide prorated health and pension benefits to part-time employees if they provide such perks to full-time workers. Hearings on the legislation are expected this spring.

[29]Another proposal, by Rep. Tom Lantos, D, seeks to end what he calls a "serious, widespread and growing" problem: the misclassification of workers as independent contractors when they are actually regular employees.

[30]Lantos says companies use this device to escape paying Social Security and unemployment compensation taxes, and to avoid the costs of withholding federal and state income taxes. The disadvantage for employees: They have to pay the employer's share (7.65 percent) of Social Security taxes, and they lose some protections of federal labor laws.

[31]The House Ways and Means Committee is planning hearings later this year on Lantos' bill and two similar proposals.

[32]Whatever happens to this pending legislation, the contingent work force will continue to grow until it accounts for one in three jobs, predicts Richard S. Belous, senior economist with the National Planning Association.

[33]This could open up new work opportunities for many older persons, Belous says. But these new positions could entail a stiff

price: a breakdown in the traditional relationship between employer and employee.

[34]Contingent work, he says, is "leading us to a world where most of us will realize there's no such thing as a corporate womb."

**Content Questions**

*True or False*

If the statement is false, rewrite it to make it true.

1. Contingent work is often good for retired people.
2. The contingent labor force grew faster than full-time employment in the 1980s.
3. On average, contingent workers earn the same pay as core workers.
4. The contingent work force is expected to grow until it accounts for half of the jobs in the U.S.
5. Most people aged 50 or older who work part-time do so by choice.

*Completion*

6. Identify four disadvantages of contingent work for employees.
7. List two advantages of contingent work for employers.
8. Why do retirees under the age of 70 often choose contingent work?
9. How would Rep. Schroeder's (D-CO) legislation help contingent workers?
10. Name four artifacts of a disposable society.

**Vocabulary**

1. burgeoning (¶6)
2. commodities (¶12)
3. augmented (¶14)
6. subsidized (¶21)
7. prorated (¶27)

**Content Analysis Questions**

1. Who is the intended audience? How do you know?
2. What is Lewis's thesis? How does he develop and support his thesis?
3. What is Lewis's point of view on contingent workers? Give examples to support your answer.
4. What is the purpose of the illustration?
5. Explain the core-ring concept.
6. Compare and contrast Lewis's article with the article "Current Situation: Contingent Work Force."

**Application Question**

1. A 52-year-old friend of yours was just notified that the plant where he's worked as a manager for the last 20 years is closing in three weeks and he will be out of a job. He asks your advice. What alternatives do you ask him to consider?

# Glossary

**annotate** a way to highlight and organize main ideas and details by writing brief, useful information in the margins of a text

**argument** the author's thesis that is intended to convince the reader, through logical evidence, to think, feel, or behave in a certain way

**bias** an author's personal slant on a topic

**caption** a brief description of the contents of a graphic

**column** vertical lines of data in a table

**comprehension monitoring strategies** tactics to make certain that the reader's understanding is satisfactory for his or her purpose

**connotation; connotative** the implied meaning of a word triggered by the feelings and emotions it creates

**context** the meaning of words taken from their context—how they are used in conjunction with other words

**context clue** information an author provides within the sentence or paragraph to help the reader understand important words

**controlling thought** what the author wants the reader to know or understand about the topic

**critical reader** one who comprehends, questions, clarifies, and analyzes in order to reach objective, reasoned judgments

**denotation; denotative** a word's literal, dictionary meaning

**description; descriptive** text that paints a picture using words

**diagram** a general term that refers to any type of drawing an author uses to help the reader understand ideas, objects, plans, processes or sequences

**directly stated main idea** the topic and controlling thought in a sentence; often called a topic sentence

**Do** the second phase of the Plan»Do»Review cycle; requires active physical and mental involvement

**evidence** the facts and opinions an author uses to support and develop a thesis or argument

**exposition; expository** text that explains, sets forth or makes clear facts, events, and ideas

**fact** objective information that is true; a fact can change over time as new discoveries are made

**figurative language** words used in an imaginative way to help the reader comprehend the message more clearly by forming a mental image, or picture, of what an author is talking about; figurative expressions often compare something the author thinks the reader knows to what he or she wants the reader to understand

**flow chart** a type of diagram that uses boxes, rectangles, diamonds, or circles with connecting lines or arrows, to show the step-by-step procedure of a complicated process

**graph** a type of graphic that uses bars or lines to show the relationships between or among quantities

**graphic** any visual that an author uses to highlight, clarify or illustrate (often through an example), summarize, or add to the text information

**implied main idea** the author doesn't directly state the main idea and leaves it up to the reader to piece together the information from all the sentences and infer, or put together, the main idea

**infer; inference** the best reasoned conclusion based on the information given

**information map** a type of graphic organizer for main ideas and details that uses different size boxes or circles and different size type to create a picture of the relationships among the ideas

**irony; ironic** text that says the opposite of what the author means

**key; legend** a reference point on a graphic that defines the codes being used

**literal meaning** dictionary definition

**main idea** the combination of the topic and the controlling thought

**major supporting detail** a specific piece of information that directly supports and explains a main idea

**map** a diagram that depicts all or part of the earth's three-dimensional surface on a two-dimensional flat surface

**metaphor** a type of figurative language that uses an implied comparison

**methods of development** how an author develops and supports the thesis or main ideas; the structure he or she gives the information. Six common methods of development are *example, comparison and/or contrast, division and classification, cause and effect, process,* and *definition.*

**minor supporting detail** a very specific piece of information that supports and explains a major detail

**multi-paragraph selection** a group of related paragraphs—each with a main idea—that supports and explains one thesis, or overall main idea; for example, an essay or text chapter

**narration; narrative** text that tells a story

**objectively analyze** impartial examination of the author's ideas and information separate from the reader's personal opinions and biases

**opinion** subjective information that cannot be proved true or false; an opinion is not right or wrong or good or bad but, depending on the amount and type of evidence the author examined before forming the opinion, it can be deemed valid or invalid

**outline** a type of graphic organizer for main ideas and details that uses differing amounts of indentation to create a picture of the relationships among the ideas

**paragraph** a group of related sentences that support and explain one main idea

**persuasion; persuasive** text that influences the reader by engaging his or her emotions or by presenting logical arguments to make the reader believe or feel a certain way or take a particular action

**pie chart; circle graph** a type of graphic that illustrates the ratio of the values of a category to the total; the whole pie or circle represents 100% and various segments, or pieces of the pie, show relative magnitude or frequencies

**Plan** the first phase of a Plan»Do»Review cycle; developing a plan is based on a reading assignment's two critical factors: (1) the purpose for reading the assignment, and (2) how difficult the material is

**Plan»Do»Review cycle** the approach that encourages the reader to become more successful at reading for learning; the reader *plans* before beginning, *does* the reading actively, *reviews* what has been read, and continues to *plan, do,* and *review* until comprehension goals are met

**point of view** the author's position or opinion on the topic

**pre-reading strategies** tactics that prime the reader's brain and give him or her a head start on good comprehension

**prefix** a word part added to the beginning of a root word to change its meaning

**preview** looking over material before beginning to read to get a general understanding of the organization and core ideas

**prose** writing other than poetry

**purpose** an author's reason for writing

**reliable** a fair analysis of the topic without undue influence from others

**Review** the third phase of the Plan»Do»Review cycle; information is put into perspective and the reader begins working to remember it; without good review, spaced over time, the reader will probably forget as much as 80% of what was read

**root word** the basic part of a word

**row** horizontal lines of data in a table

**satire; sarcasm** an ironic tone that uses ridicule, mockery, exaggeration and understatement to poke fun at people and deride foolish or dishonest human behaviors

**scale** a map element that shows the relationship between a length measured on a map and the corresponding distance on the ground

**signal word** words or phrases to point the reader in a specific direction of thought or to alert the reader to particular types of information

**simile** a type of figurative language that makes direct comparisons using the words "like" or "as"

**stance** the author's position on a subject

**strategy** an action a reader consciously selects to achieve a particular goal; strategies are means to an end

**suffix** a word part added to the end of a root word to change its meaning or the way it can be used in a sentence

**summary; summarize** a condensed version of the original; it begins with a restatement of the thesis or main idea and includes the main ideas and/or major supporting details in the same order and with the same emphasis as the original

**table** a graphic that provides several pieces of specific data, often numbers or statistics, arranged systematically in rows and columns; the information often compares qualities or quantities or shows how things change over time

**thesis** the primary idea of a multi-paragraph selection that combines the main ideas of all the paragraphs; the frame that holds the paragraphs of the essay or chapter together

**tone** the emotional feeling or attitude created with words

**topic** the *who* or *what* of the text

**word analysis** defining a word by defining its root and any prefixes and/or suffixes

# Suggested Answers for Practice Exercises

## Chapter 2

### PRACTICE: IDENTIFYING THE AUTHOR'S PURPOSE

1. exposition and perhaps persuasion
2. description
3. exposition and perhaps persuasion
4. exposition
5. narration and exposition

## Chapter 3

### PRACTICE: DEFINING WORDS USING CONTEXT CLUES

Always fit your definition back into the context to be certain it makes sense.

1. *slant*—their approach to the topic; I use punctuation as a clue
2. *Like terms* are terms that have the same variables with the same exponents; Angel gives a specific definition

3. *physical units (i.e.,* quantity of production, number of errors), *time* (i.e., meeting deadlines, coming to work each day), or *money* (i.e., profits, sales costs); Robbins gives examples to define each term

4. *tempo,* or overall speed; Politoske provides a definition

5. Computerphobia, the fear of computers, . . . This relatively recent phenomenon, also known as *cyberphobia;* authors relate word to a word they have just defined

6. Although a person who is *chronically* drunk, as opposed to the occasional drinker; author gives clue by stating the opposite

## PRACTICE: DEFINING WORDS USING WORD PARTS

Always fit your definition back into the context to be certain it makes sense.

1. *biodiversity;* (bio = living organisms; divers = different; ity = state) having a variety of living things
   *unreplaceable:* (un = not; able = capable of) cannot be replaced

2. *illiterate:* (il = not; literate = able to read and write) not able to read and write

3. *telecommunications:* (tele = over a distance; communications = exchanging/transmitting information, signals, messages) exchanging/transmitting information, signals, messages over a distance

4. *empowerment:* (em = within; ment = action) encouraging action from within the community

5. *intrapersonal:* (intra = within) communication within yourself
   *interpersonal:* (inter = among, between) communication between/among people

6. *microbial:* (micro = small; bios = living organisms; al = characterized by) populated by tiny organisms

## PRACTICE: SELECTING THE BEST DICTIONARY DEFINITION

Always fit your definition back into the context to be certain it makes sense.

1. *harmony:* definition 1—a combination of parts into a pleasing or orderly whole

2. *acute:* definition 6—very serious; critical; crucial

3. *critically:* definition 2—characterized by careful analysis and judgment

4. *front:* definition 18—the boundary between two air masses of different density and temperature

5. *radical:* definition 1b—extreme

## PRACTICE: DEFINING WORDS USING OUTSIDE RESOURCES

Always fit your definition back into the context to be certain it makes sense.

In addition to the definition, name the resource you used to find your definition.

1. *megalopolis:* a large, heavily populated, continuously urban area
   *notorious:* widely but unfavorably known
2. *Gutenberg revolution:* the invention of moveable type by Gutenberg
3. *preemptory force:* commanding presence
4. *pervasive:* dominant
   *apt metaphor:* appropriate comparisons
5. *raison d'être:* reason for being

## PRACTICE: DEFINING WORDS USING CONTEXT CLUES, WORD PARTS AND OTHER RESOURCES

Always fit your definition back into the context to be certain it makes sense.

1. *accelerating loss:* rapidly-increasing losses
2. *habitat destruction:* loss of native environments
3. *exploitation:* unethical uses
4. *predation:* killing by another animal

## PRACTICE: CONSIDERING BOTH THE CONNOTATIVE AND DENOTATIVE MEANINGS

There is not just one correct answer. Discuss your answers with your classmates and instructor.

1. a. *jock:* athlete (negative)       b. *athlete:* person trained in sports (positive)

2. a. *reserved:* self-restrained (positive)       b. *inhibited:* unresponsive (negative)

3. a. *collect:* gather (positive)       b. *hoard:* accumulate (negative)

4. a. *impertinent:* rude (negative)       b. *bold:* confident (positive)

1. *unsuccessfully peddling his idea to every monarch of Western Europe*—message: negative; more neutral phrase: unsuccessfully presenting his idea . . .

2. *crushing black leaders, inflating the images of Uncle Toms, able to channel and control the aspirations and goals of the black masses*—message: strong emotional negatives; more neutral phrases: by discrediting black leaders while encouraging . . . were able to influence many black youths.

3. *quintessential yuppie mother*—message: has many connotations—may tend to trivialize; more neutral phrase: outstanding working mother

4. *so-called God Squad*—message: negative; more neutral phrase: the commission

## PRACTICE: UNDERSTANDING FIGURATIVE LANGUAGE

Always fit your definition back into the context to be certain it makes sense. There is not just one correct answer. Discuss your answers with your classmates and instructor.

1. *hew out of the mountain of despair a stone of hope:* comparing mining a single stone out of a mountain to mining hope out of despair—both take time and a great deal of work
*transform the jangling discords of our nation into a beautiful symphony of brotherhood:* comparing humanity to music—both can be clashing and noisy at times but can also sound together in harmony

2. *performance improvement efforts . . . have as much impact on operational and financial results as a ceremonial rain dance has on the weather:* comparing performance improvement efforts and a ceremonial rain dance—both have little effect

3. *The year 2000 is operating like a powerful magnet on humanity:* comparing the year 2000 and a powerful magnet—the pull of both is great

4. *classrooms of the '90s are now more or less jam-packed with computer terminals:* comparing the rooms full of computers to a jar of jam—both stuffed full
*a spaghetti feast of electronic wiring:* comparing how the wires look to a bowl of spaghetti—both contain an intertwined maze of chords

5. *The flowering of Etruscan civilization:* comparing the development of the Etruscan civilization to the development of a flower—both open slowly and produce beautiful results

6. *Ted Turner . . . is crazy like a fox:* comparing Ted Turner to a fox—both are very crafty

# Chapter 4

## PRACTICE: IDENTIFYING DIRECTLY STATED MAIN IDEAS

Although there is not just one correct answer, you should include these ideas. Discuss your answers with your classmates and instructor.

1. To be successful in school, students must be able to understand and remember information presented in classroom lectures.

2. We created our twenty-four-hour society, in part, as a way to cut costs, a way to squeeze more output from our scarce resources.

3. The assessment of the economic status of the aged is far more complex than most popular articles and analyses suggest.

4. In spite of the good intentions of many writers, fictional characters are predominantly white and do not accurately portray reality.

5. Acne is caused by skin oils, not dirt or moisturizers.

## PRACTICE: IDENTIFYING IMPLIED MAIN IDEAS

Although there is not just one correct answer, you should include these ideas. Discuss your answers with your classmates and instructor.

1. The families portrayed in many past textbooks were not representative of American life.

2. Be sensitive to the variety of human relations challenges you will encounter on the job; give and expect equal treatment.

3. Thomas More was an extraordinary man, a true Renaissance humanist.

4. The enchanting and familiar surroundings reminded me of what I would be leaving.

5. The Federal Clean Air Act mandates are causing a variety of U.S. businesses and agencies to consider telecommuting as a work alternative.

## PRACTICE: IDENTIFYING MAIN IDEAS IN PARAGRAPHS

Although there is not just one correct answer, you should include these ideas. Discuss your answers with your classmates and instructor.

1. To keep pace with the rapidly changing workplace, business education has changed more in the last ten years than it did in the last century.

2. When your intended audience is a listener rather than a reader, you must write very differently.

3. It is generally accepted that adult behavior is acquired through a mix of genetic make-up and experience gained as the individual grows up.

4. Even if production of all ozone-destroying chemicals stopped today, those already in the atmosphere would go on destroying ozone well into the twenty-first century.

5. Although they are challenging to produce, 35mm slides usually make the best impression on an audience.

## PRACTICE: IDENTIFYING THE THESIS OF A MULTI-PARAGRAPH SELECTION

Although there is not just one correct answer, you should include these ideas. Discuss your answers with your classmates and instructor.

1. exposition

2. a. *vigorous:* lively
   b. *caloric intake and expenditure:* amount of calories eaten and used
   c. *sedentary:* not active

    d. *hydrate:* saturate with water

    e. *when no thirst sensations exist:* when you're not thirsty

    f. *electrolytes:* water, sodium, potassium, and chloride

    g. *precipitates nausea:* causes nausea

3. [1]Athletes and active individuals have a few special nutritional needs to meet the demands of *vigorous* activity, to prevent heat exhaustion and heat stroke, and to maximize and store energy from food.

4. [2]If you are neither losing nor gaining weight and have sufficient energy, you are probably taking in the correct number of calories daily.
[3]It is necessary to hydrate approximately fifteen minutes before exercising.
[4]Electrolytes should be replaced as rapidly as possible.
[5]Iron is the only nutrient that adolescent female and male athletes need in greater quantity.

# Chapter 5

## PRACTICE: DETERMINING THE RELATIONSHIPS AMONG DETAILS AND SENTENCES

Although there is not just one correct answer, you should include these ideas. Discuss your answers with your classmates and instructor.

1a. The origin of the term "Baroque" is uncertain.

1b. They provide an illustration or example; giving an example of possible derivations.

1c. It continues the thought by providing another example of a possible derivation.

2a. Couples seeking a divorce will not always find it easy to agree on issues that affect their children, but they should attempt to do so before telling their children about the impending separation.

2b. It provides specific examples of how children need to be prepared for their parents' divorce.

2c. Sentence 3 contains major details, because they directly explain and support the main idea.

3a. Various behavioral theories have been studied as they relate to health. These constructs influence how we view ourselves and also how we behave or seek to change behaviors.

3b. It provides examples of the behavioral theories that have been studied.

3c. They define each of the terms.

4a. Many North American Indian tribes made beautiful handicrafts while others lived very simply with few artifacts.

4b. It introduces a contrast.

4c. "however"

5a. Advertising plays an obvious role in the growth of the nation's economy.

5b. It summarizes.

6a. New machinery, technologies and materials permitted companies to become more efficient and productive.

6b. They provide examples of industries that became more productive.

6c. It provides examples of industries that gained efficiency from new technologies.

6d. It provides examples of industries that benefited from larger and more efficient machine tools and a wider variety of semifinished materials.

## PRACTICE: DETERMINING THE MAIN IDEA, SIGNIFICANT DETAILS, AND METHOD OF DEVELOPMENT

Although there is not just one correct answer, you should include these ideas. Discuss your answers with your classmates and instructor.

1a. The increasing age of the average worker is affecting business in two ways.

1b. Cause/effect—main idea is the cause; details are the effects

1c. "affected in two ways," "First," "And second"

1d. (1) older workers put greater demand on a company's health insurance, life insurance, and retirement benefit programs; (2) younger workers want different things from employers

2a. The most serious disciplinary problems facing managers involve attendance.

2b. examples

2c. probably the main idea

2d. probably more; you would need at least some detail

3a. Being shy can cause many problems for adults.

3b. examples of the effects of being shy

3c. being shy; excluded from social relationships, less likely to be promoted, often taken advantage of by salespeople

3d. It continues the thought by giving another effect.

4a. To be convincing, presentation graphics must be fitted to the message and to the audience.

4b. (1) develop a plan, (2) decide on one primary idea (theme), (3) state the idea in 12 words, (4) develop a complete outline, (5) decide on the time and the relative emphasis of each portion, (6) decide on the best way to illustrate, (7) draw small sketches of each visual

5a. Because public speaking differs from other forms of interaction in two important ways, communication difficulties often arise.

5b. (1) it includes two distinct and separate roles for speaker and audience; (2) the speaker carries primary responsibility

5c. communication difficulties

6a. We can influence people in our personal and professional lives in three basic ways.

6b. He divides or classifies ways to influence people.

6c. illustrations and/or examples for each of the three categories of influence

# Chapter 6

## PRACTICE: READING AND INTEGRATING A GRAPH AND WORDS

1a. temperature curves for San Diego (maritime climate) and Dallas (continental climate)

1b. to give an example of the concept

1c. You probably wouldn't need any detail from the graph. The "why" is stated in the paragraph, not in the graph.

2a. sources of money available for starting a new business and buying an existing business

2b. because it lists five specific resources

2c. personal resources

2d. lending institution

## PRACTICE: READING AND INTEGRATING A TABLE AND WORDS

3a. attitudes of entering college students in 1968 and 1987

3b. Table 3–1 adds details not covered in the paragraph.

3c. Significant increases in the categories "Improve reading and writing skills," "Get a better job," and "Make more money," (and perhaps even "Prepare for graduate or professional school")

## PRACTICE: READING AND INTEGRATING A PIE CHART AND WORDS

4a. how a typical item's price is increased from manufacturer to consumer

4b. Figure 19.2 gives an example of the concept of price markup.

4c. The manufacturer's cost for the item is $25.00. The consumer pays $60.38.

4d. Each member of the distribution chain marks up the item in order to make a profit. This information is in the paragraph.

## PRACTICE: READING AND INTEGRATING A DIAGRAM AND WORDS

5a. Figure 20.3 illustrates what the paragraph says.

5b. The map illustrates the Federal Reserve System's check clearing process.

5c. probably not; it's just to illustrate the process

5d. The author probably wants you to remember that the Fed serves commercial banks by clearing checks, and that it is a somewhat complicated process.

## PRACTICE: READING AND INTEGRATING A PHOTOGRAPH/ILLUSTRATION AND WORDS

6a. The illustration provides a specific example of the author's thesis.

6b. "What you 'see,' then, is the meaning your mind imposes on the data, and your mind can reprocess that data so that they represent something different."

# Chapter 7

## PRACTICE: ANNOTATING TEXT

Although there is not just one way to annotate this excerpt, consider these elements. Discuss your annotations with your classmates and instructor.

### READING HISTORY

*T* An understanding of the fundamentals of historical writing will make the student of history a more discerning and selective reader. Although no two historical works are identical, most contain the same basic elements and can be approached in a similar manner by the reader. When reading a historical monograph, concentrate on the two basic issues discussed in the preceding section: facts and interpretation.

*T: Understanding basics of hist writing can make me better rdr.*
*\* Most have same elements & approach is same*
*Impt: concentrate on ① facts ② interp*

*Ask: What is thesis/argument?*

***Interpretation.*** The first question the reader should ask is: What is the author's argument? What is his theme, his interpreta-
*Note:*
tion, his thesis? A theme is not the same as a topic. An author may select the Civil War as a topic, but he then must propose a particular theme or argument regarding some aspect of the war. (The most common, not surprisingly, is why the war occurred.)

Discovering the author's theme is usually easy enough because most writers state their arguments clearly in the preface to their book. Students often make the crucial error of skimming over the preface—if they read it at all—and then moving on to the "meat" of the book. Since the preface indicates the manner in which the author has used his data to develop his arguments, students who ignore it often find themselves overwhelmed with details without understanding what the author is attempting to say. This error should be avoided always.

*thesis often in preface*

The more history you read, the more you will appreciate the diversity of opinions and approaches among historians. While each

*history works can be categorized by thesis & date*

author offers a unique perspective, historical works fall into general categories, or "schools," depending on their thesis and when they were published. *DEF* The study of the manner in which different historians approach their subjects is referred to as *historiography*. Every historical subject has a historiography, sometimes limited, sometimes extensive. As in the other sciences, new schools of thought supplant existing ones, offering new insights and challenging accepted theories. Below are excerpts from two monographs dealing with the American Revolution. As you read them, note the contrast in the underlying arguments.

*ex. of differing p.o.v.*

*Degler: Revolution conserved not changed colonies*

1. "Despite its precedent-setting character, however, the American revolt is noteworthy because it made no serious interruption in the smooth flow of American development. Both in intention and in fact, the American Revolution conserved the past rather than repudiated it. And in preserving the colonial experience, the men of the first quarter century of the Republic's history set the scenery and wrote the script for the drama of American politics for years to come."*

*Jameson: Revolution major catalyst for change*

2. "The stream of revolution, once started, could not be confined within narrow banks, but spread abroad upon the land. Many economic desires, many social aspirations were set free by the political struggle, many aspects of colonial society profoundly altered by the forces thus set loose. The relations of social classes to each other, the institution of slavery, the system of landholding, of business, the forms and spirit of the intellectual and religious life, all felt the transforming hand of revolution, all emerged from under it in shapes advanced many degrees nearer to those we know."†

*\*Impt: writers have differing views— I must identify Read widely for perspective*

What you have just read is nothing less than two conflicting theories of the fundamental nature of the American Revolution. Professor Jameson portrays the Revolution as a catalyst for major social, economic, and political change, while Professor Degler views it primarily as a war for independence that conserved, rather than transformed, colonial institutions. The existence of such divergent opinions makes it* imperative that the reader be aware of the argument of every book and read a variety of books and articles to get different perspectives on a subject.

*historical bias not bad if I recognize it & if it doesn't distort*

All historical works contain biases of some sort, but a historical bias is not in itself bad or negative. As long as history books are composed by human beings, they will reflect the perspectives of their authors. This need not diminish the quality of historical writing if historians remain faithful to the facts. Some historians, however, have such strong biases that they distort the evidence to make it fit their preconceived notions. This type of history writing (which is the exception rather than the rule) is of limited value, but when properly treated can contribute to the accumulation of knowledge by providing new insights and challenging the values—and creative abilities—of other historians.

*Evidence: examine facts*

*Ask QS: type? convincing? sources? adequate?*

*\*Impt: good wk uses convincing data from comp. services*

*goal: be critical reader*

*① assess strengths & weaknesses*

*② be open-minded*

*③ do not accept all _or_ reject all*

***Evidence.*** Once you are aware of the author's central argument, you can concentrate on his use of evidence—the "facts"—that buttress that argument. There are several types of questions that you should keep in mind as you progress through a book. What types of evidence does the author use? Is his evidence convincing? Which sources does he rely on, and what additional sources might he have consulted? One strategy you might adopt is to imagine that you are writing the monograph. Where would you go for information? What would you look at? Then ask yourself: Did the author consult these sources? Obviously no writer can examine everything. A good historical work, however, *offers convincing data extracted from a comprehensive collection of materials.

As you begin to ask these questions, you will develop the skill of critical reading. Used in this sense the word critical does not mean reading to discern what is wrong with the narrative. Rather, it refers to analytic reading, assessing the strengths and weaknesses of the monograph, and determining whether the argument ultimately works. All historical works should be approached with a critical—but open-mind.

One important point to remember is that you need not accept or reject every aspect of a historical monograph. In fact, you most likely will accord a "mixed review" to most of the books you read. You may accept the author's argument but find his evidence inadequate, or you may be impressed by his data but draw different conclusions from it. You may find some chapters tightly argued, but others unconvincing. Even if you like a particular book, almost inevitably you will have some comments, criticisms, or suggestions.

*Carl N. Degler, *Out of Our Past,* rev. ed. (New York: Harper & Row, Harper Colophon Books, 1970), p. 73.
†J. Franklin Jameson, *The American Revolution Considered As a Social Movement* (Boston: Beacon Press, 1956), p. 9.

## PRACTICE: CREATING AN INFORMAL OUTLINE OR INFORMATION MAP

Although there is not just one correct answer, I think an informal outline would be more effective than an information map for this information. Consider this sample. You would include the same basic information in a map. Discuss your outline or map with your classmates and instructor.

### Informal Outline

*Understanding of the basics of historical writing will make me a better reader
  • most have the same basic elements
  • most can be approached in the same way
*When I read history, concentrate on two basic issues: facts and interpretation
  • Interpretation
    —ask "What is the author's argument/theme/interpretation/thesis?"
    -often clearly stated in preface

—historical works fall into general categories/"schools"
  -according to their thesis and when they were published
  -*historiography:* study of the way historians approach their subjects
—writers have a variety of opinions so I always have to identify the argument
—I should read several books/articles on the same subject to get different perspectives
—all historical works contain biases
  -historical bias is not in itself bad or negative; can be useful
  -but watch for biases that distort the evidence
- Evidence
  —once I identify the argument, I can examine the author's evidence
    -evidence: the "facts" that support the argument
  —questions to keep in mind as I read
    -what types of evidence does the author use?
    -is evidence convincing?
    -which sources does he rely on?
    -what additional sources might he have consulted?
    -where would I go for information? Did he?
—a good work uses credible data from a broad collection of resources

\*I should become a critical/analytical reader
- assess the strengths and weaknesses of the material
- be open-minded
- I need not accept or reject everything an author says
- I can accept some things, reject some things and suspend judgment on others

## PRACTICE: WRITING A SUMMARY

Although these are not the only words you could use to write a summary, consider this sample. Discuss your summary with your classmates and instructor.

Because most historical works have the same elements and can be approached in the same way, understanding the basics of historical writing will make me a better reader. I should concentrate on two basic issues: interpretation and facts.

To discover the author's interpretation I should ask "What is the author's argument/theme/interpretation/thesis?" The answer, the author's argument, is often clearly stated in preface. Historical works fall into general categories or "schools" of thought according to their argument and when they were published. Because of these differences of opinions, I must always identify the author's argument. I should read several books/articles on the same subject to get different perspectives. All historical works contain biases, which is not bad unless those biases distort the evidence.

Once I identify the argument, I can examine the author's evidence. Evidence refers to the facts the author uses to support the argument. Questions to keep in mind as I read include: What types of evidence does the author use? Is the evidence convincing? Which sources does he rely on? What additional sources might he have consulted? and Where would I go for information? Did he? A good work uses credible data from a broad collection of resources.

My goal is to become a critical/analytical reader. This means I assess the strengths and weaknesses of the material with an open mind. I need not accept or reject everything an author says. After careful evaluation I can accept some things, reject some things and suspend judgment on others.

# Chapter 8

### PRACTICE: IDENTIFYING POINT OF VIEW

Although there is not just one correct answer, consider these elements. Discuss your answers with your classmates and instructor.

1a. Greenberg and Dintiman appear to be against smoking.

1b. A representative of the tobacco industry would probably be in favor of smoking.

1c. You need to read more than one source for a research paper to explore a variety of points of view. You could consult sources such as medical reports, current periodicals, tobacco company reports, books on addictive behaviors, and research compilations.

2a. Trelease's point of view on watching television seems to be that critical viewing is fine; uncritical/unquestioning viewing is disastrous. Trelease is probably reliable because of his commitment to children and education it is doubtful anyone could influence him to change his mind.

2b. A television executive, an advertising person, and a politician are among the people who might have a different point of view about watching television.

2c. Answers will vary.

3a. They see a positive impact.

3b. Because people have individual reasons for prefering types of foods, it's impossible (and unwise) to generalize about the attitudes of all people who prefer "health foods or natural foods." Some might view the impact of biotechnology negatively; others might view it as a positive step; while still others might see both positive and negative aspects.

3c. A pesticide company representative might have a negative point of view about biotechnology because of its potential negative impact on the pesticide business.

### PRACTICE: DISTINGUISHING BETWEEN FACT AND OPINION

Discuss whether you think the sentences are facts, and whether the opinions are valid or invalid with your classmates and instructor.

### Paragraph 1

1. fact—whether or not more and more firms have adopted MBO can be verified

2. fact—definition of MBO can be verified

3. fact—whether this is a characteristic of MBO can be verified

4. fact—whether such a meeting usually occurs annually with focus on next year can be verified

5. fact—whether manager and subordinate are to agree on goals can be verified

6. fact—whether MBO goals are to be stated in quantitative terms and written down can be verified

7. fact—whether evaluation of MBO goals is typically done one year later can be verified

8. fact—whether MBO has been shown to be effective can be verified

9. fact—whether these companies have reported success with MBO can be verified

10. opinion—whether MBO involves quite a bit of paperwork and is used too rigidly might be difficult to verify; you would probably get different answers from different sources. If we think Griffin and Ebert are knowledgeable and reliable, we might tentatively accept their information.

### Paragraph 2

1. fact—whether such a program was initiated in 1980 can be verified

2. fact—this information can be verified

3. opinion—whether the EPA's record was disgraceful would be difficult to verify; you would probably get different answers from different sources. If we think Nebel is knowledgeable and reliable, we might tentatively accept his information.

## PRACTICE: IDENTIFYING TONE

Although there is not just one correct answer, consider these elements. Discuss your views with your classmates and instructor.

1a. Long's point of view appears to be positive toward the use and future outlook of computers.

1b. Long's tone seems to be optimistic and upbeat—any problem can be overcome.

2a. I think Barrett views Trump as a pretentious, publicity-seeking individual.

2b. Because of phrases like "smirked into a camera," "longest media dry spell," "laying claim . . . with a lordly wave," "willing to play poster-boy," I'd describe Barrett's tone as sarcastic.

3a.  I think White considers fear to be a most powerful force.

3b.  Because of phrases such as "don't underrate the power," "what devastation . . . can wreak," "damaging to our inner world," and "their dark energies," I would describe White's tone as serious.

# Chapter 9

## PRACTICE: USE YOUR CRITICAL READING STRATEGIES

There is not just one correct answer. Discuss your views with your classmates and instructor.

# *Credits*

Page 14: Allen R. Angel, *Elementary Algebra for College Students*, 3rd ed., © 1992, pp. 6–7. Reprinted by permission of Prentice-Hall, Englewood Cliffs, N.J. Reprinted with permission. © 1992 Prentice-Hall.

Page 16: Bernard J. Nebel and Richard T. Wright, *Environmental Science*, 3rd ed., © 1990, pp. 274–75. Reprinted by permission of Prentice-Hall, Englewood Cliffs, N.J.

Page 19: Daniel Politoske, *Music*, © 1992, pp. 21–24. Reprinted by permission of Prentice-Hall, Englewood Cliffs, N.J.

Page 26: John J. Macionis, *Sociology*, 3rd ed., © 1991, p. 44. Reprinted by permission of Prentice-Hall, Englewood Cliffs, N.J.

Page 36: John J. Macionis, *Sociology*, 3rd ed., © 1991, p. 5. Reprinted by permission of Prentice-Hall, Englewood Cliffs, N.J.

Page 36: Stephen P. Robbins, *Training in Interpersonal Skills: Tips for Managing People at Work*, © 1989, p. 6. Reprinted by permission of Prentice-Hall, Englewood Cliffs, N.J.

Page 37: Reprinted with permission. March 1992, Robert L. McGrath.

Page 39: Reprinted with permission. © June 1992, *Travel Holiday*.

Page 40: Irwin Unger, *These United States: The Question of Our Past*, 5th ed., © 1992, p. 4. Reprinted by permission of Prentice-Hall, Englewood Cliffs, N.J.

Page 49–52: From the book: *Webster's New World Dictionary, Third College Edition*, © 1988. Used by permission of the publisher, Webster's New World Dictionaries/A Division of Simon & Schuster.

Page 61: Reprinted with permission. © 1986 R.L. McGrath.

Page 64: Bernard J. Nebel and Richard T. Wright, *Environmental Science*, 3rd ed., © 1990, pp. 11–12. Reprinted by permission of Prentice-Hall, Englewood Cliffs, N.J.

Page 66: © 1992, *The Boston Globe Newspaper Company*. Reprinted with permission.

Page 71: Barker and Barker, *Communication*, 6th ed., © 1993, pp. 63, 67–69, 255. Reprinted by permission of Prentice-Hall, Englewood Cliffs, N.J.

Page 72: Victor Grassian, *Moral Reasoning: Ethical Theory and Some Contemporary Moral Problems*, 2nd ed., © 1992, p. 304. Reprinted by permission of Prentice-Hall, Englewood Cliffs, N.J.

Page 72: Edward F. Bergman and Tom L. McKnight, *Introduction to Geography*, © 1993, p. 21. Reprinted by permission of Prentice-Hall, Englewood Cliffs, N.J.

Pages 73–74: Jerrold S. Greenberg and George B. Dintiman, *Exploring Health: Expanding the Boundaries of Wellness*, © 1992, p. 493. Reprinted by permission of Prentice-Hall, Englewood Cliffs, N.J.

Pages 75–76: Thomas I. White, *Discovering Philosophy*, © 1991, p. 15. Reprinted by permission of Prentice-Hall, Englewood Cliffs, N.J.

**425**

## PHOTOGRAPHS

# *Index*